STANDARD ENGLISH

'This book does more than "widen the debate": it also [ ] carefully analysing the complex issues of definition and ideolog, ...ich the notion of "Standard English" presents. Its contributors provide a robust alternative, grounded in historical, sociolinguistic and descriptive perspectives, to the simplistic accounts which have been prominent in recent years. It is a timely and significant contribution to the literature on this topic.' *David Crystal*

The debates surrounding 'Standard English', grammar and correctness are as intense today as ever and extend far beyond an academic context. *Standard English: The widening debate* draws together leading international scholars who confront the issues head on.

Current debates about the teaching of English in the school curriculum and more general concerns about declining standards of English are placed in a historical, social and international context. *Standard English*:

- traces the notion of 'Standard English' from its roots in the practices of late seventeenth-century grammarians, through succeeding centuries to the present day;

- explores the definitions of 'Standard English', with particular attention paid to distinctions between spoken and written English;

- demonstrates that 'Standard English' is viewed very differently in the US and reveals how it is used as a marker for different forms of social discrimination, and draws on similar issues such as the English Only Movement and Ebonics;

- considers the relevance of 'Standard English' in the world context.

Standard English: The widening debate is an accessible, seminal work which clarifies an increasingly confused topic. It is therefore essential reading for students of English, and English in Education, and will also appeal to anyone with an active interest in the English language.

Contributors: James Milroy, Richard J. Watts, Hayley Davis, Tony Bex, Peter Trudgill, Jenny Cheshire, Ronald Carter, Lesley Milroy, Laura C. Hartley and Dennis R. Preston, Bent Preisler, Tony Crowley.

STANDARD ENGLISH

The widening debate

Edited by
Tony Bex and Richard J. Watts

London and New York

First published 1999
by Routledge
11 New Fetter Lane, London EC4P 4EE

Simultaneously published in the USA and Canada
by Routledge
29 West 35th Street, New York, NY 10001

Typeset in Goudy by
The Florence Group, Stoodleigh, Devon
Printed and bound in Great Britain by
Redwood Books, Trowbridge, Wilshire

British Library Cataloguing in Publication Data
A catalogue record for this book is available
from the British Library

Library of Congress Cataloguing in Publication Data
Standard English : the widening debate / edited by
Tony Bex and Richard J. Watts.
p. cm.
ISBN 0–415–19162–9 (hc.).—ISBN 0–415–19163–7 (pbk.)
1. English language—Standardization. 2. English
language–English-speaking countries. 3. English language—
Study and teaching. 4. English language—Foreign countries.
5. English language—Variation. 6. English language—Usage.
I. Bex, Tony, 1943– .
II. Watts, Richard J.
PE1074.7.S73 1999
428–dc21   98–36167
CIP

ISBN 0–415–19163–7 (Pbk)
ISBN 0–415–19162–9 (Hbk)

CONTENTS

List of figures and tables   vii
List of contributors   ix

Introduction   1
TONY BEX AND RICHARD J. WATTS

PART I
Perspectives on the history and ideology of 'Standard English'

Introduction to Part I   13

1   The consequences of standardisation in descriptive
    linguistics
    JAMES MILROY   16

2   The social construction of Standard English: Grammar
    writers as a 'discourse community'
    RICHARD J. WATTS   40

3   Typography, lexicography and the development of the
    idea of 'standard English'
    HAYLEY DAVIS   69

4   Representations of English in twentieth-century Britain:
    Fowler, Gowers and Partridge
    TONY BEX   89

PART II
Perspectives on the spoken language

Introduction to Part II   113

CONTENTS

5   Standard English: What it isn't
    PETER TRUDGILL   117

6   Spoken standard English
    JENNY CHESHIRE   129

7   Standard grammars, spoken grammars: Some educational
    implications
    RONALD CARTER   149

PART III
Perspectives from outside the UK

Introduction to Part III   169

8   Standard English and language ideology in Britain and
    the United States
    LESLEY MILROY   173

9   The names of US English: Valley girl, cowboy, yankee,
    normal, nasal and ignorant
    LAURA C. HARTLEY AND DENNIS R. PRESTON   207

10 Functions and forms of English in a European EFL
    country
    BENT PREISLER   239

EPILOGUE   269

11 Curiouser and curiouser: Falling standards in the stan-
    dard English debate
    TONY CROWLEY   271

    Bibliography   283
    Index   299

FIGURES AND TABLES

Figures

9.1   Mean scores for language 'correctness' by MI respondents for US English   211

9.2   Mean scores for language 'correctness' by IN respondents for US English   211

9.3   Mean scores for language 'correctness' by S respondents for US English   212

9.4   Regions ranked for language 'correctness' by OR respondents   212

9.5   Mean scores for 'pleasant' English by MI respondents   214

9.6   Mean scores for 'pleasant' English by IN respondents   214

9.7   Mean scores for 'pleasant' English by S respondents   215

9.8   Ratings for 'pleasant' English by OR respondents   215

9.9   Degree of difference between MI (the home area) and the fifty states, NYC and WDC   217

9.10   Degree of difference between IN (the home area) and the fifty states, NYC and WDC   217

9.11   Degree of difference between S (the home area) and the fifty states, NYC and WDC   218

9.12   Degree of difference between OR (the home area) and the fifty states, NYC and WDC   218

9.13   Computer-assisted generalisations of hand-drawn maps showing where MI respondents believe speech regions to exist in the US   221

9.14   Computer-assisted generalisations of hand-drawn maps showing where IN respondents believe speech regions to exist in the US   221

9.15   Hand-counted generalisations of hand-drawn maps showing where SC respondents believe speech regions to exist in the US   222

9.16 Hand-counted generalisations of hand-drawn maps
showing where OR respondents believe speech regions to
exist in the US 223
9.17 Hand-drawn map by an MI respondent 224
9.18 Hand-drawn map by an IN respondent 224
9.19 Hand-drawn map by an SC respondent 225
9.20 Hand-drawn map by an OR respondent 226
9.21 Regions of the US used in this study 227
10.1 Correlation between preference for American or British
English and interest in country music 252
10.2 Correlation between preference for American or British
English and interest in classical music 252
10.3 Histogram displaying an NKE age profile of Danes 254

Tables

9.1 Frequency of *label* category by area of respondent 228
9.2 Frequencies of labels used for hand-drawn maps for
respondents from the four areas studied 231
9.3 MI results for labelling of other US accents 231
9.4 IN results for labelling of other US accents 232
9.5 SC results for labelling of other US accents 233
9.6 OR results for labelling of other US accents 234
10.1 Extent to which English is experienced by adult Danes 244
10.2 Question about the presence of English in Danish society 247
10.3 Reasons for preference of either American or British
English 248
10.4 Survey on the relative perceived suitability of American
or British English in various contexts 249
10.5 Survey on the relative perceived suitability of American
or British English by those who like American English
better than British English 250
10.6 Reasons for learning English 255
10.7 Reaction to being addressed in a language one does not
understand 256
10.8 Extent to which respondents feel they need to know
English 256
10.9 Views on reasons for presence of the English language in
Danish society 257
10.10 Views on subtitling or dubbing of foreign TV programmes 257

CONTRIBUTORS

Tony Bex is Senior Lecturer in Linguistics and English Language at the University of Kent at Canterbury. He has published widely in the field of applied linguistics, and his recent publications include *Variety in Written English* (Routledge, 1996). He is chair of the Poetics and Linguistics Association and is currently writing a book on stylistics.

Ronald Carter is Professor of Modern English Language in the School of English Studies at the University of Nottingham. He has published widely in the fields of applied, literary and educational linguistics. Recent publications include: *Exploring Spoken English* (CUP, 1997); *The Routledge History of Literature in English: Britain and Ireland* (with John McRae) Routledge, (1997); *Investigating English Discourse* (Routledge, 1997). He is currently working (with Michael McCarthy) on a new grammar of spoken and written English to be published by Cambridge University Press in 2001.

Jenny Cheshire is Professor of Linguistics at Queen Mary and Westfield College, University of London. She has worked on a range of topics in sociolinguistics, specialising in variation and change in present-day English syntax. Her previous publications include *English around the World: Sociolinguistic Perspectives* (CUP, 1991). She is currently working on dialect levelling in British English.

Tony Crowley is Professor of English at the University of Manchester. He has published widely in the area of Language and Cultural Theory. His publications include: *The Politics of Discourse* (Macmillan, 1989); *Proper English?* (Routledge, 1992); *Language in History* (Routledge, 1996). He is currently working on *The Language and Cultural Reader* (forthcoming).

Hayley Davis is Lecturer in the English Department of Goldmiths College, London University. She has published work on morphology, lexicography and gender and discourse. Her previous publications include *Redefining Linguistics* with T.J. Taylor (eds), Routledge (1990) and 'What makes bad language bad?'

(rev. edn.) in *A first Integrationalist Reader*, ed. R. Harris and G. Wolf, Elsevier Science (1998). She is currently writing a book on lay metalanguage.

Laura C. Hartley is a Grants Officer in the Office of the Provost at Lesley College in Cambridge, Massachusetts. She holds a doctorate in Linguistics from Michigan State University. In addition to her work in Perceptual Dialectology and Language Attitudes, she is interested in cross-cultural pragmatics and intercultural communication and is currently involved in a study of face-management in complaint situations.

James Milroy is an Emeritus Professor of Linguistics at the University of Sheffield, currently attached to the University of Michigan. His main interests are in historical linguistics, sociolinguistics and the history of English and Germanic languages. His publications include 'linguistic variation and change' (Blackwell 1992) and, with Lesley Milroy, 'Authority in Language' (Routledge, 3rd edn., 1998). He is currently working on a book on the relation of social dialectology to the theory of language change (Longman).

Lesley Milroy is a Professor at the Linguistics Program, University of Michigan. She has worked on a number of topics in sociolinguistics, including social dialectology, bilingualism, conversation analysis and language ideology. She has published a large number of journal articles and several books, including (with James Milroy) Authority in Language (3rd edn.) (Routledge, 1998).

Bent Preisler is Professor of English Language and Society at the Department of Languages and Culture, Roskilde University. He is author or co-author of several books and numerous articles on topics in English grammar, pronunciation, discourse analysis, sociolinguistics, language pedagogy, and English as a foreign and international language. His previous publications include *Linguistic Sex Roles in Conversation* (Mouton de Gruyter, 1986). In recent years he has been concerned, in particular, with the social and psychological aspects of the use of English in Denmark.

Dennis R. Preston is Professor of Linguistics in the Department of Linguistics and Languages, Michigan State University. He has worked on dialectology, sociolinguistics, the social psychology of language, discourse, folk linguistics, and second language acquisition, the last particularly from a variationist point of view. His most recent book-length publications include, with Nancy Niedzielski, the soon-to-appear, *Folk Linguistics*, Berlin: Mouton de Gruyter and the in-press Handbook of Perceptual Dialectology, Amsterdam: Benjamins. He is on a survey of the degree of accommodation to the Northern Cities Vowel Shift among minority populations in southern Michigan, a research effort supported by the National Science Foundation.

Peter Trudgill is Professor of English Linguistics at the University of Fribourg, Switzerland. His work has mainly been in the fields of dialectology and socio-linguistics and his previous publications include *Sociolinguistics: An Introduction to Language and Society* (3rd edn., 1995). His current interests focus on a range of issues concerning dialect typology: the relationship between types of linguistic structure and types of society.

Richard J. Watts is Professor of English Linguistics at the University of Berne, Switzerland. His work has been in the fields of linguistic politeness, pragmatics and the sociolinguistics of English. His previous publications include *Power in Family Discourse* (Mouton de Gruyter, 1992) and, with Sachiko Ide and Konrad Enlich, *Politeness in Language* (Mouton de Gruyter, 1992). He is currently researching into alternative ways of looking at the 'history' of English and is also involved in assessing the status and significance of English within the complex multilingual framework of Switzerland.

INTRODUCTION

Tony Bex and Richard J. Watts

This collection has been compiled for a number of different reasons. The virulence of the debate about the variety of English to be taught within the National Curriculum in England and Wales during the late 1980s supplied one impetus. One of the more surprising features about that debate was the extent to which the views of professional linguists and educators were treated with contempt by the Conservative government and the popular press. This is well documented in Cox (1991) and mention of it is made in some of the chapters that follow. At about the same time, a number of papers and books appeared discussing the nature of 'Standard English' many of which were produced, or are referred to, by the authors of this volume. In the USA, there was the demand for Spanish to be given equal rights with English in at least some of the states – an issue which may seem tangential to the concerns of this book, but which inevitably affects the ways in which English is both viewed and taught within those states – and the growing interest in 'ebonics'. The immediate impetus, however, was a conversation between the editors in the early 1990s. It seemed to us that there was a need to clarify and bring into focus the diverse positions held by a number of the contributors to the debate. This need became even more pressing after the publication of Honey's *Language is Power* (1997) with its peculiar mixture of half truths and ad hominem arguments. However, when we approached potential contributors, it soon became apparent that there was no general consensus as to what constituted 'Standard English' or how best to approach the topic as a field of enquiry.

Rather than working to a pre-determined agenda, we thought it better to represent the different views and approaches which are current among linguists, and the collection is therefore deliberately heterogeneous. We have divided it into three parts, each one of which contains a brief introduction setting out the broad perspectives adopted by the different authors. Part I contains chapters investigating the different ways the notion of 'Standard English' has been constructed historically, and why the idea of a standard remains a potent force in the contemporary world. Many of these chapters touch on the ideology of 'Standard English'. This should not surprise us:

questions of language are after all essentially ideological (cf. Taylor and Joseph 1990; Woolard and Schieffelin 1994; Heller 1995; Blommaert, forthcoming). It does not follow from this that the contributors to this volume or, indeed, the volume as a whole are 'enemies' of 'Standard English', even though some may question its existence. This accusation, made by Honey (1997), and repeated in the British media, needs to be addressed; it also needs to be understood, and to be taken seriously.

Part II is more descriptive in that it acknowledges the existence of 'Standard English', although the various authors characterise it in slightly different ways, and attempt to describe it as accurately as possible from a linguistic point of view. This section deliberately resists notions of correctness, while recognising that there may be forms and usages which are more appropriate in some circumstances but not as appropriate in other circumstances. Interestingly, there is an apparent disagreement between Trudgill's position (Chapter 5) and Cheshire's (Chapter 6) and Carter's (Chapter 7), in that Trudgill tends to downplay spoken forms. Trudgill, though, is referring to phonology whereas Cheshire and Carter are both discussing the syntactic features which are likely to be present in spoken 'Standard English'. There is, then, significant agreement as to the importance of clear characterisations of standard forms, and because the bulk of Part II concentrates on speech, it seemed appropriate to title it 'Perspectives on the spoken language'.

Part III takes the debate beyond the UK. But these contributions have not been included simply because they offer an international context to the debate. What is significant about them is that they offer us three different perspectives (among several others, of course) which demonstrate that the debate is not always couched in the same terms, or necessarily seen in the same ways as in some of the earlier chapters, and which, by extension, may reduce the British debate to a 'parish pump' issue. In fact, the editors are not persuaded that this is the case, but we are convinced that the debate should be more outward looking than the purely British concerns typically allow.

In this general introduction, we intend to survey the different disciplinary perspectives that have gone into the making of this book. We also intend to indicate what general problems there are in the discussion of 'Standard English' and how we have attempted to overcome them. One of the first difficulties we had to face was how to limit the field of enquiry. Quirk, writing in 1985, commented:

> There are few enough (not least among professional linguists) that would claim the existence of a single standard within any one of the ENL[1] countries: plenty that would even deny both the possibility and the desirability of such a thing. Recent emphasis has been on multiple and variable standards (insofar as the use of the word

'standard' is ventured): different standards for different occasions for different people – and each as 'correct' as any other.

(Quirk 1985: 2–3)

Interestingly, the subtitle of the book in which Quirk's paper appears refers to the English 'language' and its 'literatures' so, at least for the British Council who sponsored the conference where Quirk delivered his talk, there was no real doubt that there was a single English language whatever might be thought about its variable standards. And, indeed, this perception is shared by most (if not all) producers of spellcheckers for word processors which regularly mark *Englishes* as deviant.

Joseph (1987: 2–3) adopts the principles of *Abstand* and *Ausbau* to iden-tify what is to count as a language, and he observes that English contains sufficient *Abstand*, or structural 'difference' from 'German and any other language of equal or higher prestige, of which one might otherwise consider it a dialect' (ibid.: 2). He also observes that 'British, American, Canadian, and Australian English do not differ enough from one another to be labeled separate languages' (ibid.). In terms of *Ausbau*, or prestigious functional diversity, he notices that American English has developed considerably 'over the last two centuries, but never enough to overcome its low *Abstand* vis-à-vis other English dialects and achieve independent status' (ibid.: 3). At first sight, then, it would seem appropriate to discuss the concept of 'Standard English' as though it were unitary and a model against which all other varieties are judged.

However, for a number of different reasons, this would be absurd. We do not need to appeal to Quirk's deliberately exaggerated characterisation of variable standards to recognise that the development of local varieties of English has been a way of marking out national identities. One way of characterising this development is to follow Kachru's (1985) useful delimi-tation of different Englishes. He distinguishes varieties primarily according to what he calls 'speech fellowships'. These roughly correspond to the geographical location of different Englishes and the ways in which their speakers construct notions of correctness. He describes these 'fellowships' as belonging to three concentric circles. The inner circle contains those speakers of English who learn it as a mother tongue, and in which the language can be used in all domains and is multifunctional. The outer circle contains those who learn English as a second language and where the language can be used for the more advanced functions (e.g. institutional and business purposes) but is restricted as to domain. Because these varieties are largely learned at school, they contain idiosyncratic features (at least as viewed by speakers from the inner circle) and are less likely to develop full functionality, although they may exhibit creativity.[2] The expanding circle consists of those countries where English is learned as a foreign language, and where its use is confined to international affairs such as diplomacy and business. Although Kachru does not mention such examples, there are also the kinds of advertising and 'sub-cultures' within this circle, some of which are referred to by Preisler (see Chapter 10 of this volume), which use and maintain English as a marker of social identity. It is quite clear that the 'standards' to which these groups appeal would not be recognised by most educational establishments within the expanding circle.

From this perspective English is 'pluricentric' (Clyne 1982: 159) in that where standardisation occurs, the models which are selected as the synecdoche (Joseph 1987: 2) derive from local varieties. Thus, for Kachru, there is a tension between the centripetal forces which hold English together (wherever we may choose to place the centre) and the centrifugal forces which are driving Englishes apart. However, he does recognise that the growth of English as an international language means that some degree of mutual intelligibility is likely to be maintained at least for those functions where English is used internationally (Kachru 1985: 123). Nevertheless, Kachru is sceptical about the ways in which 'mutual intelligibility' has typically been characterised. He comments (ibid.: 94) that some writers assert the desirability of a prescriptive norm primarily as a means of ensuring such intelligibility, but points out that such writers rarely pay attention to who is engaged in the linguistic interactions. Thus:

> in the case of English, we must be clear about whom we have in mind when we talk of participants in a linguistic interaction. What role does a native speaker's judgement play in determining the intelligibility of non-native speech acts that have intranational functions in, for example, Asia or Africa?
>
> (ibid.: 94)

Kachru, therefore, rejects a monomodel of English even for pedagogic purposes arguing that:

> the pragmatics of the uses of the English language can be understood only if a dynamic polymodel approach is adopted. What we should recognize is that at one level we have an internationally understood English, in spite of its local characteristics. In addition, there are several types of Englishes, for example in South Asia or parts of Africa, which are not meant necessarily for the consumption of a native speaker of English. They have their national or regional functions. On the cline of Englishness these may be low, but functionally they serve the purpose of communication as does any other human language.
>
> (ibid.: 123)

Kachru necessarily touches on a number of important issues which are the concern of this volume. On the one hand, he refers to pedagogical issues, and there is little doubt that, however 'Standard English' may be characterised, descriptive norms of correctness are typically promulgated through educational institutions. But he also brings into sharp focus the problems of writing about 'Standard English' as though it were a single variety. It is worth noting that there are probably more non-native speakers and learners of English in the world today than there are native speakers of the language. These surely have a right to be heard. There are also more native speakers in other parts of the world for whom the debate in Britain may seem rather less than trivial.

These confusions are apparent in a number of books that have appeared during the last decade or so. Bailey and Görlach (1982), for example, contains a number of interesting papers describing various forms of English that have developed worldwide, but the status of the national varieties they describe is not at all clear. Similarly, there is an occasional uncertainty when discussing variation. Appalachian English is contrasted with standard American English (Toon 1982: 243), whereas Jamaican English is contrasted both with standard American and Jamaican creole (Lawton 1982: 258). Platt et al. (1984) largely treat the national varieties of English they discuss as self-contained languages, as do Trudgill and Hannah (1985). Of course, there is nothing eccentric about such treatments, but any discussion of 'Standard English' needs to distinguish between endonormative and exonormative standards. In the former case, we are discussing usages which are standardised within a particular non-native variety of English, and in the latter with usages which are standardised by external reference to a native variety.

Greenbaum's (1985) collection, *The English Language Today*, deals much more directly with language attitudes and has a narrower focus in that the majority of chapters deal with English in Britain, the USA and Canada. However, an interesting, if brief, chapter by Görlach and Schröder notes that:

> a poll of English language teachers in Central Europe would probably show that the great majority consider 'good usage' to be the kind of English used by an educated Englishman in his formal and semi-formal social contacts and within his own family.
>
> (ibid.: 230–1)

If this is true, it suggests that there is a more international dimension to the debate that needs to be addressed. However we choose to characterise the processes of standardisation within an ENL or ESL (English as a second language) context, such characteristics may not be appropriate for EFL (English as a foreign language) contexts.

The editors of this volume, then, are quite clear that notions of 'Standard English' vary from country to country, and not merely in the ways in which such a variety is described but also in the prestige in which it is held and the functions it has developed to perform. We would dearly have liked broader coverage, but any attempt to have been inclusive would have led to a volume far larger than this one. Such a volume would also be competing with the excellent collection by Cheshire (1991). Indeed, it will be apparent that the majority of chapters deal with various issues concerning 'Standard English' in Britain. Nevertheless, it would have been short-sighted to have ignored some of the debates that were taking place elsewhere, and we have therefore included chapters dealing with the USA (Chapters 8 and 9). We have also included one chapter that looks at English in the EFL situation (Chapter 10). Although it would be misleading to suggest that these chapters represent the last word on the issues they address, they act as useful pointers to some of the ways in which the notion of 'Standard English' is at the centre of other kinds of debate.

Having chosen to limit ourselves in this way, we were faced with further problems. We have suggested that when Quirk referred to 'different standards for different occasions for different people – and each as "correct" as any other' (see above) he was being deliberately provocative. However, the differences he has identified do need careful consideration. If we treat 'different people' as referring to the kinds of national and international circumstances we have referred to above, then we would acknowledge that different people or, rather, groups of people, appeal to different standards. The phrase 'different occasions' requires more subtle disentanglement. There are, of course, the differences in medium and it may well be that there are different standards for speech and writing (see Carter, Chapter 7 of this volume). But, equally, there are different functions within these media. What might count as standard in a formal lecture will vary from what might count as standard in everyday speech situations. Although there may be a continuum between these different situations, it will be a continuum in terms of formality.

However, this again begs the question of how we distinguish varieties of English and, more relevantly, how we define 'Standard English'. It will be apparent from the chapters in this volume that there is no general consensus on such a definition. If it is to be defined as a sociolinguistic variety of the language, then we need to identify what features distinguish it from other varieties. These features will include specific linguistic elements such as syntax and lexis, but they will also include situations of utterance and the identity of the users. A frequent definition, used both in the Kingman Report (Kingman 1988) and more recently in Honey (1997), identifies the standard with written forms. This is broadly the position taken by Trudgill in this volume (Chapter 5). However, the close identification of the standard with written forms (see also Davis, Chapter 3 of this volume) has further consequences that require elucidation.

Quite clearly, not all writing is in the standard language, and yet to discriminate between standard and non-standard in a positive fashion at this level is not merely a descriptive exercise. It also involves a degree of prescriptivism. The sociolinguist in describing what happens in a particular speech situation is also referring indirectly to what is viewed as appropriate in such situations. And notions of appropriacy are developed by the people involved in the interactions. Therefore, any description of 'Standard English' has to take into account the people who are using it and their own reasons for adopting it.

Few of the authors represented here would deny that the standard is the prestige variety. By prestige, we mean that it is accorded a degree of respect within society as a whole. This respect is manifested in a variety of different ways. Either people orient to the prestige variety in given situations or they are encouraged to use it by those who are seen as possessing authority. Typically, the prestige variety is taught to children in schools, and a number of chapters make reference to the educational debate that has been taking place in Britain. However, notions of correctness are maintained through other agencies. Handbooks of English abound both in the USA and the UK, but the precise relationship between the prescriptivist tradition and the descriptivists needs to be treated with care.

The prescriptivists tend to start from the premise that there are certain forms which are correct because they best express the meanings intended. These forms represent the best English and are therefore to be encouraged. Generally, prescriptivists blur the distinction between syntax, meaning and social identity. So, syntactic (i.e. formal) deviation from the 'correct' usage leads to imprecision of meaning which, in turn, leads to social chaos. Prescriptivists, therefore, represent an ideological force which equates language use with social behaviour and correct usage with good citizenship. The extent to which they may be regarded as promulgators of standard forms is an open question, but they undoubtedly contribute to the debate over the existence of 'Standard English' in that they equate their notions of correctness with the standard language.

Prescriptivists frequently justify their claims with reference to what used to be the case. Part I of this volume therefore investigates the ways in which the idea of 'Standard English' has been constructed over the last three centuries. It notes among other things the ways in which past grammarians and others have described the language, the differing views they have had, and also comments on the historiography of the language. It may be thought that writing a history of the language is a relatively neutral activity but, as will become evident, historians need to select their evidence. The voices from the past they choose as being of significance represent a small percentage of the people who have discussed and attempted to shape the language, and not every variety is necessarily treated with equal respect. In fact, it could be argued that historians of the language still suffer from the 'Whig interpretation of history' (Butterfield 1931) in that they trace the history of the dominant dialect (often their own), thereby obscuring the significance of others both in the past and the present.

The descriptivists approach the issue more cautiously in that they recognise that there are prestigious usages, and that these may be of sufficient quantity to combine to form a distinct variety. However, they also recognise variation within the standard dialect. Like the prescriptivists, they tend to equate these forms with 'educated' usage. We have commented above on the common identification of 'Standard English' with written English. However, some commentators admit the existence of a spoken variety (e.g. Cheshire and Carter, Chapters 6 and 7 of this volume). Where they do this, they are at pains to demonstrate that the spoken grammars of the standard are not necessarily the same as the written grammars. They therefore resist the prescriptivists' drive to enforce one variety for use in all situations regardless of medium.

Some of the confusion which is inherent within these different positions depends on the purposes for which the descriptions are being made. Those who are heavily involved in the educationalist debates recognise that pedagogy, by its very nature, tends to be prescriptive. Their primary aim, then, is to identify those varieties which can form the basis of the school curriculum and to describe them as accurately as possible. In their eyes, that variety which best performs the higher functions of a developed society can be described as standard, although this variety will yield considerable flexibility as to forms depending on the particular function for which it is being used. In this case, the standard is potentially available to all users of English since it is not the possession of any particular regional group or social class. Although it is restricted according to function, it is comparatively open as to form. And in so far as it is the variety to be taught in schools, it should not be treated as an ideological football subject to the whims of particular social groups.

These kinds of description can be considered to be linguistically oriented but with a social dimension. They are therefore slightly different from the chapters that are more obviously within the sociolinguistic tradition. Sociolinguists typically track what people actually do (e.g. Labov 1966, 1972) and then relate clusters of linguistic features either to geographical areas or social classes (see Trudgill, Chapter 5 of this volume). There are dangers in this approach, however. The first, and most obvious, is that people's spoken and written patterns vary according to function. Any description of a social or geographical dialect (and with English it may be possible to conflate these and argue that marked geographical features tend to be associated with particular social classes) therefore has to take account of variation according to formality and according to register or style. It would be very odd to speak to one's young grandchildren in the same way as one spoke to one's parents, just as it would be peculiar to send a greetings card written in the same style as an academic paper. The other danger is to assume that social groupings are stable and easily described. This may be the case but, by and large, sociolinguists tend to rely on sociologists' descriptions of the groups they are discussing and there is no guarantee that these descriptions are accurate. One way of solving this problem is to allow the subjects to place themselves within social groupings through self-description and by observing the company they keep (L. Milroy 1987). This produces interesting data from a variationist perspective without imposing pre-selected categories on such data. Where the data concerns attitudes towards language (as in Hartley and Preston; Chapter 9 of this volume) then we can observe interesting overlaps between the prescriptivist traditions that have developed from within a particular ideological framework and pre-theoretical notions of language, or what has been called 'folklinguistics'.

This introduction can be no more than a sketch of the various positions occupied by different linguists when confronting the problem of 'Standard English', but it should go some way to explaining why it is that this volume does not offer simple solutions. We considered it important to allow the different voices to speak for themselves. Occasionally this has led to overlap between some of the chapters, although we have endeavoured to limit this as much as possible. Where overlap has occurred, it is because we considered it important to allow the individual authors to explain their own theoretical backgrounds. We also recognise that each author has problematised the issues in different ways such that there are internal contradictions within the volume as a whole. One of these contradictions is in the different orthographies used for 'Standard English'. In the editorial introductions we have chosen to adopt uppercase S and E to indicate that some authors consider the term to refer to a subvariety of English. The inverted commas recognise that for others 'Standard English' is a social myth constructed for ideological purposes. We have allowed individual authors' usages, including those of the contributing editors, to stand, and readers are invited to draw their own conclusions on what may be the appropriate way to write 'Standard English', and why. These kinds of contradictions are inevitable since if there were no disagreement there would be no debate.

Nevertheless, we would admit that there is one argument that is missing. It is best represented by Honey (1997), who has argued that 'Standard English' exists, that it is relatively simple to describe, that it is a good thing and that those who argue against such a view are either misguided or charlatans. Honey's 'arguments' are reviewed critically in Crowley's chapter (Chapter 11), which we present here as a fitting epilogue. There are, of course, frequent references to arguments of this nature in the following pages, but there are no chapters which espouse such a view since this stance attempts to foreclose the debate. Crowley uncovers the ideological bases of Honey's position and demonstrates the prescriptive nature of his proposed programme, thus linking back to Bex's chapter (Chapter 4) on the earlier prescriptivists. The epilogue is by no means the final word on the subject of 'Standard English', but we hope it will open up the debate to academically more honest and better-founded research.

Notes

1 Glossed as 'those countries where English is a native language' (Quirk 1985).
2 Interestingly, Kachru (1986) discusses the development of non-native literatures, and creativity in general, but it could be argued that these are also representative of the higher functions of a language.

Part I

PERSPECTIVES ON THE HISTORY AND IDEOLOGY OF 'STANDARD ENGLISH'

INTRODUCTION TO PART I

The chapters which make up Part I have a common ground in that they are all concerned with the ways in which the concept of 'Standard English' has been ideologically constructed. This is a strand that runs through the whole volume, but it is here where these issues are most explicitly expressed and given a historical context. The authors are not necessarily in agreement as to the precise definition of the term 'Standard English', but they do share a common perception that standardisation is best seen as a process driven by spokespeople who have successfully articulated a particular set of social values. Necessarily, such social values are rooted in history which is why each of the following chapters has a historical dimension.

In Chapter 1, James Milroy teases out a number of interwoven strands in the development of what he calls the 'standard language ideology', paying particular attention to the ways in which it has been promoted, often indirectly, by linguists' conceptualisations of language. There is a strong lay interest in maintaining certain standards of correctness through features of accent and grammatical forms. These features are often equated with the standard language, although they only represent a tiny proportion of the dialect and are often slightly antiquated. However, the stigma attached to using incorrect forms results in discrimination, and it is this interrelationship between linguistic form and social discrimination that enables us to refer to the conceptualisation of 'Standard English' as ideological in its nature. Linguists who attempt to resist the ideological underpinnings have been hampered by a set of research paradigms that have dominated linguistic study certainly during this century, and in varying forms in the preceding centuries. Milroy spells out both what these are, and how they are being challenged by new sociolinguistic research into language variation.[1]

In Chapter 2, Richard J. Watts investigates the genesis of the debate about 'Standard English' by discussing the works of some eighteenth-century grammarians. Although the 'complaint tradition' has a long history, it was only in the eighteenth century that detailed codification of English grammar was undertaken. Watts demonstrates that the codification was driven by a desire to describe a very limited dialect, and to describe it from a predominantly prescriptivist perspective. His characterisation of these grammarians as a 'discourse community' is helpful in that it shows how they appealed to a set of common discursive practices, and ones particularly related to education. Drawing on the work of Bourdieu and Berger and Luckman, he demonstrates how these writers managed to achieve symbolic capital, such that their work became institutionalised. Two features that he comments on – and these quite clearly demonstrate the ideological bases of interests in the eighteenth century as represented by these writers – are their constant references to the classical languages and their concentration on proscription. Necessarily, a knowledge of Greek and Latin implied a degree of education. By relating the parsing of English with the parsing of Latin, an indirect appeal could be made to the status that accrued to those people who had received a classical education. Further, the frequent injunctions as to what usages should be shunned constructed a view of language as social behaviour. Where 'good' language is equated with 'good' behaviour and vice versa, it is a very small step to the position where the users of that dialect which is regarded as 'good' are perceived as worthy regardless of the values they actually espouse.

In Chapter 3, Hayley Davis advances the argument from the perspective of lexicography. Like Watts, she argues that the concept of 'Standard English' was largely developed in relation to the written language. In a similar way to Milroy, she points out how the concept has been successfully maintained in part because of certain theoretical confusions within academic linguistics and, in particular, the tradition deriving from Saussure's seminal *Cours de linguistique générale* (1922). She concentrates on the compilation of the *Oxford English Dictionary* (OED), a project which had its origins in the mid-nineteenth century. Although not appealing to the same theoretical concerns as Watts, her discussion of those involved in advancing this project suggests that they too could be regarded as a 'discourse community'. Similarly, the status that the OED has achieved suggests that it, too, carries symbolic capital. The significance of the OED is twofold. On the one hand, it tends to freeze the language in that the meanings of words are no longer regarded as subject to human negotiation. Further, it indirectly fosters the view that 'visible' language (i.e. writing) is the template of language *tout court*. Her discussion also enables her to point out that the work of the lexicographers necessarily involved historical research, and that the OED is therefore a history of the language. However, as a history it contains the ideological biases of its compilers, one of which was that a 'Standard English' had always existed.

In Chapter 4, Tony Bex is less concerned with the history of standardisation than with the ways in which a group of influential writers maintained a set of language attitudes (and ideologies) throughout a significant part of the twentieth century. As with Milroy, he recognises that the usages that these writers' handbooks discuss do not necessarily represent the standard dialect as a whole. Nevertheless, he suggests that their work helped to maintain the prescriptivists' view of language standards. Although he does not argue this directly, he is interested in why these writers should have had so much more influence on the public's perceptions of English than the writings of professional linguists. As with Watts, he appeals to Bourdieu's notion of symbolic and cultural capital, and suggests that they were granted significance not merely for what they wrote, but also for who they were. Again, as with the grammarians and lexicographers discussed by Davis and Watts, it could be argued that they formed a 'discourse community', and a discourse community that was driven by very similar ideological concerns as those others. Although Bex concentrates on the contemporary representation of English within the different handbooks, he notes also their construction of a history of the language, a similar appeal to written forms and a slightly archaic classicism.

All of these chapters refer directly or indirectly to the close connections between 'Standard English' and pedagogy. Honey (1997) equates the dialect with a notion of 'educatedness', although he fails to spell out precisely what he means by this. Crowley's chapter, which appears as an epilogue to this volume, brings these issues into sharp focus from a contemporary perspective. He recognises that the confusion over the definition of 'Standard English' is troublesome for professional linguists, but he also discusses the ways in which its use by Honey and his apologists serves to distort the arguments when they enter the public domain.

Note

1   Other research paradigms which can be usefully applied to the study of 'Standard English' are discussed in Part III.

1

THE CONSEQUENCES OF STANDARDISATION IN DESCRIPTIVE LINGUISTICS

James Milroy

Introduction

Much of nineteenth- and twentieth-century linguistics has depended on the study of major languages that have been regarded as existing in standard, 'classical' or *canonical* forms. Languages such as Latin, Greek and Sanskrit, and subsequently English, Spanish, French and others, have been widely studied and often admired for their alleged elegance, expressiveness, richness or sophistication. Yet, in reality, many of these have at various times been spread by fire and sword through substantial areas of the known world. Their ecological success has arisen, not from the superiority of their grammatical and phonological structures over those of other less successful languages or from the great poetry that has been composed in them – but from the success of their speakers in conquering and subduing speakers of other languages throughout much of known history. I will refer to these as 'major' languages solely in recognition of the large number of native speakers that they have and the wide dispersal of these speakers.

This does not, of course, make these languages either good or bad, for languages are not in themselves moral objects. One language may use verbs at the end of clauses and another in the middle, but it cannot be shown that one word-order is in some way superior – more virtuous, more expressive – than the other. Much the same can be said of phonological and lexical structures. Thus (and this is the position of most professional linguistic scholars), no moral judgement or critical evaluation can be validly made about the abstract structures we call languages. It is the speakers of languages, and not the languages themselves, who live in a moral universe.

Most of the comments made so far are uncontroversial among linguists, although not to many others (including, for example, Honey 1997), and it is partly for this latter reason that these basic points must be repeatedly made.

What we are concerned about here is that the languages mentioned above can be said to exist in *canonical* forms that are *legitimised*. They exist at their highest level of abstraction in standardised forms, and these abstract objects are, in principle, uniform states. Yet, apparently paradoxically, all languages, including these major languages, are observed to be variable within themselves and not uniform at all, and they are also in a continuous state of change. For this reason the idea that languages can be believed to exist in static invariant forms may well be to a great extent a consequence of the fact that they have undergone a process of standardisation, and it is by no means clear that all languages are viewed by their speakers in this way. Strange as it may seem, there are places in the world where speakers do not seem to be conscious of belonging to a community of any particular language (see further below) and where it may not be entirely clear what language they are using (Grace 1991). Thus, the belief that a 'language' must exist in some authoritative, invariant form may not be a linguistic universal. This may also be partly attributable to the fact that languages native to language scholars themselves (which for that reason become important data-sources for linguistics) are typically languages that are viewed as existing in standardised or canonical forms. For these reasons, it should be borne in mind that if present-day English, for example, is viewed as having a canonical form, it does not follow that all languages at all times have been the same in this way, or even that speakers of the English language throughout history have been able to think of their native language in this way either.

What I am concerned with in this chapter are the consequences of the fact that these languages – including English – have undergone, and continue to undergo, the complex process that we refer to as standardisation, bearing in mind that although speakers believe in the existence of some canonical form, the language continues to vary and change. I want to consider two aspects of this. The first, which I shall consider only briefly, is the interaction between scholarly linguistic attitudes to language and the publicly expressed attitudes of non-linguists and critics of linguistics. The second arises from the first. It is that the consequences of standardisation are discernible in the attitudes of linguistic scholars themselves: their judgements as to what the object of description consists of have been influenced by their knowledge that a standard form exists in some abstract dimension and by some consequences of the ideology of standardisation. Weinreich, Labov and Herzog (1968) showed very eloquently how dependent linguistic theory had become on the idea that linguistic structures are uniform (when they are in reality frequently variable), and I am interested here in taking their argument a little farther. I want to consider how far this emphasis on unique invariant forms can be shown to be wholly or partly a consequence of standardisation – specifically a consequence of the fact that the languages most studied have been standard languages, and of the fact that when non-standard varieties have been studied they too have often been studied as though they had invariant canonical forms. English dialect-ology, for example, has often concentrated on eliciting what are regarded as the 'genuine' dialect forms, and intrusions from outside have sometimes been treated as 'contaminations' of the 'genuine' dialect. Indeed, it is the 'standard' language that usually takes the blame for these intrusions (for exam-ples of these tendencies see, among others, the collection in Wakelin 1972b).

One of the main assumptions I make in this chapter is that standard languages are fixed and uniform-state idealisations – not empirically verifi-able realities. That is to say, if we study the speech of people who are said to be speaking a standard language, it will never conform exactly to the idealisation. It is also true that any variety delimited and described by the linguist is an idealisation, and that the usage of an individual speaker will not conform exactly to that idealisation. However, a standard language has properties over and above those of non-standardised varieties, the chief one of which is existence in a widely used written form. For this reason we have found it preferable (Milroy and Milroy 1991) to treat standard varieties as not being mere 'varieties' on a par with other varieties, even though in a strict non-evaluative linguistic sense that is precisely what they are. If, however, they are treated within a taxonomy of varieties and viewed in a dichotomy of *standard/non-standard*, important generalisa-tions are missed that are accessible when standardisation is treated as a process that is continuously in progress. A lot of the linguistic approaches that have been used have been mainly taxonomic and product-based. As for the standard, what is described in a linguistic account as standard English is not in fact the English language as a whole, which is a much more vari-able and unstable phenomenon. I will try to show some ways in which linguistic research paradigms, including variationist approaches, are nonethe-less influenced by assumptions that originate in, or are related to, the ideology of the standard language (Milroy and Milroy 1991: 22–5). I will also suggest that some of these assumptions have been handed down from older gener-ations of scholars and are still with us.

A second assumption I make here is that in what I shall call 'standard-language cultures' the awareness of a superordinate standard variety is kept alive in the public mind by various channels (including the writing system and education in literacy) that tend to inculcate and maintain this knowledge – not always in a very clear or accurate form – in speakers' minds. The main effect of these is to equate the standard language – or what is believed to be the standard language – with the language as a whole and with 'correct' usage in that language, and this notion of correctness has a powerful role in the maintenance of the standard ideology through prescrip-tion. It is this general notion that correct invariant forms exist that we turn to first, comparing the principles affirmed by some structural linguists with views, including popular views, that have been expressed from a non-linguistic or non-structuralist perspective.

Linguists and non-linguists on 'correctness' and standard English

When present-day language scholars write about standard languages and prescriptive rules, they often distinguish two types of people who display attitudes towards language use. On the one hand, there is the general public, many of whom have strong attitudes towards linguistic correctness, and who keep writing to the newspapers denouncing trivial mistakes in usage. On the other hand, there is a group of people who are said to have more enlightened attitudes based on scholarly research on the structural properties of languages. These are, of course, present-day experts in linguistics and language studies, who are often sociolinguists. Some of these experts have felt that, as a matter of scientific responsibility, they have had a duty to venture outside narrowly academic concerns in order to promote public tolerance of variation in language and to point out that it is wrong to discriminate against individuals on linguistic grounds, just as it is wrong to discriminate on grounds of race or colour of skin. There are now many examples of language discrimination in the literature. V. Edwards (1993: 235) quotes a letter from an interview panel to an unsuccessful candidate for a teaching appointment openly stating that despite excellent qualifications he has been rejected because of minor aspects of his spoken English (essentially a London accent). See also especially Lippi-Green (1997) for many striking examples of language discrimination in the USA – in law-courts and elsewhere. More generally, anyone brought up in Britain in the 1950s will remember patronising comments about localised accents and the extreme class-consciousness of these judgements. In a prescient essay first written in 1951, Abercrombie (1965) was able to comment that in Britain at that time, the 'accent-bar' was as strong as what was then referred to as the 'colour bar'. There was no exaggeration in this: the accent-bar was overtly and widely used to exclude people with localised accents from professional advantage, and it was thought to be reasonable even by some of those who were disadvantaged by it. Its aim appeared to be to protect the interests of powerful social networks by maintaining their traditional routes to wealth and privilege. Although other factors were also involved, the standard accent (RP) served as a symbolic affirmation of the right to govern and control, and it was accepted as reasonable that, for example, the 1955 British Cabinet should consist mainly of Old Etonians (former pupils of a single high-status school who – naturally – had the 'right' accent).

Linguists who have written books and papers on correctness have sometimes denounced this discriminatory stance as based on a set of unfounded beliefs about language, much as Christian missionaries denounced the religious practices of pagans. A classic example of a linguistic polemic on the subject is Robert A. Hall's *Leave Your Language Alone!* (1950). Hall assured general readers that there was nothing wrong with the way in which they were using their language and that there was nothing 'good or bad, correct or incorrect, grammatical or ungrammatical in language'. In so far as these views were directed at the general reader, they were ideological rather than strictly linguistic. Although based on analysis of language as a formal structure, they were focused on usage and 'acceptability'. Such views represent a strong reaction against traditional views of correctness and, when viewed in that context, they are not innocent linguistic pronouncements. They are overtly and deliberately ideological, and it is disingenuous to pretend otherwise.

To judge by recent developments in Britain (and for an illuminating discussion see Cameron 1995), attempts by linguists to change public attitudes have had rather little success. On the contrary, in Britain and North America their arguments have been perceived as an attack on 'standards' and have often drawn forth quite hysterical objections from 'language guardians' (for example Simon 1980, and see the discussion by Pinker 1994), who identify tolerance of variation with 'permissiveness' and further identify linguistic 'permissiveness' with moral permissiveness. Some commentators denounce descriptive linguistics as a dangerous heresy that undermines the social fabric. For Simon (1980), it is 'a benighted and despicable catering to mass ignorance under the supposed aegis of democracy'. In extreme cases such as this (these intemperate remarks are seemingly induced by the misplaced apostrophe), the tone is quasi-religious – even apocalyptic: it envisages a battlefield in which the forces of good and evil fight for supremacy and in which there is an evil conspiracy gnawing at the roots of society. The power of the rhetoric resides in the myth of the battle against evil and corruption that underlies it. More generally, language guardians (otherwise 'shamans': Bolinger 1981; or 'mavens': Pinker 1994) are following out what we have called 'the complaint tradition' in language (Milroy and Milroy 1991) – a tradition that has changed little since the early eighteenth century. Their public salience and influence, however, amount to much more than mere complaint in that their principles of linguistic correctness and uniformity, while failing to influence actual usage very deeply, have enormous social, educational and political implications. They cannot be successfully countered with the strictly linguistic answer that all languages and varieties are grammatical, structured systems (true as that is). The ideological basis of the most extreme complaints in this tradition (which begins with Swift's *Proposal* of 1712) is authoritarian and, seemingly, transcendental. Ultimately, although arguments from logic and Latin grammar have been used, the rightness of the 'correct forms' does not need to be justified by any truly linguistically based argument: they are assumed to be *obviously* correct, and alternative forms are equally obviously considered to be incorrect.

Authority and morality in language pronouncements

Although English language guardians see themselves as maintaining and defending a glorious heritage that carries all that is precious in our culture, their agenda is authoritarian, and condemnation of the usage of fluent native speakers can serve as an instrument of power. From this perspective, a language is not seen as the possession of the communities that use it – this is essentially what Hall (1950) was proposing – but as the property of small elite groups who have a moral duty to pronounce on language behaviour much as they might pronounce on moral behaviour. These pronouncements are seen as protecting the future of the language as part of the future of the nation or the culture, and these guardians feel further entitled to prescribe what constitutes the 'grammar' of the language – usually without having studied that grammar in any depth or having a clear notion of what 'grammaticality' is. As there is a morality involved, it becomes, in this view, morally right to use various sanctions against those (normally a majority of speakers) who do not conform to prescriptive pronouncements (which are described – incorrectly – as 'rules of grammar'). This is often justified on the basis that these sanctions are being used for the greater good of the community and the people, and are morally justified for that reason. One current argument in Britain is that prescriptive teaching of 'standard English' will be of benefit to the working classes, who have allegedly been denied access to it and who are also allegedly being cruelly disadvantaged by the arguments of certain linguists (Honey 1997). False claims of this kind are quite characteristic of the guardians: standard English norms have been taught in all schools for as long as English has been a school subject, and this will continue. No one opposes the teaching of standard English. The effect of this 'access to standard English' argument is not likely to be to benefit the underprivileged, but to maintain the authority of the canon of correct English. The method of inculcating the 'standard' (in so far as this can be defined) involves correcting offences against linguistic authority much as offences against legal authority are corrected – penalising a child in schoolwork, for instance, for misplacing an apostrophe or uttering the sequence *you was*. The authoritarian nature of the orthodoxy is clear in the underlying assumption that hundreds of millions of fluent native speakers cannot be trusted to use their own native language. In this moral universe, instituting classroom drills to stop children saying *I seen it* and *you was* is seen as sane and reasonable, and not as the time-wasting absurdity that it really is. The reality is that a language must meet the communicative and social needs of all its speakers, and not only those of the guardians, whose qualifications to judge 'correctness' are often highly dubious anyway. Furthermore, the role that prescription should legitimately play in language teaching is an important educational matter that can be discussed rationally. Discussion is not part of the agenda of the prescriptive grammarian.

The quasi-religious aspect of the prescriptive orthodoxy extends into moral questions, as it becomes possible from this sense of moral rectitude and dutiful responsibility to denounce those who may have different views and deny them the moral right to hold their own views. Opponents become, in effect, heretics, and those whose research appears, however unintentionally, to challenge traditional authority are seen as contributing to the heresy. For John Honey, for example, many linguistic researchers can be identified by name as 'the enemies of standard English'. The list of 'enemies' makes entertaining reading, as it contains some strange bedfellows, including, astonishingly, Noam Chomsky, whose theories of the 1960s and 1970s appeared to be based entirely, and very narrowly, on standard English. The fact that these 'enemies' may themselves have done a great deal of research on the history and use of standard English and that they have taught their students the use of correct standard written English, is apparently, in this moral crusade, of no relevance at all. To suggest that the traditional defenders of prescriptive norms may not always have had morality on their side is in itself a moral offence – all the more dangerous in that it has so much intellectual force and realism behind it.

The general public tends to accept the authority of many prescriptive pronouncements. Most people claim to believe that there are correct and incorrect ways of speaking and may well accept, quite wrongly, that their own speech – to the extent that it is non-standard – is 'ungrammatical'. Very approximately, the forms that they *believe* are 'correct' are roughly equivalent to 'standard', careful or literary forms. It does not follow that people necessarily use these standard forms themselves (and careful forms are not generally favoured in casual speech by any speaker), or even that they are always aware of exactly what these forms are, but they are often keenly aware that to use non-standard forms is undesirable for broadly social reasons, and they want their children to be taught 'correct' English. In other words, most speakers of English and other major languages are strongly influenced by some aspects of the standard ideology, and this seems to be true at all levels of educational attainment. It is true of the privileged and the unprivileged, but the attitudes are promoted and kept alive by those who are among the most powerful – for example, journalists and newspaper editors (Cameron 1995 cites striking examples) and British Government Ministers who have been involved in debates about the teaching of English in the National Curriculum. Thus, whatever the level of education or social status, people will generally claim to share the overt prescriptive attitudes that are enshrined in the handbooks in the belief that these constitute 'common sense' and are desirable. Political affiliations to the left or the right seem to make little difference: there is agreement on both sides of the Houses of Parliament, and no 'official Opposition'. This does not, of course, alter the fact that the driving ideology behind these views, whoever may hold them, is overtly authoritarian. It accepts that the standard canon must be vigilantly maintained by guardians who have privileged access to transcendental norms of correctness and that all should obey.

In debates about language use and language teaching, language experts seem often to have played into the hands of those who support narrowly 'correct' usage by giving too little attention to the fact that what is involved is only superficially a debate about language and is more fundamentally a debate about ideologies. In some cases, by making statements to the effect that it is 'a scientific fact' that all languages are equal, they have contributed to the confusion and misunderstanding that have characterised the debate. Of course, this is not 'a fact', and it is not 'scientific': it is not possible to demonstrate empirically that forms of language are either equal or unequal, or even that 'some are more equal than others' purely as linguistic objects. A claim of this sort is ideological, just as the claims that are made against it are ideological, and it is unwise for linguists to make public claims about linguistic equality unless they are aware that such claims will be interpreted as ideological. To point out that there is nothing 'ungrammatical' in some particular non-standard usage and that 'dialects' have 'grammars' is not ideological. However, to suggest that such usage is or should be generally socially accepted is just as much an ideological claim as to suggest that it is not acceptable: it is an attempt to influence social attitudes.

Despite all this, there can be no compromise on the methodological rigour of linguistic analysis and theory. Although varieties of language are not necessarily socially equal, what the descriptive linguist is obliged to do in analysing language is to assume that all varieties are equally valid as specimens of human language, regardless of how these varieties are publicly evaluated. Although we shall see that linguists have sometimes made pre-judgements that in principle they should perhaps not have made, one can find recurrent claims of this sort in the literature for well over a century. But the claims are ultimately concerned with analytic methodology and are devoted to the advancement of theory: they are not prescriptions or anti-prescriptions about attitudes to language and are irrelevant to public evaluations of language use. Public evaluations will be made, whatever professional linguists may say about them, and they will take rather predictable forms in cultures advocating standard language. On the other hand, linguists could not pursue their subject successfully if the linguistic forms that served as input to their analysis had first to be approved as legitimate by the high priests of correctness. Prescription is simply irrelevant in determining the database of serious linguistic research, and this is where many of the miscommunications between linguists and others originate. We can clarify this by using a transcription from conversational speech: the speaker is an intelligent middle-class 18-year-old female student at a leading American university:

And so – I mean – you know – I was puny in eighth grade – smaller than I am now, not that I'm all that big anyway, and – um – this was a big guy. Anyway, he was like: you called my mom a [sound effect] bitch, and I was like: No-o-o, and I was like: I didn't – I was

like: I don't know what you're talking about. I didn't say anything,
I was like: don't bother me . . .

A linguistic analysis of this passage (and other similar passages) will attempt
to work out the grammatical and conversational functions of the word *like*
and contribute to our knowledge of how the spoken language is used and
how it is changing. A prescriptivist will condemn it as bad English and
reject it, thereby implicitly condemning much of the casual spoken usage of
many millions of fluent native speakers. He or she may also see it as proof
that the language is declining and that people simply don't know how
to speak their own language any longer. Therefore, according to the prescriptivist, people must be prevented from speaking in this way. But any
attempt at this is doomed to failure. In Samuel Johnson's words (cited
in Milroy and Milroy 1991: 35): 'to enchain syllables, and to lash the
wind, are equally the undertakings of pride unwilling to measure its
desires by its strength'. As for 'Standard English', a conversational text
of this kind draws attention to the pointlessness of classifying it as being
either in standard or non-standard English. It is typical of current spoken
English among a certain age group: that is all. It is the ideology of standardisation as a process that is relevant, not the taxonomic definition of
specimens of conversational speech.

The standard ideology in linguistic theorising

The statement about 'scientific fact' in the previous section of the chapter
is drawn from a list of citations in Honey (1983) which purport to show the
general irresponsibility of 'linguists' in statements about the language faculty
and in the practical recommendations about language teaching that some of
them have made. The remainder of this chapter is based on the idea that
attacks of this sort on linguistics are intellectually misguided. The main point
that I wish to consider here is that, despite the linguist's avoidance of overt
issues of correctness, some of the basic ideas that drive linguistic science are
themselves offshoots of, or related to, the standard ideology – the same
ideology that is espoused by the supporters of authority in language. Linguists
who have chosen to make public appeals to egalitarian ideals in the use of
language are the exception rather than the rule and do not represent all the
principles that have guided linguistic theorising: they represent only part of
the argument, which is that *all languages and varieties of language are structured entities*. In principle it has been assumed that prior evaluations of a
social kind are not appropriate in determining the database of linguistic
analysis.

Apart from this general claim about the structured nature of all forms of
language, some of the assumptions that have underlain linguistic theorising
in this century have actually subscribed to the standard ideology – in some

important cases quite directly, but in most cases quite indirectly. We shall see that in certain respects it can be argued that they have in effect shared the popular view that some forms of language are legitimate and others illegitimate. One direct appeal to the standard ideology is that of Chomsky and Halle (1968) who state that the grammar of English that they are assuming is a 'Kenyon–Knott' grammar (this being a pedagogical account of standard English used in American high schools). A more specific example from generative grammar studies, in which the influence of standardisation seems to be clear, is Creider (1986), who discusses double embedded relatives with resumptive pronouns of the type *It went down over by that river that we don't know where it goes*. These are commonly found in quite formal styles (one of Creider's examples is from the speech of a US presidential candidate on television), and he describes them as 'hopelessly and irretrievably ungrammatical' in English. However, he further comments that 'such sentences may be found in serious literature in Spanish and Norwegian where there can be no question of their grammaticality' (Creider 1986: 415). This gives the impression that the occurrence of these sentences in serious literature is the criterion for grammaticality rather than the intuitions of the native speaker. Additionally, their existence as named classes ('knot sentences') in Danish and Norwegian grammar books can be taken to confer *legitimacy* on this type of sequence at least in those languages. However, we do not know if the native speaker regards them as ungrammatical in English, and if he or she does, it may well be because they do not occur in formal written styles and are not in grammar books. It is this dependence on formal literary criteria and grammar book legitimacy that demonstrates the influence of standardisation in such judgements.

The dependence for data on the 'intuitions' of the linguist (Radford 1981) also tends to lead to allegations that perfectly grammatical sequences are 'ungrammatical'. Scholars do not always seem to have been observant about the language used around them, and at various times and places sequences such as: *he did it already, they've won the cup last year, the eggs is cracked, where's it?, there's it* have been defined as ungrammatical despite daily use by numerous native speakers in different varieties and styles of English (see J. Milroy 1992 for a discussion). Generally speaking, these 'ungrammatical' sequences are not part of the standard or literary language, and linguists' 'intuitions' have plainly been affected by their knowledge of standard English and their assumption that English is much more uniform than it actually is. The attempt to distinguish between 'grammaticality' and 'acceptability' never seems to have been entirely successful, and theorists generally do not explicitly acknowledge that 'acceptability' must be a speaker-based criterion: it must therefore be social and *normative* because language is necessarily, amongst other things, a normative phenomenon. One of the failings of non-social linguistics is its insensitivity to the existence of the norms of language as observed by speakers. Judgements of grammaticality by theorists are also implicitly normative, but this is not admitted into the theory. To say that they are 'normative' is not, of course, to imply that they are intended prescriptively.

These judgements have another more general effect. They appear to elevate a particular variety (Southern British or mainstream American English) to authoritative status, and in that respect can be seen as part of the legitimisation process of the standard ideology. The language described in these sources is a uniform-state language, with limited provision for optionality (but within one 'variety'), and the model of language that is set up as the point of reference and database of the theory is standard English, represented simply as 'English'. The idea that linguists are 'enemies' of standard English (Honey 1997), while generally ludicrous, is actually the opposite of the truth in such cases. Through their authority their work contributes to the legitimacy of the standard variety, and they give no sign at all of opposing the standard ideology.

These tendencies can be seen as consequences of language standardisation, arising ultimately from the fact that linguistic scholars, like everyone else involved in the debate, have lived in standard language cultures, in which the standard language is very highly valued, identified with the language as a whole, and supposedly accessible in codified form in grammars and handbooks of usage. It is partly for this reason that linguistic theorists have so often treated languages as if they were uniform entities, rather than variable entities and, following from this, standard languages, as idealisations, are the most uniform entities of all. To the extent that this has been done, however, it can be objected to from a strictly intellectual point of view because no language is uniform, and, as noted above, it may well be that the standardised languages of Europe have properties special to standard languages only that are not present in the many languages of the world. If it is the case that standard languages have special properties, and if some of these properties are not language-internal, but socio-political, then it is important that linguistic scholars should investigate these properties and distinguish external from internal criteria. This is especially important in cases where linguists rely on uniform-state idealisations for their database. These additional properties that standard languages possess, over and above the 'dialects' of languages, are, in a broad sense, socially based. Before going on to review specific instances of the effects of standardisation on linguistic description and theory, I now briefly summarise some of the main characteristics of standardisation.

1   *The chief linguistic consequence of successful standardisation is a high degree of uniformity of structure.* This is achieved by suppression of 'optional' (generally socially functional) variation. For example, when two equivalent structures have a salient existence in the speech community, such as *you were* and *you was* or *I saw* and *I seen*, one is accepted and the other rejected – on grounds that are linguistically arbitrary, but socially

non-arbitrary. Thus, standard languages are high-level idealisations, in which uniformity or invariance is valued above all things. One consequence of this is that no one actually speaks a standard language. People speak vernaculars which in some cases may approximate quite closely to the idealised standard; in other cases the vernacular may be quite distant. A further implication of this is that, to the extent that non-standard varieties are maintained, there must be norms in society that differ from the norms of the standard (for example when the dialect of some British city is an [h]-dropping dialect). These must be in some way maintained over time in social groupings, and in standard language cultures they are effectively in opposition to the norms of the standard. In a chapter about ideologies, it is relevant to point out that this vernacular maintenance also implies competing ideologies that are in opposition to standard (or, more generally, institutionalised) ideology.

2   *Standardisation is implemented and promoted through written forms of language.* It is in this channel that uniformity of structure is most obviously functional. In spoken language, uniformity is in certain respects dysfunctional, mainly in the sense that it inhibits the functional use of stylistic variation. Until quite recently, linguistic theorists have not in the main used data from spoken interaction as their database. A well-known history of English, for example (Strang 1970), uses dialogue from published novels and plays to exemplify the norms of spoken conversational English. I presume I need not point out in detail how unsatisfactory this is. Thus, the grammars of languages that have been written define formal, literary or written language sequences as 'grammatical' or well formed and have few reliable criteria for determining the grammaticality or otherwise of spoken sequences. (The discipline of Conversational Analysis has much to say about this: see for example Schegloff 1979.) Despite this linguists often characterise certain sequences that occur frequently in spoken interaction as ungrammatical or ill formed. The association of standardisation with writing further suggests that standard varieties, in so far as they can be said to exist, are *not* parts of the speech community in precisely the same way that other varieties are.

3   *Standardisation inhibits linguistic change and variability.* Changes in progress tend to be resisted until they have spread so widely that the written and public media have to accept them. Even in the highly standardised areas of English spelling and punctuation, some changes have been slowly accepted in the last thirty years. For example, in English composition textbooks around 1960, the spelling *all right* was required, and *alright* (on the analogy of *already*) was an 'error'. It was required that a colon should be followed by a lower-case letter: the 'erroneous' use of a capital letter after a colon is, however, now accepted and sometimes required. The changes had taken place in some usages before the standard language accepted them. Standardisation inhibits linguistic change, but it does not

prevent it totally: to borrow a term from Edward Sapir, standardisation 'leaks'. There should, however, be no illusion as to what the aim of language standardisation actually is: it is to fix and 'embalm' (Samuel Johnson's term) the structural properties of the language in a uniform state and *prevent* all structural change. No one who is informed about the history of the standard ideology can seriously doubt this. It follows that the many languages of the world that are not standardised, or not heavily standardised, are not subject to this pressure.

In what follows we shall chiefly bear in mind the points about uniformity of structure and the transmission of standardisation through written forms of language – these being the most uniform. But we shall also bear in mind another important aspect of the ideology of standardisation – the idea of legitimacy. Much of the legitimisation of the standard variety is in fact achieved through creating a history for the standard language – a process that we can reasonably call *historicisation* (involving the creation of a legitimate historical canon). Metaphorically, this process makes it possible to think of the standard language as a legitimate offspring of noble ancestors, and by implication non-standard vernaculars become *illegitimate*. It is appropriate, therefore, to turn first to the work of the scholars who have built up the tradition of descriptive historical accounts of English. I have elsewhere (J. Milroy 1995) pointed out the continuing intellectual importance of this tradition and its ideological underpinnings (see further Crowley 1989).

The standard ideology and the descriptive tradition

The groundwork of comparative (and to a great extent, structural) linguistics was laid down in the nineteenth century, and English philology was effectively a sub-branch of this, applying its principles to the description of the history of English. The ideological underpinnings of much of this are more apparent in retrospect than they were at the time, and the ideology with which we are principally interested here is the development of strong nationalism in certain northern European states and the identification of the national language as a symbol of national unity and national pride. One side-effect of this ideology was a strong Germanic purist movement in England and other northern European countries and an insistence on the lineage of English as a Germanic language with a continuous history as a single entity (for relevant discussions see Leith 1996; J. Milroy 1977, 1996). This in itself can be seen as a late stage in establishing the legitimacy of a national standard language by historicisation, and many published histories of English have served the purpose of establishing its Anglo-Saxon heritage. One consequence of all these influences is the strong tendency to describe structural changes in the history of English as internally induced rather than influenced by language contact or dialect mixing. Moreover, despite the massive structural differences between Anglo-Saxon and present-day English, the language is generally extended backwards in historical accounts to AD500 in a continuous line and its ancient pedigree is emphasised. It becomes a thoroughbred of noble line. The retrospective myth of the history of English, created to suit Victorian ideologies, certainly continues well into the twentieth century.

Apart from the nationalism common to all nation states, there was an additional powerful ideological influence on nineteenth-century English: this was the movement to establish and legitimise standard English (the Queen's English) as the language of a great empire – a world language. To cite Dean Alford:

> It [the Queen's English] is, so to speak, this land's great highway of thought and speech and seeing that the Sovereign in this realm is the person round whom all our common interests gather, the source of our civil duties and centre of our civil rights, the Queen's English is not a meaningless phrase, but one which may serve to teach us profitable lessons with regard to our language, its use and abuse.
>
> (Alford 1889)

It would be wrong to suppose that these Victorian sentiments have been entirely superseded, and the morality of 'use' and 'abuse' is still clearly present in prescriptive pronouncements. Alford's objections to dropped [h] and intrusive [r] are moralistically phrased. Victorian scholarship broke into two streams that, on the face of it, appear to be divergent. On the one hand there was a tremendous interest in rural dialects of English, largely because these were thought to preserve forms and structures that could be used to help in reconstructing the history of the language (a Germanic language) on broadly neogrammarian principles and extend its pedigree backwards in time. On the other there was a continuing drive to codify and legitimise the standard form of the language, and this is especially apparent in the dictionaries, handbooks and language histories of the period. Among the eminent scholars of the time there were many who advocated both Anglo-Saxon purism and dialect study. The advocates of the superiority of standard English could also ascribe to this purism. An important example of this is Oliphant (1873), whose account of Standard English includes many lamentations at the damage done to English by the influence of French. According to him the 'good old masonry' of Anglo-Saxon had been adulterated by 'meaner ware imported from France'. Sweet (1964: 244–5) advocated that schoolchildren should not be taught Latin and Greek until late in their schooling, if at all, and that they should be taught Anglo-Saxon early. 'The only dead languages that children ought to have anything to do with are the earlier stages of their own language ... I think children ought to begin with Old English.' Sweet, however, like Oliphant, was also a strong defender of Standard English and an opponent of dialect study. Writing in 1899, he presents the dialects of

English as degenerate forms in opposition to the work of his Oxford rival, Joseph Wright.

> Most of the present English dialects are so isolated in their develop-
> ment and so given over to disintegrating influences as to be, on the
> whole, less conservative than and generally inferior to the standard
> dialect. They throw little light on the development of English, which
> is profitably dealt with by a combined study of the literary docu-
> ments and the educated colloquial speech of each period in so far
> as it is accessible to us.
>
> (Sweet 1971)

I do not have space here to tease out the manifold implications of this important passage by the greatest English language scholar of the time. It is echoed by Wyld a generation later (1927: 16), and I need hardly comment that to the variationist it seems extraordinarily wrong-headed. The ideologic-al stance is, however, clear, and the history of English is a history of 'educated speech'. It is as if the millions of people who spoke non-standard varieties over the centuries have no part in the history of English. It is certainly pos-sible to find the same bias in favour of 'educated speech' in many respectable English scholars until rather recently, even if it is less overtly stated, and the general pro-standard flavour is of course enhanced in many histories of English by the necessary reliance on written and formal data-sources.

The distinction between 'legitimate' linguistic change and 'corruption' or 'decay', which follows rather obviously from Sweet's pronouncement, is also frequently made. Marsh (1865) – an American scholar – warns against con-founding 'positive corruptions, which tend to the deterioration of a tongue' from linguistic changes 'which belong to the character of speech, as a living semi-organism connatural with man, and so participating in his mutations'. Corruptions (but presumably not changes) arise 'from extraneous or acci-dental causes'. To Marsh it appears that linguistic change is not only 'natural' but internal to language, and the extraneous and accidental factors appear to be envisaged as broadly social. Although present-day scholars would be unlikely to speak of 'corruptions' in quite this way, the distinction between internal and external factors is very much alive (with internal explanations preferred by theorists); in some influential quarters, social explanations for linguistic changes are still strongly resisted (Lass 1987, 1996). But the effect of Marsh's distinction is surely to smuggle in a social judgement by the back door: to judge by the remainder of his discussion, 'corruptions' are colloquial usages by lower-class speakers, and legitimate changes arise in educated usage – the usage of the elite. He goes on to advocate resistance to these corrup-tions: 'To pillory such offences . . . to detect the moral obliquity that often lurks beneath them, is the sacred duty of every scholar'. It is interesting that in the nineteenth century American scholars were very similar to English scholars in their class-oriented views (but see further L. Milroy in Chapter 8 of this volume).

There is another strand in the condemnation of Victorian corruptions – the denunciation of 'journalese' or newspaper 'jargon' (Oliphant 1873) and, for the poet Hopkins, this aspect of Victorian usage was 'a bad business' (see J. Milroy 1977). Needless to say, a number of the corruptions that Marsh and others complained about have long since become linguistic changes. Marsh's distinction is also found in Whitney (1897: 155–6). He mentioned 'offenses against the correctness of speech', but he also knew that the 'corruptions' often fed into the future of the language and, once adopted, were no longer corruptions. The general effect of the distinction, however, is clearly to make a prior social judgement on what constitutes the legitimate form of the language and what constitutes a linguistic change, and the habit continues. As late as 1962, W. P. Lehmann in his first edition of the standard textbook, *Historical Linguistics*, commented that non-standard forms are used by 'rustics, criminals and the rebellious younger generation'. One gets the impression that these authors considered that such people should certainly not be allowed to take part in the process of language change.

Most of the authoritative histories of English since Sweet's time until quite recently (the breakthrough came with Leith 1980) have been retrospective histories of one elite variety, used by a minority of the population. After 1550, the story is normally exclusively a story of the development of what is called standard English (often ambiguously conceived of as a socially elite variety as well as a standard language), and dialectal developments are neglected, confined to footnotes or dismissed as 'vulgar' and 'provincial' forms. This is quite usual in the very important work of E. J. Dobson (1968) on the pronunciation of Early Modern English. His aim is exclusively to describe the pronunciation of early modern Standard English, and it is taken for granted that there actually was such a variety and that it can be retrospectively defined. There has been much excellent work on the origins of the standard, and to describe its origins is an important task. However, the history of standard English is not the history of the English language, and to dismiss the dialects as irrelevant is to ignore the variable nature of language in use. Some pronunciations that later became standard English certainly originated in non-standard usages (see, for example, Mugglestone 1995 for the probable Cockney origins of RP 'broad' /a/).

A very influential scholar in this elitist tradition was H. C. Wyld, whose work has recently come under scrutiny by Crowley (1989, 1991). His comments on the irrelevance of the language of 'illiterate peasants' and the importance of the language of 'the Oxford Common Room and the Officers' mess' are now notorious (Wyld 1927). Wyld's concept of 'Received Standard' included not only the grammar and vocabulary, but pronunciation (now known as 'Received Pronunciation' or RP), and the effect of this was to restrict the standard language to a very small elite class of speakers, probably never numbering more than 5 per cent of the population. Otherwise it was the 'Modified Standard' of 'city vulgarians'; these later became the 'non-U' speakers of Ross's famous essay (1954). Wyld was a very great historian of English and a leader in the field of Middle English dialect study. It now seems paradoxical that he could set such a high value on variation in Middle English and make such an original contribution to the study of variation in Early Modern ('Standard') English, while at the same time despising the modern dialects of English. It is probably not accidental that a competing tradition of dialectology had been represented at Oxford by Joseph Wright, who rose from the status of an illiterate woollen-mill worker to become the Professor of Anglo-Saxon, and not entirely irrelevant that he was appointed to that Chair in preference to Henry Sweet. However, the ideological bias is clear, and the association of the standard language with the idea of grades of social prestige appears in Wyld's work, as it also does in American scholarship of the same period (see, for example, Sturtevant 1917: 26). The concept of the speech community that underlies this is one in which an elite class set the standard (the word 'standard' here being used in the sense of a desirable level of usage that all should aspire to achieve), and in which the lower middle classes constantly strive to imitate the speech of their 'betters'. Labov's famous graph of the 'hypercorrection' pattern of the Lower Middle Class and his focus on the class system as the scenario in which change is enacted had certainly been anticipated.

What these scholars did was to equate a standard language with a prestige language used by a minority of speakers and thereby introduce an unanalysed social category as part of the definition of what, in theory, should be an abstract linguistic object, characterised especially by uniformity of internal structure. As Crowley has recently shown, Wyld was especially important in the legitimisation of the 'Received Standard' as the prestige language in that he gave 'scientific' status (Crowley 1991: 207–9) to what he thought was the *intrinsic* superiority of that variety (Wyld 1934). He did this by citing phonetic reasons. According to him this pronunciation has 'maximum sonority or resonance' and the 'clearest possible differentiation between sounds'. But what Wyld is describing here is an idealisation and not a reality. It is unlikely that his views could be confirmed by quantitative analysis of the output of large numbers of speakers, and these would have to be pre-defined as speakers of the variety in question: a partly social judgement as to whether they were speakers of received pronunciation (RP) would already have been made. The question of stylistic levels is also vitally important here. In empirical studies it has generally been found that in casual conversational styles there is close approximation and overlap between realisations of different phonemes (J. Milroy 1981, 1992), and there is no reason to suppose that the casual styles of RP would be much different. Thus, we have a third strand in the definition of the standard. The standard language is uniform, it has prestige, and it is also 'careful'. Wyld's idealisation is not merely a uniform-state

32

idealisation: it is also social and communicative, and it depends on ideologies of social status and what is desired in public and formal non-conversational language – carefulness and clarity of enunciation. The rise of sound broadcasting is also very relevant here. In order to speak this variety it is considered that you must have a rich voice, a good microphone manner and wear a dinner suit even when you can't be seen. However, a non-standard variety can certainly be spoken in careful style, just as RP can. What is more dubious is whether Wyld's idealised Received Standard can be spoken in a casual style. His references to 'poetry' and 'oratory' make it very clear that he is thinking of public language enunciated in a formal style, and this form of language does not greatly resemble the casual speech of anyone. Such careful high-status speech was considered part of formal politeness and good manners, like dressing for dinner and opening the door for a lady.

Although few subsequent scholars of ability have gone as far as Wyld, the consciousness of a canon of linguistic behaviour that is based on the continuity of a Received Standard has continued up to the present day in some approaches to English. Many historical studies of English refer routinely to 'good' English very much in the Wyld tradition. The tradition is, arguably, present also in, for example, the teaching of English phonetics, where RP is taken as the model accent. The influential phonetics textbooks of Daniel Jones and A. C. Gimson are avowedly descriptions of this variety. Other phoneticians have since given great attention to RP, and have tended to define it as a continuing entity by distinguishing categories such as 'Conservative' RP and 'Advanced' RP. There is every reason, however, to suppose this regionless variety is sharply recessive and that it no longer has the social function it used to have. It is, effectively, dead or dying. This RP industry has been fuelled by the need to teach English to overseas learners and is justifiable in this context, but it is also true that overseas learners of British English have thus been taught a conservative pronunciation that they will now seldom hear except in the public pronouncements of the Prince of Wales and other dignitaries. More generally the codifications of Standard English grammar such as those by Quirk and his colleagues are also responses to the need to teach a generally uniform state form to non-native learners of what is now a major world language. Although it is questionable whether RP should now be taught as a clearly focused variety, it is reasonable that the grammar taught should be standard English in so far as this is close to the usage of many speakers and is used in writing.

It is an open question to what extent the focus on uniform states that has been characteristic of linguistics for over a century is a product of the existence of standard ideologies or a product of internal descriptive requirements within linguistics – the need to focus on a definable idealisation. Yet, it seems that the existence of standard languages of European nation states has had a considerable indirect influence on the investigation of less well-known languages. It is worth considering that it may not be inherent in the nature of language as a phenomenon (in the form of grammars, lexicons and phonologies) to split up into distinct 'languages', and that these languages are largely the products of socio-political factors among which standardisation can be extremely important. The effect of Western ideologies of language on the study of Pacific languages has been discussed by Mühlhäusler (1996), who calls attention to some remarks by other scholars. Grace comments (1991: 15): 'One of the things I found most puzzling was that in some areas the people seem to have no conception of what their language is and no sense of belonging to a linguistic community'. It is not precisely that they don't know which language they are speaking: the concept of a language community has not even occurred to them. Heryanto (1990: 41), cited by Mühlhäusler, points out that language 'is not a universal category or cultural activity though it may sound odd, not all people have a language in a sense of which this term is currently used in English'. If our studies are to be about 'language', and not merely about particular languages that happen to have been most studied, we may have to rid ourselves of some of the basic assumptions we make about what kind of objects languages are, and it is clear that the ideology of the standard language has played some part in conditioning the methodologies and theoretical views that are currently in fashion.

There is much to be said about this, and I can only make a few suggestions here. One case in point, to which I have referred above, is some aspects of 'grammaticality' judgements as they have been made by generative linguists. These are often influenced by knowledge of the standard language, especially the literary standard, and they often seem to be inappropriate in the study of variable spoken language (for relevant comments see Milroy and Milroy 1991: 78–9; J. Milroy 1992: 6–9). Similarly, when linguists claim that the input to child learning is 'degenerate', one wonders how this degeneracy is to be defined, and there is a suspicion that anything that does not conform to the careful sequences of literary grammar is what is meant by 'degenerate'. If this is correct, some basic claims of an influential paradigm are affected by the ideology of standardisation. It looks from this point of view as if the Chomskyan claim about degenerate input to child language learning is a continuation of the distinction between legitimate and illegitimate forms and the dismissal of attested forms that are labelled 'careless' or 'vulgar'.

I now turn briefly to historical work, in which textual editors and others seem to have been influenced very strongly by the idea of uniformity and invariance and by notions of correctness of a kind that the original scribes knew nothing of. I have discussed this elsewhere (J. Milroy 1983, 1992), and mention it only briefly here.

Textual normalisation

The idea that a spelling system should ideally be invariant is a post-eighteenth-century notion, but it has had quite considerable effects on the judgements of editors of early English texts. In order to justify the reconstruction of invariant systems and dismisss evidence that is thought to be corrupt or unreliable, a very influential argument has been that many Middle English scribes were Anglo-Norman and not native speakers of English. They therefore wrote it incorrectly. This leads to normalisation of the spelling of these texts: if the word 'right', for instance, appears variably as *riht*, *richt*, *rith*, *ricth*, *rit*, *rist*, then it is normalised to *riht*, and the spelling–phonology relationship is sealed off from further investigation. The scribes are said to have been 'careless' or poorly acquainted with English and the variable texts are valued less highly than texts that exhibit little variation. As late as 1966, Bennett and Smithers could still comment that the 'philological value' of the *Peterborough Chronicle* extensions is 'reduced' by 'a disordered system of spelling', when this variation might be quite revealing if analysed. These arguments (and particularly the Anglo-Norman one) are clearly extensions of the view that some attested forms are illegitimate and can be dismissed. The notion of correctness, the belief in the value of 'pure' dialects and the insistence on uniformity are all part of the ideology of standardisation – projected backwards in these examples to a time when the ideology did not exist.

Of course the transmission of Middle English (ME) texts has often been very complex, and many genuine errors can be identified. However, in the Skeat–Sisam (1915) edition of *Havelok* the Anglo-Norman argument is set out in detail and accepted as 'fact' (many variant spellings in the text are specified, without clear justification, as Anglo-Norman and therefore mistakes) when there is no evidence that the scribe was a non-native English speaker and little reason to believe that by 1300 or so he was not an English speaker. Anglo-Norman had always had a restricted currency in the speech community and was dying out by 1300 anyway. In the *Havelok* edition, the systematic variation concealed by the normalisation appears to constitute evidence that in the underlying dialect certain changes had already occurred or that newer forms were present in alternation with older forms (sociolinguists have found this to be a common scenario), and that sound changes dated much later in what is known as 'standard' English were already present in certain communities. Clearly such a conclusion depends on the idea that language always incorporates variation, and it follows that an argument that [h]-dropping in English, for example, could not have occurred before the period of colonisation (as it is not generally found today in colonial varieties) is not a valid argument. Changes do not happen overnight in a language: they are initiated in a speech community and not in the whole language and, if successful, they spread in the form of alternants through speech communities and beyond them. The emphasis on orderly heterogeneity seems to be capable of giving us some insights and helping to repair the damage caused by inappropriate use of the standard ideology.

I now turn to variation studies, which recognise the importance of heterogeneity in language, but in which some traces of the standard ideology may still remain.

Sociolinguistics, structuralism and the standard ideology

All new intellectual paradigms, however innovative, necessarily carry with them some of the assumptions of their predecessors. This was true of early generative grammar, which carried on some aspects of mid-century structuralism, and it is also true of quantitative sociolinguistics. Structuralist ideas are basic to many aspects of the argumentation used, including the concept of the linguistic variable – a concept that is also present in the structuralist idea of the phoneme and its variants (allophones), whatever the superficial differences may be. The fact that sociolinguists *count* the variants whereas structuralists generally did not does not affect the common structuralist origin of both concepts. Here I will mention particularly the concept of *orderly* or *structured heterogeneity* (Weinreich, Labov and Herzog 1968), which is correctly seen as an important innovation. To show that variation in speaker usage is not necessarily random and accidental, but orderly and patterned, is a tremendous advance that seems on the face of it to reject the dominance of the standard ideology. It has certainly given us a springboard for investigating the way in which human beings actually do interact in language – in non-standard varieties and casual styles. Yet, if the claim about structured heterogeneity were taken to a logical extreme, and we were to claim that *all* heterogeneity in a dialect or language is structured, we would be subscribing to the Saussurean view that a language is a self-contained structured entity of totally interdependent parts, and we would effectively be implying that change is impossible (the 'Saussurean paradox'). The grammars of variation that we produce do not logically replace uniform and categorial grammars (as Chambers 1995 has claimed) because by this logic they become categorial grammars of variation, and this applies despite the fact that they are arrived at by quantitative means. Thus, although these variationist approaches have made a breach in the wall of the idea of self-contained languages and varieties and standard ideologies, the underlying assumptions, being structuralist, do not completely break free from these ideas. Furthermore, the quantitative methodology has been almost entirely applied to speech communities that use well-established languages – English, French, Spanish – in which the standard ideology is present, and these have usually been treated as monolingual. To judge by Mühlhäusler's (1996: 325–39) comments, variationist studies of language communities that are not affected by standardisation of the native language will require different methods and different underlying assumptions about the concept of 'a language'. This is not to say that we can totally reject the insight that languages incorporate structure in some sense and to some degree. It is the strong underlying assumption of intra-linguistic structuralism in quantitative sociolinguistics that needs to be reconsidered, and in this we need to remember that many of its insights are based on the study of communities affected by standardisation. We now finally turn to the methods of interpreting data that are used in sociolinguistics, focusing on the social category of *prestige* and its relationship to the standard ideology.

Prestige as explanation in sociolinguistics

As we saw above, the tradition in English philology assumed an identity between the standard language and the 'prestige' language. In Britain this identification was particularly strong because of the rigid class or status distinctions inherited from the nineteenth century and before, and it is still much more influential than in many other western countries. In historical description, therefore, the notion of prestige was widely appealed to as a form of explanation for language change. But the concept was never carefully analysed, and the paradox that changes in the history of English did not seem to emanate from the highest status groups was never resolved. It is by no means clear that the 'standard language' at any given time is a direct product of the language of the highest status groups (this seems often to be recessive), and the identification of the standard language with the highest prestige language clearly needs further analysis. To start with, it may be suggested that the standard language originates in the need for widespread communication in written form and that, although the highest prestige forms may affect it, the forms adopted are adopted primarily because they are the ones that are most likely to be widely accepted or understood in writing. It is in legal and administrative documents that the need for standardisation is strongest and not in the elite literary tradition, because these have to be very precise and not subject to differing interpretations.

If historical linguistics were uncritical about the concept we might expect sociolinguistics to be more critical, but this has not always been so. The idea of prestige is still used rather routinely, and there are many instances in the literature where it is assumed that a scale of prestige parallel to a scale of social status is the same thing as a scale from non-standard to standard. This tendency probably arises from the fact that most of the early quantitative work explored variation in the dimension of social class (Labov 1966; Trudgill 1974a), partly continuing the emphasis on social class so prominent in the work of Wyld (but without its assumptions about the 'best' English, 'vulgar' English and so forth). Furthermore, the division of prestige into 'overt' and 'covert' prestige does not seem to get us much further in explanation, as this binary split does not in itself face the problem of what precisely is meant by 'prestige'. How far does it reside in economic power and wealth and how far in subjective perceptions of individual speakers? Why should speakers in their daily life figure forth an abstract class system in their conversations with friends, neighbours and strangers? How far are they motivated by 'prestige' when they use more geographically widespread linguistic forms to communicate with relative outsiders and how far by communicative needs, negative politeness, identity roles, or a host of other possibilities? What is the role of language standardisation in enabling these geographically widespread forms to be used, and if standardisation has a role, what does this have to do with prestige? These unanswered questions come to mind, and there could be many more.

When sociolinguists use prestige explanations, as they often do, the assumption often seems to be that if a given change cannot be explained by overt prestige, then the explanation must be 'covert' prestige. Labov's distinction between 'change from above' and 'change from below' takes us somewhat further, as it is based on the idea of social awareness of variants, rather than class. In practice, however, it is nearly always assumed that 'change from above the level of awareness' is the same as change emanating from the higher social classes, and vice versa. Indeed, Labov (1994: 78) has recently stated that these labels refer 'simultaneously to levels of social awareness and positions in the socio-economic hierarchy'. There is no obvious reason to suppose that these two things are the same, and this dictum clearly ties us to a socio-economic model of interpretation. Changes *must* be enacted primarily within the social class hierarchy rather than in other social dimensions, and these other dimensions become subsidiary to social class as interpretative categories. This, as we have noted, is effectively a continuation of the model of the speech community that was envisaged by older historians of English. But – to return to the notion of the standard language – the many commentaries and projects that identify prestige forms with standard forms do not derive this directly from Labov. He has never included the idea of standardisation in his conceptualisation of the speech community and has almost nothing to say directly about it as a process.

The converse social category to prestige is *stigma*, and I will end this discussion by commenting on this. If we focus on stigma rather than prestige we can gain at least one insight that is not so readily accessible in the notion of prestige alone, and that is that high-status dialects can be stigmatised (i.e. avoided) in the speech community just as low-status dialects are. The speech of speakers of high social status and, supposedly, high prestige, can be – apparently – stigmatised. If this were not so, the elite dialect of the Elizabethan Court would have controlled the future of English rather than the dialects of the business and administrative classes that superseded it. Stigmatised features of upper-class language may sometimes have been the same as those used in lower-class language, as suggested by the anecdote about King Edward VII who, on meeting the author Frank Harris, is alleged to have said *Mornin'*, *'Arris. Goin' rattin'*? In the late twentieth century, conservative RP is receding in the younger generation and formerly stigmatised features, including glottal stops, are entering their speech (Wells 1982). The vowels of the Royal Family are parodied with spellings such as *hice*, *abite* for 'house, about'. Some of the 'U' (upper-class) forms advocated by Ross (1954), such as *looking glass* for 'mirror' are now merely viewed as quaint archaisms. Thus, salient forms that are generally viewed as standard, or mainstream, are not necessarily those of the highest social classes, and they probably have not in the past originated as innovations by those classes. Thus, it seems (1) that those with highest social prestige are not necessarily accorded prestige for their use of language, and (2) that a prestige language is not identical in every respect with an idealised standard language. Prestige (as it is normally used) and standardisation are concepts of different orders – the one being social and speaker-based, and the other socio-political and institutional. In interpreting the findings of variationist studies, it is important to keep them separate and define them more precisely, and to investigate the subtle relationship between them. The term 'prestige', as used by social and historical linguists, is particularly in need of clarification.

In this chapter I have attempted to show that, although linguists often disapprove of popular attitudes to correctness, they are themselves in some respects affected by the ideology that conditions these popular views – the ideology of language standardisation with its emphasis on formal and written styles and neglect of the structure of spoken language. This ideology has arguably strengthened the tendency to think of languages as wholly separate pre-defined entities, consisting of sequences that can be defined as 'grammatical', and the belief in uniformity and self-containedness of language states seems to have been incorporated into structuralist views of language – views that continue to affect research paradigms. The identification of standardisation with 'prestige' is so strong in the descriptive tradition as represented by Wyld and others that, as I have tried to show, it still influences our thinking. In sociolinguistic research, it is important to separate these concepts. It is also important to allow for the fact that the speech communities that have been studied have usually been within cultures that are perceived to have a standard language, as this affects the claim to universality of the diachronic processes identified. The speakers in such cultures are liable to be influenced by the standard ideology, and this cannot be wholly irrelevant to their usage. The sense in which it is relevant, however, will never be precisely understood until the separate concepts of prestige and standardisation, and the subtle effects of one on the other, are more fully explored than they have been to date. Above all, it should be borne in mind that standardisation is not an 'unnatural' process that distorts the 'natural' use of language in speech communities. It is a natural socio-political process, whose role in determining speaker usage must be taken into account in assessing the results of our findings. In standard language cultures, standardisation is heavily involved in linguistic change and is not irrelevant to it. What I have suggested here and elsewhere (J. Milroy 1992) is that it is desirable for this to be taken more fully into account and its consequences for a theory of linguistic change more fully investigated. Finally, I have tried to show that just as linguistic change is a process, so standardisation is a process, and that a process-based model of interpretation is capable of giving important insights that are not easily accessible in the 'product' models of language change that have been traditional in the subject.

2

THE SOCIAL CONSTRUCTION OF STANDARD ENGLISH: GRAMMAR WRITERS AS A 'DISCOURSE COMMUNITY'

Richard J. Watts

1 Social constructivism and Standard English as the 'legitimate language'

In tracing out the historical development of British Standard English (SE) there is general agreement about the central importance of the first sixty years of the eighteenth century in creating the conditions under which an 'ideology of linguistic prescriptivism' became the dominant conceptual framework for setting up the notion of a national standard language (cf. Smith 1984; Watts 1990, 1996; Mugglestone 1995; Leith 1997; Milroy and Milroy 1998). The eighteenth century was a period in which explicit connections were being made between mercantilism and imperialist ambitions, on the one hand, and the nation-state and a 'national' language, on the other (Hobsbawm 1990).

However, in the welter of books and pamphlets of different kinds that were published on the subject of language in the first half of the eighteenth century, we tend to lose sight of the significance of certain powerful social institutions through which dominant social values were not only constructed and diffused throughout society but were also built into and made part of the hegemonic practices of government and the administration. The most influential of these social institutions was that of 'public' education in the form of schools and universities, and it is with that institution, and the grammars of English that were written specifically for it from the turn of the eighteenth century till 1762, that I shall be concerned in this chapter.[1]

I shall argue that it is only by understanding how these social values came to be constructed and so successfully diffused that we will be able to understand the powerful lay conceptualisations of SE. These conceptualisations led to the recent fight over the National Curriculum for English language teaching in Britain, in which ideas of 'correct English' and 'proper English' with their connotations of 'perfection', 'excellence', 'unity', 'unchangeability', etc. prevailed over alternative notions such as 'variability', 'development and change', 'flexibility', 'alternative standards', etc. The social values diffused through the education system have a long history and are firmly entrenched in the minds of non-linguists concerned with the teaching of SE. Linguists and sociolinguists would be well advised to understand those values before suggesting any further educational strategies. Two concepts lie at the heart of the present analysis of eighteenth-century grammars, the concept of 'social institution', which I have already mentioned briefly and which I derive from the work of Berger and Luckmann (1991), and the concept of 'symbolic capital' as developed by Pierre Bourdieu and his associates.

Berger and Luckmann maintain that all socio-communicative interaction takes place within social institutions which are constructed in the course of time through face-to-face contacts. Social institutions are continually reproduced and, in the process, adapted to changing needs. During the individual's socialisation via the dialogic medium of language, he or she objectifies inter-personal, interactional experiences into a conceptualisation of 'reality' which is essentially a social construct. In doing so the individual structures a system of social roles, ethics and constraints to which values are assigned and re-affirms these values by accepting (or even rejecting) those aspects of 'social reality'. Berger and Luckmann call this process 'institutionalization', which they define as 'a reciprocal typification of habitualized actions by types of actors' (1991: 72). In order for a typification process to constitute an insti-tution, it must be repeated frequently; it must acquire its own historicity. As Berger and Luckmann point out, 'institutions have a history, of which they are the products' (1991: 94). In addition they imply social control.

Thus, at one and the same time, institutions are cultural products and essential constitutive factors that help us to define a culture. To challenge the 'reality' of an institution is to threaten an important element of the culture itself, which implies that social institutions are particularly resistant to change and reform.

One of the most important and influential social institutions in any cultural group is that of 'public' education, comprising schools, classrooms, governing bodies, control assessment bodies (like school inspectorates), sets of legally binding statutes and decrees, groups of people to whom these laws apply (e.g. parents, children), agents of the institution (like teachers, school prin-cipals, school boards, etc.), bodies responsible for the production of knowledge to be disseminated through the institution (e.g. teaching materials, training institutions, teaching aids, etc.). Clearly, the 'reciprocal typifications of actions' that go to make up the institution of public education are myriad and constitute an immensely complex 'history'.

In Bourdieu's terms, a culture functions by producing and reproducing three different kinds of capital: *material capital* (involving the economy and the production of material goods), *cultural capital* (involving different forms of knowledge, acquired abilities, competence and skills) and *symbolic capital* (involving social status, honour, fame, respect, prestige, etc.), all of which function in different kinds of 'marketplace'. To acquire these forms of capital different kinds of resource are necessary, and within the area of symbolic capital one of the major types of *symbolic resource* is language. However, the types of resource necessary to acquire capital can vary in their forms and each form can have a greater or lesser value than another form. This is also the case with language, so that highly valued forms of language can allow the user of those forms to gain access to economic and cultural marketplaces. For example, with a knowledge of the appropriate kind of language to use in a job interview and the ability to manipulate this resource, access can be gained to the job market, hence to the acquisition of economic capital. With reference to the linguistic marketplace Bourdieu talks of 'legitimate language', i.e. that language which has acquired a place of pre-eminence through forms of institutional discourse.

Clearly individuals can be socialised into the ways in which they should comport themselves within any one marketplace, whether economic, cultural or symbolic. The 'feel' for a situation which an individual can gain and the ways in which she or he accordingly reacts are referred to by Bourdieu as a *habitus*. In reference to language Bourdieu and Passeron (1994: 8) state that this is 'the most active and elusive part of the cultural heritage', thereby implying that the 'linguistic habitus' is one of the most salient in social interaction and one of the most difficult to change.

A further major concept in Bourdieu's work is that of *field*, by which he understands the social space for action within an institutional framework, i.e. the hierarchical structure of the institution and the qualifications required to manipulate the institution to gain forms of capital. For Bourdieu one of the most significant fields within the area of symbolic capital is the education system, and it is at this point, in the social institution of public education, that the theory of social construction and reproduction interlocks with the theory of the linguistic marketplace.

Within the education system, Bourdieu's term 'legitimate language' refers not only to a highly valued, officially sanctioned linguistic code, but also to the forms of discourse which characterise that social institution. They are those forms of language use which have become 'reciprocal typifications' of habitualised language behaviour in the institutional field of social action represented by the public education system. Now, as in the eighteenth century, the legitimate language code in education is SE and the legitimate forms of language behaviour are those which define the various types of habitus within the institution, e.g. the pupil, the teacher, the materials' writer, the school inspector, etc. The forms of discourse that have become 'legitimate language' thus characterise what I shall call a 'discourse community', a term which I shall define more closely in the following section. I shall argue that grammar writers during the eighteenth century constitute just such a discourse community and that by studying their discourse more closely we can trace the development of an ethos of prescriptivism in the social construction of SE.

2 The notion of 'discourse community' and its application to the discourse of eighteenth-century grammar writers

I define the term 'discourse community' as a set of individuals who can be interpreted as constituting a community on the basis of the ways in which their oral or written discourse practices reveal common interests, goals and beliefs, i.e. on the degree of institutionalisation that their discourse displays. The members of the community may or may not be conscious of sharing these discourse practices. Thus, a discourse community may show strong or weak member affiliation to the values of the community, and the community itself may only become 'visible' through the course of time. In this sense, of course, a discourse community might also be defined as an embryonic institution with its own historicity.

If we use this definition to evaluate whether grammar writers in the first sixty years of the eighteenth century can be classified as a discourse community, we need to know the following:

1   What aspects of the discourse observable in their grammars allow us to posit a degree of homogeneity, even over a relatively long period of time?
2   Is it possible to assess from the written discourse who the intended addressees were, and do those intended addressees constitute a relatively homogeneous group?
3   Is it possible to interpret the features of that discourse as forming part of the legitimate language of the social institution of 'public' education, i.e. as constituting a significant part of the symbolic resource of language?

In looking at the discourse practices of eighteenth-century grammarians, we can observe a shift towards a prescriptive stance in the legitimate language of public education.

The grammars I have examined are listed below. They are not all fully representative of the discourse community, but those that are less so still contain clear features of the legitimate language:

James Greenwood, *An Essay toward a Practical English Grammar*, 1711
Hugh Jones, *An Accidence to the English Tongue*, 1724
Daniel Duncan, *A New English Grammar*, 1731
Samuel Saxon, *The English Scholar's Assistant*, 1737
Robert Lowth, *A Short Introduction to English Grammar*, 1762

In addition, I shall also refer at various points to John Wallis's *Grammatica Linguæ Anglicanæ*, 1653, and Guy Miège's *The English Grammar*, 1688.

The most salient types of discourse practice which indicate membership in a discourse community are explicit references to earlier works and the reworking of sections of text from earlier works, with or without acknowledgement of the source. Both types of discourse practice represent forms of intertextuality which allow us to trace the lines of a common discourse. Looked at from the perspective of the eighteenth century the practice of reusing excerpts from earlier authors was almost certainly not considered as plagiarism, although Greenwood does acknowledge his English translation of Wallis's long preface by giving this section of the grammar the title 'Dr. *Wallis*'s PREFACE • With Additions. The *Additions* have this Mark before them (")' and by warning the reader in his own short preface that 'I have in this Book taking [sic] in every Thing that was Material from Dr. *WALLIS*, but He Writing for Foreigners and in *Latin*, I have not pursu'd his Method; as not being every way answerable to my Design.'

As the eighteenth century progressed grammar writers tended to refer their readers more frequently to models of language usage, all of them from the written language. In the earlier part of the century newspapers and reviews like *The Tatler*, *The Spectator*, *The Examiner* and others were also offered as models of the legitimate language, and by the time we reach Lowth's grammar in 1762 we find that poets and prose writers are not only held up as models to be followed but also as examples of what not to do. Not all of the grammars in the selection given above make use of this discourse strategy. Duncan's and Saxon's grammars, for example, make no explicit reference to 'good' authors, probably because they are more specifically aimed at a younger audience. The nearest that Saxon gets to referring to models of written English is to suggest in his section on 'Figurative Syntax' (ibid.: 79), by which he means inverted word order, that it 'is mostly used in Poetry'. Duncan simply contents himself, in his discussion of 'the Regimen of Adjectives' (ibid.: 54), with some advice to the learners of grammar that knowing which prepositions to use after which adjectives is 'nothing but the Study of the best Use of the Language can teach', although he does not say where the 'best Use' of English is to be found.

The intended audience of all the grammars, with the possible exception of Jones's, is schoolboys within the social institution of 'public' education, i.e. at charity schools, public schools, grammar schools, etc. There are a number of common discourse strategies which reveal this to be the case, including the following:

- frequent comparison with Latin, often revealing the explicit aim of enabling the pupils to learn Latin more easily by tackling grammar in English first
- commonly shared assumptions concerning ways in which the grammars

should be structured, e.g. that there are eight parts of speech, divisible into two groups, the declinables and the indeclinables; that there are no cases in English but that case is signalled through prepositions; that the variety of tenses in Latin is signalled through the use of auxiliary verbs; that the nouns are divisible into 'nouns substantive' and 'nouns adjective', etc.

- frequent confusion between language structure and language usage, so that what is commonly presented as a grammatical 'rule' is in fact a rule of 'good' style and what is offered as a grammatical explanation turns out to be semantic or pragmatic
- a tendency to present the structures of English to native English-speaking pupils as if they were learning a 'foreign' language
- (in some, but not all, of the grammars) lengthy meta-discursive commentaries on the grammatical explanations given and/or lists of test questions and model answers
- frequent instructions to the 'learners' on what to avoid, or what not to do to be a 'good' speaker or writer of SE.

In the following section I shall take a closer look at two of these common features to answer Question 1 above. However, the grammars themselves are textual structures functioning on a number of different discourse levels. The similarities between those levels are also indicative of a common set of beliefs about language and didactic goals with respect to language which were a major force in moulding the legitimate language of public education, i.e. SE, within a normative, prescriptive framework. In Section 4 I will focus on those levels in an attempt to answer Question 2 above. In Section 5 I shall argue, in response to Question 3, that it is indeed feasible to suggest that the discourse features I shall look at form part of the legitimate language of the social institution of public education. In Section 6, the concluding section of this chapter, I shall go one step further and argue that the normative, prescriptive framework within which SE was socially constructed in the social institution of 'public' education in the eighteenth century is still the dominant ideology of SE today. I shall reiterate my plea to linguists, sociolinguists and educational linguists to try to understand as fully as possible the historical reasons for the strength of that ideology so that more constructive and more flexible ways of altering it might be suggested in the future.

3 Common aspects of the grammar writers' discourse

Examples of all the discourse features listed in the previous section can be found in the restricted set of grammar writers I have chosen from the eighteenth century, but space will not allow me to deal with them all in detail. I have thus chosen two of those general features to discuss in this section:

commonly shared assumptions concerning ways in which the grammars should be structured, in which I will focus on the authors' definitions of the term 'grammar' itself and the perspective from which they view the problem of parts of speech, and references that the authors make to Latin.

One of the most salient points at which significant similarities as well as differences can be observed is when grammar writers introduce the term 'grammar' itself and the problem of 'word classes' or 'parts of speech'. After his own short preface and an English translation of John Wallis's 'Preface' with additions, Greenwood introduces the reader to the general field of language. In this 'Introduction' he says the following:

> Mens Intentions in Speaking are, or at least should be, to be understood; which cannot be, where Men do not use their Words according to the Propriety of the Language in which they speak; for Propriety of Speech is that which gives our Thoughts Entrance into other Mens Minds with the greatest Ease and Advantage; and therefore deserves some Part of our Care and Study.
>
> (ibid.: 33–4)

Greenwood looks at language from a prescriptive point of view here, stating what 'Mens Intentions' should be in using language, i.e. 'to be understood', rather than what they are, and suggesting that this goal is unattainable if speakers do not 'use Words according to the Propriety of the Language in which they speak'. The typical conduit metaphor Greenwood uses to refer to language – i.e. language is a vehicle to express our thoughts and if we want to access the thoughts of another, which are themselves contained within our minds, we have to use that vehicle – is given a prescriptive twist. We can only gain access if we use words properly, 'according to the Propriety of the Language', i.e. only if we use the legitimate language.

This idea is picked up in his first chapter 'Of *Grammar* and its *Parts*' where he gives the following asterisked subheading to the chapter: '*Grammar is the Art of Speaking rightly'. (Greenwood uses the asterisk as a typographical device to highlight that section of his text.) At the end of each chapter Greenwood gives a set of model questions and answers, presumably as a way of testing what the learners have learnt, and the very first set of questions gives further evidence for the prescriptive stance of the author:

Q. *What is* Art?
A. *Art* is a Method or Way of doing any thing well. Therefore the Word *rightly* might have been omitted in the Definition of *Grammar*; for no one would suppose that Art is doing any thing *ill*.
Q. *What do you learn* Grammar *for?*
A. To learn to speak rightly.

Q.   *What do you mean by speaking rightly?*
A.   Speaking *properly* and as we ought to speak.

(ibid.: 35)

Learning how to speak well, learning the institutionally legitimate forms of discourse, is thus implicit in the very notion of grammar, and speaking well means speaking properly.

In Chapter II, 'Of the Eight Parts of Speech' we read the following:

> To signify the Difference of our Thoughts or Notions in any Language, there is need of several Sorts of Words: Now every Word being considered as a Part of Speech or Discourse; the *Grammarians* (or they who write of Grammar) do reckon up eight Sorts of Words of a different Nature, which they call, *Eight Parts of Speech.*

> * The Eight Parts of Speech are,
> *Noun,*   *Adverb,*
> *Pronoun,*   *Conjunction,*
> *Verb,*   *Preposition,*
> *Participle,*   *Interjection.*

The 'eight parts of speech' correspond exactly with those proposed for the grammar of Latin, and they are simply taken over and applied to English. What is more interesting in this quotation, however, is that Greenwood actually recognises a community of 'Grammarians (or they who write of Grammar)', with whom he would probably have identified and from whom he has taken over the eight parts of speech.

Like Greenwood, Jones first presents a very short introduction to the study of grammar before going into 'Part I', which runs as follows:

> English *Grammar* teacheth the *Grounds,* and *Use* of the English *Language.*

> I[st].   The *Grounds* consist in these *Five Things.*
> 1st.   *Letters.*
> 2[dly]. *Syllables,* made of Letters.
> 3[dly]. *Words,* made up of Syllables.
> 4[thly]. *Sentences,* made up of Words.
> 5[thly]. *Discourses* or *Speeches,* made up of Sentences.

> II[dly]. The *Use* of Grammar is *threefold,* shewing
> I[st].   How to *Read* well.
> 2[dly]. How to *Write correctly.*
> 3[dly]. How to *Talk properly.*

(ibid.: 1–2)

Once again, the construction of a legitimate language in Bourdieu's sense of the term is unmistakable in Jones' grammar. The grammar is said to 'teach', and what the learner should learn is to 'read well', to 'write correctly' and to 'talk properly', although, as with Greenwood, no set of guidelines is laid down to determine how the terms 'well', 'correct' and 'proper' should be defined.

When Jones finally determines the 'parts of speech' for English in 'PART III. *Of English Words*' (ibid.: 20), we find him suggesting a breakdown of just three:

> There are three *Kinds of English Words* or *Parts of our Speech*, 1. *Nouns*; 2. *Verbs*; 3. *Particles*.

Included within the class of nouns, however, are 'Nouns Substantive', i.e. common, proper nouns and pronouns, and 'Nouns Epithets', among which we find the adjectives and participles. The class of particles comprises 'Particles relating to Verbs', i.e. adverbs, 'Particles relating to Nouns', i.e. prepositions, 'Particles relating to Sentences', i.e. conjunctions, and 'several *Interjections*'. So the full range of eight parts of speech is again represented in Jones' work, although somewhat covertly.

Saxon starts numbering the parts of his text from 'Part II' on, leaving us to assume that 'Part I' deals with the sounds and 'letters' of English but, analogous to Greenwood and Jones, he begins with a short introduction to grammar entitled '*Of* ENGLISH GRAMMAR *and its* PARTS', the first paragraph of which reads as follows:

> GRAMMAR is an Art which teacheth to write or speak any Language truly and properly, as the *English Tongue, &c.* and consists of four Parts, *viz.* Letters, Syllables, Words, and Sentences.
>
> (ibid.: 1)

The similarities with Greenwood and Jones are striking. Grammar is said to be an 'art'; a grammar 'teacheth to write or speak any Language truly and properly'; and grammars have four parts, rather than Jones' five. What is missing here is Jones' insistence on 'discourses' or 'speeches' which occupy him for over a third of the space of his 'grammar'.

'PART III. *Of the* Various Words *or* Parts of Speech' in Saxon's grammar begins as follows:

> A Word is the Sign of a Thought, and Part of a Sentence or Speech; and is that which conveys something to the Understanding.
>
> The Words or Parts of Speech are Four, *viz. Noun, Adnoun, Verb,* and *Particle*.

Under the *Adnoun* are comprehended *Pronoun* and *Participle*, commonly called two distinct Parts of Speech.

(ibid.: 34)

Like Greenwood, Saxon considers words to signal thoughts and to be the vehicle by which thoughts are 'conveyed ... to the Understanding'. The category of nouns in Saxon includes that of adjectives, so that if we count what he considers to make up the class of 'adnouns', i.e. pronouns and participles, and what he considers to make up the class of particles, i.e. adverbs, conjunctions, prepositions and interjections, we reach exactly the same number of parts of speech as Greenwood.

Duncan differs from Greenwood, Jones and Saxon in not beginning the body of his text with a definition of grammar, but rather by starting immediately with a short introductory paragraph on the parts of speech. His preface, however, includes references to 'Mr. Walker' (presumably William Walker, the author of *Some improvements in the art of teaching especially in the first grounding of a young scholar in grammar learning* in 1669), 'Mr. Greenwood' and the author 'of the Grammar, approved by Bickerstaff' (John Brightland and Charles Gildon, the authors of *A grammar of the English tongue, with notes, giving the grounds and reason of grammar in general*, 1711), so that we can assume Duncan not only to accept those authors' definitions of grammar, but also to be constructing a discourse community of grammarians reaching back into the seventeenth century. The short paragraph on the parts of speech on page 1 runs as follows:

MEN, to express their Thoughts, make use of eight Kinds of Words, called the eight Parts of Speech, namely,

Once again we have the idea, albeit very succinctly expressed, that 'men' express their thoughts by means of words. We also have exactly the same number of parts of speech as in Greenwood and, by extension, in Jones and Saxon.

Lowth also begins the body of his text with a brief definition of grammar, but he follows it with a comment on 'Universal Grammar', which remains implicit in Greenwood's text:

Grammar is the Art of rightly expressing our thoughts by Words.
Grammar in general, or Universal Grammar, explains the Principles which are common to all languages.

> The Grammar of any particular Language, as the English Grammar, applies those common principles to that particular language, according to the established usage and custom of it.
>
> (ibid.: 1)

Most of the themes which I have discussed in reference to the definition of grammar re-emerge in succinct form in Lowth. Grammar is an 'art'; grammar indicates how we can express ourselves 'rightly'; thoughts are conveyed by words. The only idea that is missing here is that of grammar 'teaching' the 'art', but Lowth deals with the supposed didactic usefulness of grammar teaching in his preface.

Lowth increases the parts of speech from eight to nine. The adjective now appears as a word class in its own right and partially subsumes the former word class 'participle'. All the other word classes are retained and 'article' is added to the list. The way in which Lowth introduces the section on 'WORDS', however, is clearly indicative of the degree to which he makes use of the discourse features constituting the 'legitimate language' of grammar writers in the eighteenth century:

> WORDS are articulate sounds, used by common consent as signs of ideas, or notions.
>
> There are in English nine Sorts of Words, or, as they are commonly called, Parts of Speech ...
>
> (ibid.: 7)

As we would expect in the discourse community of grammar writers, words are taken to be the 'signs of ideas, or notions', i.e. it is through words that ideas or thoughts are conveyed from a speaker to a hearer. The expression 'as they are commonly called' reveals that Lowth is conscious of working within a discourse tradition, just as Greenwood's reference to 'grammarians' does.

One of the surest signs that the grammars under examination here were meant for study within the social institution of 'public' education is the frequent references to Latin. This is not quite so explicit in all the grammars. In a grammar of just sixty-nine pages in length, Jones, for instance, takes up 27 per cent of the total length dealing with questions of pronunciation and spelling and roughly 30 per cent dealing with prescriptive rules for the production of good written texts and 'polite' conversation, leaving only 17 per cent of the grammar for questions of syntax and 26 per cent for the parts of speech. Since this part of his grammar only covers twenty pages, there is only one explicit reference to Latin when he deals with the derivation of the English vocabulary:

> As to the Derivation of *English Words*;
> 1   *Scripture Names* are of *Hebrew, Greek,* or *Latin Derivation.*

2   *Terms of Art and Science* are chiefly *Greek*.
3   Abundance of *common Words* are of *Latin Extraction*, as
    Names ending in (*ion*) and (*ty*) as *Nation, Station, Humanity,*
    Christianity, which are made *Latin* by leaving out the (*n*) in
    the former, and changing (*ty*) into (*tas*) in the latter.

(ibid.: 20–1)

The assumption behind this statement seems to be that the reader will also
need to know how to work from English to derive the Latin nouns. In any
case, Jones presents his description of the parts of speech in essentially the
same way as all the other grammar writers in our corpus. In other words,
despite the fact that Latin is not mentioned explicitly apart from the quotation given above, the way in which the sections on the parts of speech and
syntax are presented are clearly based on the model of Latin grammar.

In his preface, Lowth, who does at least try in a much longer grammar
than Jones to describe the structures of English on their own terms without
reference to Latin, makes the following statement:

> If this method were adopted in our Schools; if children were first
> taught the common principles of Grammar by some short and clear
> system of *English* Grammar, which happily by its simplicity and facility
> is perhaps of all others the fittest for such a purpose, they would
> have some notion of what they were going about, when they should
> enter into the *Latin* Grammar; and would hardly be engaged so many
> years, as they now are, in that most irksome and difficult part of
> literature, with so much labour of the memory, and with so little
> assistance of the understanding.
>
> (ibid.: xii–xiii)

For Lowth, as for all our grammar writers with the possible exception of
Jones (see above), the ultimate goal for schoolboys is to acquire a knowledge
of Latin, and the best way to do this is to learn the grammar of their native
language before doing so.

Hence the most highly valued form of language as symbolic capital is that
which can only be acquired through a Latinate grammar and a comparison
of English with Latin. A classical education is that through which the legitimate language may be acquired and the study of English grammar is a means
to that end.

Lowth's grammatical categories are so similar to those of Greenwood, Saxon
and Duncan that we can only conclude that they form part of the legitimate
language of grammar writers, deriving as it does from Latin grammar. For
example, like all the other grammar writers in our restricted corpus, he takes
prepositions to indicate case differences in the English noun system and
compares this way of 'marking' case with the Latin method of suffixation:

The English Language, to express different connexions and relations of one thing to another, uses, for the most part, Prepositions. The Greek and Latin among the antient, and some too among the modern languages, as the German, vary the termination or ending of the Substantive to answer the same purpose.

(ibid.: 24–5)

Lowth goes beyond a consideration of Latin (and Greek), however, and erroneously mentions German as being a language which marks case distinctions by varying 'the termination or ending of the Substantive'.

Saxon, like Lowth, takes the nouns in English to have six cases, but is also compelled to admit that case is only apparent, in the Latinate system that he proposes, through the accompaniment of 'signs', most of which turn out to be prepositions:

Nouns, &c. are declined with six Cases; the *Nominative, Genitive, Dative, Accusative, Vocative* and *Ablative*; so called from the *Latin*.

(ibid.: 40)

DECLENSION is the varying of a *Noun, Adnoun,* &c. by six Cases.

An *English* Noun is declined, not by altering or changing its Theme any further than to distinguish its Number; for (strictly and properly speaking) nothing more is necessary than to know its ending in the singular and plural Number, and the Particles or Signs *a, an, the, of, to, O, in, with, thro', from, by,* &c. as used in varying the following Noun *Boy.*

(ibid.: 41)

The second area of grammar in which Saxon, like Duncan and Greenwood, has explicit recourse to Latin is that of verb tenses. For example, in presenting the various tenses of English, he feels it necessary to add the following note:

Note, To these, Grammarians add two more, (in Imitation of the Latin,) *viz.* the *Imperfect* and *Pluperfect.*

(ibid.: 56)

Saxon refers, as do Greenwood, Lowth and Duncan, to a group of 'Grammarians', thereby explicitly referring to the discourse community, but it is not clear whether he means that the English language has imitated Latin or that the 'Grammarians' have added the two tenses to English in imitation of the grammar of Latin. The latter interpretation seems far more likely here, which would be an open acknowledgement of one of the most salient discourse practices of grammar writers, viz. to invent the existence of a structure which is not in evidence in English simply because it happens to exist for Latin.

Duncan does exactly this in his explanation of the ablative case in English:

> The *Ablative Case* in *English* is that, which turn'd into *Latin*, would be an Ablative, by reason of some Preposition that governs it, or some *Latin* Idiom that requires it so. As the Comparative Degree governs the Ablative in *Latin*, therefore Grammarians have made the Particle *than*, that follows the Comparative in *English*, a Sign of the Ablative Case. For that same Reason the Prepositions *from*, *by*, *of*, *in*, *with*, *through*, *for*, &c. are deemed Signs of this Case, because the *Latin* Prepositions answering to them govern it.
>
> (ibid.: 6–7)

The ablative case in English is only present because, if the relevant English structure were translated into Latin, the Latin ablative case would have to appear. This forces Duncan into the familiar makeshift solution of suggesting that prepositions are 'Sign[s] of the Ablative Case'.

Of the five grammarians considered here Duncan makes the greatest number of references to Latin. In his preface he is quite explicit about his didactic aims. Pupils need to learn English grammar as an introduction to the grammar of Latin. He mentions at the end of the preface that if a second edition of his grammar is called for, he will also provide an accompanying Latin grammar to go with it. Hence, throughout the text he is concerned to make the bridge explicitly from English to Latin at the expense of inventing structures which simply do not appear in English. A further example of this tendency can be found in his explanation of verbal inflections in Latin, in which he credits English with exactly the same distinction of tense, mood and voice as Latin:

> 1 THE various Inflexion is the distinguishing Mark of Voice, Mood, Tense, Number and Person in *Latin*.
> 2 This Language has, like the *English*, its Active, Passive, and Neuter Verbs; and besides them a fourth Sort called Verbs Deponent, which are conjugated like Passives, and have a Signification either of a Verb Active or Neuter.
>
> (ibid.: 36)

Greenwood is much more explicit on the subject of cases:

> As the Mind is not always employ'd about single Objects only, but does likewise compare one thing with another, in order to express the *Relation* and *Respect* that Things have to one another.
>
> In the *Latin* and *Greek* Tongues, they make different Endings of the same *Noun*, to denote these *References* or *Respects*, and these different *Endings*, are called Cases. The *Latins* have six in each Number, whose Names are as follow,

The *Nominative*, The *Accusative*,
The *Genitive*, The *Vocative*,
The *Dative*, The *Ablative*.

But the *Respect* of *Things* to one another in our Language, is shewn by the help of certain Words called *Prepositions*; such are *of*, *to*, *from*, &c. So that we have no *Cases*, except the *Genitive*, whereby we are freed from a great deal of Trouble and Difficulty that is found in other *Languages* from these Things.

(ibid.: 51–2)

The reader is left to puzzle why, if English has no cases but the Genitive (and one assumes also the Nominative), the author goes to the trouble to list the six cases in Latin. Is it because the learner will already have studied Latin and will therefore be familiar with Greenwood's breakdown of cases, or is it rather because Greenwood, like Duncan, is deliberately using English to prepare the way for the learner to tackle Latin grammar? The important point to make, however, is that Greenwood, like all the other grammar writers in our selection, considers prepositions to indicate 'the *Respect* of *Things* to one another'. It would therefore appear that the latter interpretation is more likely and that it was one of the discourse practices of eighteenth-century grammar writers explicitly to relate English grammar to Latin grammar because of the need to learn Latin.

With respect to the question of verb tenses, Greenwood uses the same strategy. But this time he appears to suggest that English is in some sense deficient in having only two tenses (which is in fact a very perceptive and highly modern way of looking at the English verb system) and that by using auxiliary verbs English can be made to have the same number of tenses as Latin. Latin is therefore held up as the grammatical model for the legitimate language SE:

As for the *Tenses* or *Times*, the natural and proper Number is three because all *Time* is either *past*, *present*, or *to come*. That is
I   The *Present Time*, that *now* is.
II   The *Preter time*, that is *past*.
III The *Future Time*, that is yet *to come*.
In *Greek* the Number is increased to Eight or Nine, in *Italian* to Seven, in *French* and *Spanish* there are Six, in *English* (as in *Dutch*) we have properly but Two; but by the Help of Auxiliary or assistant *Verbs*, we make up as many as there are in *Latin*, that is Six.

(ibid.: 113–14)

Summary

To summarise this section, both the insistence on referring to Latin and also the definition of grammar and of the parts of speech show a relatively high level of consistency in the discourse practices of grammar writers throughout the period from 1711 to 1762. This is certainly not accidental. In the following section I shall deal with the problem of identifying the assumed addressees of the various sections of each grammar writer's text and I shall also mention briefly examples of explicit or implicit references to or reworkings of sections of earlier works.

4 Addressees and textual sources

Like most other written texts, we can expect grammars to contain a number of different 'voices' addressed to different imagined readers (cf. Watts 1995) and for the texts themselves to have passed through a complex process of writing, correcting, printing, advertising, etc. There will therefore be a number of different communicative levels in grammars, on which we can recognise not only the different intended addressees, but also different authorial intentions.

If we take Saxon's grammar as an example, we find

- a frontispiece containing the title of the work, the name of the author, the printer of the book and the names and locations of various book-sellers selling the book, and a brief list of contents
- a preface addressed to the 'Masters *of* English Schools, Mistresses, Parents, Young Ladies, *and* Foreigners'
- a more detailed list of contents
- a list of errata
- a note labelled 'N.B.' giving the author's credentials (where he teaches, what he teaches, etc.)
- the body of the text
- a set of questions in a smaller print size after every section called an 'INTERROGATORY'
- an appendix containing the Lord's Prayer and a set of questions, not all of which are grammatical, e.g. 'How many Petitions are there in the Lord's Prayer?', 'What's the Doxology, or Conclusion of the Lord's Prayer?', etc.

On some of the different textual levels, the intended addressee is clearly indicated. For example, the first paragraph of the appendix runs as follows:

> Masters, Mistresses, or Parents, may exercise their Scholars and Children in the Use of this Grammar, after the following Manner, let the Number be more or less. *viz*.
>
> (Saxon 1737: 99)

In the preface we have not only an explicit addressee (see above) but also information about who the author is and where he now teaches:

And being now engag'd in a Charity-School, and confin'd to the teaching only the English tongue, writing, and accompts, &c. have attempted (at my vacant hours) more accurately to methodize this epitome of English grammar, purely for the benefit of those under my care, whose parents (being indigent) can't bestow on them a more liberal education.

(ibid.: iv)

It also contains information about potential buyers of the book, whom he has secured by means of setting up a subscription list of more than 200 people. A list of subscribers who were virtually certain to buy the book once it had been printed assured the author of being able to cover the printing costs and of being able to pay the debts he might have incurred to the booksellers. This was a common method of guaranteeing an adequate readership in the eighteenth century:

And having met with great encouragement by the subscription of more than two hundred divines, gentlemen of my own profession, ladies, &c. (many of whom have perus'd the manuscript) have now ventur'd to make it publick, and do recommend it to those gentlemen engag'd in the like profession with myself; to gentlewomen employ'd in teaching the fair sex; to young ladies and to foreigners.

(ibid.: iv)

In the body of the text we find that the addressee is frequently referred to with the second person pronoun 'you' when Saxon wants to give specific advice to the reader. From time to time he also refers the addressee to other works which he or she might find helpful. We can thus infer that the intended reader at this communicative level, which occupies the bulk of the overall text, is a learner, probably a schoolboy. The 'interrogatories' which follow every section not only confirm this impression, but they also help to characterise the voice at this textual level as that of a teacher. Consider advice given to the reader:

Thus *altar* for *sacrifice*, and *alter* to *change*; *arrant*, *notorious*; *errant*, *wandring*, and *errand*, a *message*; *boar*, a *beast*; *boor*, a *clown*, and *bore*, a *hole*, &c. These and innumerable more, you'll meet with alpha-betically ranged in *Cole's Dictionary*, and in most of the common Spelling Books: and would you avoid the Errors that these Similitudes of Sounds are apt to betray you into writing, you must be very careful in your Observations thereupon.

(ibid.: 27)

The tone here is clearly prescriptive. The learner must 'avoid the Errors that these Similitudes of Sounds are apt to betray you into writing'. He or she is

56

warned to be very careful in 'your Observations thereupon'. On the other hand, no concrete didactic advice is given as to how the reader is meant to use the grammar as a whole.

Duncan's text contains the following communicative levels:

- a frontispiece
- a dedication to John Oxenford, Esq.
- a preface, presumably addressed to all those who are likely to buy the grammar
- the body of the text

There are no questions on the text in Duncan's grammar and no direct references to the reader with the pronoun 'you'. Liberal use is made of passive structures, a discourse strategy which conveniently masks both the intended addressee and to a certain extent the speaker. The impression given by the text is that it is not aimed directly at the learners, who are taken to be beginners, but rather at the teachers:

> An accurate Treatise of Particles would be too extensive for this small Tract. However we will add the few Observations following, which may be sufficient for Beginners.
>
> (Duncan 1731: 64)

As in the case of Saxon, however, the tone used by Duncan clearly indicates a prescriptive stance:

> Note that an Adverb is not to be placed too far from its Verb; and that when it is join'd either to a Noun or an Adverb, no other Word is to be put between them.
>
> (ibid.: 64)

The most explicit reference to the intended reader, however, is contained in the very first paragraph of the preface, in which the 'voice' evaluates the learning of dead languages as being a 'yoke' and suggests that it would be easier for the learner to approach the grammar of Latin by learning English grammar first:

> The Learning of dead Languages is a Yoke, that neither we nor our Fore-fathers could ever bear, when we were Children. And, I fancy, the Loathsomness of that dry Study comes for want of reasoning previously with them enough about the Nature of Words, and their Dependency on one another, in their own Mother Tongue.
>
> (ibid.: v)

The clue to interpreting the intended addressee is the pronoun 'we' in the clause 'when we were Children', which includes the 'voice', or Duncan, in a set of adults all of whom have had to learn Latin grammar at some time in their lives.

Jones' grammar is structured according to the following set of communicative levels:

- a frontispiece, in which the author's prescriptive intentions are explicitly stated, viz. 'BEING A *Grammatical* ESSAY UPON OUR LANGUAGE, Considering the true Manner of *Reading, Writing,* and *Talking* proper *English*'
- a dedication to 'Her Royal Highness Wilhelmina Charlotte, Princess of Wales'
- the table of contents
- the body of the text

Of all five grammars, Jones' *Accidence* is the most blatantly prescriptive. Just over 30 per cent of the overall text is contained in Part V, 'Of English Discourse, or Speech', indicating that the legitimate language for Jones consists in producing socially acceptable prose and poetry and being thought of as producing the kind of 'conversation' acceptable in the 'polite' circles of society.

During Part V the 'voice' at this communicative level in the text adopts an overtly elitist stance, largely using the pronoun 'we' to indicate what the members of 'polite' society would write or say and how they would write and say it. If we consider the intended readership of the grammar as defined in the frontispiece ('CHIEFLY For the Use of such BOYS and MEN, as have never learnt *Latin* perfectly, and for the Benefit of the FEMALE SEX: Also for the *Welch, Scotch, Irish,* and *Foreigners*'), the 'we' becomes exclusive rather than inclusive. In addition, the amount of detail Jones gives as to how one should behave 'properly' is likely to have been comprehensible only to a member of polite society, and even then only with great difficulty. Consider the socially discriminating tone in the following extract:

> Some talk well, that can neither write nor read, (or but indifferently;) such are Persons of good natural Parts, who have been deprived of the Advantage of a Learned Education.
>   Some can write correctly, that can neither read nor talk distinctly, or without some Tone or Brogue. But ready and proper Expression is excellently beneficial. Reading promotes profitable and pleasant Learning and Knowledge: a fine Hand is beautify'd with good Composure; and an elegant Composition is compleated by handsome Delivery. So that good Manners, correct Writing, proper English,

and a smooth Tongue, are requisite Qualifications, sufficient to render a Person (of but tolerable good Endowments) compleatly accomplished for Conversation.

(Jones 1724: 64–5)

Jones presents to the reader models of good prose style such as Addison, 'Clarendon's History, the Tatler, Spectator, Examiner, and Entertainer'. The poets 'which *strike* the *deepest Impression* upon my *Fancy* are, *Milton* in his *Paradise Lost, Cowley, Philips, Prior, Addison*, and *Pope*; and *Dryden* for *Translations*' (ibid.: 63). But most of his prescriptive statements on how to comport oneself well in polite society have little or nothing to do with language and are long lists of evaluative statements which even a member of polite society would have great difficulty in interpreting.

Lowth mentions the same authors as Jones, but he does so not only to recommend them as models of good style (or, as he would have it, good grammar). Much of the time Lowth uses examples from the works of those authors, and also from the works of Shakespeare and the Bible, as illustrations of what the learner should *not* do. The normative tendencies of grammar writers have by this time taken them so far that they put themselves above the models of literature they propose, as arbiters not only of good taste, but of what is correct and what is not. The prescriptivist urge in Lowth results in him evaluating who shall and who shall not be considered part of the canon of English literature (cf. Crowley 1989).

Lowth's grammar also has a frontispiece and a preface, but the body of the text is punctuated by notes, some of which run over several pages. In fact the amount of space taken up by the notes is almost as voluminous as the body text itself. The addressee of Lowth's preface is not quite so clearly delineated as that of Saxon's, but there are clear instances in which Lowth gives readers advice on how to teach grammar. The purpose of the grammar is still didactic. Like Duncan, however, Lowth also considers the study of the grammar of English to be the best way into the study of Latin. He adds to this the opinion that it will also stand the learner in good stead in learning a modern foreign language:

Besides this principal design of Grammar in our own Language, there is a secondary use to which it may be applied, and which, I think, is not attended to as it deserves: A good foundation in the General Principles of Grammar is in the first place necessary for all those who are initiated in a learned education.

(Lowth 1762: xi)

When he has a competent knowledge of the main principles, the common terms, the general rules, the whole subject and business of grammar, exemplified in his own Language; he then will apply himself with great advantage to any foreign language, whether ancient or modern.

(ibid.: xii)

In Lowth's discussion of verb conjugations we find an interesting example of possible cross-referencing involving the grammar writers considered here. In a discussion of the past tense forms of *be* in the indicative and subjunctive moods he inserts a long note in which he quotes sections from Milton, Dryden, Addison, Prior and Pope, all of whom use *thou wert* in a clearly indicative rather than subjunctive context. His comment is as follows:

> Shall we in deference to these great authorities allow *wert* to be the same with *wast*, and common to the Indicative and Subjunctive Mode? or rather abide by the practice of our best antient writers; the propriety of the language, which requires, as far as may be, distinct forms for different Modes; and the analogy of formation in each Mode; I *was*, Thou *wast*; I *were*, Thou *wert*? all which conspire to make *wert* peculiar to the Subjunctive Mode.

(ibid.: 52, note)

The ironic tone in the phrase 'in deference to these great authorities' is interpretable through the fact that we are confronted with a rhetorical question here. The reader is expected to answer, 'No, of course not.' Lowth does not mention which 'antient writers' he is thinking of, but perhaps he has no one in particular in mind. If he had, he would surely have mentioned them by name. The overall tone is normative and prescriptive – e.g. 'the propriety of the language' – and the attitude he is taking to the 'great authorities' is decidedly condescending.

Could it be that Lowth in 1762 has picked up on a comment by Duncan in 1731 in which exactly the same problem is dealt with?:

> *Were* and *wert* are made use of by some instead of *was* and *wast*; whether they speak good English or not in so doing, is the Question; *was* and *wast* however is the most used.

(Duncan 1731: 28)

There is of course no way of knowing, and in any case Duncan refrains from taking a stand on whether or not this is 'good English'. But this does provide evidence that Lowth knew what earlier grammarians had written and that he is conscious of being a member of the discourse community of grammar writers. Indeed, he too explicitly mentions 'the grammarians' as a group of scholars whose terminology he has taken over.

Of the five grammars under discussion Greenwood's is the most complex with respect to the levels of communication contained within it. The following set can be identified:

- a frontispiece which indicates that Greenwood is not only concerned with English grammar, but also that he has a secondary purpose in writing the 'essay', viz. to provide 'a Rational and Plain Account of GRAMMAR in General, with a Familiar Explanation of its Terms';
- a dedication to Dr. Richard Mead, 'Physician of St. *Thomas's-Hospital*, and FELLOW of the ROYAL SOCIETY';
- Greenwood's own preface;
- a table of contents;
- the translation of John Wallis's 'Preface';
- Greenwood's additions to Wallis's preface, which are clearly marked in the text;
- the body of the text;
- notes leading the reader into a consideration of 'grammar in general';
- questions on certain sections of the text, aimed at the learner of English grammar rather than at the reader of the notes.

The frontispiece makes reference to the 'Genius and Nature of the English Tongue' which echoes statements made in earlier grammars, e.g. Guy Miège's *The English Grammar* in 1688, which reprinted almost word for word in its preface Richard Carew's text of 1586, entitled 'The Excellency of the English Tongue' in William Camden's *Remains Concerning Britain*. The dedication to Dr Richard Mead extolls the latter's virtues as a champion and patron of learning and reason, and it is certainly not insignificant that Mead was a member of the Royal Society.

Greenwood addresses his preface to those responsible for the education of the young, and the perspective from which he views language education is explicitly normative:

> Yet I do not see how they should write any thing with a tolerable Correctness, unless they have some tast of *Grammar*, or express themselves clearly, and deliver their Thoughts by Letter or otherwise, so as not to lay themselves open to the Censure of their Friends, for their blameable *Spelling* or false *Syntax*.

Like the other grammar writers, he also champions the learning of English grammar before tackling Latin. In order to back up his argument he quotes from a letter by the '*Ingenious Author* of the *TATLER*' (Addison?) and acknowledges his debt to John Wallis, 'Dr. *HICKS*, Dr. *KENNET*, Dr. *GIBSON*, Mr. *BENJAMIN MORLAND*, and some others that I could name', Bishop Wilkins's *Real Character* and 'Mr. *LOCK*'. These points, together with the fact that he prints the whole of John Wallis's preface in English with his own, sometimes rather lengthy additions, are clear indications that we are confronted here with a tradition in grammar writing and writing about the English language which justifies my interpretation of these writers as constituting a discourse community. The body of the text is aimed at two types of potential reader. On the one hand, the learner is addressed, and it is also to the learner that the questions are aimed. On the other hand, the teacher is addressed in the notes, which aim to enrich the reader's understanding of grammar as a universal phenomenon.

Summary

Perhaps more than any of the other grammarians in our corpus, Greenwood provides evidence that the legitimate language of 'public' and private education is a form of SE which has already acquired, and throughout the eighteenth century will continue to acquire, standards of correctness which can be used to discriminate against those who are not members of 'polite society' (cf. Jones's text). The social institution of public education is instrumental in prescribing which forms of SE are socially acceptable and which are not, and the discourse community of grammar writers are instrumental in deciding on what those forms will be and how they should be described. The link with Latin is an indication that the institution aimed at a 'learned education' in which Latin, and to a lesser extent Greek, were still valued linguistic assets which were at least on a par with a knowledge of SE even if they were not still a little superior to it. The legitimate language of education was a socially conscious language, a language of social exclusion, and a language of elite social values. To support this argument, I shall briefly consider in the next section how Question 3 in Section 2 (Is it possible to interpret the features of that discourse as forming part of the legitimate language of the social institution of 'public' education, i.e. as constituting a significant part of the symbolic resource of language?) might be answered. Following this I shall draw some pertinent conclusions with respect to the present-day situation of SE in the public education system in Section 6.

5 The legitimate language of 'public' education

The evidence I have given in Sections 3 and 4 in support of the argument that we are dealing with a discourse community when examining the grammars of English written in the eighteenth century could be multiplied almost endlessly. I have also indicated how the discourse strategies of the members of the community are firmly rooted in the traditions of 'public' education and grammar writing, traditions that go back at least 300 to 350 years prior to 1800. But this still leaves one major question open. At the end of the previous section I argued that SE was the legitimate language of the 'public' education system. I need to modify that slightly here and to provide support for my argument. My modification is aimed at showing that it is not SE as such which is the legitimate language but the social construction of what SE was meant to be in terms of the various marketplaces that were dominant in the eighteenth century. As a topic this is large enough in itself to write a book-length analysis, and I will have to restrict myself to a few brief remarks.

In Section 1 I argued that Bourdieu sees culture in terms of a complex set of marketplaces in which material capital, cultural capital and symbolic capital are produced and reproduced. The most important form of symbolic resource is language. It is through the acquisition and application of forms of language that access can be gained to cultural marketplaces such as education, professional training, the acquisition of specialised skills, etc., and it is through the different forms of cultural resource that access can be gained to material marketplaces. Forms of language representing linguistic capital which can be used in other marketplaces have greater or less value, the most highly valued form being the legitimate language within a field, or the social space for action within an institutional framework. Since education is one of the most highly valued types of cultural resource, the legitimate language which is used in that field is likely to be one of the most, if not the most, highly valued forms of language in the linguistic marketplace.

One of the most important material marketplaces in the first half of the eighteenth century was represented by imperialist expansion, which was predicated essentially on opening up and controlling new world markets, i.e. on seeking to create wealth in the core area of a far-flung empire by manipulating the cheap labour and material resources of the periphery. The eighteenth-century strategy for capitalising on the material wealth of the periphery was to colonise territory and control the markets by exercising power. That strategy placed an increased demand on human resources from the core area (i.e. in our case Britain) to control and administrate new colonial territories. It also placed an increasingly heavy demand on military institutions to control those territories physically. Civil servants and army officers were produced through the 'public' education system (including the universities) and were the representatives of British national power. As Hobsbawm (1990) shows, standard languages became the most potent symbols of that power, so it is clear not only that the demand for SE increased considerably throughout the eighteenth century, but also that it became a metaphorical standard bearer for British imperial power.

If we take SE to be a set of standardly accepted, non-local forms of language, then there is absolutely no reason to argue that those forms should not be variable and changeable. But the legitimate language of 'public' education in the eighteenth century was constructed according to beliefs about language which would not allow for variability or the propensity for change and development. The type of SE constructed for and within the educational framework was continually reproduced along lines set out by grammarians, lexicologists,

63

orthographers, elocutionists, etc., i.e. in a word by all those who were set up as or who set themselves up as 'experts' on language. Some of the beliefs which make up what we might call the 'ideology of SE' are explicitly expressed in the practices of the discourse community of grammar writers, but many of them lie below the surface and inform the discourse in more devious ways. Among these beliefs we have the following.

- One of the characteristics of the habitus of a well-educated person is that he or she should have received a learned education, i.e. should have a knowledge of classical Latin and possibly also Greek and be well versed in the literature of one or both of these, and that a knowledge of SE should precede that of Latin or Greek.
- The structure of SE should therefore be presented with the same grammatical terminology and in the same order as that of Latin and Greek to enable the learner to move from his or her mother tongue to these two languages.
- Since the study of Latin and Greek was (and still is) the study of written texts enshrined in the canon of literature set up for the classical period, the study of English should also be able to fall back on 'good' literary models from the past.
- The study of classical written texts involved the opportunity to display metalinguistic knowledge of those texts by being able to parse their grammatical structure. Hence a knowledge of SE should similarly enable learners to parse written texts in English.
- The study of English grammar should enable the learner to achieve 'perfection' in the language and to use English 'correctly'. By 'correct' the grammar writers dealt with in this chapter understood questions of social appropriateness as well as grammatical correctness, such that a knowledge of English grammar should ultimately lead the learner to a position from which he or she could enter and function adequately within 'polite' social circles. There were in other words grammatical and social norms to achieve for which the learner needed prescriptive rules.
- The structures of SE, once they have reached a state of 'perfection' (and most eighteenth-century writers believed that SE had reached that state), should not be changed. Any variability and/or change could only be change for the worse.

If we take these beliefs about language and transform them into a set of learning goals, we are justified in asking whether or not the intended addressees, if they were the learners themselves (as in Jones, Saxon and Greenwood), would have been able to achieve those goals or, if the intended addressees were the teachers (as in Lowth and Duncan), whether they would have been able to help their pupils to reach those goals.

All of the grammarians in this study present the grammar of English as if English were a classical language. Greenwood explicitly mentions the fact that Wallis's grammar was written in Latin for foreign learners of English and puts forward the opinion that learning English as one would learn a foreign language will help the learner when he or she tackles a foreign language. But, despite occasional references to French, Italian, Spanish and Dutch, the term 'foreign language' here meant Latin or Greek. The major problem was that the 'learner' had already acquired some form of English, so that learning about the parts of speech, the syntax and the pronunciation of the language (which generally meant learning how to spell 'properly') was in effect learning the metalanguage of the education system, and this attitude is echoed in the numerous statements about learning the grammar of English before going on to the grammar of Latin.

Summary

Part of the 'legitimate language' was therefore learning how to talk *about* English as if it were a classical language using an extremely esoteric meta-language. There are, for instance, long lists of 'prepositions' in Lowth and Greenwood giving their meanings but with no indication of why a prefix like *pre-*, for instance, should be considered to belong to the same part of speech as the preposition *before*. Duncan states that there are no grammatical cases in the English noun and that it cannot therefore be declined. But he then proceeds to 'prove' that there are as many cases as in Latin, except that English signals them with a range of 'particles', prepositions in the case of the genitive and ablative and the interjection *o* for the vocative. The most telling point about all the grammars is their injunctions about what the learner should avoid. In most cases we are not confronted with a grammar at all, but with advice concerning 'polite' usage. This reaches its absolute hiatus in Jones' grammar.

The conclusion we are forced to reach is that the learner may, with the help of a diligent teacher, have learnt a great deal about a particular way of looking at English, but that he or she could never have 'learnt' English. However, that certainly was not the point of the grammars in any case, despite statements to the contrary by the authors themselves. The 'legitimate language' included this metalinguistic knowledge and only those who could show that they possessed it were able to progress in the education system.

6 Lessons for the present

The 'legitimate language' of 'public' education in the eighteenth century, which I consider to be a social construct reproduced through generations of learners by schools and teachers, received a large part of its legitimacy through the discourse community of grammarians in the eighteenth century. Throughout the rest of the eighteenth century, the whole of the nineteenth century and the first half of the twentieth century that part of the legitimate language which included a knowledge of and ability to manipulate the metalinguistic discourse of classical Latin and Greek grammar has been continually reproduced as a mainstay of English teaching within the education system. In fact, we can trace its roots at least as far back as the first half of the sixteenth century. The Royal Grammar – which was published in 1549 as the only grammar of Latin to be used in English schools by order of Edward VI and was put together from a grammar of Latin by William Lily and an addition by John Colet – was a model for grammar writers of the late sixteenth century and the seventeenth century and is frequently referred to.

The tradition of normative grammar in English schools is thus long and extremely well established. The tedious exercise of parsing English sentences and texts is firmly fixed in my own memory as part and parcel of English language teaching at grammar schools in the 1950s, and I feel sure that it is just as firmly in the minds of many of my contemporaries, whether linguists or non-linguists, as being an integral and definitive aspect of 'doing school' – regardless of whether or not it was popular or whether or not it had any effect on making us better users of 'proper English'. That tradition was extended during the nineteenth century into the realm of pronunciation, involving lessons in elocution, and reading and reciting literary texts aloud in an almost fruitless effort to get 'learners' of English to produce the legitimate form of spoken SE, viz. RP (Received Pronunciation). This latter part of the tradition in turn found its way into the phonetics courses of British university English departments and from there into coursebooks on English as a foreign language.

It is, in other words, a deeply entrenched tradition, one which might even be called a 'social institution' with its own long historicity, in that it reveals 'reciprocal typifications of actions', to use Berger and Luckmann's (1991) terminology. It would be foolhardy of us to think that we can break out of this institutionalised form of educational discourse without trying to understand, as fully as possible, the history of how it came to be as powerful as it is. In this sense I do not have any ready-made solutions. But I do believe that we might profitably turn our minds to considering the following types of question.

- If the social construction of SE involves setting up a powerful language ideology as the backbone of the 'legitimate language', what are the beliefs that constitute that ideology and what are the historical origins of those beliefs, i.e. what are the myths on which the ideology is constructed? In a chapter in Wright (i.p.) I discuss a selection of the myths that form part of the ideology of the standard. Most of these can be traced back in statements on language made through the centuries prior to the eighteenth century, and some of them have remained remarkably stable till the present day.

- Have any of those myths been inverted and, if so, when and why? It is interesting to note at this point that one myth, the myth of the variety of the English language which looked on dialect variation as a positive factor, was indeed inverted some time between 1710 and 1720, such that, in terms of the legitimate language, dialect speakers were castigated as being degenerate.
- How has the social construction of SE been affected by significant socio-historical developments, e.g. the building of an empire, the growth of urban centres and the relation between them and their hinterlands, sudden changes in market economy (particularly in the eighteenth and nineteenth centuries), the development of an ideology of social class, etc.? Answering this question would require a full-length monograph, but interesting indications concerning the close association between the development of the ideology of the standard and socio-cultural factors in the eighteenth century are given by L. Milroy in Chapter 8 of this volume. (See also Watts, to appear in Wright i.p.)
- How can a socio-historical study of SE, involving links with several other disciplines such as history, geography, economics, political science, sociology, etc., help us to answer the problems we as linguists and socio-linguists have with non-linguistic conceptualisations of SE?

Answering at least the last two questions would entail full-scale research with inordinate amounts of funding, but I should like to close with a suggestion that the answer to my second question is definitely in the affirmative. However, as an example of where one might look to tackle the question of inverted myths, consider the following statement by Thomas Sheridan on different dialects of English in his lectures on elocution in 1762:

> Thus not only the Scotch, Irish, and Welsh, have each their own idioms, which uniformly prevail in those countries, but almost every county in England has its peculiar dialect. Nay in the very metrop-olis two different modes of pronunciation prevail, by which the inhabitants of one part of the town, are distinguished from those of the other. One is current in the city, and is called the cockney; the other at the court-end, and is called the polite pronunciation. As amongst these various dialects, one must have the preference, and become fashionable, it will of course fall to the lot of that which prevails at court, the source of fashions of all kinds. All other dialects, are sure marks, either of a provincial, rustic, pedantic, or mechanic education; and therefore have some degree of disgrace annexed to them.
>
> (Sheridan 1762: 30)

In 1586, however, Richard Carew was able to write the following:

Moreover the copiousness of our Language appeareth in the diversity of our Dialects, for we have Court and we have Countrey English, we have Northern and Southern, gross and ordinary, which differ each from other, not only in the terminations, but also in many words, terms, and phrases, and express the same thing in divers sorts, yet all write English alike.

(Carew 1586: 44)

We can of course dispute the truth of Carew's final statement here, but 'copiousness' is one of Carew's 'four wheels' on which English is felt to have reached perfection and there is no doubt that he considers diversity of dialects to be a positive point. What happened between the time of Carew and the time of Sheridan? And what might this tell us about lay conceptualisations of SE? I will not answer these questions here but will leave them pending investigation along with many others.

Note

1   I do not mean to suggest that there was a state system of education in the eighteenth century. 'Public' education was offered in the form of various kinds of schools, ranging from expensive fee-paying schools right down to charity schools run by various religious denominational groups. In the eighteenth century the state was conspicuous by its absence in the institutional organisation of schooling (cf. Porter 1982).

3

TYPOGRAPHY, LEXICOGRAPHY AND THE DEVELOPMENT OF THE IDEA OF 'STANDARD ENGLISH'

Hayley Davis

It is a widely held assumption that a standard variety of English has been in existence for the past four hundred years or so (see p. 71 below). This view, however, appears to confuse the idea of language standardisation – involving *inter alia* a uniformity of orthographic, typographic, grammatical and lexical practices – with the belief that there is a superior variety of English spoken by those belonging to the 'educated' classes. This confusion has been further compounded by a recent proposal by John Honey for a National Language Authority on the lines of the French Academy:

> What the English language needs is a form of authority that can easily be appealed to for guidance as to the uses which are acceptable compared with those which are not – an authority based not on an individual's irrational likes and dislikes but on the genuine consensus of educated opinion.
>
> (Honey 1997: 163)

Most discussions of 'standard English', although appearing to focus on a variety of differing issues, are alike in their conflation of a number of different uses and understandings of the term. This is largely because the various participants in such debates have thought it unnecessary to adopt an historiographical approach to the subject. Such an approach, as I will demonstrate, will also show up the fruitlessness of Honey's proposal.

In the first place, in many contemporary debates involving standard English, it is not made clear whether theorists are discussing lexis, pronunciation, orthography or grammar. And second, standard English is nothing like the Académie's model of standard French, the latter being an artificial language spoken by no one. Third, and more importantly, standard French is completely unenforceable: in France it is only the Ministry of Education and the National Assembly, not the French Academy, which have any legal power to enforce linguistic prescriptions. But in practice the 'linguistic rules' laid down by such bodies are ignored by everyone.

Another problem with the twentieth-century idea of standard English is that it is often unclear whether linguists are referring to a spoken linguistic reality, a written variety of English, or an idealisation, as is evidenced in the following quotations.

> By standard English I mean the language in which this book is written, which is essentially the same form of English used in books and newspapers all over the world.
>
> (Honey 1997: 1)

> In theory, at least, standard English can be spoken in any accent of English, though in practice it is seldom (indeed perhaps never) spoken in the broadest forms of regional accent.
>
> (ibid.: 3)

> Standard English is that variety of English which is usually used in print, and which is normally taught in schools and to non-native speakers learning the language. It is also the variety which is normally spoken by educated people and used in news broadcasts and other similar situations. The difference between standard and non-standard, it should be noted, has nothing in principle to do with differences between formal and colloquial language, or with concepts such as 'bad language'. Standard English has colloquial as well as formal variants, and Standard English speakers swear as much as others.
>
> (Trudgill 1995: 6–7)

Trudgill and Honey here seem of the opinion that it is both a written and a spoken variety of English, whereas Fromkin and Rodman below claim that it is neither, since it is only an 'ideal' spoken variety (whatever that implies).

> SAE [Standard American English] is an idealisation. Nobody speaks this dialect; and if somebody did, we would not know it, because SAE is not defined precisely. Several years ago there was an entire conference devoted to one subject: a precise definition of SAE. This meeting did not succeed in satisfying everyone as to what SAE should be. It used to be the case that the language used by national broadcasters represented SAE, but today many of these people speak a regional dialect, or themselves 'violate' the English preferred by the purists.
>
> (Fromkin and Rodman 1993: 284)

As Carter writes in *Keywords in Language and Literacy*:

> The term 'standard' is protean. It is simultaneously 'distinctive', 'correct', 'authorised', 'accepted', 'ordinary', 'superior', 'measurable'. It is perhaps not surprising that so many confusions and disagreements exist in discussion of Standard English.
>
> (Carter 1995: 150)

Crowley accordingly writes in *The Politics of Discourse* (1989) that the term 'standard . . . has a complex recorded history in that it demonstrates at least two major senses (a uniform practice and a level to be reached) amongst the variety of its uses' (Crowley 1989: 1). And these uses are not only about language but also about social and cultural identity. Because such uses both take their impetus from and give rise to social and cultural changes, they also have different forms of discourse[1] relating to them. This chapter will thus examine the different ways in which 'standard' has been used since the seventeenth century when referring to language and communication in lexicographical and lexicological contexts. It will also examine various cultural developments that provided the impetus for language standardisation.

Honey claims in *Language is Power* that a standard variety of English was in common currency before the end of the sixteenth century:

> A standard variety of English, both spoken and written, was recognised as existing before the end of the sixteenth century, in the sense of an *authorised*, *delimited* and *unitary* standard, but that recognition of the 'unitary' character of that standard English – i.e., that it involved an essential unity of language – continued to be a matter of contention for a further two centuries.
>
> (Honey 1997: 75)

However, it is only when language becomes the object of a field of study containing a set (or sets) of criteria for its institutionalised codification, that we arrive at what we understand to be 'standard English'. This understanding owes its development to the inception of general linguistic theory with Saussure's concept of *la langue* (1922) and to the proposal for a new historical dictionary, later the *Oxford English Dictionary* (*OED*), in 1858 (Davis 1994). Indeed, prior to the publication of the *OED*, 'standard English' was a relatively unknown phrase. And, according to the *OED* supplement of 1933, the first attestation of the expression 'standard English' came from the text for its original proposals in 1858. Without a standard, codified language supposedly allowing all speakers at least the possibility of arriving at the same, unambiguous linguistic message, there would be no justification for the proposal that all members of a community should have access to this form of communication, whether it be 'superior' or 'ordinary'. It is only when a

71

society accepts that members of a speech community can understand each other *because* they share the same set of words with the same set of meanings, that we start talking about *using* a standard language. As Alfred Schutz wrote in 1962, 'to be successful, any communicative process must . . . involve a set of common abstractions or standardizations' (Schutz 1962: 323). And the veteran linguist John Lyons believes that the possibility of communication depends upon the existence of a 'common core' of language (Lyons 1968). This view of language and communication, although appearing plausible and commonsensical, only really came into existence as a theoretical postulate with the first publication in 1916 of Saussure's *Course in General Linguistics*. Here, Saussure provides an account of what he calls the 'speech circuit' (Saussure 1922: 27).

> In order to identify what role linguistic structure plays within the totality of language, we must consider the individual act of speech and trace what takes place in the speech circuit. This act requires at least two individuals: without this minimum the circuit would not be complete . . . The starting point of the circuit is in the brain of one individual, for instance A, where facts of consciousness which we shall call concepts are associated with representations of linguistic signs or sound patterns by means of which they may be expressed . . . The sound waves are sent from A's mouth to B's ear . . . Next, the circuit continues in B in the opposite order . . . The individual's receptive and co-ordinating faculties build up a stock of imprints which turn out to be for all practical purposes the same as the next person's.
>
> (Saussure 1922: 27ff)

Saussure was the first person to attempt to make the study of language into an autonomous, and hence scientific, discipline and partly occasioned the muddled views surrounding standard English discussed above. His speech-circuit model assumes that a language is a fixed code which A and B share. And this theory assumes that exactly the same linguistic knowledge must be assigned to A and B if communication is to be successful. This model of communication was later taken up by Chomsky when he wrote of an 'ideal speaker-listener living in a completely homogeneous speech community' (Chomsky 1965). But languages as we know them are not fixed codes. If they were, we would be unable to engage in our day-to-day metalinguistic activities such as asking another person the meaning of a word or introducing a new word. If these linguistic activities are taken to be legitimate means of language using and language learning, then languages are manifestly not fixed codes. A further objection to this fixed-code theory is the problem of ascertaining how the codes were established in the first place. Saussure and his successors have felt it unnecessary to deal with such matters.

This difficulty has been further complicated by Saussure's (and subsequent linguists') theoretical confusion about the relationship between writing and speech. The argument about standardisation and standard English is basically an argument about the history of writing and prescription, with the consequent idea that words somehow have 'true' meanings. In order to 'fix' the form and meaning of words, there must presumably be some invariable criteria for setting down the orthography and denotation of words. Despite Saussure's condemnation of grammatical prescriptivism (Saussure 1922: 13), his theory appeared to support the nineteenth-century desire for the sociopolitical ideal of 'one nation: one language' (R. Harris 1987: 112). It is thus easy to see how the Victorian case for prescriptivism became indistinguishable from the case for standardisation.

Muddling speech and writing

Related to the notion of the fixed-code theory and the reaction against prescriptivism is the idea that speech is the primary concern of the linguist. Writing is said, by the majority of linguists, to hold a merely derivative function. But in the absence of any way of codifying language, such as writing, the idea of any standard of language would collapse.

For the majority of present-day linguists, speech has primacy over writing: 'speech is prior to writing not only historically but also genetically and logically' (Bolinger and Sears 1981: 274). Lyons (1972) spells this out in greater detail, advancing arguments that have a tradition dating back to the nineteenth century in language study, a tradition which, although antedating the sound spectrograph, was reacting against the non-scientific prescriptivism according to which the written language of certain authors embodied 'correct' language. This reaction against writing in part explains why some theorists wish to deny that writing is language (Bloomfield 1935: 21). Lyons claims that the spoken language is *prior* to the written 'in the sense that the latter results from the transference of the former from its "natural", or primary, medium to a secondary medium' (Lyons 1972: 62). He lists four relevant kinds of priority: (1) phylogenetic, that historically the written language is derived from speech; (2) ontogenetic, that a child learns the spoken language before the written; (3) functional, that the 'spoken language serves in a wider range of communicative functions than does written language'; and (4) structural, that the 'basic units of the script can be put into correspondence (not necessarily one-to-one correspondence) with units of the spoken language' (ibid.: 63).

What such linguists generally fail to acknowledge is that without writing the very identification of linguistic units is problematic: since every utterance varies acoustically, and since speaking is not just effected by the vocal organs but involves the total context, including the whole body (R. Harris 1986: 99), the criteria for grounding the identity of linguistic units would be, at best, very insecure. And then the idea of a standard language could not even get off the ground. Despite his insistence on the primacy of speech, Saussure comes close to acknowledging this fact, claiming that it is through writing that linguistic signs are made 'tangible' (Saussure 1922: 32). He still insists, though, that a language and its written form 'constitute two separate systems of signs. The sole reason for the existence of the latter is to represent the former' (ibid.: 45).

The misconceptions surrounding the relationship between writing and speech stem from the belief that the Western tradition has a Euro- and ethno-centric view of writing imbued with 'romantic' misconceptions and fallacies (R. Harris 1989: 99). These misconceptions are based on the fact that 'true writing' involves the use of the alphabet. And this, in turn, is tied up with the concomitant idea that a standard language involves the 'correct' use of the alphabet – i.e. correct spellings.

The principal misconceptions surrounding this view of writing are that (1) writing represents speech; (2) writing originated as a communicational substitute for spoken messages; and (3) letters of the alphabet provide a one-to-one relationship with sounds (R. Harris 1986, 1989). As the third misconception implicitly subsumes (1) and (2), the alphabet is taken to be the system of writing *par excellence*, despite the fact that it appeared late in the development of writing systems. Even when it did appear it did not imme-diately 'catch on'. As Havelock notes, even though the alphabet converted the Greek 'spoken tongue into an artefact, thereby separating it from the speaker and making it into a "language", that is an object available for inspec-tion, reflection, [and] analysis' (Havelock 1982: 8), it took 300 years of usage before it became an object of discourse. The reason for this is that there is no such thing as a 'blind technology' (Finnegan 1989: 116), that is to say, technological developments such as writing systems do not occur in a cultural vacuum: 'the actual development and usage of communication media are inextricably entwined in the social and political constitution of the society in which they are used' (ibid.: 116). 'The usage and importance of these technologies are governed by social, economic, political, and ideological factors' (ibid.: 117). This may explain why, in what is known as the High Classical Greek period (the fifth century BC), there was no discussion of citi-zens being literate or illiterate. Instead they were often spoken of as educated, uneducated, musical or unmusical; and 'literacy' and 'cultivation' were not necessarily felt to be synonymous (Havelock 1976: 3). Today, on the other hand, 'incorrect' spelling is usually an indicator of non-standard English, which it was not in, say, Shakespeare's day.

One factor in the 'institutionalisation' of the alphabet was the development in the seventeenth century of the practice of printing the monolingual dictionary in alphabetical order. Even a hundred or so years after the introduction of printing, alphabetical order was not yet considered fully familiar to the general literate public. It seemed at that time to be strangely arbitrary or random in the way that it brought together words that were unrelated semantically. In the preface to his dictionary *Table Alphabeticall* (Cawdrey 1604), Cawdrey has to explain what he means by the alphabet:

> If thou be desirous (gentle Reader) rightly and readily to understand, and to profit by this Table, and such like, then thou must learne the Alphabet, to wit, the order of the Letters as they stand, perfectly without booke, and where every letter standeth: as (b) neere the beginning, (n) about the middest, and (t) toward the end. Nowe if the word, which thou art desirous to finde, begin with (a) then looke in the beginning of this Table, but if with (v) looke towards the end . . .

As with most institutions, given the right climate, it does not take long for them to become 'a way of life', or 'psychologically real' in the Saussurean sense.[2] Spelling reforms of the seventeenth and eighteenth centuries helped the general public to become aware of the alphabet. Until the eighteenth century, there was a great deal of uncertainty about what letters constituted the alphabet: whether, for example, *i* and *j*, *u* and *v* were distinct, and if so what was their 'correct' alphabetical order. But by the nineteenth century, the alphabetical ordering was accepted as 'natural', as the concept of standard English would become in the twentieth century.

The important question to be considered concerning the relationship between writing and speech is how writing affects the whole framework of communicational concepts available to a community. Writing radically altered our concept of what language is by drawing a distinction between language and speech, a distinction not recognised in an oral society, and one which has subsequently been oversimplified by many linguistic theorists. Writing, in fact, ultimately destroyed the equation of language with speech; hence the four kinds of priority suggested by Lyons (see p. 73 above) concerning the primacy of speech fail to confront the question of how the concept of a language is defined, or rather redefined, by writing. Viewed from this perspective, writing becomes influential in the identification of linguistic units within linguistic theory. Writing is also important in fostering the idea of 'levels' of linguistic analysis, since a language can be seen as composed of words which, at one level, have predictable combinatorial properties leading to the study of syntax and, at a lower level, are made out of individual sounds studied by phonology (expressed in Saussure's principle of the linearity of the linguistic sign; Saussure 1922: 103). Thus, in advocating the primacy of speech by claiming that orthography correctly identifies the units of speech, linguists were launching linguistics on its 'crypto-scriptist' path (R. Harris 1980: 18).

Different standards of lexicography

If writing plays such a large part in the identification of linguistic units, it is the development of printing and, more specifically, of lexicography that has 'institutionalised' words. And again, the 'correct' use of words is taken to be an indicator of using standard English.[3]

As Aarsleff notes, 'the study of language in any period is intertwined with events in the larger cultural context, such as developments in natural science, in philosophy, and even in political and religious thought' (Aarsleff 1983: vii). A corollary of this point is that literacy and printing have been major influences on linguistic theories: 'Language is, to some extent, defined by the medium in which it is produced and received' (De Maria and Kitzinger 1989: 83).

With the introduction of the printing press into Europe in the fifteenth century, the problem for the new printers was that of deciding what words to use to make the printed books widely comprehensible. To achieve this, it was necessary to suppress variability as far as possible. Eisenstein claims that 'typography arrested linguistic drift, enriched as well as standardised vernaculars, and paved the way for the more deliberate purification and codification of all major European languages' (Eisenstein 1980: 117). 'Individualism' as redefined by the new authors came to mean 'deviation from the norm and divergence from the type' (ibid: 23). The psychological implications for the 'print culture' in pedagogic areas were substantial:

> A 'mother's tongue' learned 'naturally' at home would be reinforced by inculcation of a homogenised print-made language mastered while still young, when learning to read. During the most impressionable years of childhood, the eye would first see a more standardised version of what the ear had first heard.
>
> (ibid: 118)

Similarly, as a result of typographical practice, the dictionary, over the centuries, gradually came to be seen as embodying the 'correct' spelling of words. With the introduction of the *OED*, a word's existence in a particular orthographic form became sanctioned or validated purely by being included in a dictionary. But this was not always the case with earlier monolingual dictionaries. The status and function of words has not remained stable.

The *OED* differs drastically in its aims and presuppositions from the first monolingual dictionary as well as from the *OED*'s immediate precursors. The first English monolingual dictionary (Cawdrey 1604), alphabetically ordered and written in the 'hard-word' tradition, was not a scholarly record of all the words in the language, but was written to help the uneducated, or as Cawdrey put it in his preface, 'for the benefit and helpe of ladies, Gentlewomen, or any other unskilfull persons' (Cawdrey 1604). Since by this time Latin was losing its dominance, some scholars were reacting against the fixity and stability of language that the dominance of Latin had implied for centuries. Definitions given in this earlier period seem to the modern reader rather naive: *auburne* is glossed by Cawdrey merely as 'colour', *Clicketing* by Coles in 1676 as 'when a Fox desires copulation, he goes a Clicketing'. Proper names were also included, glossed as, for example, 'the name of a man' (Coles 1676). 'Correctness' or 'accuracy' in defining words was not the aim of early lexicography; these early discussions of lexis were bound up with views of language origins and functions. Consequently, before the OED there was no standard English vocabulary.

Modern lexicography, especially the OED, has had far-reaching influences on twentieth-century discussions of language. Although the printed mono-lingual dictionary had been in existence since at least the beginning of the seventeenth century, the theories of language on which such dictionaries were based, and which were in turn consolidated by lexicographical work, remained to all intents and purposes fundamentally the same: specifically, words were thought to have some sort of representational relationship to things or ideas. Dictionaries increasingly came to be seen as authoritative guides to linguistic usage because of changes in society, education, and developments in the sciences, so that when Saussurean theory first appeared, it was taken as reflecting a fundamental truth about language. Saussure could thus claim without fear of ridicule that 'a language, as a collective phenomenon, takes the form of a totality of imprints in everyone's brain, rather like a dictionary of which each individual has an identical copy' (Saussure 1922: 38).

The principle underlying the OED, as it underlies Saussurean theory, is that it is a repository of *all* the words in the language, all of which are known by the collectivity of English speakers, although not all are known by any individual. Similarly, the words in the OED are unchangeable by individual whim. To be acceptable for inclusion in the OED a word has to appear in print, and not just any piece of print, but in the work of those whom the compilers of the OED deem to be reputable authors.

The chief impulse that led to the compilation of the OED was an attempt to turn the lexicographer into a historian of the language. This was a reaction against earlier lexicographical practice of selecting only the 'good' words of the language. This approach brought with it a marked change in the status and understanding of the concept 'word'.

In the seventeenth century, language was deemed to be Adamic in origin. Much of the scholarship in Britain at this time, fostered by the newly formed Royal Society, was to equip language for science by reorganising it, using various notational devices in order to capture its true essence. By stripping the language of synonyms and words not conforming to things, an ideal language could, it was suggested, be created and rationally taught, a language whose every element corresponded to something in the real world. Languages were thought to be not arbitrary, as in Saussurean theory, but rather naturally related to the world. A language was thus an aggregate of signs rather than a system, and attention was focused on the thing represented by the sign. Nothing was further from Saussure's conception of linguistic signs. The preface to Phillips's dictionary of 1658, *A New World of English Words*, reveals how influential this view of language was in the compilation of his dictionary:

> The very Summe and Comprehension of all Learning in General, is chiefly reducible into these two grand Heads, *Words* and *Things*: and though the latter of these two be, by all men, not without just cause, acknowledged the more solid and substantial part of Learning; yet since, on the other side, it cannot be denied but that without Language (which is as it were the *vehiculum* or conveyencer of all good Arts) *things* cannot well be expressed or published to the World, it must be necessarily granted, that the one is little lesse necessary, and an inseparable concomitant of the other; for let a Subject be never so grave, never so useful, carrying in it never so clear and perfect a demonstration, yet if it be not pertinently worded, and urged with a certain power and efficacy to the understanding, but in a forced, tumultous, or disjointed phrase, it will either not be understood, or so slightly and with such indifference regarded, that it will come short of working that effect which it promised to itself.
>
> (Phillips 1658)

During this time, as I have indicated elsewhere (Davis 1994), a dictionary came to mean not only a word-book, but also an alphabetically ordered reference book. Furthermore, so many unfamiliar words were being introduced from other languages that, as one contemporary lexicographer writes, 'few, without the help of a Dictionary, would be able to understand our ordinary English books' (Blount 1656). Adopting a prescriptive approach, Blount professes that he is not too fond of the state of the language, the affectation of 'novelty in speech', and the use of 'uncouth words'. There is, he writes, 'presumptuous, and far fetching of words: And some therefore that think it a grace, if their speech hover, and thereby hold the hearer in suspense'.

A few years later, both Locke in 1690 and the Port Royal Grammarians of 1660 rejected the proposal for a completely rational language representing reality. These scholars now concentrated on ideas, rather than things, as being represented by words. For Locke, language was heavily connected with the need for communication, and words were invented to make one's thought known. Any abuse of words would result in erroneous ideas, and the 'imperfection of words' causes want of knowledge.

Locke felt that because one could never be sure that a word ever produced the same idea in the speaker and the hearer, language had its imperfections. For everyday conversation he felt that language was adequate, but when scientific matters needed to be discussed, exactness was required. His remedy for these imperfections was definition, which was 'best made by enumerating those simple *Ideas* that are combined in the signification of the term Defined' (Locke 1690: III.iii, p. 413). He claimed that 'if we could trace them back to their sources, we should find, in all languages, the names which stand for Things that fall not under our Senses, to have had their first rise from sensible *Ideas*' (ibid.: III.i, p. 403). For Locke, a definition is nothing else but 'the shewing the meaning of one Word by several other not synonymous Terms' (ibid.: III.iv, p. 422). A language was now a social institution, not an Adamic creation. It was Locke's solution to the imperfections of language that probably gave rise to both etymological and prescriptive dictionaries, lending support to the view that words had 'true' meanings. Yet Locke's *Essay Concerning Human Understanding* (1690) was not an essay on language itself, but on epistemology, the acquisition of knowledge, in line with the aims of the Royal Society of London for the Improvement of Natural Knowledge, 1662. The Royal Society was the closest body, at this time, to producing a language-legislating institution in England. Even this could not compete with the Académie Française's dictionary project of 1635, which succeeded in providing French speakers with a national dictionary (*Dictionnaire de la langue française* 1694). The aim of the Académie Française was a prescriptive one, viz. 'to remedy those disorders which the civil wars ... have brought into [the language]'.

In early eighteenth-century England, the literati were envious of the success of the Académie's *Dictionnaire de la langue française* (1694), and so writers such as Swift, Pope and Addison busied themselves with their ideas about 'fixing' the English language. The most famous declarations came from Jonathan Swift's *Proposal for Correcting, Improving and Ascertaining the English Language* (1712), in his attempt to 'fix the language forever'. In the meantime, others were less interested in surpassing the 'Frenchies' than in pursuing more populist and commercial aims. There was also in the eighteenth century a desire for correctness in spelling and writing. Bailey in the Preface to his *Universal Etymological Dictionary* (1721) declares:

> Words are those Chanels by which knowledge of Things is convey'd to our Understandings; and therefore upon a right Apprehension of them demands the Rectitude of our Notions; and in order to form our Judgements right, they must be understood in their proper Meaning, and us'd in their true Sense, either in Writing or Speaking. For if the Words of the Speaker or Writer, tho'ever so apposite to the Matter be taken in a wrong Sense, they form erroneous Ideas in the Mind concerning the Thing spoken or written of; and if we use Words in a false and improper Sense, this causes Confusion in the Understanding of the Hearer, and renders the discourse unintelligible.
>
> (N. Bailey 1721)

Many of the words Bailey included were there just to show their etymologies, their 'true' and 'proper' meanings, so as, Bailey hoped, to facilitate intelligible communication. For instance, *spinage* is glossed as 'an Herb well known', from the French *espinars* and *To Spin Out* as '[*spingere*, Ital.] to burst out as Blood out of a Vein'.

It was these projects that ended up providing the impetus for the lexicographical programme which ultimately achieved the 'gold standard'. And so, in the eighteenth century, there was a strong movement to produce a 'standard' dictionary of English to register 'proper' usage. Samuel Johnson was the man who was eventually contracted to compile such a dictionary. In 1747 his *Plan of a Dictionary of the English Language* was published. Many of the goals expressed in this Plan eventually proved to be unworkable in practice. Like the Académie Française, Johnson aimed to 'fix' or 'standardise' the language in order to preserve its 'purity'. But in the absence of any official codification, there was a problem as to where a 'standard' for the language could be found. The generally accepted answer at this time was that certain texts should be held up as linguistic models, and it was thought that biblical and other religious texts would be the best exemplars.[4] Johnson was eventually forced to abandon as impossible his original goal of 'fixing' the language, and to adopt the lesser aim of 'stalling' it, although he did still hope to go some way in preventing the influx of foreign words introduced by translators.

Given such lexical developments, a division between a dictionary and a grammar was inevitable, although it was not seen as a divide with hard and fast boundaries. As Johnson puts it, irregular constructions such as *oxen, brought, sheep*, etc. 'cannot be reduced to rules', and 'must be learned from the dictionary rather than the grammar' (S. Johnson 1816: 17).

That Johnson considered words to have original meanings is seen in his ordering of the different 'senses' of the words:

> In explaining the general and popular language, it seems necessary to sort the several senses of each word, and to exhibit first its natural and primitive signification; as, To *arrive*, to reach the shore in a voyage: he *arrived* at a safe harbour.
> Then to give its consequential meaning, *to arrive*, to reach any place, whether by land or sea; as, he *arrived* at his country seat. Then its metaphorical sense, to obtain anything desired; as, he *arrived* at a peerage.
>
> (S. Johnson 1816: 20–1)

Thus 'every word will have its history' (ibid.: 28). In the Preface, Johnson states that by tracing every word to its origin and by not admitting any word of which no origin can be found, he could 'secure our language from being over-run with cant, from being crowded with low terms' (ibid.: 16). Like Locke, he felt that words named ideas, and he was therefore sceptical about the possibility of synonyms: 'Words are seldom exactly synonimous; a new term was not introduced, but because the former was thought inadequate: names, therefore, have often many ideas, but few ideas have many names' (ibid.: 47). In his letter to Lord Chesterfield, he said that his Plan for a dictionary was to 'preserve the purity, and ascertain the meaning of our *English* idiom' (ibid.: 6). However, when it came to writing the dictionary, he felt that the Plan was too ambitious, since languages change, and so words cannot be preserved indefinitely: 'we laugh at the elixir that promises to prolong life to a thousand years' (ibid.: 60). In the Preface he wrote:

> When I took the first survey of my undertaking, I found our speech copious without order, and energetick without rules: wherever I turned my view, there was perplexity to be disentangled and confusion to be regulated: choice was to be made out of boundless variety, without any established principle of selection: adulterations were to be detected, without a settled test of purity; and modes of expression to be rejected or received, without the suffrages of any writers of classical reputation or acknowledged authority.
>
> (ibid.: 32)

Although Johnson was forced to admit that there were no lexical rules governing the definition and use of words, his ordering of the different 'senses' of words was later adopted by the initiators of the *OED*. But those who first undertook work on what became the *OED* eventually rejected Johnson's 'notion of a dictionary as a means of teaching "correct" usage in favour of a historical and non-judgemental approach' (Berg 1993: 137).

Locke's concept of definition might have influenced Johnson's definition of *explanation*, which

> requires the use of terms less abstruse than that which is to be explained, and such terms cannot always be found; for as nothing can be proved but by supposing something intuitively known, and evident without proof, so nothing can be defined but by the use of words too plain to admit a definition.
>
> (S. Johnson 1816: 46)

Furthermore, Johnson claims that the 'signification' of some verbs such as *bear, come, get,*

> is so loose and general, the use so vague and indeterminate, and the senses destorted so widely from the first idea, that it is hard to trace them through the maze of variation . . . or interpret them by any words of distinct and settled meaning.
>
> (ibid.)

So for Johnson, words were products of history, showing the changes in human institutions and society, displaying the long tradition of 'English riches'. It was for this reason that, unlike his predecessors, he now considered change and variation to be 'virtues worth recording'. The idea that words have 'true meanings' became increasingly influential during the mid-eighteenth century and it still holds force in contemporary discussions of standard English.

Charles Richardson, whose work of 1836 was also influential in the proposal for the *OED*, criticised Johnson's lexicographical work for giving numerous explanations of the same word 'founded upon no etymological or radical meaning', and for not distinguishing between literal and metaphorical significations: 'How is it possible that any word should have such a variety of separate meanings?' (Richardson 1836: 46).

> The lexicographer can never assure himself that he has attained the meaning of a word until he has discovered the thing, the sensible object . . . the sensation caused by that thing or object (for language cannot sever them), of which that word is the name. To this, the term *meaning* should be strictly and exclusively appropriated; and this, too, may be called the literal meaning.
>
> (ibid.: 43)

Richardson's *New Dictionary of the English Language* showed strong support for Horne Tooke's philosophical philology as expressed in *The Diversions of Purley* (1786). Richardson followed Tooke in his attachment to the view that every word had only one immutable meaning. Tooke's philology attempted to demonstrate, by using etymological arguments, that thought was dependent on language. He also claimed that all words and all parts of speech could be traced back to primary nouns that named concrete objects or actions with single immutable meanings. The majority of his etymologies, however, were speculative and rather fanciful: A *bar*, he wrote, 'in all its uses is a *defence*', a *barn* is 'a covered enclosure in which the grain, etc. is protected from the weather', a *baron* is 'an armed, defenceful, powerful man', a *barge* is a 'strong boat', a *bargain* 'a conformed, strengthened agreement', a *bark* 'a stout vessel', and the *bark* of a tree is its 'defence' (Richardson 1815: 51). By giving the individual meanings of words in this way, Richardson thought he could prevent his dictionary becoming replete with redundant information.

Despite their methods of attempting to ascertain the original, true meanings of words, both Richardson and Tooke adopted a historical approach in order to develop a new theory of language. For Richardson, as for Tooke, the 'first aim of language is to communicate thoughts: the second, to do it with dispatch' (Richardson 1815: 22). This view justifies the theory that many words 'are just abbreviations, and signs for other words' and not immediately the signs of ideas. This latter purpose of speech has a much greater share in accounting for the different sorts of words (ibid.: 22).

Arguing against Johnson's ten distinct explanations of the word *sad*, Richardson demonstrates that it is really a derivative of *sat*, 'by the mere change of *t* into *d*', from the Latin word meaning *set, settled* and metaphorically *sedate* (Richardson 1836: 46). Again, that *sex* is from the Latin *secus*, meaning *cut*, because an 'animal is cut (*secatur*) or divided into male and female'.

Rigorous alphabetical order was now abandoned by Richardson: for example, *Go* and *Goer* are listed in one entry before *Goad*. (This practice of listing words according to their senses had been employed in the seventeenth century, but only to avoid 'vain and tedious repetitions' (Coles 1676): 'you will often meet with words explain'd in their dependence and relation to one another, and the sense compleated by taking them together', as for example *Lupa, Lupercal, Lupercalia, Luperci*.)

It was Archbishop Trench who, influenced by Johnson's and Richardson's lexicographical work, finally inspired the undertaking that led to the compilation of the *Oxford English Dictionary*. Richardson and Tooke helped bring about a change in language study, divorcing it from the study of mind, 'from *a priori* speculation to *a posteriori* proof'. Words now become 'context-free through an analysis of their roots, paving the way for the study of language itself' (Davis 1994). For Trench, etymology should be employed to trace a word back to its original, 'true', divine origin; not, as in the theories of Tooke and Richardson, to show the history of the language. Etymology, as Trench saw it, was not about the mind but rather about spiritual and moral truths. The impossibility of inventing a language was sure proof for Trench that a language had a divine origin; a view similar to that of some seventeenth-century philosophers: 'Words often contain a witness for great moral truths – God having pressed such a seal of truth upon language, that men are continually uttering deeper things than they know' (Trench 1851: 7); '[words] ... are not merely arbitrary signs, but living powers ... intertwining themselves with all that men have been doing, thinking and feeling from the beginning of the world till now' (ibid.: 43–4).

Trench presented two papers to the Philological Society, later published under the title *On Some Deficiencies in Our English Dictionaries* (1857). One of Trench's most important observations was that a dictionary should be an objective 'inventory of language', and it should not contain subjective opinions on word meanings, as Johnson's dictionary had. A dictionary should also, he thought, use quotations that might assist in illustrating a word's first introduction, etymology and meaning. This would provide for an objective way of ascertaining a word's true meaning.

> A Dictionary is an historical monument, the history of a nation contemplated from one point of view, and the wrong ways into which a language has wandered, or attempted to wander, may be as instructive as the right ones in which it has travelled.
>
> (ibid.: 6)

In effect, this formed the basis of the *Proposal for the Publication of a New English Dictionary by the Philological Society* in 1859, later to become the *OED*: to define all the words which make up the English language, and to be based on historical principles, 'so as to bring into clear light the common thread which unites all together' (Philological Society 1859).

By the time the Philological Society conceived of this lexicographical idea, comparative philology had replaced the old 'philosophical' philology of Horne Tooke. Comparative philology was systematically comparing languages and grammatical forms by analysing the inflections of words. Now, the meanings of words were no longer analysed, and nor were roots often inspected for etymology, as they had been in Tooke's and Richardson's theories; instead, it was more usual for formal patterns of grammatical elements to be analysed. A word, as in Saussurean theory, now was a form compared to other forms. Language was studied as natural history, a process subject to invariable laws.

It was not until the second half of the nineteenth century that the results of comparative philology were put into historical perspective. Sound changes were conceived as regular, so that if at a certain time in a given dialect a sound in a certain position of a word changed into a different sound, this change would affect the 'same' sounds in the 'same' positions in other words of the same dialect. Languages were now conceived to be subject to 'laws' having no exceptions. These were no longer divine laws, but their own innate laws; hence, for the first time, the possibility of a science of language. Evolutionary linguistics replaced the Adamic theory of language. This was occasioned in part by Darwin's evolutionary theory, and in part by the introduction of mechanistic physics and other sciences, with the concomitant growth of industrialisation and technology.

In 1876, James Murray was approached to be the editor of the *New English Dictionary*, the purely historical project initiated by Trench. Murray, however, found the task rather daunting. In a letter to Henry Sweet, he wrote 'I shall have to do the best I can at defining probably 80,000 words that I never *knew* or *used* or *saw* before . . . I have no "natural" pronunciation and no intuitive knowledge' (quoted in K. Murray 1978: 190–1). Unlike the present editors of the *OED*, who claim to be describing the standard[5] language of literature and conversation, he did not wish to prescribe pronunciation.

> Language is mobile and liable to change . . . and a very large number of words have two or more pronunciations current . . . a man may call a *vase* a *vawse*, a *vahse*, a *vaze*, or a *vase*, as he pleases. And why should he not? We do not all think alike, walk alike, dress alike, write alike, or dine alike; why should we not use our liberty in speech also . . . ?
>
> (K. Murray 1978: 189)

He also found the question of how many words were in the language 'of Englishmen' an impossible one:

> Of some Englishmen? Or of *all* Englishmen? Is it *all* that *all* English-men speak, or some of what *some* Englishmen speak? Does it include the English of Scotland, and of Ireland, the speech of British Englishmen, and American Englishmen . . . ?
>
> (ibid.: 193)

Thus for the first volume of the dictionary, Murray could claim with conviction that the English language had no well-defined circle. He claimed that all that could be expected was just one way of recording some facts, and his method was 'not an unreasonable way of exhibiting the facts' (J. Murray 1884).

However, once lexicographers agreed upon a 'standard' way of listing, de-fining, and spelling a finite, complete set of words of the English language, it did not take long for this to give rise to the view that a standard language had always been in existence. Just as illusory as this is the concomitant belief that, underlying the multifarious uses of words, there has to be some under-lying sameness of form and meaning in order to explain how language makes communication possible.

Yet the term 'Standard English' is not a harmless 'descriptive' term at all. It has sense only within a strict form of prescriptivism, and is 'used to the benefit of specific social interests and against other such interests' (Crowley 1987: 199). It prescribes 'the discourse of one class of speakers by proscribing the discourse of others' (ibid.). In effect, the term also arose from the pronun-ciation dictionaries of the early twentieth century, as in the works of Daniel Jones. These texts were originally devised to teach the native, as well as non-native speakers, 'the language'. What was therefore needed was a standard to chart English sounds and transcribe texts. This was achieved by abstracting from the total varied empirical uses of spoken language a small number of ' "typical", "representative", "average" (and so on) sounds that would count as English' (ibid.: 201). Despite Jones's denial that there was a 'standard spoken English':

> [RP means] widely understood pronunciation. . . . I do not hold it up as a standard which everyone is recommended to adopt. . . . I have no intention of becoming either a reformer of pronunciation or a judge who decides what pronunciations are 'good' and what are 'bad'.
>
> (D. Jones 1917: xvi)

His pronunciation dictionaries, along with Murray's lexicographical work, nevertheless have the effect of bringing in the idea of a 'standard'.

We can see how these lexicographical developments gradually influenced what we now know as the *OED*, and what we now understand by 'standard English'. It is interesting to note Berg's comment in *A Guide to the Oxford English Dictionary*:

> In lexicographical terms, [the OED] is a *diachronic* dictionary; that is, it not only defines the language of the present day, it also records its use at any period within the Dictionary's coverage. The diachronic, or historical, approach benefits users in several ways. First, in addition to explaining what a word form means, it also, by documenting its history, explains *why* it has come to have a particular meaning.
>
> (Berg 1993: 3)

Berg also claims that

> contrary to the popular view of the *OED* as an authority on the 'correct' usage of the language, the Dictionary is intended to be *descriptive*, not *prescriptive*; it records, non-judgementally, the history of the language as mirrored in the written words of a democratic mix of novelists, playwrights, journalists, scholars, scientists, legislators, politicians, diarists, saints, and philosophers.
>
> (ibid.: 5)

However, she still charts the changing policy for the inclusion of taboo and offensive language (ibid.: 181). It is difficult to see how such an inclusion or exclusion can be a 'non-judgemental' decision. Weiner, the co-editor of the second edition of the *Oxford English Dictionary*, states that the new edition differs from Murray's in that the original dictionary had 'cultural filters' such as printed sources which 'screened out all that was unacceptable for printed publication' (Weiner 1990: 494). But the lexicographers of today, because 'all sorts of words' are permitted in print, have to draw the boundary lines themselves, i.e. not just between 'nonce' words and established words, but between 'American' and other forms. This further complicates the issue of standard English just as in the expansion of boundary lines to include a variety of different standard Englishes, as we have seen with Murray's self-questioning and in the varied definitions of standard English quoted at the start of this chapter. Standard English today includes a multitude of standards in countries where English is the official or national language.

The concept of standard English, then, is a confused and confusing one. Since the seventeenth century it has referred to a 'common core of language', an ideal or value to be met, the 'true' meanings behind words, the language of the literati, and those items of vocabulary listed in the *Oxford English Dictionary*. More often than not, however, linguists and educationalists attempt to unite all these senses, giving rise to paradoxical and confusing theses. Ricks in *The State of the Language* identifies one of the reasons why any idea of Standard English in our society will always have double standards:

> For the meaning of the word is not a matter of fact (which is why an argument about it can't be settled by recourse to the dictionary), and it is not a matter of opinion (which is why an argument about it mustn't be unsettled by a refusal to have recourse to the dictionary). The meaning of a word is a human agreement, created within society but incapable of having meaning except to and through individuals.
>
> (Ricks 1980: xi)

Although there is no way of enforcing or maintaining a linguistic standard, we can, by a process of conceptual clarification, arrive at a clearer understanding of why some are continually trying to set up such untenable 'standards' for English. This would be a first step towards regulating the 'perplexity and confusion of our speech' (S. Johnson 1816).

Acknowledgement

I would like to thank Chris Baldick for his helpful comments and suggestions on an earlier draft of this chapter.

Notes

1 The systems by which language and discourse are classified, ordered, distributed, etc.
2 'In order to determine to what extent something is a reality, it is necessary and also sufficient to find out to what extent it exists as far as the language users are concerned' (Saussure 1922: 128).
3 It is for this very reason that John Honey believes that England [sic] needs an official body effectively to manage and control linguistic change:

> traditionally, any new use [of words], whether by some scholar, or, more commonly, by groups of less educated people, must pass through the filter of educated people generally. It is the task of the dictionary-makers to monitor that approval, and the grammarians to describe the extent to which new uses are widely acceptable among educated people. That filter, and that criterion – acceptability to the educated – constitute for English the mechanism authority, and embody the notion of prescription which is then codified by the dictionary-makers and grammarians.
>
> (Honey 1997: 147)

4 'The Vulgar Translation of the Bible ... is the best standard of our language' (Lowth 1762: 89). The language of the Bible is 'the standard of our language as well as of our faith' (Monboddo 1792, Vol. 1: 479). 'The English Bible is practically the standard of our language' (Higginson 1864).

5   Although not outwardly as exhaustive as the professed aim of Murray's original dictionary, which

> seeks not merely to record *every* word that has been used in the language for the last 800 years, and its written form and signification, and the pronunciation of the current words, but to furnish a biography of each word, giving as nearly as possible the date of its birth or first known appearance [my emphasis]
>
> (Murray 1900: 47)

the editors of the second edition of the *OED* make claims which are more explic- itly wedded to the notion of a standard:

> The aim is to present in alphabetical series the words that have formed the English vocabulary from the time of the earliest records down to the present day, with all the relevant facts concerning their form, sense- history, pronunciation, and etymology. It embraces not only the standard language of literature and conversation, whether current at the moment or obsolete, or archaic, but also the main technical vocabulary, and a large measure of dialectal usage and slang.
>
> (*OED*, 2nd edn., 1989)

4

REPRESENTATIONS OF ENGLISH IN TWENTIETH-CENTURY BRITAIN: FOWLER, GOWERS AND PARTRIDGE

Tony Bex

The publication of the *Kingman Report* in 1988 was greeted with considerable attention by the British public. Matters of language seem to be of perennial concern within Britain and, when this concern was coupled with a prospectus for the future of English language education, it was not surprising that the report should have been the object of much discussion and criticism. From the comments that were made it would appear that, at least within the United Kingdom, there is a general consensus that there is something that might best be called 'correct', or 'standard' English, and that this is what should be taught to our children.[1]

The committee responsible for this report largely confirmed this view. They took it as axiomatic that something called 'standard English' both existed and that it should form part of the school curriculum. Their attempts to define what they meant by standard English were guided by various submissions from the general public as well as from specialists, and the committee itself consisted both of those professionally engaged in language study and of lay people.[2] Not surprisingly, the definition of standard English is both confused and confusing. 'Standard English' is 'the language which we have in common' but which we 'can only have partial access to'. It is variously equated with 'all the words in the Oxford English Dictionary' and 'the written form used by all writers of English'. It is not a dialect, although it developed from a dialect, and it is 'used to communicate across local areas and between regions in a spoken form' (Kingman 1988: 14).

I mention the membership of the committee in part because the presence of non-linguists may have been instrumental in the construction of such a woolly definition. I am not suggesting that such members were at all insincere in their submissions, but the extent to which they lacked a thorough grounding in the kinds of problem outlined in this volume indicates that they derived their ideas from more populist views of what is meant by the English language, and more particularly 'standard' English. Crowley (1997) has discussed the ways in which the term 'standard' can be defined in three relatively distinct ways, and how the elisions between such definitions (or re-definitions) can lead to confusion. I would suggest that the unclear definition of standard English within the *Kingman Report* derives from the elision of 'standard' as 'uniform' and 'standard' as 'excellent'. On the one hand, they were attempting to prescribe a set of usages that might be thought common to all varieties of English, while on the other they were recommending a variety that was perceived both as multi-functional and, to some extent, 'cultured'. This was not surprising since the Kingman committee was established because standards of English were felt to be falling and part of its brief was necessarily to encourage both uniformity and excellence. The report is therefore a contribution to the 'complaint tradition' (Milroy and Milroy 1991: 31–6) which surfaces on a regular, if more informal, basis in the columns of national newspapers and (particularly) radio programmes (cf. Bex 1996: 44–5).

A recent addition appeared in the *Independent* newspaper (24/6/97) as part of a continuing correspondence discussing an article on grammar that had appeared two weeks previously:

> Sir: May we return to the matter raised by Walter Roberts ('Grammarians Weep', 14 June), about which I have a question: are there any people who, having been taught to speak grammatically, then decide arbitrarily to ignore the rules they learnt and make up their own, and follow the example of those who have not had their advantage? I think not.
>
> The people whose speech is lamented by Mr. Roberts (among others) are unfortunate enough never to have been taught the rules in the first place. If we are invited to see this usage as a 'rich and fascinating phenomenon' (Letters, 16 June) and adopt it, then ignorance has the last word. A bleak prospect indeed.
> Sheelagh Flawn
> *East Preston, West Sussex*

The writer seems to be arguing that English has rules that can be taught (rather than those that may be immanent in a language) suggesting that correct English is nobody's birthright, but something that has to be (laboriously?) learned. But in making such an assertion, the correspondent obviously has in mind the existence of an authority who not only 'knows' the rules but has the right to impose them on those who do not.

Of course, it is always possible to dismiss such beliefs as belonging to 'folk' linguistics and therefore as being of little significance to the study of language. However, as Cameron has pointed out, this view can only be sustained if we consider that 'ordinary' people's views of language are not also a fact of language and a contribution to the ways in which languages change historically (Cameron 1990: 92–3). It becomes interesting therefore to consider who is supposed to possess such knowledge and how it is typically represented. By and large, it would appear not to be academic linguists. Indeed, Honey's recent book *Language is Power* (1997), a populist account of the failure to offer an English syllabus which concentrates on standard English (which he appears to equate with educated usage, although he fails to define what he means by either of these terms), has a running refrain which suggests that academic linguists are chiefly responsible for encouraging the 'fall in standards' implicitly referred to in the quoted correspondent. The most likely candidates for possession of this education would therefore include school teachers (and their associated text books), respected authors (and particularly those who make up the canon[3] that is taught in schools and universities), and compilers of reference works about the language (particularly lexicographers, but also those who offer help on nice points of usage).

Of these three groups, the first are currently constrained by the demands of the National Curriculum which has specific targets of correctness in language use deriving from the Kingman Committee as adapted by Cox and further modified by the Department of Education and Employment (Cox 1991). However, it is worth pointing out that these constraints only apply to the state schools. The second group typically contains those authors whose writing is studied for examination purposes. Although there are a number of contemporary authors, the majority are drawn from the earlier part of the century or before. The models of English presented are therefore slightly dated. The third group is the more interesting since it is not entirely clear how its members have achieved the standing they appear to have, nor how they have been selected to be arbiters of correct English. Widdowson (1993: 322) has suggested that: 'the sub-set of reliable informants is self-selected, and self-appointed as the custodians of correct English'. But this is surely *faux naïf*. While it is true that anybody can assert their linguistic preferences, only some of these people are taken seriously. To achieve authority, one has to be granted authority and such authority derives from society at large. For this reason it becomes important to investigate both those who appear to possess such authority and to establish what it is that they have in common such that they are treated as authorities by 'ordinary' members of the public. This chapter concentrates on three such authorities – Fowler, Gowers and Partridge – and attempts to show how they typically described the language, and why they were accorded the authority they achieved. Although they may not have contributed significantly to the academic debate as to what constitutes standard English, I maintain they have been of immense significance in shaping lay people's perceptions of what counts as 'good' English, and therefore, by default, in establishing what may be regarded as popular notions of standard English.

In the middle of the twentieth century, the relationships between these authorities and the teaching of English in schools were blurred. The *Newbolt*

Report of 1921 established English as a new subject within the curriculum. Protherough and Atkinson (1994: 7) argue that this 'newly minted subject was invested with the resonance of "Englishness", defined through the English language and supremely through the heritage of English literature'. They further claim that:

> the novelty lay in bringing together under the title of English, 'taught as a fine art', four separate concepts: the universal need for literacy as the core of the curriculum, the developmental importance of children's self-expression, a belief in the power of English literature for moral and social improvement, and a concern for 'the full development of mind and character'.

The first and third of these concepts inevitably privilege the written mode and the lexicon and grammars associated with it, while the second and fourth concentrate on psychological aspects of self-development. What is not obviously present is any interest in the language and its workings for their own sake, and in this respect the Report is similar to the *Kingman Report* of seventy years later. One consequence of these emphases is that grammar tended to be taught prescriptively as an aspect of 'style', and particularly literary style. Teachers, and their pupils, were typically encouraged to believe that there were 'right ways' of saying things, and that these 'right ways' were encoded in the works of prescriptive grammarians or other authorities in the language. Within the classroom there were textbooks which listed errors, demonstrated correct usage and had exercises to test the pupils' knowledge. An example by Hewson, published as late as 1955 and intended as a textbook for GCE examination classes, contains the following example exercise:

> Correct these sentences. Briefly give a reason for the correction.
> 1 (a) I wonder if it was her.
>   (b) Neither of you are very good singers.
>   (c) Who shall we send?
>   (d) He is one of the few players I know who plays that shot well.
>   (e) What our team wants are five new forwards.
>   (f) Seated on the top of a camel, the eye of the Arab watched the horizon.
>   (g) He is a better cricketer than I have ever seen.
>   (h) Either of the men were eligible for re-election.
>   (Hewson 1955: 18–19)

To the modern eye there is nothing particularly exceptionable about the majority of these sentences, although (f) reads rather oddly. No doubt in the 1950s most of them would have been perfectly acceptable in everyday speech in spite of breaching some of the shibboleths that applied to written usages. The preceding section of the book merely lists the rules which are assumed to apply in such cases (though no doubt some additional explanations would have been added by the classroom teacher). Exceptions are duly noted but none of this is clearly rooted in a discussion of the language or where these rules emanate from. Not surprisingly, grammar was often seen as arbitrary and boring.[4] Nevertheless, the interrelationships between correct usage and self-development suggested by the *Newbolt Report* inevitably led to anxieties by those who wished to appear educated. And these anxieties could only be resolved if there were authorities who could be consulted and relied upon to offer clear non-technical guidance on difficult matters of style and grammar.

The primary members of this group include H. W. Fowler, Ernest Gowers and Eric Partridge. The doyen of this group has to be H. W. Fowler with his two books *The King's English* (co-authored with F. G. Fowler, his brother) and *Dictionary of Modern English Usage* (MEU). The former was published in 1906 (two editions) and further editions appeared in 1930 and 1973. MEU first appeared in 1926 and subsequent editions or reprints were produced in 1930, 1934, 1952, 1958, 1959, 1965 (revised by Ernest Gowers), 1966, 1968, 1977, 1978, 1982, 1983, 1984, 1988, 1994 and 1996 (further revised by Robert Burchfield). Such a publishing history indicates a perennial appeal. Gowers (1957: 14) estimates that more than half a million copies had been sold by 1957 and in the preface to his edition mentions the story of Churchill complaining about a member of his staff for using *intensively* in place of *intensely* and referring the unfortunate to *MEU* for advice. Burchfield, in his preface, comments on known users of the book, including a judge, a colonel and a retired museum curator (ibid.: ix). On purely anecdotal evidence, I have discovered that many of my contemporaries are familiar with *MEU*, but largely as a volume that occupied the family bookshelf alongside the Bible and a dictionary. However, whether used or not, it clearly has the status of an authority and this is borne out in Sutcliffe's comment in his discussion of the circumstances surrounding its original appearance: 'Yet nobody can safely disregard Fowler's warnings' (1978: 220), or more recently in Enright's rather wistful comment: 'One may have been writing (not to say talking) all one's life, and one still gets things wrong' (1997: 6), with the implication that Fowler will be the policeman (or, perhaps, nanny) who identifies and corrects one's mistakes.

Fowler's original issue of *MEU* makes no mention in the preface of its intended audience. However, in the third edition of *The King's English* he observes that he (and his by then deceased brother) were gratified to notice 'that some of the conspicuous solecisms once familiar no longer met our eyes daily in the newspapers' (Fowler and Fowler 1931: 4). That such a modest man should impute, however tentatively, the changes in the language of the press to the influence of his writings suggests the underlying pedagogic purpose behind his various projects. This is reflected in his academic career. Born in

1858, he completed his secondary education at Rugby, a leading public school and went up to Oxford to read classics. He then taught at Sedburgh until 1899 when a fundamental disagreement with his friend and headmaster led to his resignation. These biographical details are significant in that they indicate the social and cultural backgrounds which formed his tastes, and which inevitably found their way into his descriptions (and prescriptions) of the language. They represent a moment in the social history of the ways in which the English language has been described.

Of course, a usage guide is not intended necessarily to be a grammar of the language. Its functions are more diverse and more likely to be subject to the whims of its compiler. As Borroff (1985: 353) points out:

> It can take time out to talk, can become an articulate presence, holding forth not merely about this or that word, idiom, or grammatical construction, but about language itself, what it is and what it ought to be.

In this respect, such usage handbooks – unlike grammars which offer guides to syntactic combinations, or dictionaries which indicate the range of meanings of individual words – more obviously possess a dual function (and therefore a dual power) in that they are more than simply language about language because they both instruct and exemplify at the same time.[5] In the quote above, the shift from descriptive 'is' to prescriptive 'ought' underlines the view of language as a form of social behaviour. Borroff (1985: 358) suggests that to speak with impropriety is to commit a misdemeanour, and it is clear that Fowler would agree with her.

MEU's primary concern was with style rather than grammatical description. This is self-evident from the entry on *Elegant Variation* (Fowler 1926: 130–3). One of the longest entries in the work, it identifies most clearly the targets Fowler had in sight and the methods by which he wished to eliminate them. In it, Fowler discusses choice of vocabulary, aspects of syntax (especially relating to pronouns and relatives) and literary style. Little, if any, mention is made of the spoken language and the article revels in exemplifying the various faults he wishes to eradicate both from journalism and more elevated literary works. In this respect, he is a direct inheritor of the eighteenth-century tradition of prescriptivism which instils anxiety in its followers by demonstrating that even respectable authors are capable of error. Fowler mentions Thackeray specifically, though he reserves special odium for 'minor novelists and reporters' (ibid.: 131). Their chief fault is that they are 'intent rather on expressing themselves prettily than on conveying their meaning clearly'. In itself this seems a venial sin but, as I intend to show later, Fowler equates the 'correct' use of English with the public school virtues of manliness and lack of vulgarity. Transgressing these articles of faith is to commit an act of social impropriety.

This aspect of his work is particularly apparent in his response to Jespersen's attack on him as an 'instinctive grammatical moraliser' for rejecting the construction he called the *fused participle* because it could not be classified within his own Latinate grammatical system. Fowler replied 'our grammatical conscience has by this time a Latin element inextricably compounded in it' (Gowers 1957: 11). The choice of the phrase *our grammatical conscience* is instructive in two ways. The first is that, however metaphorically, he clearly appears to believe that a person who employs a grammatical solecism (however defined) should feel guilty. Bad English is thus equated clearly with bad behaviour. As Gowers writes, Fowler's aim 'was, in his own words, to tell the people not what they do and how they come to do it, but what he thinks they ought to do for the future'.

The second is more complex. By using *our*, he is appealing to an unspecified social group. Exactly which speakers he has in mind is never made clear. However, by a (possibly unconscious) elision he has managed to suggest that those who have had a classical education, or been taught English according to Latin principles, have the right to regulate the usage of those who have not had such an advantage.

It would, however, be an error to suggest that Fowler had a clear ideological intent behind his entries. Many of them are idiosyncratic while others represent the received wisdom of the period. A peculiar mixture of these two facets can be found in his entry for *England, English(man)*. Although too long to be quoted in full, the following extracts indicate the personal prejudices that often inform his opinions:

> The incorrect use of these words as equivalents of *Great Britain, United Kingdom, British Empire, British, Briton* is often resented by the Scotch, Irish, & Welsh; their susceptibilities are natural, but are not necessarily to be deferred to ... How should an Englishman utter the words *Great Britain* with the glow of emotion that for him goes with *England*? He talks the *English* language; he has been taught *English* history as one tale from Alfred to George V; he has known in his youth how many Frenchmen are a match for one *Englishman*; he has heard of the word of an *Englishman* & of *English* fair play, scorns certain things as *unEnglish*, & aspires to be an *English* gentleman.
>
> (Fowler 1926: 139)

This passage deserves analysis not so much because of the prejudices which it reveals, but because of the way in which they are constructed. The first, and most obvious, point is that the main protagonist is identified as a male and not simply as the 'generic' masculine. This is clear from the final clause. The second, and equally obvious, point is the dismissive references to the 'Celtic' fringe. Although they are allowed a sense of nationhood, they are a colonised group whose 'susceptibilities . . . are not . . . always to be deferred to'. Slightly less obvious is the construction of English history. The continuity referred to ignores the Norman invasion, but it also elides the various internal divisions between different social groups as to what constitutes 'Englishness'. As Crowley (1996: Chapter 5; see also Leith 1997; Joseph 1987) has pointed out, the historiography of the nation is intimately connected to the historiography of the language and is an essential part of the standardisation cycle. For Fowler, this history is so selective as to be almost derisory. Of course, it might be argued that a reference work such as *MEU* could not be expected to deal with the complexities inherent in any accurate historical account. However, the verb choices within the quoted passage suggest that Fowler was not entirely unconscious of the problems implicit in his account. His putative Englishman may actively *speak* English and *scorn* things *unEnglish*, but he has passively *been taught* English history. Similarly, he *has known* about the weakness of the French, and *has heard* of English honour. No doubt it is because of his insecure grasp of these English truths that he can only *aspire* to be an English gentleman.

Interestingly, Gowers' 1965 revision of Fowler alters this entry in revealing ways. Although the Scotch, Irish and Welsh become 'other nationals of the U.K.' (Fowler 1965: 156), the sense of English nationhood is enhanced by references to the 'Queen of *England*' (ibid.: 157) and a quotation from Leo Amory: 'Speak for *England*' (ibid.: 157) uttered on 2 September 1939. In this way, the history has been updated although not fundamentally altered. And this is in marked contrast to the entries under *Feminine Designations* (Fowler 1926: 175–6; 1965: 194–5). Whereas Fowler's article argues for an increase of nouns ending in -*ess*, Gowers recognises that 'feminine designations seem now to be falling into disuse' (ibid.: 194). Fowler's own position again seems to depend on a particular view of the ways in which the language is a social construct. Arguing against those women who object to feminine endings, he states:

> These ladies neither are nor pretend to be making their objection in the interests of the language or of people in general; they object in their own interests only; this they are entitled to do, but still it is lower ground, & general convenience & the needs of the King's English, if these are against them, must be reckoned of more importance than their sectional claims.
>
> (ibid.: 175)

Fowler does not construct his argument on the assumption of women's inferiority, although there are moments when he comes very close to it, but on the need to maintain distinctions. Later, in the same article, he states that 'everyone knows the inconvenience of being uncertain whether a doctor is a man or a woman' (ibid.: 176). This is offered without explanation, and I can only assume that Fowler feels that there are appropriate, but different, ways of addressing men and women. Correct speech and social distinction are in a symbiotic relationship. By 1965, this particular distinction was falling into desuetude, leading Gowers to comment that 'it symbolizes the victory of women in their struggle for equal rights; it reflects the abandonment by men of those ideas about women in the professions that moved Dr. Johnson to his rude remark about women preachers' (ibid.: 194–5). Nevertheless, even Gowers seems to restrict his comments to the professions, suggesting that distinctions of class still applied.

Having said this, it is clear that Fowler's ideal was male speech. Two entries exemplify his view that women's speech was essentially inferior. Under *aggravate, aggravation* (1926: 13) he asserts:

1 The use of these in the sense *annoy, vex, annoyance, vexation* should be left to the uneducated. It is for the most part a feminine or childish colloquialism, but intrudes occasionally into the newspapers.

Similarly, he claims that *clever* 'is much misused, especially in feminine conversation, where it is constantly heard in the sense of learned, well read, bookish, or studious; a woman whose cleverness is apparent in all that she does will tell you that she wishes she were *clever*' (ibid.: 79). Perhaps it is not entirely surprising that some women whose gender has been equated with uneducated childishness might feel that they are not 'clever'. Again, there are revealing differences in Gowers' revisions for these two entries. He rewrites *aggravate, aggravation* (Fowler 1965: 13) completely, omitting all reference to education, women and childishness. By implication, he suggests that Fowler was fighting a lost cause and that the sense of these words as 'annoy or exasperate' was both so ingrained and historically justified within the language as to warrant retention. However, he leaves Fowler's entry for *clever* untouched; whether this is because he agrees with it or because he feels it to be an interesting example of Fowler's eccentricity is not clear.

So far, then, I have argued that Fowler's view of the best English (and, to that extent, 'standard' English) is that which is identified with a particular construction of English (rather than British) history. Further, it is largely derived from male patterns of speech and writing. I have suggested that his primary sources are literary and that the majority of the solecisms that he quotes also derive from written texts. However, he does not ignore the spoken language entirely as can be seen from his detailed entry on *pronunciation* (ibid.: 466–7) and various individual entries on disputed articulations.[6] Given his intended non-specialist readership, he does not use the IPA (International Phonetic Alphabet) but borrows the system used by the *Oxford English Dictionary*. At first sight, this seems a perfectly reasonable choice but it does lead to an inevitable circularity in that readers have to know already the intended phonological values of the illustrative words in order to be able to apply those values to disputed items. A further problem is that specific issues in pronunciation tend to be treated as though the written form were primary and the spoken form derivative. Fowler, for example, refers to the silent 't' and the silent 'h' (ibid.: 467) as though they are spectres waiting to materialise. This privileging of the written form is, however, tempered by a recognition of the uneasy relationships that hold between spelling and pronunciation, allowing him to write: 'Some good people, afraid that they may be suspected of not knowing how to spell, say the t in self-defence' (ibid.: 467).

It is not clear what models of pronunciation Fowler used. Giles (1987: 5–6) has argued:

> Though most people can both standardize and broaden their most usual way of speaking (i.e. their *idiolect*) at least slightly, it is also true that some people are practically immobile in this respect due to the limitation of their early vocal environments (for example, ghetto children; but, perhaps even more so, public school children).

While it is true that Fowler had a public school background, it is also true that he recognised and, to some extent, applauded the process of accommodation (Giles *et al.* 1991). He advises people to 'pronounce as your neighbours do, not better; for words in general use, your neighbour is the general public' (Fowler 1965: 467). However, the general public talk with a variety of dialects and Fowler recognises this when he distinguishes between northern and southern pronunciations (ibid.). So one is entitled to ask which subsection of the general public he is referring to. Although not entirely clear on this point, there is some evidence from his discussion of grammar that he had in mind a very limited subsection of the people.

Fowler's grammatical paradigms are not easy to untangle and his discussions are often confused. He has been accused, most noticeably by Jesperson (see above), of viewing English through the spectacles of Latin but this accusation is slightly misleading. In his entry on the *split infinitive* (Fowler 1926: 558–61), he gives no indication that this particular shibboleth derives from an attempt to force English syntactic structures into Latin corsets. His own aversion to the splitting of infinitives is based on grounds of good taste and the construction of unambiguous meanings. On the other hand, in his discussion of *Preposition at end* (ibid.: 457–9) he takes Dryden and Gibbon to task for adopting 'deliberate Latinism', arguing that:

> Those who lay down the universal principle that final prepositions are 'inelegant' are unconsciously trying to deprive the English language of a valuable idiomatic resource, which has been used freely by all our greatest writers except those whose instinct for English idiom has been overpowered by notions of correctness derived from Latin standards.
>
> (ibid.: 458)

It would appear, then, that he was flexible in his views as to the relation-ships that hold between English and Latin grammar. This is largely borne out in his discussion of *Saxonisms* (ibid.: 514–15). Here, he rejects the prac-tice of replacing Latinate words by coinages or resurrections of words etymologically related to Anglo-Saxon. His argument is that 'conscious delib-erate Saxonism is folly, that the choice of particular words should depend not on their descent but on considerations of expressiveness, intelligibility, brevity, euphony or ease of handling' (ibid.: 515). Nevertheless, it is clear that he assumes a knowledge of Latin among his readers for in his entry under *Analogy* (ibid.: 20–2) he refers (again) to word formation. Recognising that a major element in lexical productivity involves suffixation by analogy, he refers to a newspaper article which coined the term *abstentients*. Fowler suggests that the writer, in searching for a term that did not put us in mind of alcohol, coined the word by analogy with *dissentients*. However, he continues:

> the correspondence between *abstention* and *dissension* is not quite so close as he assumed; if he had remembered *dissentire* and *abstenire*, analogy would have led him to *abstinents* instead of to *abstentients*.
>
> (ibid.: 20–1)

The choice of *remember* here is significant because it underlines how Fowler takes it for granted that his readers are familiar with Latin vocabulary and its declensions and conjugations.

As an original thinker about English syntax, Fowler is neither clear nor particularly interesting. His discussion of the *fused participle* (ibid.: 205–8) is a genuine attempt to classify a construction which he believed was 'rapidly corrupting modern English style' (ibid.: 206). He argues that such construc-tions – exemplified here in the sentence 'Women having the vote reduces men's power' (ibid.: 206) – 'defy grammatical analysis' (ibid.: 207). Yet, that he has analysed it (albeit unsatisfactorily) and then rejected his own analysis as inconsistent with his own grammatical prejudices indicates that he does have firm ideas as to what *ought* to count as grammatical. Furthermore, in contrast to some of the observations I have quoted above, in this instance it is quite clear that he rejects the fused participle as a legitimate grammatical construction in English simply because its supposed analogy with Latin 'sense fusion' (ibid.: 207) is false. We have, then, the interesting paradox that Fowler will appeal to Latin analogies when it suits his purpose and reject them when it does not.

Although Fowler's analyses are logically inconsistent, they are not without interest because they demonstrate some of the points I have been making about the sectional nature of his views. In *The King's English* (Fowler and Fowler 1931, originally published in 1906), he attempts to distinguish between *shall* and *will*. His opening remarks are particularly revealing:

It is unfortunate that the idiomatic use, while it comes by nature to southern Englishmen (who will find most of this section superfluous), is so complicated that those who are not to the manner born can hardly acquire it; and for them the section is in danger of being useless.

(ibid.: 142)

The message this conveys, that 'true' or 'correct' English is that spoken by southern Englishmen, is repeated in *MEU* under *shall & will, should and would* (Fowler 1926: 526–9) where Fowler quotes Bradley approvingly: 'To use *will* in these cases is now a mark of Scottish, Irish, provincial, or extra-British idiom' (ibid.: 526).

Without too much risk of caricature, it can be seen that Fowler's influential work characterised 'correct' English as that used in the writings of educated men from the south of England. To gloss this slightly, although some mention is made of speech forms, the dominant mode used in exemplification of good practice is the written mode. 'Educated' is necessarily a loose term, but Fowler's constant reference to Latin and his assumption that his readers would be familiar with Latin grammar and vocabulary suggests at least a grammar school education and more probably a public school one. 'Men' hardly needs any expansion. Fowler rarely mentions women's writing except to disparage it by innuendo (cf. Fowler 1926: 176). The south of England is slightly misleading in that many boys who were educated in public schools were not so geographically restricted, but in so far as it refers to a dialect which developed from the East Midland dialect it is a satisfactory designation. It could be objected that because Fowler was writing a reference work concerned largely with matters of style rather than a descriptive grammar, much of this is irrelevant. However, because his works were influential in establishing a standard by which people's speech and writing were to be judged, his selective use of the evidence becomes highly significant.

I have referred to some of the revisions made by Ernest Gowers in his edition of Fowler. Gowers has a dual significance in this portrait of the ways in which an image of the English language was constructed and then reflected back to the general public in the twentieth century. Not only did he keep the memory of Fowler alive, he also published two influential books of his own. His early background was remarkably similar to Fowler's. Born some twenty-two years later, he also studied at Rugby and continued by reading classics, though at Cambridge rather than Oxford. He then had a distinguished career in the British civil service where he was asked to write a handbook on correct usage for his co-employees. The two books he produced, *Plain Words* (1948) and *The ABC of Plain Words* (1951), were eventually combined to form *The Complete Plain Words* (1954). Although arguably less popular than *MEU*, *CPW* has been through three editions and numerous reprints partly because, as Burchfield, the reviser of Fowler, comments in his entry for Gowers in the

Oxford Dictionary of National Biography: 'In an age of possibly declining standards of written English Gowers provided clear guidance to anyone who turned
to him for a ruling on matters of linguistic dispute.'

   The view that standards were in decline was evidently also held by Gowers,
who wrote in his account of Fowler (1957: 14):

> Strange things are happening to the English language; the revolt
> against the tyranny of the old grammarians seems to be producing a
> school of thought which holds that grammar is obsolete and it does
> not matter how we write so long as we can make ourselves understood.

   As with my comments on Fowler, this also is revealing. It suggests a direct
line of thought between the two writers. But it also indicates a peculiar view
of what is meant by grammar and the relationship that is supposed to hold
between grammar and meaning. The notion that there can be a language
that is not organised grammatically harks as far back as Bullokar (1586),
whose own *Pamphlet for Grammar* refers on its title page to 'languages ruled
or not ruled by grammar'. It is fairly clear that Bullokar was referring to
languages that were not descendants of Latin or Greek and it is at least
arguable that Gowers, with his classical background, was also unconsciously
thinking of English as modelled on Latin and that a language whose constructions could not be described in terms previously used to describe Latin was
in danger of losing its grammar.

   However, Gowers rarely appealed to Latin paradigms in the advice he gave.
Rather, he tended to assume that his readers would be aware of classical
models. So, in his comments on syntax he mentions that:

> In Latin, the subject of the verb will have a form that shows it is
> 'in the nominative', and the object one that shows it is 'in the
> accusative'; you may arrange them as you like, and the meaning will
> remain the same. In the two sentences 'Cain killed Abel' and 'Abel
> killed Cain' the words are the same, but when they are reversed the
> meaning is reversed too.
>
> (Gowers 1954: 122)

For the speaker of English who has no knowledge of Latin, the first of
these sentences will be only mildly informative, whereas the second will
be stating the banally obvious.[7] Nevertheless, although Gowers' book is part
of the same discourse inhabited by Fowler, there are important differences.
The first of these is that it was written 'as a guide to officials in the use of
English' (ibid.: 196). It was commissioned as a direct result of the growth
of the executive following the Second World War. Gowers mentions that
'*De facto* executive power, which during the seventeenth and eighteenth
centuries moved from the King to Ministers, is being diffused lower still by

the growth of social legislation. ... So many people have to read so many official instructions' (ibid.: 197). The implication here is that the expansion of the Civil Service has not only increased the number of official documents which need to be read, but that the growth of the executive has widened the social base of its recruits, the result being that these documents are being written by people who are less well-educated in literacy skills. Gowers' brief was to advise them in how to construct documents that were transparent in their meanings.

The Complete Plain Words is more discursive than *MEU*, although it does contain lists of errors and areas of potential difficulty. Its avowed prescriptive nature, however, does not interfere with Gowers' occasional discussions of a more general nature. Oddly, in the 'Epilogue', he appears to contradict the position he adumbrated in the lecture he gave to the English Association in 1957. He states (Gowers 1954: 198): 'It does not seem to me to be true that the language itself is in decay. Its grammatical and syntactical usages are carefully preserved, perhaps too carefully.' This may, however, only be an apparent contradiction and largely the result of the different audiences he was addressing. In discussing 'The Handling of Words' (ibid.: 119), he suggests that 'Grammar has fallen from the high esteem that it used to enjoy'. In the brief history he offers of the decline of grammar it becomes clear that he is referring to the inappropriate attempts of grammarians to force English into a Latin mould. This leads him to declare (ibid.: 120):

> The old-fashioned grammarian certainly has much to answer for. He created a false sense of values that still lingers. I have ample evidence in my own correspondence that too much importance is still attached to grammarians' fetishes and too little to choosing the right words. But we cannot have grammar jettisoned altogether; that would mean chaos. There are certain grammatical conventions that are, so to speak, a code of good manners.

These various statements can, I think, be reconciled if we imagine Gowers picking his way delicately through a number of conflicting claims. Besieged by correspondents who wished him to interdict various usages on the grounds that they violated 'rules' they had learned at school,[8] he wished to defend the language against ossification. On the other hand, he was not prepared to reject the view that older grammarians had useful things to say about the language and, indeed, quotes Cobbett approvingly (ibid.: 119). This attitude fits well with his view that the following of grammatical conventions, however they are described, is on a par with good manners.

It is not difficult to see why Gowers' work has managed to be sufficiently popular as to go through three separate revisions. On the one hand, there had been a significant increase in the number of clerical jobs following the war, particularly in the newly nationalised industries. The management structure in these organisations broadly replicated the class structure in Britain as a whole (Marwick 1982: Chapter 2) and many of the new, junior staff needed specific advice on how to write business letters and other official documents in the style of their superiors. Gowers filled that need in ways that a descriptive grammar could never manage. However, at a deeper level, his work maintained the popular notion that 'correctness' was derived from the written language. This is not surprising for a handbook on writing, but the popular idea that the grammar of speech was somehow secondary is not an easy notion to shift and the appearance of another book on correct usage helped subtly to reinforce it. Further, the image of the language that was reflected back to the public was one that had a heritage, if no longer quite so classically based, embodied in the literary canon leading Sir Bruce Fraser to observe in his revised edition of 1973:

> The nature of education has changed greatly since the late 1940s and it seems to me here and there Gowers assumes in his readers a more literary education than most readers now have. I have reluctantly cut out a number of literary allusions which, though apt and charming, may (to quote one of my correspondents) 'look highbrow and irrelevant in the swinging and illiterate seventies'.
>
> (Gowers 1973: iv)

And finally, it privileged the dialect, if not quite so much of the public school, of those senior civil servants whose education would have been similar to that of Gowers and Fowler.

The third of the popular writers on English usage in the middle of the century had a slightly different background from the others. Born in New Zealand in 1894, Eric Partridge came to Oxford where he studied literature. He worked briefly as a lecturer in English literature between 1925 and 1927 before devoting his life to lexicography and other works on the English language. *Usage and Abusage* was first published in Britain in 1947 since when it has gone through many editions including publication by Penguin Books, a sure sign of its popularity. Partridge supplies no preface to indicate who might be his intended readers although it follows a format similar to that of *MEU*. Under the entry *Grammar*, however, he does state that 'in this book a knowledge of the essentials of accidence and the simplicities of syntax has been assumed' (Partridge 1947: 136). A significant number of the entries cover ground already described by Fowler, who is extensively quoted. The section on *Fused Participles* (ibid.: 121–7), for example, is essentially a brief essay on Jespersen's and Onions' dispute with Fowler with liberal interventions of Partridge. As he explains (ibid.: 122):

> The fused participle has caused much heartburning. There are two main schools of thought: The Fowlerites, who consider it the

abomination of abominations; the Onions men and the Jespersenites, who, on certain points, oppose the Fowlerites with a most English sturdiness.

This is a revealing paragraph. The fused participle can only give rise to passion in one of two ways. On the one hand, scholars of the language might dispute the term as an inadequate description of a syntactic construction. And this was broadly the position taken by Jespersen. On the other, prescriptivists might dispute passionately as to whether it is a construction that should be allowed into 'polite' usage. As quoted by Partridge, Onions clearly belongs to the camp that feels it has earned its historical right to be recognised. Lurking behind this discussion is the old bugbear as to whether English constructions should obey Latin rules; hence Partridge's reference to 'English sturdiness'.[9]

At the root of this dispute is a confused notion of grammatical rules which can best be exemplified through Partridge's brief entry on *Grammar* (ibid.: 136–7):

> Grammar is based on language – the particular language concerned – grammar has no existence apart from language; grammar is a set of rules codifying usage, not a code superimposed on language and pre-determining usage; in short, grammar must modify itself if language changes, grammar being made for man, not man for grammar. Nevertheless, where grammatical rules make for a clarity that would disappear with the disappearance of rules, it is better to preserve and maintain the rules – until, at least, a simpler or more satisfactory rule is devised or (more probably) evolved.

The first part of this quotation establishes grammar as a description of the language. However, Partridge then moves to a most peculiar position for, if grammatical rules are immanent within the language, 'rules' being roughly equivalent to 'laws' in the natural sciences, they cannot 'disappear'; however, they may change over time. I presume it is to account for historical change that he mentions the evolution of new rules. Nevertheless, the relationship that is supposed to hold between 'clarity' and grammatical rules is deeply obscure. 'Clarity' must be clarity for some speakers. In the example of the fused participle, it is reasonable to assume that those who used the construction were perfectly well aware of what they meant by it as were their interlocutors. In this sense, it did not lack clarity even though it offended against Fowler's rules. The same is true for most of the offensive constructions listed in all three books.

Interestingly, where there are constructions which do 'break' the rules, but which Fowler, Gowers or Partridge regard as acceptable, all three authors tend to appeal to the notion of 'idiom'. Partridge (1947: 148) quotes Pearsall

Smith's claim that '*idioms* are "those forms of expression, of grammatical construction, or of phrasing, which are peculiar to a language, and approved by its usage, although the meanings they convey very often are different from their grammatical or logical signification" '. Gowers (1954: 121), in discussing two particular idioms, comments: 'That the first is logically nonsense and the second a grammatical howler is neither here nor there; idiom makes light of such things.' Fowler (1926: 251) observes that 'grammar and idiom are independent categories; being applicable to the same material, they sometimes agree & sometimes disagree about particular specimens of it'.

Of these three authors, Partridge is the only one who has an entry on *Standard English* (Partridge 1947: 304–8). As in many of his entries, Partridge quotes extensively from other sources, and we can assume that he agrees with what he cites. He distinguishes between three types of standard: Received Standard, Modified Standard and Literary Standard. The first two occur both in speech and writing while the third is limited exclusively to writing, and largely the writing of the 'best' authors (ibid.: 304). For the first of these he follows Wyld in asserting that it is:

> the best, that form which has the widest currency and is heard with practically no variation among speakers of the better class all over the country. This type might be called Public School English.
>
> (ibid.: 306)

Modified Standard is:

> Standard English, modified, altered, differentiated by various influences, regional and social. Modified Standard differs from class to class, and from locality to locality; it has no uniformity, and no single form of it is heard outside a particular class or a particular area.
>
> (ibid.: 306)

Although Partridge does not distinguish clearly between accent and dialect in his article, it does seem clear that he regards Received Standard as containing a uniform accent and a fixed syntax. And, as the quotation indicates, it is both male and class-based. Modified Standard, so defined, is so vague as to be incapable of clear description. In so far as we can guess what he had in mind, it would appear to be a version of Received Standard spoken by relatively well-educated English speakers who had not had the advantages of a public school education. However, in spite of citing Wyld's definitions of Received and Modified Standard English, Partridge later asserts that 'a language cannot be at the same time entirely standardized and truly vital' (ibid.: 306); 'No standard language exists on its own capital; no standard language can thus exist, – if it is to continue to be a language and not become a mausoleum' (ibid.: 307).

These contradictions are interesting for they show the difficulties faced by any handbook writer who, in selecting what they believe to be the best usage, have then to decide how to classify what has been omitted. Partridge, as a keen lexicographer of slang, was fully aware of this dilemma which was why he had to argue that there both was and was not a standardised English.

As stated at the beginning of the chapter, I have concentrated on these three authors for two reasons. First, their immense popularity, as measured by the numbers of editions which each book had throughout the twentieth century, suggests that they were catering to a real need. They were, therefore, far more influential in constructing a model of the language than any professional linguist. The model constructed was, as I have argued, male, class-based, largely drawn from the written mode, and appealed to a particular view of history that privileged the English. Second, their contribution to linguistic thought tends to be largely ignored by linguists,[10] but if a language is best seen as the possession of its speakers, what these speakers think about their language is an important feature in its development and use.

The tradition of writing handbooks on usage continues,[11] which suggests a deep seated anxiety among (British) English speakers about what counts as 'correct'. This is borne out by the regular appearance of an advertisement in the press headed 'Shamed By Your Mistakes In English?' and which continues: 'Indeed thousands of talented, intelligent people are held back at work and socially because their command of English does not equal their other abilities.' However, if 'correct grammar' is regarded as a social marker, it still remains to be seen why Fowler, Gowers and Partridge should be treated as the leading guides in this area.

Part of the answer lies in their remarkably similar backgrounds. The extent to which the speech and writing habits developed in the major public schools were homogeneous is open to question; but that there was thought to be a public school 'speech' is well attested in the quotations above (see also Crowley 1989, 1996). As Bourdieu and Passeron (1994: 8) point out:

> In secondary and higher education it is taken for granted that the language of ideas elaborated by the academic and scientific traditions and also the second-order language of allusions and cultural complicities are second nature to intelligent and gifted individuals; or better, that the ability to understand and manipulate these learned languages – artificial languages, *par excellence* – where we see the natural language of human intelligence at work immediately distinguishes intelligent students from the rest.

The development of the public schools in the nineteenth century developed just such a language and range of cultural allusions which was maintained at the universities. This was achieved by inculcating a measure of respect for the models of the earlier (Roman) empire, tempered by a Greek humanism filtered through a Christian morality and sensitivity. In this sense, these writers shared a common discourse which, as we have seen, inevitably found its way into their writings on language.

None of this strictly indicates why their works should have achieved such authority. For this we have to appeal to Bourdieu's (1991) notions of 'symbolic capital'. The social discourses of which all these writers were a part carried just such capital. Oxbridge and the great public schools are regarded as having prestige (and this prestige, in the case of the universities, is transferred to their publishing houses). Negative evidence for this can be seen in Harris's (R. Harris 1988: 17) comment on Murray:

> Murray began his career as a more or less taught schoolmaster from the Borders, who clearly regarded himself as a mere outsider seeking admittance to the inner sanctum of English language and culture, and who equally clearly believed in authority in the matter of laying down rights and wrongs on English usage.

Fowler, Gowers and Partridge possessed the authority. However, they still required a public willing to recognise it. Bourdieu makes the point (1991: 51) that individuals' reactions to symbolic domination are variable depending on their 'predispositions to feel it'. In a society still largely governed by class differences, modes of speech were significant markers as can be seen from the reactions to Mitford's article on U and non-U speech (Marwick 1982: 45). For those who wished to 'better' themselves, it was important to speak (and write) 'properly'. To do this, people needed guidance and it is not surprising that they turned to writers who possessed the symbolic capital of an Oxbridge and public school background. Nor is it surprising that their mentors defined 'correct usage' as, in Bourdieu's (1991: 61) words:

> the product of a competence which is an *incorporated grammar*, the word grammar being used explicitly (and not tacitly, as it is by the linguists) in its true sense of a system of scholarly rules, derived *ex post facto* from expressed discourse and set up as imperative norms for discourse yet to be expressed.

It remains to be seen whether these various works have had an impact on professional linguists and, if so, what kind of an impact. I believe the answer to be a tentative 'yes', at least within Britain. And I would suggest this influence shows itself in two different ways. On the one hand, there are those linguists like Greenbaum and Crystal who continue within the prescriptivist tradition. And there are those descriptive linguists who are engaged in producing grammars of the language. Such grammarians (even with the advent of large corpora) cannot hope to describe and systematise all the idiolects of those people who claim to speak English. They are therefore forced back into a selection which becomes, in Joseph's words (1987: 58), synecdochic of the language as a whole. The varieties they select from tend towards those of their class and workplace. It is, for example, noticeable that in many universities which offer English language as a discipline there is a distinction made between dialectology and straightforward grammar of English. This suggests that there is a grammar of English against which all other grammars are classified as dialects. Although it would be unfair to castigate such departments for not covering the full subject area, it is worth noting that the variety which is typically selected as synecdochic tends to be that represented in the written form (but see Carter, Chapter 7 of this volume). That, at least, is certainly the impression one receives from the standard textbooks in the area.[12]

Nevertheless, this is not clear evidence that any of these authors have been directly influenced by the prescriptivists. It does, however, relate to my earlier point about symbolic capital. All these writers, by virtue of their position (and possibly their schooling) now belong to the class which maintains the superiority of certain usages. It is, therefore, not entirely surprising that they should take as their model the dialect with which they are most familiar and then generalise it to English as a whole. Thus, it could be argued that they have been influenced by such writers as Fowler and Gowers by subtle indirection.

Notes

1 For an interesting, and ultimately unsatisfactory, attempt to define 'standard' English in the educational setting see Perera (1994: 81).

2 One of these, A. S. Byatt, had previously been a lecturer in English literature. Her recent novel, *Babel Tower*, presents a fictionalised account of a committee investigating the teaching of English. She prefaces her book with a quote from Nietzsche: 'I fear we are not getting rid of God because we still believe in grammar.'

3 I do not mean to refer solely to the canon of English literature, though this is likely to predominate. I have in mind also other respected writers within the humanities, including historians and philosophers.

4 See also some of the comments below offered, and those by Gowers in particular.

5 I would not want to suggest that grammars and dictionaries are not also normative but that their normativity is less apparent on the surface.

6 See particularly his discussion of *LU* (Fowler 1926: 335–6).

7 In the revised edition (1973), Sir Bruce Fraser emends this passage by inserting ' "Amor vincit omnia" means exactly the same as "Omnia vincit amor". (Love conquers all things)' (Gowers 1973: 113). That he chooses a relatively well known phrase, but also gives us the translation, suggests that the assumption that a significant number of civil servants had received a classical education could no longer be held. This revision was retained by Greenbaum and Whitcut in the third edition of 1986.

8 On almost every page where he discusses disputed usages, Gowers refers to correspondents who belong to the 'complaint tradition'.

9 The futility of this discussion can be observed from the fact that there is no mention of the term in *Oxford English* (Dear 1986), although there is a brief

discussion of the different nuances of meaning between the NP + *ing* construction and the Possessive + *ing* construction (ibid.: 120).

10 R. Harris (1988), for example, makes no mention of them.

11 See, for example, Burchfield's updating of Fowler (1996); Greenbaum and Whitcut's *Longman Guide to English Usage* (1988); Dear's *Oxford English* (1986); Crystal's *Who Cares About English Usage* (1984). Indeed, Greenbaum (1986) has argued that grammarians should be prescriptive in certain circumstances.

12 See, for example, Burton-Roberts (1986); Halliday (1994); Huddleston (1984).

Part II

PERSPECTIVES ON THE SPOKEN LANGUAGE

INTRODUCTION TO PART II

In planning this volume it became clear to us that one aspect of the debate has always evinced virulent reactions from both sides of the divide: the question of whether or not we can talk about 'standard spoken English'. For this reason we have devoted Part II, containing three chapters, to the discussion of spoken English, although several of the other contributors touch upon this subject to a greater or lesser degree in their respective chapters (e.g. Richard Watts, James Milroy, Lesley Milroy, Laura Hartley and Dennis Preston).

We begin with Peter Trudgill's chapter (Chapter 5), since he presents what is probably the linguistically best motivated set of arguments against the notion of 'standard spoken English' if what we understand by that term is a set of highly codified rules of pronunciation. Trudgill's chapter, however, does not just argue against a process of standardisation for the phonology of spoken English. In common with all the other contributors to this volume Trudgill posits that 'Standard English' is 'the variety of English normally used in writing', that it is 'the variety associated with the education system in all the English-speaking countries of the world' and that it emerged as the variety 'associated with the social group with the highest degree of power, wealth and prestige'.

Trudgill's wider aim is to characterise 'Standard English' by outlining what it is not, and in so doing he touches on levels of formality for which speakers need to develop as wide a range of styles as possible. He argues that, within the education system, it is desirable to make that wide range of styles explicit to the learners whilst also giving them a greater exposure to styles that are situated at the more formal end of the continuum. He raises the question as to whether the National Curriculum document for English in England and Wales (DfE/WO 1995) can identify what is meant by the vocabulary of standard English and indicates some of the obvious problems which would arise if any such definition of the term were attempted.

The crux of his argument, however, is that 'Standard English is simply "a sub-variety of English", differing from regional varieties of the language in being a "social dialect"'. There is thus no one accent which is associated with it. From a sociolinguistic point of view the argument cannot be flawed although the reader might wish to challenge Trudgill's claim that there is general agreement amongst linguists in Britain that 'Standard English' has nothing to do with pronunciation. The chapters by James Milroy

(Chapter 1) and Lesley Milroy (Chapter 8) certainly do challenge his point of view. In addition, at least two book-length publications (Crowley 1989 and Mugglestone 1995) have been devoted to examining the rise of RP (Received Pronunciation) as a prestige accent. Trudgill sets up three stages in the standardisation process: (1) *determination* of which forms are deemed to be 'standard', (2) the *codification* of those forms and (3) their *stabilisation* through prescriptive methods in the education system. In this respect it is particularly important to assess the degree of codification and stabilisation in the area of phonetics and phonology, since Crowley and Mugglestone clearly show that RP had been 'determined' as the socially desirable accent at least as early as the nineteenth century, but also because many of those with a 'degree of power, wealth and prestige' today, and a large number of people who do not possess those attributes, are also convinced that RP represents the standard phonological form of spoken English. Trudgill's chapter is thus the ideal starting point for carrying this aspect of the debate further.

The chapter by Jenny Cheshire (Chapter 6) takes the discussion of spoken English a step further by considering the problems of the syntax of spoken forms of English. She admits that there is still considerable debate about whether or not Trudgill's exclusion of accent from the definition of 'Standard English' reflects a non-linguistic perception of 'spoken Standard English'. For her, however, it is more appropriate to focus attention on the field of education, in particular to the National Curriculum document on Standard English (DfE/WO 1995), since the terms 'spoken and written forms' might lead the reader to suppose that the two are very similar.

Like Trudgill she is concerned that our beliefs about the written forms of 'Standard English' might lead us to overlook syntactic structures that regularly occur in a wide variety of speaking styles in the spoken language. The sort of structures which she illustrates with data from spoken English corpora have not been adequately dealt with in linguistic descriptions of spoken English, and she attributes this to the influence of three linguistic traditions:

1   the generative tradition, in which a description of the competence of the idealised native speaker/hearer based on idealised, intuited sentences in fact turns out to involve standardisation, since linguistic variation attributed to social facts about the speaker is ignored
2   the lay tradition, outlined by Milroy and Milroy (1998) in their description of 'authority in language', in which the historically developed links between standardisation, nationalism and literacy lead to the tendency for speakers to think of the development of language through time as leading to a 'summit' of excellency, as being distinct from other languages and dialects, and as being the only 'proper' form of the language
3   the sociolinguistic tradition, in which researchers attempt to provide a socially grounded definition of Standard English.

In the second tradition of defining 'Standard English' linguistic variation has been given short shrift by those demanding codification. The problem with the third tradition is that its proponents end up by analysing social facts rather than linguistic facts and defining what is *not* Standard English rather than what *is*. In doing so they tend to refer to data-generated grammatical descriptions of English such as Quirk et al. (1985a), which, in the last resort, are flawed by a tendency to represent the spoken English of very restricted groups of speakers in more formal than informal speech styles. Like Trudgill, she points out that 'the majority of adult speakers, however, will need a wider stylistic repertoire'. It is thus not particularly helpful if the National Curriculum leads us to the assumption that the syntax of spoken and written styles of English are essentially the same.

Cheshire then illustrates the kinds of syntactic structure that regularly occur in a wide variety of styles of spoken English and which have not received much if any attention from the three linguistic traditions outlined above. It is important to bring these facts to the notice of linguists and teachers alike since the simple branding of syntactic variants as 'non-standard' which has now begun to occur since the implementation of the National Curriculum has 'important real-world implications'. We find ourselves in complete agreement here and can only deplore a situation in which the debate about Standard English has reached a personalised, politicised level at which these 'important real-world implications' are being conveniently glossed over or hidden.

In Chapter 7, Ronald Carter's discussion overlaps partially with Cheshire's, but it also carries the debate squarely into the English-language classroom. Carter states clearly what some of Cheshire's 'important real-world implications' might be. He suggests that the view of standard spoken English projected by the National Curriculum document is one in which 'an artificial and unnatural English' is required of the majority of learners leading to a new form of oral illiteracy for speakers of English. If we use Trudgill's definition of Standard English as a 'social dialect', the National Curriculum assumes that children are willing to do what any child psychologist knows they will not do, i.e. 'to learn a dialect associated with a group with which they do not wish to be associated'. The reason is quite simple: the kind of shift from an assumed non-standard to a standard spoken dialect that this entails amounts to a devaluation of their own local variety of English in favour of another. Indeed, the consequences outlined by Carter and hinted at by Cheshire are so serious that one wonders why so much emphasis should be placed on spoken standard English in the National Curriculum when 'so little appears to be known about what exactly it is'.

Like Cheshire, Carter presents some of the attestable evidence that is so sadly lacking in the debates on literacy in many countries, to show that there is a wide range of structures which we can expect to find only in the spoken medium. His examples are taken from the CANCODE corpus of spoken

English encompassing, to date, some 5 million words. The structures that he presents can be shown to be produced by speakers involved in real-time spoken discourse in different contexts in which forming and restating interpersonal relationships and aligning oneself to the physical conditions of the discourse context are more significant than 'speaking like a book'. Again like Cheshire, he, too, argues against the intuitively invented example sentences of the generativists, since the kinds of introspection are inapplicable to describe and explain naturally occurring spoken data. The constraints of face-to-face, online verbal interaction lead to radically different mechanisms of processing and storing of information according to the requirements of individual speakers.

The evidence indicates very clearly that the syntactic structures presented are not only used regularly and in a wide range of speech styles by speakers, but also that they are used strategically within the discourse. Carter suggests that the structures he deals with are all 'forms of spoken English which are perfectly standard and which are indeed grammatically correct', but that, since they do not figure in standard grammars of English, they are easily judged to be non-standard and even ungrammatical. This is clearly an area in which a great deal more work is needed from linguists, but it is, fortunately, one in which a start has already been made in the USA (see Schegloff, Ochs and Thompson 1997).

Carter's final point is that pedagogic processes can gain a great deal not only from looking at this kind of data-driven research on oral corpora but also by comparing and contrasting spoken and written texts. In doing so, it will be seen that both media encompass a very wide range of genre types in which a wider set of variations must be allowed than the minimal variation in written English acceptable to the National Curriculum, and that the number of genre types in the oral medium will be far greater than those in the written medium. Carter is certainly not against teaching 'Standard English'. Not to teach standard written English would be to disregard the need to teach English internationally as a second or a foreign language and it would 'seriously disadvantage and disempower' the native speaker. But to teach standard spoken English requires that we take on the task of showing what it is.

The aspect of the debate which involves the spoken language is thus of central significance, and it will involve taking the data out to those who set themselves up as the guardians of 'Standard English' and allowing them to compare their own oral performance with those we have on tape. The argument might be: 'Never mind what you think you say or should say. Focus on what you and others like you actually do say!'

5

STANDARD ENGLISH: WHAT IT ISN'T

Peter Trudgill

There is a reasonably clear consensus in the sociolinguistics literature about the term *standardised language*: a standardised language is a language one of whose varieties has undergone standardisation. *Standardisation*, too, appears to be a relatively uncontroversial term, although the terminology employed in the discussion of this topic is by no means uniform. I myself have defined standardisation (Trudgill 1992) as 'consisting of the processes of language determination, codification and stabilisation'. Language determination 'refers to decisions which have to be taken concerning the selection of particular languages or varieties of language for particular purposes in the society or nation in question' (ibid.: 71). Codification is the process whereby a language variety 'acquires a publicly recognised and fixed form'. The results of codification 'are usually enshrined in dictionaries and grammar books' (ibid.: 17). Stabilisation is a process whereby a formerly diffuse variety (in the sense of Le Page and Tabouret-Keller 1985: 70) 'undergoes focussing and takes on a more fixed and stable form'.

It is therefore somewhat surprising that there seems to be considerable confusion in the English-speaking world, even amongst linguists, about what *Standard English* is. One would think that it should be reasonably clear which of the varieties of English is the one which has been subject to the process of standardisation, and what its characteristics are. In fact, however, we do not even seem to be able to agree how to spell this term – with an upper case or lower case <s>? – a point which I will return to later. Also, the use of the term by non-linguists appears to be even more haphazard.

In this chapter, I therefore attempt a characterisation of Standard English. It should be noted that this is indeed a characterisation rather than a strict definition – language varieties do not readily lend themselves to definition as such. We can describe what Chinese is, for example, in such a way as to make ourselves very well understood on the issue, but actually to define Chinese would be another matter altogether. The characterisation will also be as much negative as positive – a clearer idea of what Standard English is can be obtained by saying what it is not as well as by saying what it is. My discussion of this topic will be both a sociolinguistic and a linguistic discussion. (But it will be specifically linguistic: the word 'ideology' will not appear again in this chapter.) And it will also, I hope, be informed by references from time to time to the nature of standard and non-standard varieties in language situations beyond the English-speaking world.

Standard English is not a language

Standard English is often referred to as 'the standard language'. It is clear, however, that Standard English is not 'a language' in any meaningful sense of this term. Standard English, whatever it is, is less than a language, since it is only one variety of English among many. Standard English may be the most important variety of English, in all sorts of ways: it is the variety of English normally used in writing, especially printing; it is the variety associated with the education system in all the English-speaking countries of the world, and is therefore the variety spoken by those who are often referred to as 'educated people'; and it is the variety taught to non-native learners. But most native speakers of English in the world are native speakers of some non-standard variety of the language, and English, like other *Ausbau* languages (see Kloss 1967), can be described (Chambers and Trudgill 1997) as consisting of an autonomous standardised variety together with all the non-standard varieties which are heteronomous with respect to it. Standard English is thus not *the* English language but simply one variety of it.

Standard English is not an accent

There is one thing about Standard English on which most linguists, or at least British linguists, do appear to be agreed, and that is that Standard English has nothing to do with pronunciation. From a British perspective, we have to acknowledge that there is in Britain a high status and widely described accent known as Received Pronunciation (RP) which is sociolinguistically unusual when seen from a global perspective in that it is not associated with any geographical area, being instead a purely social accent associated with speakers in all parts of the country, or at least in England, from upper-class and upper-middle-class backgrounds. It is widely agreed, though, that while all RP speakers also speak Standard English, the reverse is not the case. Perhaps 9 per cent–12 per cent of the population of Britain (see Trudgill and Cheshire 1989) speak Standard English with some form of regional accent. It is true that in most cases Standard English speakers do not have 'broad' local accents, i.e. accents with large numbers of regional features which are phonologically and phonetically very distant from RP, but it is clear that in principle we can say that, while RP is, in a sense, standardised, it is a standardised accent of English and not Standard English itself.

This point becomes even clearer from an international perspective. Standard English speakers can be found in all English-speaking countries, and it goes without saying that they speak this variety with different non-RP accents depending on whether they come from Scotland or the USA or New Zealand or wherever.

Standard English is not a style

There is, however and unfortunately, considerable confusion in the minds of many concerning the relationship between Standard English and the vocabulary associated with formal varieties of the English language. We characterise *styles* (see Trudgill 1992) as varieties of language viewed from the point of view of *formality*. Styles are varieties of language which can be arranged on a continuum ranging from very formal to very informal. Formal styles are employed in social situations which are formal, and informal styles are employed in social situations which are informal – which is not to say, however, that speakers are 'sociolinguistic automata' (Giles 1973) who respond blindly to the particular degree of formality of a particular social situation. On the contrary, speakers are able to influence and change the degree of formality of a social situation by manipulation of stylistic choice.

All the languages of the world would appear to demonstrate some degree of stylistic differentiation in this sense, reflecting the wide range of social relationships and social situations found, to a greater or lesser extent, in all human societies. I believe, with Labov (1972), that there is no such thing as a single-style speaker, although it is obviously also the case that the repertoire of styles available to individual speakers will be a reflection of their social experiences and, in many cases, also their education. It is of course important here to distinguish between individual speakers of languages and those languages themselves, but it is clear that languages too may differ similarly in the range of styles available to their speakers. In many areas of the world, switching from informal to formal situations also involves switching from one language to another. In such cases, it is probable that neither of the two languages involved will have the full range of styles available to speakers in monolingual situations.

English as it is employed in areas where it is the major native language of the community, such as in the British Isles, North America and Australasia, is a language which has the fullest possible range of styles running from the most to the least formal. This obviously does not mean to say, however, that all speakers have equal access to or ability in all styles, and it is generally accepted that one of the objectives of mother tongue education is to give pupils exposure to styles at the more formal end of the continuum that they might otherwise not gain any ability in using.

Stylistic differences in English are most obvious at the level of lexis. Consider the differences between the following:

Father was exceedingly fatigued subsequent to his extensive
   peregrination.
Dad was very tired after his lengthy journey.
The old man was bloody knackered after his long trip.

Although one could argue about some of the details, we can accept that
these three sentences have more or less the same referential meaning, and
thus differ only in style – and that the stylistic differences are indicated
by lexical choice. It is also clear that native speakers are very sensitive to
the fact that stylistic variation constitutes a cline: some of the words
here, such as *was*, *his* are stylistically neutral; others range in formality from
the ridiculously formal *peregrination* through very formal *fatigued* to interme-
diate *tired* to informal *trip* to very informal *knackered* and tabooed informal
bloody. It will be observed that, as is often the case, the most informal or
'slang' words are regionally restricted, being in this case unknown or unusual
in North American English. It will also be observed that there are no strict
co-occurrence restrictions here as there are in some languages – one can say
long journey and *lengthy trip* just as well as *lengthy journey* and *long trip*.

   Formality in English is, however, by no means confined to lexis. Grammatical constructions vary as between informal and formal English – it is
often claimed, for instance, that the passive voice is more frequent in formal
than in informal styles – and, as has been shown by many works in the Labo-
vian secular linguistics tradition, starting with Labov (1966), phonology is
also highly sensitive to style.

   As far as the relationship between style, on the one hand, and Standard
English, on the other, is concerned, we can say the following. The phonological sensitivity to stylistic context just referred to obviously has no
connection to Standard English since, as we have noted, Standard English
has no connection with phonology.

   Let us then examine lexis. I would like to assert that our sentence

   The old man was bloody knackered after his long trip.

is clearly and unambiguously Standard English. To assert otherwise – that
swear words like *bloody* and very informal words like *knackered* are not Standard
English – would get us into a very difficult situation. Does a Standard English
speaker suddenly switch out of Standard English as soon as he or she starts
swearing? Are Standard English speakers not allowed to use slang without
switching into some non-standard variety? My contention is that Standard
English is no different from any other (non-standard) variety of the language.
Speakers of Standard English have a full range of styles open to them, just
as speakers of other varieties do, and can swear and use slang just like anybody
else. (It will be clear that I do not agree with the contention which is sometimes heard that 'nobody speaks Standard English'.) Equally, there is no need

for speakers of non-standard varieties to switch into Standard English in order to employ formal styles. The most logical position we can adopt on this is as follows:

The old man was bloody knackered after his long trip

is a Standard English sentence, couched in a very informal style, while

Father were very tired after his lengthy journey

is a sentence in a non-standard (north of England, for instance) variety of English, as attested by the non-standard verb form *were*, couched in a rather formal style. It is true that, in most English-speaking societies there is a tendency – a social convention perhaps – for Standard English to dominate in relatively formal social situations, but there is no necessary connection here, and we are therefore justified in asserting the theoretical independence of the parameter standard–non-standard from the parameter formal–informal. This theoretical independence becomes clearer if we observe sociolinguistic situations outside the English-speaking world. There are many parts of the world where speakers employ the local dialect for nearly all purposes, such as Luxembourg, Limburg in the Netherlands, and much of Norway. In such situations, a visit to the respective Town Hall to discuss important local political problems with the mayor will not elicit a switch to Standard German or Dutch or Norwegian, but it will produce styles of greater formality than those to be found on Friday night in the local bar amongst a group of close friends. Stylistic switching occurs *within* dialects and not *between* them.

This theoretical independence of the notion of Standard English from style does not mean that there are not problems in individual cases of distinguishing the two, as Hudson and Holmes (1995) have pointed out. For example, I tend to regard the use of *this* as an indefinite in narratives as in

There was this man, and he'd got this gun, . . . *etc.*

as a feature of colloquial style, but other linguists might regard it as a non-standard grammatical feature.

Standard English is not a register

We use the term *register* in the sense of a variety of language determined by topic, subject matter or activity, such as the register of mathematics, the register of medicine, or the register of pigeon fancying. In English, this is almost exclusively a matter of lexis, although some registers, notably the register of law, are known to have special syntactic characteristics. It is also clear that the education system is widely regarded as having as one of its

121

tasks the transmission of particular registers to pupils – those academic, technical or scientific registers which they are not likely to have had contact with outside the education system – and of course it is a necessary part of the study of, say, physical geography to acquire the register – the technical terms – associated with physical geography.

It is, however, an interesting question as to how far technical registers have a technical function – that of, for example, providing well-defined unambiguous terms for dealing with particular topics – and how far they have the more particularly sociolinguistic function of symbolising a speaker or writer's membership of a particular group, and of, as it were, keeping outsiders out. Linguists will defend the use of 'lexical item' rather than 'word' by saying that the former has a more rigorous definition than the latter, but it is also undoubtedly true that employing the term 'lexical item' does signal one's membership of the group of academic linguists. And it is not entirely clear to me, as a medical outsider, that using 'clavicle' rather than 'collar-bone' has any function at all other than symbolising one's status as a doctor rather than a patient.

Here again we find confusion over the term *Standard English*. The National Curriculum document for English in England and Wales (DfE/WO 1995) talks frequently about 'Standard English vocabulary'. It is not at all clear what this can mean. I have argued above that it cannot mean 'vocabulary associated with formal styles'. Is it perhaps supposed to mean 'vocabulary associated with academic or technical registers'? If so, this would not make sense either, since the question of register and the question of standard versus non-standard are also in principle entirely separate questions. It is of course true that it is most usual in English-speaking societies to employ Standard English when one is using scientific registers – this is the social convention, we might say. But one can certainly acquire and use technical registers without using Standard English, just as one can employ non-technical registers while speaking or writing Standard English. There is, once again, no necessary connection between the two. Thus

There was two eskers what we saw in them U-shaped valleys

is a non-standard English sentence couched in the technical register of physical geography.

This type of combination of technical register with a non-standard variety is much more common in some language communities than others. In German-speaking Switzerland, for example, most speakers use their local non-standard dialect in nearly all social situations and for nearly all purposes. Thus it is that one may hear, in the corridors of the University of Berne, two philosophy professors discussing the works of Kant using all the appropriate philosophical vocabulary while using the phonology and grammar of their local dialect.

It would, of course, be possible to argue that their philosophical vocabulary is not an integral part of their native non-standard Swiss German dialects and that the professors are 'switching' or that these words are being 'borrowed' from Standard German and being subjected, as loan words often are, to phonological integration into the local dialect. This, however, would be very difficult to argue for with any degree of logic. All speakers acquire new vocabulary throughout their lifetimes. There seems no reason to suppose that technical vocabulary is the sole prerogative of standard varieties, or that while, if you are a non-standard dialect speaker, it is possible to acquire new non-technical words within your own non-standard dialect, it is sadly by definition impossible to acquire technical words without switching to the standard variety. After all, dialects of English resemble each other at all linguistic levels much more than they differ – otherwise interdialectal communication would be impossible. There is no reason why they should not have most of their vocabulary in common as well as most of their grammar and most of their phonology. If the Swiss example tells us anything, it tells us that there is no necessary connection between Standard English and technical registers.

So what is it then?

If Standard English is not therefore a language, an accent, a style or a register, then of course we are obliged to say what it actually is. The answer is, as at least most British sociolinguists are agreed, that Standard English is a dialect. As we saw above, Standard English is simply one variety of English among many. It is a sub-variety of English. Sub-varieties of languages are usually referred to as *dialects*, and languages are often described as *consisting of* dialects. As a named dialect, like Cockney, or Scouse, or Yorkshire, it is entirely normal that we should spell the name of the Standard English dialect with capital letters.

Standard English is, however, an unusual dialect in a number of ways. It is, for example, by far the most important dialect in the English-speaking world from a social, intellectual and cultural point of view; and it does not have an associated accent.

It is also of interest that dialects of English, as of other languages, are generally simultaneously both geographical and social dialects which combine to form both geographical and social dialect continua. How we divide these continua up is also most often linguistically arbitrary, although we do of course find it convenient normally to make such divisions and use names for dialects that we happen to want to talk about for a particular purpose *as if* they were discrete varieties. It is thus legitimate and usual to talk about Yorkshire dialect, or South Yorkshire dialect, or Sheffield dialect, or middle-class Sheffield dialect, depending on what our particular objectives are. Standard English is unusual, seen against this background, in a number of ways. First, the distinction between Standard English and other dialects is not arbitrary or a matter of slicing up a continuum at some point of our own choice, although as we have seen there are some difficulties. This is inherent in the nature of standardisation itself. There is really no continuum linking Standard English to other dialects because the codification that forms a crucial part of the standardisation process results in a situation where, in most cases, a feature is either standard or it is not.

Second, unlike other dialects, Standard English is a purely social dialect. Because of its unusual history and its extreme sociological importance, it is no longer a geographical dialect, even if we can tell that its origins were originally in the southeast of England. It is true that, in the English-speaking world as a whole, it comes in a number of different forms, so that we can talk, if we wish to for some particular purpose, of Scottish Standard English, or American Standard English, or English Standard English. (Bizarrely, the British National Curriculum document suggests that American and Australian English are not Standard English!) And even in England we can note that there is a small amount of geographical variation at least in spoken Standard English, such as the different tendencies in different parts of the country to employ contractions such as *He's not* as opposed to *he hasn't*. But the most salient sociolinguistic characteristic of Standard English is that it is a social dialect.

At least two linguists have professed to find this statement controversial. Stein and Quirk (1995) argue that Standard English is not a social-class dialect because the *Sun*, a British newspaper with a largely working-class readership, is written in Standard English. This argument would appear to be a total non-sequitur, since all newspapers that are written in English are written in Standard English, by middle-class journalists, regardless of their readership.

Stein and Quirk also fly in the face of all the sociolinguistic research on English grammar that has been carried out in the last quarter of the twentieth century (see for example Cheshire 1982). Standard English is a dialect which is spoken as their native variety, at least in Britain, by about 12 per cent–15 per cent of the population, and this small percentage does not just constitute a random cross-section of the population. They are very much concentrated at the top of the social scale (or, as some would prefer, 'the very top'). The further down the social scale one goes, the more non-standard forms one finds.

Historically, we can say that Standard English was selected (though of course, unlike many other languages, not by any overt or conscious decision) as the variety to become the standard variety precisely because it was the variety associated with the social group with the highest degree of power, wealth and prestige. Subsequent developments have reinforced its social character: the fact that it has been employed as the dialect of an education to which pupils, especially in earlier centuries, have had differential access depending on their social-class background.

So far we have not discussed grammar. When, however, it comes to discussing what are the linguistic differences between Standard English and the non-standard dialects, it is obvious from our discussion above that they cannot be phonological, and that they do not appear to be lexical either (though see below). It therefore follows that Standard English is a social dialect which is distinguished from other dialects of the language by its *grammatical* forms.

Standard English is not a set of prescriptive rules

We have to make it clear, however, that these grammatical forms are not necessarily identical with those which prescriptive grammarians have concerned themselves with over the last few centuries. Standard English, like many other Germanic languages, most certainly tolerates sentence-final prepositions, as in *I've bought a new car which I'm very pleased with*. And Standard English does not exclude constructions such as *It's me* or *He is taller than me*.

Grammatical idiosyncrasies of Standard English

Grammatical differences between Standard English and other dialects are in fact rather few in number, although of course they are very significant socially. This means that, as part of our characterisation of what Standard English is, we are actually able to cite quite a high proportion of them.

Standard English of course has most of its grammatical features in common with the other dialects. When compared to the non-standard dialects, however, it can be seen to have idiosyncrasies which include the following:

1   Standard English fails to distinguish between the forms of the auxiliary verb *do* and its main verb forms. This is true both of present tense forms, where many other dialects distinguish between auxiliary *I do*, *he do* and main verb *I does*, *he does* or similar, and the past tense, where most other dialects distinguish between auxiliary *did* and main verb *done*, as in *You done it, did you?*
2   Standard English has an unusual and irregular present tense verb morphology in that only the third-person singular receives morphological marking: *he goes* versus *I go*. Many other dialects use either zero for all persons or *-s* for all persons.
3   Standard English lacks multiple negation, so that no choice is available between *I don't want none*, which is not possible, and *I don't want any*. Most non-standard dialects of English around the world permit multiple negation.
4   Standard English has an irregular formation of reflexive pronouns with some forms based on the possessive pronouns, e.g. *myself*, and others on the objective pronouns, e.g. *himself*. Most non-standard dialects have a regular system employing possessive forms throughout, i.e. *hisself*, *theirselves*.

125

5   Standard English fails to distinguish between second-person singular and second-person plural pronouns, having *you* in both cases. Many non-standard dialects maintain the older English distinction between *thou* and *you*, or have developed newer distinctions such as *you* versus *youse*.

6   Standard English has irregular forms of the verb *to be* both in the present tense (*am, is, are*) and in the past (*was, were*). Many non-standard dialects have the same form for all persons, such as *I be, you be, he be, we be, they be*, and *I were, you were, he were, we were, they were*.

7   In the case of many irregular verbs, Standard English redundantly distinguishes between preterite and perfect verb forms both by the use of the auxiliary *have* and by the use of distinct preterite and past participle forms: *I have seen* versus *I saw*. Many other dialects have *I have seen* versus *I seen*.

8   Standard English has only a two-way contrast in its demonstrative system, with *this* (near to the speaker) opposed to *that* (away from the speaker). Many other dialects have a three-way system involving a further distinction between, for example, *that* (near to the listener) and *yon* (away from both speaker and listener).

Linguistic change

There is also an interesting problem concerning which grammatical forms are and are not Standard English which has to do with linguistic change, in general, and the fact that, in particular, there is a tendency for forms to spread from non-standard dialects to the standard. Just as there are some difficulties in practice in distinguishing between features of non-standard dialect and features of colloquial style, as was discussed above, so there are difficulties associated with standard versus non-standard status and linguistic change. Given that it is possible for non-standard features to become standard (and vice versa), it follows that there will be a period of time when a form's status will be uncertain or ambiguous. For example, most Standard English speakers are happy to accept the new status of *than* as a preposition rather than a conjunction in constructions such as:

He is bigger than me.

but less happy, for the time being, to do so in:

He is bigger than what I am.

Similarly, American Standard English currently admits a new verb *to got* in

You haven't got any money, do you?

126

but not (or not yet) in

You don't got any money, do you?

Non-standard lexis

I have argued above that there is no necessary connection between formal vocabulary or technical vocabulary and Standard English. That is, there is no such thing as Standard English vocabulary. There is an interesting sense, however, in which this is not entirely true. We can illustrate this in the following way. It is clear that there is such a thing as *non-standard* vocabulary. For instance, in the non-standard dialect of Norwich, England, there is a verb *to blar* which means *to cry, weep*. Not only is this verb regionally restricted, to the dialects of this part of the country, it is also socially restricted – the small proportion of the population of Norwich who are native speakers of Standard English do not normally use this word, although they are perfectly well aware of what it means. This means that there is a sense in which we can say that *to cry* is a Standard English word, whereas *to blar* is not. However, *cry* is by no means *only* a Standard English word, since there are very many other non-standard dialects elsewhere in which it is the only word available with this meaning, and even in the working-class non-standard dialect of Norwich, *to cry* is a perfectly common and frequently used word. Because Standard English is not geographically restricted to any particular region, its vocabulary is available to all. There are in any case also, of course, many cases in which Standard English speakers in different parts of England employ different but equivalent words, and hundreds of cases in which the vocabulary of English Standard English and American Standard English differ, as is very well known. The usage in the National Curriculum of the term 'Standard English vocabulary' in the sense of 'vocabulary that occurs in the Standard English dialect and no other' thus remains problematical.

Conclusion

From an educational point of view, the position of Standard English as the dialect of English used in writing is unassailable. (We should perhaps add, however, that it has nothing whatsoever to do with spelling or punctuation!) As far as spoken Standard English is concerned, we could conclude that the teaching of Standard English to speakers of other dialects may be commendable – as most would in theory agree, if for no other reason than the discrimination which is currently exercised against non-standard dialect speakers in most English-speaking societies – and may also be possible – which I am inclined, for sociolinguistic reasons (see Trudgill 1975) to doubt.

Either way, however, there is clearly no necessary connection at all between the teaching of formal styles and technical registers, on the one hand, and the teaching of the standard dialect, on the other.

6

SPOKEN STANDARD ENGLISH

Jenny Cheshire

1 Introduction

The introduction of the National Curriculum for English in England and Wales (DfE/WO 1995) has highlighted, for linguists at least, the fact that we know relatively little about the syntactic structure of spoken English. One of the requirements of the programme of study for Speaking and Listening is that children 'should be taught . . . to be confident users of standard English in formal and informal situations' (DfE/WO 1995: 18). This requirement presupposes that the concept of a spoken standard English is unproblematic. The reality, however, is that not only is the concept of spoken standard English problematic in itself, but the grammatical structure of spoken English generally is far from being well understood. This is especially true of the English that is spoken in informal situations, if we assume that these give rise to spontaneous conversational speech. Our conventional descriptions of English syntax fit written English (and, perhaps, the speech produced by educated speakers in formal situations) better than the speech that we produce in more informal styles, a point that has been made by many scholars who have worked on spoken English (see, for example, Crystal 1980; Stubbs 1983; Carter and McCarthy 1995; Milroy and Milroy 1998). In this chapter I will not attempt to deal with the educational aspects of these issues, important though they are; instead I will confine my discussion first to some of the reasons for our failure to describe adequately the grammar of speech, and then to a brief account of some of the grammatical structures that are typical of spontaneous informal spoken English. I will conclude by briefly examining the implications for the meaning of the term 'spoken standard English'.

2 Problems in analysing the syntax of spoken English

An important reason for our failure to understand the nature of spoken syntax is that our frameworks of analysis conform to the views of language that we have acquired during our education rather than to the variety of language that we produce during face-to-face interaction. Strive as we may to be objective analysts of language, complete objectivity can never be possible, for linguists, like everyone else, are social creatures whose behaviour is influenced by our social background and governed by social norms. We face the same problems in our analysis of language as sociologists do in their analysis of social behaviour (see, for discussion, Garfinkel 1967).

In this context the most relevant aspect of our social background is that linguists have necessarily had many years of formal education and exposure to standard English. Standard English, as is well known, has been heavily influenced by written English. Its origins lie in writing: more precisely, in public official documents, a genre produced in circumstances as far removed as possible from the spontaneous interaction of informal speech. Written English has continued to be the reference point for the standard variety, with grammarians during the eighteenth century codifying the forms used in writing (Cheshire and Milroy 1993: 7). Literacy remains the major influence in promoting awareness of the standard today (Milroy and Milroy 1998).

For present-day English many linguists now accept a link between written English and the spoken English of 'the educated', as can be seen from definitions of standard English as 'educated English' (Quirk et al. 1985a: 18) or as 'the set of grammatical and lexical forms which is typically used in speech and writing by educated native speakers' (Trudgill 1984: 32). The set of forms includes variants that have been codified as 'standard', and therefore reflects the factors that have influenced their selection. In general these factors have been appropriate for written language, but less so for speech, especially informal speech (see Cheshire and Stein 1997; Stein 1997). For example, forms that encode detachment (such as the indefinite pronoun *one*) were preferred to forms encoding involvement; forms that express affective meaning were neglected; and there was a drive to reduce variation, in keeping with the spirit of the 'age of reason' (Stein 1994, 1997). For at least some educated speakers the set may include other forms and structures that have developed as part of written English: as Brown and Yule (1983: 14) point out, the people who typically write descriptions of language are middle-aged academics who have spent long years immersed in written language and whose speech, therefore, is likely to have a great deal in common with written forms. If Brown and Yule are correct, this means that we cannot assume that the speech of academics is necessarily representative of the speech of other educated speakers of English who may have less exposure to the written language. If we wish to determine the syntactic structure of spoken English, then, we need to widen the database of 'educated speech' that has so far provided the basis for the linguistic description of standard English. The accepted reference grammars for English – A *Comprehensive Grammar of the English Language* (1985b), formerly A *Grammar of Contemporary English* (1972), both by Quirk et al. – claim to be based to some extent on corpora of spoken English, but most of the speakers in these corpora are university dons (see Carter 1997: 58). Corpora that are representative of the wider population do now exist, and are being analysed (see, for example, the work of Carter and his colleagues, e.g. Carter 1997; Carter and McCarthy 1995), but for the time being the accessible descriptions of English syntax rely heavily on the speech and writing of academics. They also rely on their intuitions, and our intensive association with written language is likely to result in the structures of written English being more accessible to our intuitions than the structures of speech. In short, linguists have inevitably had a long-standing and intensive contact with standard English. The nature of standard English as primarily a written variety, together with the immersion of academics in written English, does not augur well for their recognition of structures that may be more typical of spoken English than written English.

A related issue concerns the extent to which it is possible for researchers to escape from the ethos of linguistic correctness to which we have inevitably been exposed during our education. Lakoff stated as long ago as 1977 that the distinction between description and prescription was still blurrier than we might like 'particularly in areas where we have been brought up to make value judgements before we learned to be disinterested academic observers' (1977: 82). Lyons (1977: 586–7) makes a similar point. Almost twenty years further on, the issue was still relevant, as Meechan and Foley (1994: 83) point out in their discussion of existential *there* (to which I will return in Section 3): 'even the most careful introspection', they conclude, 'can fail to filter out the effects of prescriptive grammar'.

Problems arising from the use of introspection are often thought to apply mainly to researchers working within the generative tradition, where intuitions have an explicit methodological status. It is less often recognised that they also have an important role in descriptive grammars. Consider, for example, the reference grammars mentioned above. The Introduction to the 1972 edition of Quirk et al.'s *Grammar* explains that it is based on the authors' own experience as teachers and speakers of the language, augmented with research on corpora and data from elicitation tests (Quirk et al. 1972: v). The later edition also makes use of the findings of research carried out in the intervening period between the two editions (Quirk et al. 1985: v); this includes research in the generative tradition, for the *Grammar* is suitably eclectic in its choice of sources. The illustrative examples in the *Grammar* have been adapted and edited 'for reasons of simplicity and economic presentation' (1972: v) – an understandable and perhaps necessary strategy, but one that inevitably results in the authors consulting their intuitions.

Intuitions may also come into play in analyses of non-standard varieties of English, if the analysts make their own decisions about which are the 'non-standard' features to be analysed (this was the case, for example, in the research described in Cheshire 1982 – but I am by no means alone in this practice). This does not invalidate the description of the morphological and syntactic features of these varieties if, for example, a variationist analysis is performed: it is simply the labelling of some variants as 'standard' and others as 'non-standard' that is in question. With the implementation of the National Curriculum, this labelling now has potentially important real-world implications. The issue is relevant to all descriptions of non-standard varieties of English that do not have a matched set of control data from educated speakers, since they take as their baseline for describing a spoken variety of 'non-standard' English the analyst's intuitions about what is 'standard' English.

I do not wish to imply that intuitions should not be part of linguistic data, nor that existing analyses of English are invalid. It is pointless, for example, to complain that the generative tradition has failed to identify the syntactic structures typical of speech, since generativists systematically exclude spoken language from their field of enquiry, seeing it as irrelevant to the aim of discovering the core grammar underlying language behaviour. We do, however, need to consider some of the specific ways in which our conventional frameworks for analysing language have been influenced by our beliefs about language, and the effect that this may have had on our understanding of the syntax of spoken English.

3 Some syntactic structures of spoken English

I argued in the previous section that our intuitions about language are likely to be influenced by the structure of the written variety, as well as by prescriptive norms. If we accept these arguments, it becomes possible to identify some features that are typical of spoken English, by systematically considering the views about language that have arisen as part of the standardisation process. If we look on these as potential blinkers that may obscure the form of spoken language, we can consider the alternative views of language that emerge as we look beyond them.

One form, one meaning

Standardisation typically results in morphological variation and some kinds of syntactic variation being reduced in the standard variety, as I mentioned in the previous section. For example, eighteenth-century grammarians were concerned to promote the use of a single past tense verb form rather than several different forms for the same verb: thus *saw* has become the past tense form for SEE in standard English, and *seed, seen, sawed* and *see* are no longer used in writing or by speakers who wish to appear educated (though these forms survive elsewhere). The drive to reduce variation seems to have responded in part to a desire to eliminate what was seen as redundancy in language: a single meaning should be expressed by a single form, and vice versa. The result is that variation is now relatively unusual in standardised English and, where it does exist, it tends to attract the attention of analysts. It is not surprising, therefore, that analyses have been carried out on variable relative pronoun forms (Quirk 1957; Sigley 1997) and on the presence or absence of complementizer *that* (Thompson and Mulac 1991). Researchers have also analysed morphological and syntactic variants that are not used by educated speakers, such as multiple negation or double modal constructions (as in *A good machine clipper would could do it in half a day*; Beal 1993: 196), or that are used by a restricted set of educated speakers, such as the Irish 'hot news' perfect (for example *She's after selling the boat*; Harris 1993: 141). Features such as these are readily observable as different from those that have been codified as 'standard', because their variants, whether 'standard' or 'non-standard', can be seen as different ways of saying the same thing (see Cheshire 1987: 260): they clearly contravene, in other words, the principle of 'one form, one meaning'. Thus the hot news perfect is one of a number of ways of expressing the perfect tense; and *would could do it* seems to correspond to standard English *would be able to do it*. Far less attention has been paid – until relatively recently, at least – to features whose meaning varies depending on the linguistic contexts in which they occur: features, in other words, that are more typical of spontaneous speech than of writing (Cheshire and Stein 1997) and that are less open to perception as different ways of saying the same thing. These are less suitable for variationist analyses, and less noticeable, it seems, to researchers.

A case in point is *never* functioning as a negative marker. As a quantifier, its scope is determined by the linguistic context in which it occurs, and the syntactic and semantic relationships into which it enters can only be determined by considering it in context. These relationships do not seem to be accessible to our intuitions. The conventional analyses see *never* as an indeterminate, equivalent to *not ever*, in the same way that *none* is equivalent to *not any*. However, *never* cannot be seen as equivalent to *not ever* in contexts where the time reference is to a restricted period of time, as in *I never went out last night*: here the tense of the verb and the adverbial *last night* specify the time reference, or the scope of the quantifier, and limit it to a short period of past time. Conventional analyses miss this point. Instead, they frequently label *never* in these contexts as 'non-standard', despite the fact that the contexts occur in educated speech and in writing (see Cheshire 1997 for analysis and discussion). Conventional analyses also miss the fact that *not ever* seems to be a feature of written English rather than spoken English: there is only one occurrence of *not ever*, but 78 tokens of *never* in 50,000 words drawn from the London–Lund corpus of educated adult speech (Tottie 1991). Using intuitions, then, can point to features typical of written English, but they are less reliable when it comes to spoken English.

In the past scholars have had similar blind spots about other features typical of speech. Features such as *you know*, *I mean* or *oh* were once dismissed as mere fillers and fumbles, but rigorous analyses of their use in interaction have now revealed that they have important, and varied, functions (see, for example, Coates 1987; Holmes 1986, 1989; Schiffrin 1987). Their polypragmatic functions are not, it seems, accessible to intuitions.

Tag questions are another feature of this type: early studies assigned them a single function, that of expressing speaker insecurity, but later, more careful, analyses have revealed a range of meanings and functions (see for example, Cameron et al. 1988). Conventional approaches to linguistic analysis, then, predispose us to look for a 'one form, one meaning' relationship, and we risk overlooking the features typical of spoken language, whose meaning is pragmatically determined.

Equally, the conventional frameworks of analysis and description have no way of accounting for words that are becoming grammaticalized and whose meaning is therefore involved in grammatical change; examples in present-day English are *going to* as a future time marker (Tagliamonte 1997), or *like* as a marker of reported speech and thought (Romaine and Lange 1991). They also have no way of accounting for variation in general, though this is often grammatical in the sense that it conforms to systematic linguistic constraints.

Structural oppositions

Idealised 'one form – one meaning' relationships make it possible to set up discrete, static categories and to look for structural oppositions between them. Joseph (1987: 38) claims that this stems directly from the literate tradition:

> what is transferred to the standard language is really something more significant: an entire way of thinking about language, as a medium composed of discrete units, able to be isolated in time.

Cheshire (1996) argues that for at least one feature of English, *that*, this way of thinking about language has resulted in the semantic and pragmatic functions of the form being seriously misunderstood. Previous accounts have assumed that the fundamental meaning of *that* is a distal spatial one, in opposition to the proximal meaning of *this*. In fact, however, a spatial meaning for *that* comes into play only when it is in implicit or explicit opposition with *this*, as it seems to be when we consult our intuitions. When we look for structural oppositions we have to focus on one syntactic category at a time; but by taking a more comprehensive approach it is possible to explain several problems that have beset previous analyses of *that*, such as how to explain the so-called 'empathetic' *that* in examples like *how's that throat?*, uttered to an addressee known to have a sore throat (Lakoff 1974). By considering *that* in all the syntactic categories in which it occurs in spoken English, including, therefore, the complementizer, the relative pronoun, the intensifier and more, it is possible to identify a basic interactive function for *that* which has been obscured in previous analyses.

It can also be revealing to look beyond the categorisation of language into discrete varieties, registers or styles. The point has been made by Berrendonner and Reichler-Béguelin (1997: 215–16) in their analysis of left dislocation in French; see also Cheshire and Stein (1997: 9–10). Discrete varieties are, of course, artefacts of analysis – a heuristic procedure that helps impose order on language, defining the limits of our investigations. But the boundaries that we impose may hide regularities; in particular, including typically spoken forms in an analysis can provide a new perspective, with implications for linguistic theory. Seppänen (1997) provides an example of this. He analyses the genitive forms of relative pronouns in what are usually considered to be regional, colloquial and formal varieties of present-day English. As he points out, it has been usual to distinguish two radically different types of relativisation structure in English, one relying on the use of *wh*-relativizers to introduce the clause while the other relies on a 'gapped variant' employing either no overt relativizer, or *that* (or *as*, *at* or *what* in the 'non-standard' varieties). There has been much discussion in the literature concerning the syntactic status of *that* in these constructions (see Cheshire 1996 for a summary). Seppänen identifies a formal identity in the mode of relativisation used across the different varieties, which seriously questions the accepted view that there are two distinct modes. Had spoken and 'non-standard' variants been included from the outset, then the conventional view of relative constructions may well have been different; it would certainly have fitted the structure of spoken relatives rather than the intuitions of linguists.

Concord

A further principle that has been important to grammarians who codified standard English is concord, or agreement. Sundby *et al.*'s *Dictionary of English Normative Grammar 1700–1800* (1991) has an entire section devoted to concord as a guiding principle in language prescription, and the continuing influence of this principle for present-day linguists has been shown by Meechan and Foley (1994) in their work on existential *there* constructions. I will discuss existential *there* in some detail, as it provides a clear example of the way in which present-day linguists may be led to overlook the functions that specific features have in speech.

Existential *there* occurs with singular concord in spoken English, as in examples 1 and 2 below:

(1) There's hardly any berries.

(Meechan and Foley 1994: 74)

(2) There's lots of museums.

(Reading corpus; see Cheshire 1982)

Its occurrence has been analysed in empirical studies of the English spoken in several parts of the world, including York, England (Tagliamonte in press), Sydney, Australia (Eisikovits 1991) and Ottawa, Canada (Meechan and Foley 1994). Quirk et al. (1985a: 1405) note that existential *there* with singular concord occurs in informal styles, but the fact that it occurs frequently in relatively formal sociolinguistic interviews in Canada suggests that here, at least, it is typical of more formal styles also: 72 per cent of existential *there* constructions with a plural noun showed singular agreement in Meechan and Foley's data.

Theoretical accounts of existential *there*, however, rely on introspective data, and analysts have assumed that verbal agreement is a requirement in these constructions, just as it is with other subject–verb constructions in English. Intuitions, in other words, yield only constructions such as:

(1a)   There are hardly any berries.

(2a)   There are lots of museums.

and not constructions with singular concord, such as (1) and (2) above.

Existential *there* poses a number of problems for syntactic theory, as Meechan and Foley explain. Nominative case, which is linked to agreement in English, is normally assigned to the noun phrase (NP) in preverbal subject position (as it is in *The berries are plentiful*, for example), but with existential *there* constructions the subject is postverbal (since *there* is an empty or dummy subject). Analysts, therefore, have to account first for how a postverbal NP can acquire case and, second, for how an NP in this position can control agreement. Meechan and Foley discuss some of the complicated solutions that analysts have devised. As I pointed out above, however, the intuitions that require these solutions are at odds with the ways in which speakers actually use the constructions for, if the distribution in Meechan and Foley's study is typical (and there is a similar distribution in Tagliamonte's corpus) in the majority of cases, there is no plural agreement to be accounted for.

Nevertheless, within the framework of Government and Binding Theory it is still necessary to account for the fact that there is no variation when the postverbal NP is singular: in other words, it is necessary to explain the non-occurrence of utterances such as:

(3)   *there are a museum

Meechan and Foley do this by assuming that plural reference on the noun is important in triggering plural agreement, and they offer an explanation in terms of the interface between syntax and phonological form. Their solution is in line with Chomsky's (1995) minimalist approach: the morphological requirements for case for the postverbal NP are satisfied prior to the assignment of phonological form (PF); this takes place at a post-syntactic level that interfaces with the sensory motor system.

If we start with the empirical facts, however, we can relate the existential *there* construction more directly to the conditions of speaking, and avoid the machinations needed to account for the non-occurrence of examples such as (3). For example, Meechan and Foley's variationist analysis finds that in the context of contraction (in other words, in examples with *there's* rather than *there is*) the frequency of singular agreement increases to 92 per cent. This too can be accounted for within Government and Binding Theory, this time in terms of movement of a contracted form before LF (logical form) raising of the postverbal NP (assuming that a copula cannot remain in inflection (INFL) in contracted form because there is no full lexical item to which it can attach). But it can also be taken as a simple indication that invariant *there is* or *there was* is a typical phenomenon of spoken language, since contraction is a phonetic phenomenon. This means that we should look for an explanation for the lack of agreement in the circumstances in which spontaneous speech occurs. The theoretically motivated account considers examples such as (1) and (2) above in isolation from their discourse context and assumes a canonical Subject–Verb structure from which all structures must be derived. It then becomes necessary to account for a subject that is postverbal, and to see it in terms of movement from a previous preverbal position. An approach oriented to spoken language, on the other hand, may simply note that the structure regularly occurs, and then look at how it relates to factors that we know to be important to speakers.

One such factor is the presentation of information. Spontaneous spoken language is produced as chunks of information rather than as the sentence structures so loved by philosophers and theoretical linguists. In these sentences every argument of the verb is a full referential lexical phrase. In speech, however, there is a preference for clauses to have light subjects (light both phonetically and in terms of information content; see Chafe 1994) and for new information to be presented at the end of a clause. The existential *there* construction fits into this pattern, with an empty subject and an empty verb preparing the way for the focused presentation of new information.

Like many of the features typical of speech, the construction is multifunctional. This has been shown by Schiffrin (1994), who analyses existential *there* within a conversation analysis perspective – not commenting therefore on the question of agreement, which is irrelevant to her concerns. In her data, the existential *there* construction leads hearers towards the identification of a referent. It also has a role in turn-taking: almost all of the 60 examples that she analyses were produced under a single intonation contour, suggesting a preference for the construction to be issued as a single turn constructional unit (Schiffrin 1994: 253). Like left dislocation, another syntactic construction typical of spoken English (Pawley and Syder 1983: 561), existential *there* can be seen as a way for speakers to take the floor quickly and easily in lively conversation. Clearly, it would be functional for such a useful construction to be stored and accessed as a prefabricated phrase, rather than as a structure that is generated anew each time that it is used. It would then be comparable to French *il y a* or German *es gibt*, neither of which exhibits agreement with the following noun phrase. In more formal speech styles, where speakers have time to plan what they intend to say, and where speaking turns may be distributed more routinely than in informal conversation, the expression of grammatical agreement could become more important than the communicative need to take or keep the floor whilst preserving the pace of speech – particularly for speakers who have been exposed to prescriptive norms of subject–verb agreement. In these styles, the option of choosing a prefabricated phrase could be bypassed.

With this account, we would expect agreement in existential *there* construc-tions to occur variably: more frequently in formal speech styles than in informal styles, and more frequently in the speech of educated speakers. Meechan and Foley's analysis did in fact find a correlation between the education of speakers and the frequency of occurrence of the construction. The generative tradition intentionally takes no account of social and styl-istic variation, as I pointed out in Section 2. It is significant, though, that their intuitions have led analysts working within this tradition to identify the variant that does exhibit agreement and that is used more frequently by educated speakers, and to fail to identify the variant that does not show agreement.

In fact, lack of agreement on features that serve the discourse function of introducing a topic in fast speech may be a more general characteristic of spoken English. It also exists in Reading English for what Schiffrin (1987: 267–89) terms the *you know X* construction. Examples (4) and (5) illustrate the construction; they are taken from the corpus of adolescent speech that I recorded in Reading in the late 1970s (see Cheshire 1982).

(4)   you know that hill down there?

(5)   you know your mum . . . you know that bike she had?

The Reading corpus contains many features of non-standard English, one of which is the variable use of an -*s* suffix on present tense verbs, as in examples (6) to (9):

(6)   some girls at our school gets it on the knuckles

(7)   I loves Elvis, he's great

(8)   you knows him don't you Nod?

(9)   he says to me look over here and see if I knows you

The frequency of occurrence of the -s suffix on lexical verbs with non-third-person-singular subjects is approximately 56 per cent for the 24 speakers analysed in the study. The lexical verbs include KNOW, as examples (8) and (9) show. There are 24 tokens of KNOW as the *you know* X construction, introducing a topic for discussion; here there is no variation, and the suffix never occurs (as in examples (4) and (5) above).

Thus, for both standard and non-standard varieties of English, there are certain structures with communicative functions in topic management and in turn-taking which appear to occur as unanalysed wholes. They do not, that is, have agreement between the verb and the subject. As so often happens, an organising principle is the same for both the standard and the non-standard varieties (see Cheshire and Stein 1997: 9–10). I did not see this constraint on variation when I carried out the earlier analysis of the Reading data. For the same reason, it seems, as analysts who did not see the absence of agreement on the existential *there* construction, our intuitions about syntax do not extend to the functions that syntactic features may have in speech. Consequently, we do not discover a discourse function and its effect on variation unless we specifically set out to look for it. For the Reading data, there are theoretical implications for the general interpretation of the -s suffix which, as Cheshire and Ouhalla have recently argued, does not appear to be a present tense suffix, as I first supposed (Cheshire and Ouhalla 1997).

Infrequent constructions

Existential *there* constructions and *you know* X constructions occur relatively frequently in speech, as do other multifunctional constructions typical of spoken syntax (left dislocation is a further example). However, there are other constructions which occur less frequently and which it is all too easy, therefore, to discount as performance errors. Lack of frequency, then, may be a further reason why some of the structures characteristic of spoken English syntax have been overlooked in the past. One such construction is what I will term a 'fused construction', after Montgomery (1989). The construction is illustrated in examples (10–13) below:

(10)   that's really what Professor Galbraith was talking about is
       that there's a huge knock-on effect
                          (BBC Radio 4, *Today* programme)

(11)   it's just a bunch of baloney is what it is
                          (university-educated US speaker)

(12)   that's what the Mark Thomas crew were doing something
       really interesting today
                          (university-educated speaker from London)

(13)   that's what worries me is that they don't really understand
the issues
(university-educated speaker from Northern Ireland)

These examples are all from educated speakers of English, but they do not
fit conventional frameworks for analysing syntax, which do not allow for a
single constituent to straddle two clauses, as does *what Professor Galbraith was
talking about* in (10), *a bunch of baloney* in (12), *the Mark Thomas crew were
doing* in (13) and *what worries me* in (14). Moreover, they do not seem to
conform to our norms about standard English: the people on whom I informally tested the grammaticality of these examples were baffled by them and
assumed that I had invented them. Each of these utterances was expressed
with a single intonation contour; descriptively, then, there seems to be a dual
structure within a single intonation and information unit, with the middle
section belonging both to what precedes it and to what follows. Each example,
that is to say, seems to be a blend of two separate clauses, as below:

(10a) that's really what Professor Galbraith was talking about

(10b) what Professor Galbraith was talking about is that there's a
huge knock-on effect

(11a) it's just a bunch of baloney

(11b) a bunch of baloney is what it is

(12a) that's what the Mark Thomas crew were doing

(12b) the Mark Thomas crew were doing something really
interesting today

(13a) that's what worries me

(13b) they don't really understand the issues

Similar constructions are discussed by Halford (1990), who gives (14) as
an example of 'oral syntax' (1990: 34). The subordinate clause *because I am
in a bad mood* could be dependent on either of two main clauses, one preceding
the subordinate clause and one following it. Halford points out that, although
intonation could be used to disambiguate the clausal structure, the ambiguity
is in fact retained: it is, it seems, an ambiguity that is functional:

(14)   I hate sitting around here because I am in a bad mood I'll
go home

Constructions of this kind are not confined to English: Berrendonner and Reichler-Béguelin (1989) give the examples which I reproduce below as (15) and (16): in (15) the middle section, *dans ce film*, is part of the same intonation contour as the preceding and following clause, as in (10–13), whereas in (16) the middle section, *même si W.H. se dit athée*, is in a separate intonation unit:

(15)   parce qu'il y a beaucoup d'ironie dans ce film y a y a de l'ironie
(because there's a lot of irony in this film there's there's irony)

(16)   c'est vraiment au fond c'est très chrétien ... même si W.H. se dit athée ... peu importe c'est un mystique
(it's really in fact it's very Christian ... even though W.H. says she's an atheist ... it doesn't matter she's a mystic)

Like existential *there* constructions, examples such as these could be accommodated within existing syntactic frameworks. Chomsky (1995) suggests that the computational system of language (i.e. syntax) does not determine word order: this is determined by discourse considerations, at the PF level. Since the principles which determine PF are not syntactic, they can be expected to override patterns of organisation determined by syntax. Jamal Ouhalla (personal communication) further points out that this possibly includes merging two separate syntactic descriptions (i.e. two sentences) into a single string of words in circumstances that might be required by a given discourse context.

One such discourse context appears to be the desire to clarify connections between what has been uttered and what the speaker intends to utter next. Example (12) was uttered by a speaker who was aware that I happened at the time to be writing about the syntax of spoken English. On reflection he explained that he had realised that his *that* maybe did not refer after all to what he had just been saying, and so he then went on to make the topic clearer. Examples (10) and (13) may well serve the same function of striving for clarity in the ongoing production of speech; the construction, as Berrendonner and Reichler-Béguelin (1989: 109) point out, is an efficient compromise between operating cost and effectiveness (and conforms to the predictions of Relevance Theory; Sperber and Wilson 1986). Example (11), however, seems to have an emphatic function, and the marked construction presumably enhances the emphasis. Examples (10–13) all occurred at the beginning of a speaker turn, and (11), (12) and (13) were in conversations involving several speakers: like left dislocation and existential *there* constructions, then, fused constructions may be a resource that speakers can use in order to seize the floor in lively conversations. Anaphoric *that* or *it* indicate that there is a link with what has just been said, and the construction allows the speaker time to make the link explicit.

141

Montgomery (1989) mentions his corpus of more than 50 examples of this type of fused construction, all beginning with *that*. He finds that speakers use the construction to cohere foregoing and following discourse (ibid.: 250), and that it also occurs when they sum up what they have been saying and 'create order out of chaos' (ibid.: 251). His example (23) (reproduced as (17) below) pulls out and condenses the most important information from what had been a long rambling answer to the fieldworker's question 'what do you do for a good time?'

(17)   that's the best way I ever found to think is just to walk
       back up through the woods or something

Fused constructions, then, are multifunctional: they can help speakers to seize the floor, express emphasis, ensure coherence and, as summary constructions, impose a hierarchic organisation on the necessarily linear development of discourse. Schiffrin (1987) has demonstrated that discourse markers can have both local and global functions in the emerging discourse: but discourse markers are not the only features of spoken language that work in this way. Certain types of clause structure, notably fused constructions, may have similar functions.

Genre-specific constructions

Other types of syntactic structure that may not be accessible to our intuitions are those that occur more frequently in certain genres than in others. Carter and McCarthy (1995: 144) have pointed out that grammatical features are not always distributed equally across different genres; for example, in the mini-corpus which they analyse in their 1995 study they find that left dislocation occurs more frequently in narratives. In the Reading corpus of adolescent speech there is a structure that occurs in those parts of conversations where speakers are taking part in joint remembering (Edwards and Middleton 1986), such as when they are reminiscing about films or TV programmes that they have all seen and enjoyed. I will term this a *wh*-descriptive clause: this occurs as an independent construction in the turn of a single speaker, as in the extracts given as examples (18) and (19). In these extracts a group of four 12–14-year-old speakers were discussing *The Hunchback of Notre Dame*, a film that had been shown on television recently.

In these conversations the reminiscences proceed by speakers nominating parts of the film that they have enjoyed, as the extracts below show. One way in which they do this is with a lone *wh*-descriptive clause. These clauses are usually uttered with level tones on all but the last syllable of the final noun phrase. This syllable has a falling tone and is often lengthened. The clause seems to function as a bid for a topic to be discussed, a bid which is sometimes taken up by the other speakers, as is Johnny's *when he took that*

142

woman up into that bell thing. This is accepted by Nicky, with *yeah*, and Johnny goes on to describe the scene more fully, joined by Patsy and Jacky. The topics of the *wh*-descriptive clauses are not always taken up by the group, however; this is the fate of Nicky's *and when he took her up*, which he then abandons for a different topic. When he falters Johnny leaps into the conversation with his own suggested topic, which is then taken up by the others, as we have just seen.

(18) *The bell scene*
    Darren: we watch Hunchback we do
    Patsy: *Hunchback of Notre Dame*
    All: yeah
    Patsy: it was good that was
    Darren: where that man is all hunchback ... looking
        through all those cracks
→Nicky: and when he took her up ... I saw that other one
        when ... [er
→Johnny: [when he took that woman up into that
        bell thing
    Nicky: yeah ... you know ... all big bells
    Johnny: I like the bit where he swings down to where she's
        gonna be hanged and [she
    Patsy: [yeah he swang down and
        caught her by one hand didn't he
    Jacky: he had one eye down here and one eye up there

Four further examples of *wh*-descriptive clauses can be seen in (19) and (20) below:

(19) *The bowl of acid*
    Darren: there was this other man ... his master
    Patsy: and there was a man couldn't get him as long as
        she was in the em ... church
→Nicky: when he tipped that acid down
    Patsy: oh yes I hated that part
    Nicky: there was this big bowl of acid ... and then all
        these men were down there trying to get in ...
        and he tipped it didn't he and it went all down
        and all big rocks fell out
    Darren: and a couple throwed rocks down in it

(20) *The bells again*
    Patsy: I thought he was gonna fall when he was treading
        on the em er edge

→*Johnny*: when he was on them bloody bells swinging about
    Patsy: yeah
    Johnny: and he knocked ... and he knocked his master
              down didn't he from the galleries ... wooo ...
              crash!
→*Darren*: when he was gonna em [
→*Patsy*:   [when he told that girl he
              was deaf ... he got deaf by the ... that bell
    Nicky: but he was still there
    Patsy: I know

The first two bids for discussion topics, Nicky's and Johnny's, are successful, as can be seen from the turns that follow. The third, Darren's, is not. We can see clearly here how fast is the pace of speech in these multi-party conversations – a momentary stumble, like Darren's *em*, and the speaker loses the floor. The fourth bid, Patsy's, is not really successful either: after a pause she adds some detail, but the topic is not elaborated on by the others, and Nicky's contribution is negative.

It is difficult to know how to describe clauses such as these: it is tempting to see them as adverbial clauses because they typically begin with *when* or *where*, indicating a time or a scene in the film, but conventional frameworks, both descriptive and theoretical, would expect an adverbial clause to be dependent on a main clause, and here they are not. An alternative analysis, perhaps, is to see them as the syntactic object of an underlying or 'understood' clause *do you remember*. However, the intonation is not that of a final clause element; instead, the lengthened final syllable resembles the drawl which speakers sometimes use to indicate that they are ready to yield their turn (Duncan 1972). This reflects the discourse function I identified above, of enabling a speaker simultaneously to propose a topic and invite the other speakers to take it up.

It is relevant that the determiner in the *wh*-descriptive clauses is almost always *that* rather than *the* (note how Patsy moves from *the* to *that* in (20)). *That* is a way of foregrounding a referent, putting it into high focus (Ehlich 1982; Cornish 1988). It frequently occurs in a cluster of features expressing interpersonal involvement (Cheshire 1996: 380): in the two extracts above there are, for example, tag questions, many intensifiers including the quantifier *all* and 'metaphorical' *this*. The *wh*-descriptive clauses, then, can be seen as an involvement strategy, a strategy which is necessary for the joint construction of shared remembering.

This construction has not, as far as I am aware, been reported elsewhere, and I do not know whether it is more typical of younger speakers than older speakers, nor whether it occurs in the speech of speakers who are more influenced by education than those I recorded in the adventure playgrounds in Reading. In other words, it is not yet clear whether this should be included in a description of spoken standard English. What *is* clear is that it is a feature of spoken rather than written syntax, fulfilling multiple functions in turn-taking and the creation of interpersonal involvement; and it is one more syntactic feature that may not be accessible to the intuitions of the educated linguist.

4 Conclusion

The features of spoken English syntax that I have discussed are well adapted to the circumstances of speaking. They are polypragmatic and multifunctional, responding to speakers' needs to plan simultaneously as they go; to take, keep or signal their intention to yield the floor; to present information in manageable chunks; to create interpersonal involvement; to introduce conversational topics and, perhaps, to also perform other conversational tasks not mentioned here. Features that can simultaneously perform functions such as these tend not to be found in our descriptions of standard English. I argued in Section 2 that this is because the origins and continuing influences of standard English lie in formal written English rather than speech, and these influences then affect the intuitions of linguists, and our beliefs and behaviour about language. These, in turn, affect the models and frameworks that we have developed to analyse language; and they constitute an important reason for our ignorance about the structure of the syntax of spoken English.

Our understanding of spoken syntax should, however, increase rapidly as work continues on the analysis of corpora of transcribed speech. The syntax of speech is not, I have argued, the mystery that it has sometimes been supposed to be: many of the constructions I have discussed in the previous section can be analysed using conventional theoretical and descriptive models, as I have shown – though this does not mean that these models are necessarily the most appropriate ones to use. However, there remains the possibility that we will overlook the recurrent structures of spoken syntax because our beliefs about language encourage us to look for discrete categories with a single function, or to assume that principles of linguistic organisation that have been important during standardisation (such as concord) are equally important during speaking.

Should the features that I have discussed in this chapter be considered to be part of standard English? For linguists working within the generative tradition, the question is presumably irrelevant, for these features do not appear to be accessible to our intuitions, and it is not possible, therefore, to use them for grammaticality judgements. This does, of course, beg the question of the status of grammaticality judgements that are based on intuitions.

For descriptive linguists who accept a definition of standard English as the set of features used in the speech and writing of educated speakers, the answer seems to me unclear because, with the possible exception of *wh*-descriptive clauses, the features I have identified occur in 'educated' speech, but not in writing. For a feature to be considered 'standard', must it occur in both these varieties? I said at the beginning of the chapter that the concept of spoken standard English is problematic, as indeed is the concept of a standard language generally. Macaulay (1973: 1331) stated that one reason for the difficulty of precisely defining a standard language is that the evidence lies at the intersection of two distinct areas of investigation. The first, he says, is the description of the language, including all its varieties. The second is the description of the norms of speech for specific communities including the significance of the use of a particular variety in a specific situation. In my view, however, the main problem is not that the evidence lies at the intersection of these two distinct areas of investigation, but that it is difficult to keep these two areas distinct, because of the prestige of the standard variety and the influence of language norms on our descriptions of the varieties. My own preference is to use the term 'standard English' to refer to the set of norms to which speakers and writers conform to a greater or lesser extent (see Milroy and Milroy 1985: 22–3). This view takes account of the historical development of these norms; Downes (1984: 34), for example, stresses the links between standardisation, nationalism and literacy. The features I have discussed here would not then be considered as part of the standard, since they have had no role in any of these three processes.

At the very least, it seems necessary to draw a clear distinction between spoken standard English and written standard English, and between formal and informal styles of both speaking and writing. The features discussed in this chapter can then be identified as more likely to occur in spoken face-to-face interaction in informal settings. It also seems necessary to recognise that the formality continuum overlaps with the continuum between planned and unplanned discourse (Ochs 1979). Formal speech can often be relatively more planned because the situations which call for formal styles may allow speakers to take their time, pausing to collect their thoughts. In these situations individuals tend to respect each other's speaking rights, and to conform to a one-at-a-time model of turn-taking (Coates 1997); there may even be predetermined routines for speaker turns, as in the question and answer formats of interviews. Sometimes speakers will have planned their contributions in advance or will have spoken on similar topics before. These circumstances could hardly differ more from those where we produce the fast spontaneous unplanned speech of informal conversation, where multifunctional, polypragmatic features are so useful. Speakers who spend much of their time speaking in formal situations may carry over the linguistic features and constructions typical of formal styles to their conversational speech styles, especially if they are treated with the same respect in their private lives that they command in their professional roles. The majority of adult speakers, however, will have a wider stylistic repertoire.

Given the social prestige of written language, of the set of forms that have been accepted as standard English and of the individuals who command respect in their professional life, it could be difficult to convince the general public, let alone those responsible for the requirements of the National Curriculum for English, that the features discussed in this chapter are not 'bad English' or performance errors, but structures that are functional and appropriate for the situations in which they occur. It is difficult enough attempting to explain that forms such as multiple negation, though not 'standard', are grammatically well-formed and, though stigmatised, often appropriate to the situations in which they occur.

It is most unfortunate, therefore, that the National Curriculum for English in England and Wales implies that formal and informal styles of speaking call for identical forms of English. This institutionalises the ideas about language that, I have argued, prevent us from perceiving the syntactic structure of spoken English. It seems, however, from the examples of standard English that are given in the policy document, that the policy makers had in mind here the use of features that have been codified as standard, and that they do not consider standard English to consist of more than this. They mention, for example, 'how pronouns, adverbs and adjectives should be used, and how negatives, questions and verb tenses should be formed' (DfE/WO 1995: 3). This is continuing the legacy of the nineteenth century, which is when the concept of a spoken standard English seems to have been introduced. Partly as a consequence of the industrial revolution, a new middle class emerged who were insecure of their social position and looked to pronouncing dictionaries and grammars for guidance in their linguistic behaviour (see, for discussion, Leith and Graddol 1996: 161). The heightened awareness of social status differences contributed to the spread of 'politeness' as a social ideal; for language this gave rise to the idea that to use the 'correct' form was the mark of a polite, cultivated person, and specific issues of usage, such as the choice of *who* or *that* as a relative pronoun or the use of contracted verb forms, became seen as 'morally, socially or politically charged' (Klein 1994: 43). It is no coincidence that, although the contracted form *ain't* was once used by both the upper and lower classes in English society, it is now confined only to the lower classes. The demands of the National Curriculum would institutionalise this view.

It is unlikely, however, that sensitive schoolteachers who are familiar with local grammatical forms will discriminate against pupils who use the charged forms, if they express themselves clearly and articulately when speaking. But the National Curriculum still stands as a public statement of the national view of the English language; and it continues the tradition of a nation that is remarkably ill-informed about the nature of English, both standard and non-standard, and both spoken and written – though especially, at present, spoken.

Acknowledgement

I am grateful to Nik Coupland, John Rickford, Sali Tagliamonte and Jamal Ouhalla for their comments on this chapter, which have greatly improved it.

7

STANDARD GRAMMARS, SPOKEN GRAMMARS: SOME EDUCATIONAL IMPLICATIONS

Ronald Carter

> To be unable to write Standard English or to use its spoken forms in appropriate public contexts is to be disenfranchised, to be deprived of true citizenship. ... Where it is appropriate to use the standard, you use it but there are many uses where other forms, or other languages, are as appropriate. ... It is astonishing to reflect that no linguistic theory has ever begun to pose the question of the permissible range of variation within a standard although it is obvious even from the history of English that the range is not fixed.
>
> (McCabe 1990: 11)

1 Grammar and speech: Terms and determinations

The following extract from a conversation was recorded as part of the CANCODE research project,[1] a multi-million word computational linguistic research investigation of naturally occurring spoken British English based in the Department of English Studies at the University of Nottingham. The speakers are both educated speakers of English. The setting is an informal one in a village pub on an exceptionally hot summer's evening in the mid-1990s. The speakers, who are both male, are good friends and are 'catching up' on each other's news, having not spoken at length to each other for some time.

Example dialogue:

```
1   <S 01>   Are you still playing er
2   <S 02>                   Gui-tar
3   <S 01>   Irish music, yeah
4   <S 02>   No I don't play very much now, no, not at all
5   <S 01>                                   I thought you
6            were touring the country at one point
```

```
 7   <S 02>   [laughs]                    No, I er ... we go,
 8            we listen to it quite a lot, every time we go to Ireland
 9            we erm, you know, seek out good musicians and er
10            do quite a lot of listening and of course we still buy
11            a lot of records, bought a lot of records over the last
12            few years, but erm, there's not actually anybody to
13            play with around here, you know [<S 01> Mm] there's
14            a there's a session every Sunday night in Cambridge
15            in a pub and that's erm about it ... do you still listen
16            to Scottish music?
17   <S 01>   Ver ... since this pair have arrived [<S 02> Mm] very
18            very little, cos you just don't have the time, and with
19            the new house, and with the garden [<S 02> Mm]
20            occasionally I take fits of putting stuff on, not as much
21            as before
22   <S 02>   They do I s'pose take up a lot of time, don't they
23            kids
24   <S 01>                                              They
25            take up a lot of, I mean, normally, you get, if you're
26            lucky they're all tucked up in bed by eight-thirty
27            [<S 02> Mm] ... that's if you're lucky, and then er
28   <S 02>   Do they sleep all night without erm waking up, did
29            they wake up last night, they didn't [<S 01> No] did
30            they, no, [<S 01> No] didn't hear a thing
31   <S 01>   Jamie normally, you put him in his cot and he's ...
32            he's gone [<S 02> Mm] he sleeps he's very good
33            at sleeping [<S 02>Mm] Thomas is a bit of a pain
34            [<S 02> Ah] all sorts of things frighten him, you
35            know [<S 02> Yeah] wakes up with nightmares and
36            that [<S 02> does he] Some nights we change beds
37            about three or four times, he comes into our bed and
38            there's not enough room and so I go into his bed and
39            he comes back in so to my bed and his bed and chop-
40            ping and changing
41   <S 02>   It's extraordinary to think they have bad dreams, well,
42            I suppose they dream of images they've seen during
43            the day, probably dream of that bloomin' duck or
44            something
45   <S 01>   Or it just might be a car, noisy car going past the
46            window or something, wakes them up [<S 02> Mm]
47   <S 02>   It's going to be hot tonight ... in bed, isn't it
48   <S 01>   Mm
```
(CANCODE data; see also Carter and McCarthy 1997: 42 ff)

The recorded extract reveals a number of features which have been frequently commented upon in discussions of spoken discourse. There are, for example, instances of back-channelling; false starts and hesitations; extensive use of spoken discourse markers and vague language such as *all sorts of things, sort of, I mean, I suppose, well, or something*; a choice of lexical items which are less likely to be found in written contexts such as: *bloomin', chopping and changing, a bit of a pain* and so on. These are features which allow for the fact that spoken discourse such as this is constructed in real time and which are integral to the informality and interpersonal symmetry of the speaker's relationship as well as to the physical environment of their conversation. Such features have been described in numerous recent studies, usually undertaken from within the discipline of discourse analysis. For a review of such work and of differences and distinctions between written and spoken English see McCarthy and Carter (1994: especially Chapter 1). Perera (1994) comments on the ways in which such features of ordinary and often interpersonally sensitive language use have been construed by media and government as examples of 'sloppy' or 'lazy' speech.

1.1 Heads and tails

What is less frequently commented upon are the *grammatical* features which characterise spoken English discourse. Here are some features which can be observed in the above data.

- *Heads*, an example of which is:
  Jamie, normally, you put him in his cot and he's . . .
  (lines 31–32 of example dialogue)

This is an example of a grammatical structure which Carter and McCarthy (1995, 1997) have termed a *head*. Normally, the use of a head structure with a pronoun (here *him*) repeats the topic word (here *Jamie*) and serves to give emphasis to *Jamie* as the new topic or sub-topic.

Heads perform an orienting and focusing function, identifying key information for listeners and establishing a shared frame of reference for what is important in a conversational exchange. Heads are almost exclusively nouns or noun phrases and are placed at the front of a clause, anticipating a structure which then forms the main subject of the clause. Here are a few examples of heads, which are italicised in the following:

> *That chap over there*, he said it was ok.
> *This friend of ours, Carol, her daughter*, she decided to buy one.
> *The women in the audience*, they all shouted.
> (CANCODE and author's data)

Heads are almost exclusive to informal spoken standard English. They parallel *tails* (see below) although tails generally serve a much more affective purpose.

- *Tails*, an example of which is:
  They do, I suppose, take up a lot of time, don't they, kids?

  (lines 22–23 of example dialogue)

This is an example of a different grammatical structure which Carter and McCarthy (1995, 1997) have termed a *tail*. This term describes the slot available at the end of a clause in which a speaker can insert grammatical patterns which amplify, extend or reinforce what a speaker is saying or has said. Examples of tails (italicised) include:

She's a really good actress, *Clare*
I'm going to have haddock and chips, *I am*
They haven't mended the road yet *haven't those workmen*
They complain about it all the time *they do*
He must be quite a comic *that fellow*, you know
It's not actually very good is it *that wine?*

(CANCODE and author's data)

We should note also the extent to which such examples cluster with different kinds of tags, hedges and modal expressions and how they often serve to express, on the part of the speaker, some kind of affective response, personal attitude or evaluative stance towards the proposition or topic of the clause.

It is, of course, not wholly accurate to say that such features as *tails* and *heads* have not been observed or commented upon previously, although observations have tended to come from the field of discourse analysis rather than from the field of grammar studies. Terms used to describe them, such as right- and left-branching or left- and right-dislocation (see Gelyukens 1992), are revealing as metaphors but suggest that they are an oddity not in the main line of usage or that they are in some way 'broken' or 'damaged' structures. There are several reasons for such metaphorical phenomena but principal among them is the establishment of written usage as the norm against which other usage is set. Furthermore, the need to invent new terms at all is symptomatic of a descriptive situation in which there are no other established, standard terms available.

The written language has formed the basis of exemplification for linguistics for much of the twentieth century and for the study of grammar for the past 2000 years. Written or 'literary' language has been posited therefore as the best usage, forming itself in the process almost as an evaluative category to the extent that *literacy* is seen as competence in reading and writing rather than competence in speaking and listening. Standard grammars which have, in turn, formed the basis for judgements and subsequent curricular policing in schools of what constitutes standard English have been based more or less exclusively on written evidence. And it is therefore no surprise that defini- tions of standard language, standard grammar and standards in language use have come irresistibly to merge with the written language data used as the main basis for exemplification;[2] (see Carter (1995) for discussion of 'standard words' and other 'keywords' in language and literacy debates). In educational contexts there is the consequent paradox of having to develop a new term, 'oracy', for a process which is more natural than literacy (by comparison, literacy has to be much more formally learned) but which is accordingly downgraded as a capacity less worthy of attention, which is less easily testable and which is certainly less socially prestigious.

It is, of course, unfair to criticise linguists for not examining data which is not readily available, for it is only with the invention of the tape-recorder and its related developments that access to naturally occurring spoken data has been afforded. But the preoccupation with the sentence as the basis for examples, the tendency to dismiss whatever did not occur in the written form of a language as ill formed, and simplistic assessments of what is non- standard can be traced to such research contexts and determinations. The whole machinery of linguistic exemplification, based mainly on invented, introspective data – at least within most generative and cognitively oriented traditions – also works against the use of naturally occurring spoken data for purposes of illustration, analysis and argument.

Such a descriptive position certainly raises questions about the some- what unthinking and determined use of the equation between speech and standard English in discussions concerning the teaching of English. For example, it is interesting to note how frequent are the references to gram- mar and to spoken standard English in the latest documents guiding the teaching of English for the National Curriculum in England and Wales. For example:

> In order to participate confidently in public, cultural and working life, pupils need to be able to speak . . . standard English fluently and accurately.
>
> (DfE/WO 1995: 2)

> Pupils' . . . use of standard English should be developed by involve- ment in activities that . . . demand the grammatical constructions of spoken standard English.
>
> (DfE/WO 1995: 12)

> Pupils should be taught to be fluent, accurate users of (spoken) stan- dard English grammar.
>
> (DfE/WO 1995: 18)

We can only conclude from statements such as these that the requirement is for pupils to speak in the same way as they write.

Another way in which such phenomena as heads and tails can be dismissed as peripheral is for it to be said that they are infrequent or, more dismissively still, for it to be claimed that they belong only within regional dialects and are not therefore of especial significance in the use of spoken national forms of the standard dialect which is normally the major focus for description and, in educational contexts, learning. A related argument is that such differences between spoken and written forms are minor and are restricted to a few (again infrequent) forms.

In CANCODE data heads and tails are neither isolated nor peripheral phenomena. Not only can their frequency be attested but their even distribution across a range of social, interactive, generic and geographic contexts can also be demonstrated. For example, certain tails *are* regionally restricted in Britain and Ireland. In the northwest of England a single pronoun tail is common:

> I'm going to have a gin and tonic, *me*.
> We're always getting into trouble, *us*.

(CANCODE data)

However, tails of the kind and variety described above and illustrated in the CANCODE data are widespread and are neither regionally nor socially restricted. They are examples of *standard spoken English*.

1.2 Other grammatical features

It should not be thought that heads and tails are the only features of spoken standard English which can be identified in data such as that collected for the CANCODE corpus. In terms of frequency and distributional criteria other features which are of significance are those listed below:

- *Ellipsis*, an example of which is:
  . . . it might just be a car, noisy car going past the window, wakes them up

(lines 46–47 of example dialogue)

Ellipsis of the type illustrated here is pervasive in spoken discourse. It occurs in writing but functions textually to prevent repetition where structures would otherwise be redundant. For example, in the sentence *we ran for the bus but missed it* where it is clear that *we* remains the subject of both clauses; or in the sentence *The chair was broken and the table too* where it is clearly redundant to repeat the verb phrase *was broken*. Ellipsis in spoken English is mainly situational (i.e. affecting people and things in the immediate situation) and frequently involves the omission of personal subjects, again where it is obvious that the references will remain unambiguous. Such a feature is also especially common with verbs of mental process; for example, *think so, wonder if they'll be coming to the party, guess they won't be ringing after all* and so on. Such ellipsis occurs with main or auxiliary verbs where meaning can be relatively easily reconstructed from the context. For example:

A: What's the matter?
B: Got an awful cold.
A: Just seen Paco.
B: Did he say anything?
A: Nothing.
B: Interesting isn't it?

(CANCODE data)

Ellipsis only rarely occurs with modal auxiliary verbs, however, so that, while pronoun subjects are omitted, the force of the modal is normally retained (e.g. *must be difficult, might be the right thing to do*). Several elliptical structures are almost, as it were, fixed expressions, occurring as frozen lexical routines (*sounds strange, seems worth it, absolutely right, good job you did that*) and so on. Collectively, ellipsis of this kind is situationally rooted but is not random. It occurs across most speech genres and in almost all cases marks a degree of informality and social symmetry between speakers. Ellipsis is treated in many standard grammars but the different speaker choices in using situational ellipsis are not normally considered. Ellipsis is generally less common in the genre of spoken narrative, however, where the speaker is constructing a world within which shared coordinates are less obvious and where too great a degree of ellipsis can therefore be disorientating (see Carter and McCarthy 1995).

* *Word order* is differently inflected in speech and writing, particularly in reported speech structures: for example, *wh*-clefts are more widespread in spoken English:
  What fascinates me with that is the way it's rolled.
  That's what she said was the biggest shock.
  Why I rang you was that I needed to check something.
  Where we always go wrong is that we forget it's a one-way street.

(CANCODE data)

The *wh*-type clauses are fronted for emphasis, but they may also be used to signal an evaluation or to contradict an expected response from the interlocutor. Clauses with *why* and *how* often anticipate questions and try to provide an answer or explanation in advance. As is the case with heads, tails and ellipsis, this kind of word-ordering is interpersonally sensitive. There is a concern to balance the communication in the interests of the dynamics of interpersonal exchange as much as there is with the transmission of prop-

155

ositional content. Inevitably, such concerns are less salient in written communication.

In general, fronting operates differently in spoken discourse compared with written discourse, not least because the demands of face-to-face communication require information to be stored and processed differently by interlocutors, and speakers are sensitive to such requirements by emphasising key topics at salient clausal (and, of course, intonational) junctures. Other related examples found in the CANCODE corpus include *it* themes and the regular fronting of objects and complements, as in:

> *Two free air tickets* they were going to give us.
> *It's ten by seven* you want yeah.

A range of other features are being observed (almost daily) as part of ongoing data collection and analysis in CANCODE research. The following are merely observational statements at this stage and require more extensive analysis before either the provenance of the features or their equivalences in written form can be accounted for. And in some cases there are no written equivalences.

- *Clause components*

The status of the clause is less clear in spoken discourse. CANCODE data certainly bears out Halliday's (1989) observations that there are in speech many more clause complexes and clauses characterised by embedding than in writing. For example, clauses such as the following are not uncommon:

> There's so many things I'm going to be able to tell you if we get
>   time to meet up on the Monday.
> That's the bit they've always promised to tell us more about but
>   keep forgetting.

Sometimes it is far from clear what actually functions as a clause and what can be interpreted as a form of ellipsis. The following example may in fact be a use of present participles endemic to narrative recounting:

> So I go into his bed and he comes back in so to my bed and his
>   bed and chopping and changing.
>   (lines 38–40 of example dialogue)

Carter and McCarthy (1995) raise further questions about the usefulness of the clause as a descriptive category for spoken grammar.

- *Double negatives for emphasis*

Double negation is common in spoken English. It contrasts markedly with written English, where it can be used to signal non-commitment to propositions, either for reasons of politeness, guardedness or sometimes for ironic purposes (for example, *This is a not uninteresting essay*). Great sensitivity surrounds the structure, however, since in British English it is associated with non-standard dialects. A negative structure, doubled with an end-placed mental process verb (not infrequently clustering with question tags) is so common across the full range of CANCODE data that it can only be described as standard spoken English:

> She's not going into town, I don't think.
> He's not going to university this year, I don't believe, is he?

* *Plurals, singulars and standards*

The whole area of plural and singular forms is problematised by real evidence from spoken corpora. For example, the form *There's* is used standardly in spoken English irrespective of whether the following subject is singular or plural.

> There's two directions you can take her.
> There's a cafe up there to the right.
> There's a problem with the wheel cylinder, I'm afraid.
> There's problems with the argument which you don't really seem
> to deal with.

Yet plural/singular distinctions with nominal or pronominal subjects are much more clearly differentiated with distribution in CANCODE data that is related more explicitly to region and social class. There are complex issues to do here with perceptual salience, articulation (*there's* is easier to say than *there are*) and a long history of public 'correction' of such forms, an issue which will not be considered in this chapter. *Subject verb concord* figures prominently in recent national curriculum requirements in the UK for speaking and writing 'standard English'.

1.3 Grammar, speech and writing

It is frequently the case that literacy debates, particularly as conducted in the national media of many different countries, take place in the absence of attestable evidence, thus ensuring that rising or declining standards of literacy are simply established by the clearest assertions, by the most forceful anecdotes, or by governmental insistence. However, it is also not unusual for debates internal to the profession to be conducted without detailed scrutiny of language data. It seems appropriate therefore for the discussion in this chapter to be based on real data. The main CANCODE example on page 159 below is additionally drawn from material collected in the course of the Language in the National Curriculum Project (LINC) between 1989 and 1992.[3]

It is difficult to draw precise boundaries between spoken and written standard English and it is both unduly naive and relativistic to assume that all spoken forms are equally acceptable. However, the generally stigmatised uses are few (see again Perera 1994) and are greatly outnumbered by specifically standard spoken English forms. One main danger, therefore, is that spoken English continues to be judged by the codified standards of written English, and that teaching pupils to speak standard English may, in fact, be to teach them to speak in formal written English. A test of spoken English may, therefore, become a test of one's abilities to speak a very restricted code – a formal English used routinely by dons, civil servants and cabinet ministers. It is not very far removed from the language of formal debate. Such a view of spoken English can produce an artificial and unnatural English and can even promote a kind of *illiteracy* which is as damaging for users of English as not being able to write literate English: to have everyone speaking and writing only one code – a standard written English code – generates an illiteracy almost as grave as would be the case if everyone were only able to use a single regional dialect. And, as we have seen above, it may produce speakers whose discourse is divergent and distant rather than speakers who can use language for convergent and interpersonally sensitive purposes.

To summarise, it has been argued so far:

- that there is a close relationship between standard English and the written language
- that there are forms of spoken English which are perfectly standard and which are indeed grammatically correct. These forms do not appear in standard grammars, however, and it is easy, therefore, for them to be judged as non-standard and ungrammatical.
- that there are dangers inherent in teaching children to speak using formal written English structures or indeed testing them for their ability to speak, in effect, like a book.

In addition, it is also important to emphasise that grammar is only one part (though an important part) of standard English. Discussions of children's spoken and written language use involves consideration of other components of standardness such as vocabulary, orthography, punctuation and the influence of articulation on spoken and written representation.

It is vital that teachers know more about this sort of issue for they will then be better equipped to help pupils to know more about one of the most central features of language and literacy. It has been argued that such understandings are best promoted by pedagogic processes which involve regular comparison and contrast of spoken and written texts and not by processes which focus on one to the exclusion of the other (Carter 1997: Chapter 4).[4] It is also important for teachers to know more about the ways in which spoken and written forms intersect, to differentiate more systematically between standard and non-standard spoken forms and to work with the different *values* which different forms can carry in different communicative contexts.

2 Working with standard English: A classroom case study

The following extract is from a classroom discussion between an English teacher and a small group of Year 10 (aged 14–15) secondary-school pupils in the West Midlands of England. The teacher has asked them to consider how they would spend £10,000 'for the benefit of the local community', and makes it clear, in response to a question, that this 'community' included people of their own age (curly brackets '}' indicate two speakers talking at the same time).

Teacher: Well, if you had this £10,000, then, which someone's going to give, what could you do with that £10,000 to make life rather better for you, to give you more things to do?

Pupil 4:   They could make it a place for body-poppers to go and, like a youth club and . . . special room for all that . . .

Pupil 2:   Leisure Centre.

Pupil 4:   Yeah.

Teacher: We're having a big leisure centre which is costing millions but you'd like to have a building where you could go yourselves, would you?

Pupil 2:   Yeah . . . in the nights, like, when, it's cold.

Pupil 1:   And you could sleep there.

Pupil 2:   Mm.

Teacher: You could stay there as well? So what kind of things would you like to see in this building that you could have? Body-popping is one – a room for that . . .

Pupil 3:   Space invaders . . . stuff like that.

Teacher: But you can't get these in . . . in arcades in town? Or do you have to be . . .

Pupil 3:   Yeah – but you've got to be older.

Pupil 4:}   You got to be 18.

Pupil 3:}   You got to be over 18.

Teacher: So you'd like to have an arcade where you could go . . . without having to be over 18.

Pupil 3:   Yeah.

Pupil 4:   Not gambling machines, though, just the games.

Teacher: Just the Space Invader games. You like those.

Pupil 4:   Mm.

Teacher: You think they'd be popular? *(pause)* That's £10,000, I don't think it would cost £10,000 just to have body-popping and Space Invaders; what else could you have?

Pupil 4: You could have a variety of things

Pupil 2: Snooker tables . . .

Teacher: Yes?

Pupil 2: Table tennis . . .

Teacher: Do you think people would go there to play table tennis and snooker?

Pupil 2: Yes.

Teacher: Do many people go and watch the body-popping down there?

Pupil 3:} Quite a lot

Pupil 4:} Quite a few . . . yeah . . .

Pupil 3: Every Saturday they has a challenge at Maskell's Leisure Centre.

Teacher: So you're saying there are a lot of young people your age, then, who have nowhere to go and nothing to do.

Pupil 4: Mm. There's loads of people who does it . . . but . . . there's nowhere to go . . . really . . . and . . .

Teacher: So you'd have table tennis, snooker there, body-popping . . . somewhere to stay overnight as well you think.

Pupil 2: Mm.

Pupil 1: Yeah. Got to.

Teacher: Why do you think that's necessary?

Pupil 1: Something to do, init? Nothing to do. You know.

(LINC/CANCODE data; see also Carter and McCarthy 1997: 121ff)

Some features of spoken discourse which might be noted as significant in the light of the foregoing discussion of spoken grammar and for purposes of evaluating successful spoken communication are discussed below. It is not uncommon in spoken discourse for clauses to be chained together in parallel structures, such as:

to make life rather better for you, to give you more things to do

Such patterning allows the speaker the opportunity to reformulate, refine or otherwise be more precise than composing in real time normally allows. Chaining of this kind occurs in writing, not uncommonly to create a more spoken, 'interactive' rhetorical structure for the writing. (In writing, however, the reformulations normally lead to additional information content rather than simple topic restatement.)

Like is used in the phrase *in the nights, like, when it's cold*, informally, as an alternative phrasing for *for instance* or *for example*. Such uses of *like* would not normally be appropriate in most standard written English.

Stuff, as in *stuff like that* is a common 'vague' word in conversational English (see Channell 1994). In such contexts too great a degree of precision would be likely to sound excessively impersonal and authoritative. Similar 'vague' expressions and discourse markers are found in structures such as *things like that* or *something like that*. As mentioned, such usage is often regarded as 'sloppy'; yet scrutiny of real data in context reveals the communicative effectiveness of much of such language.

Sets of expressions, such as *quite a lot/quite a few*, are relatively common in informal spoken English, and they are further examples of 'vague' language. In most conversations very imprecise reference to numbers and to quantities allows speakers deliberately to hedge or to add emphasis without expecting to be taken literally.

As we saw in Section 1, rules for subject–verb concord vary in different dialects of English. In the example *There's loads of people who does it*, *people* is accompanied by what would be plural verbs in most standard written dialects of English. There is, however, extensive evidence to suggest that *there's* is a more frequent structure in English than *there are* and is used irrespective of the noun or nouns which follow it. The singular form of the verb with *people* is, however, unusual in such a context and belongs more centrally within a non-standard dialect form (here a regional West Midlands dialect). Note that the teacher uses *there are* in the previous turn. The contrasts in grammatical choices do not get in the way of sustained discussion as the choices express each speaker's perception of the relative formality of the context and of their own role within it. It would be interesting to assess the impact on the discussion if the teacher chose to intervene to 'correct'.

Got to is another example of ellipsis (from several lines in this interchange) in which the normal subject and auxiliary verb are deleted. The use of ellipsis is appropriate to the informal, interpersonal context of the discussion which the teacher has created and which is clearly conducive to pupils speaking openly and without too great a degree of inhibition. *Nothing to do* is another elliptical construction which marks deliberate casualness in the reply.

In sum, the efforts of the speakers here are invested as much in the relationships engendered by the discussion as they are in the transmission of content and ideas. Overall, we have to recognise that the language choices, often ungrammatical according to 'standard' definitions, largely reflect and encode such interpersonality, and that the speakers achieve their communicative goals effectively.

The complexities attendant on any assessment of the effectiveness of pupils speaking standard English and on the selection of appropriate pedagogies for teaching and studying standard spoken and written English are, it is to be hoped, clear. There is little doubt, however, that much is to be gained from a recognition that standard spoken and standard written Englishes are in important respects different (for further methodological exemplification see Bain et al. 1992; Woods 1995; Wilkinson 1995).

3 Conclusions: An educational view

Glottal stops ain't allowed no more
The latest suggestion that schoolchildren should speak Standard English – even in the playground's rough and tumble – has generally been received as a good thing by the world of adults.

From the age of five, the nation's children may now be encouraged to pick up their aitches and drop the ubiquitous glottal stops, *aints* and other manifestations of non-U grammar. With regional accents allowed to remain, the result is likely to be that BBC English is once again a model for the nation.

(*Times Educational Supplement*, 25 September 1992)

3.1 Words and nations

The above quotation illustrates something of the complexities and confusions concerning standard English and spoken English; the issues are, of course, not helped by such statements appearing (as they regularly do) in reports specifically aimed at school teachers. The overall issues are well-rehearsed but they can be briefly summarised in relation to this newspaper report, as follows:

1   Accent variation is seen as crucial in popular definitions of standard English (though standard English, definitions of which are largely a matter of grammar and lexis, can be spoken in any accent).

2   Such public reports and pronouncements rarely show any understanding or toleration of language variation. Centripetal forces (Bakhtin 1981) predominate at the present time, creating considerable psychological pressure for there to be single, definable, unchanging, unitary and non-'regional' forms. There is no recognition that double negatives or the use of certain forms of the verb 'to be' (*aint*) may be bound up with an individual's identity as a member of a particular social and cultural group or groups. There may be an underlying and implicit statement that non-standard language use equals non-standard people (or here school children).

3   Identity is a matter only of national identity. Yet the national curriculum to which the newspaper report refers applies in Britain only to England and Wales (not to Scotland or Northern Ireland). Also, there is no recognition of the existence of other languages in the country. English (BBC English) is the language of those living within the geographical boundaries of Britain; paradoxically, therefore, Welsh, the languages of Scotland and Ireland and major languages (such as Punjabi) which are spoken by those who are British are by omission discounted in almost all British national curriculum documentation. (For further discussion of the issues in relation to language planning, see Stubbs 1993.)

4 The preoccupation with what are felt to be salient non-standard forms draws attention to *oppositions* rather than continuities between 'standard' and 'non-standard' forms. The preoccupation has been reinforced by studies commissioned by government agencies (e.g. Hudson and Holmes 1995) into 'spoken standard English' in which only what are categorised as non-standard forms are itemised for teachers' scrutiny and, it is implied, for their curricular policing.

5 The term 'non-standard' carries very definite negative connotations. Linguists and educationalists should consider replacing it with a more positive term.

The national and nationalist concerns with standardness have been deconstructed in major work by sociolinguists in Britain (several of whom are represented in this volume) and central insights into the way in which nonstandard dialects are rule governed have been made. There is little doubt that teachers are helped by such knowledge. There is a concern, however, that such accounts have not always taken full cognisance of standard spoken grammar, and that variation theory, however extensively refined by linguists, has not penetrated in any way laypeople's understanding of language. Issues concerning standard English have also remained an easy target for ideologically motivated centripetal tendencies which have presented non-standard varieties as 'unhygienic' (Cameron 1995).

3.2 Schools, curricula and standard Englishes

There are a number of complex linguistic, cultural and pedagogic issues surrounding the teaching of standard English in schools. There is little doubt that standard written English should be taught in schools and that curriculum documents are right to stress its importance. Standard English consists of a set of forms which are used with only minimal variation in written English and in a range of formal spoken contexts in use around the world. Such forms constitute the basis for the teaching of English internationally. Standard English should, therefore, be taught and, where appropriate and at appropriate developmental stages, taught explicitly, for not to learn to write standard English is to be seriously disadvantaged and disempowered.

The issue here is that to become a *speaker* of standard English is to become a speaker of a clearly marked, socially symbolic dialect; and a long tradition of sociolinguistic research suggests that, whatever the teacher may do in the classroom and whatever the overall implications for assessment, children will not learn a dialect associated with a group with which they do not wish to be associated. By contrast, it is clear too that the minority of pupils who are already speakers of standard English as a social dialect are unfairly advantaged. (As already stated, standard English can be spoken with any regional accent.)

The shift from non-standard to standard dialects can also become one which implies a devaluation of one dialect (and the identity derived from its use) in favour of another. Teachers know at first hand the consequences that there can be for some students, particularly those at an early age, in any attempt to replace the language of home and local community: a complex dynamic of identity, value and self-confidence can be at the same time affected by any such replacement. The pedagogic reality for many has been well described by Perera:

> Pupils who speak non-standard English do so not because they are unintelligent or because they have not been well taught, but because it is the variety of English used all the time by their family and friends. Any assessment of spoken English, therefore, which gives undue weight to Standard English, is measuring not the school's effectiveness, not the pupil's ability, but their social background.
>
> (Perera 1993: 10)

and by Stubbs:

> It is very much more doubtful whether children should be explicitly taught spoken SE [Standard English]. They must be able to under-stand it, of course, but it is doubtful if schools should try to teach or insist on production in standard English. First, such an insistence is unlikely to be successful. Children know that not everyone speaks SE, and an insistence that they should speak it is likely to alienate them from the school or their family or both. In any case, the habits of the spoken language are usually so deeply ingrained that they are impervious to conscious teaching for a few hours a week in school. People need to be very highly motivated in order to change their native dialect. Writing depends much more on conscious language behaviour, and is therefore open to explicit teaching in a way in which the spoken language is not.
>
> (Stubbs 1986: 95–6)

The achievement of competence in standard English, it is strongly argued by many teachers, is best brought about on the basis of pupils' understanding of and respect for their existing language competences, and on the basis of teachers' respect for and interest in those varieties. Such is the central nature of standard English to the latest national curriculum documents in England and Wales that it is presented as if there should be no contaminating connec-tions with other varieties of the language. It is presented as a curiously pure and disinfected domain of language study and it is presented insistently; polit-ical emblem overrides classroom realities and the discourses of 'verbal hygiene' (Cameron 1995) prevail.

It has been argued in this chapter that the situation is only complicated further when the precise nature of spoken standard English remains to be more fully clarified and defined and when there is an absence of any extensive evidence from spoken data in our standard grammars and reference authorities (see McCabe 1990, cited in the epigraph to this chapter). It is unduly ironic in this context, however, that there should be so much emphasis on spoken standard English in the National Curriculum for England and Wales (DfE/WO 1995) and that pupils should be assessed on their ability to speak it, when so little appears to be known about what exactly it is and when it is defined only as 'not speaking non-standard English'.

In the light of such confusion the only realistic course of action is to reduce drastically references to speaking standard English in national curriculum documents. Given both the state of linguistic research and the public perceptions on such matters, it is difficult not to argue that the same should not apply to curricular documents in other parts of the world.

This chapter has raised issues about the definition of standard English, with particular reference to grammar. It is argued that there is still some way to go before a more comprehensive description of standard spoken grammar may be offered and, until that point is reached, considerable confusions and complexities will continue to prevail. However, descriptions and definitions of spoken standard grammar in relation to non-standard spoken grammar and in relation to standard written grammar do exhibit tendencies, and probable patterns can be located. Teachers and pupils could be made more aware of these tendencies and probable patterns. There are also, of course, some formal occasions in which pupils may need to speak a version of the language close to a standard written version. In the meantime, the importance of standard written English cannot be denied and the complexities in helping the majority of pupils to learn it cannot be underestimated.

The cultural power of written discourse and of the standard English associated with it will continue to prevail. However, speaking such a variety in a number of informal and interpersonally rich contexts, or refusing to speak it, are *choices* that education systems should do all in their power to preserve. And in this respect the greatest investment for curriculum designers is in actual spoken data and real instances of use, in stretches of talk rather than in decontextualised sentences, and in the values of *chosen* rather than imposed spoken discourses.

Notes

1   CANCODE stands for Cambridge Nottingham Corpus of Discourse in English. At the time of writing the project has assembled almost five million words of spoken English from a variety of different speech situations with speakers drawn from different parts of Great Britain and with due attention given in corpus construction to representative sociolinguistic profiles such as gender, age, class and social context. Sample data and analysis is provided in Carter and McCarthy

(1997); particular descriptions of generic classification systems and processes of data collection are provided in McCarthy (1998: Chapters 1 and 2). I am grateful to my close colleague, Michael McCarthy, for discussion of the issues raised in this paper and for allowing me to use data initially collected by him.

2   Such a situation may be illustrated further with reference to Quirk et al.'s *A Comprehensive Grammar of the English Language* (1985b), a grammar which is innovative in the use of corpus data for purposes of exemplification. However, the grammar draws its spoken data from a relatively small corpus of words (500,000 words). The corpus mostly consists of written text and the small amount of spoken data is based mainly on tape-recorded formal English conversation between, for example, university dons in a University of London common room in the 1960s. It may be doing such users of English a disservice, but it would be surprising if the English used in such contexts was anything other than a quite restricted code. It is in most manifestations a code in which there is minimal variation between spoken and written forms. Yet that restricted code is nevertheless used to illustrate and further reinforce definitions of what standard English grammar is. To a considerable extent standard English grammar may be best defined as the grammar of standard written English. Recently, however, even more innovative extensions to the research and descriptive principles of Quirk et al.'s grammar have been undertaken by one of the co-authors of the grammar, Professor Sidney Greenbaum. *The Oxford English Grammar* (Greenbaum 1996) makes extensive use of corpus data, including a multi-million word corpus of international English (the ICE corpus), which includes an extensive spoken component. Not unsurprisingly, such a grammar records evidence of heads, tails, situational ellipsis and *wh*-cleft fronting in its account (although Greenbaum's terminology is, not unsurprisingly, different; see, for example Greenbaum 1996: 230–1), where 'heads' are discussed with reference to terms such as appositives, left-dislocation and anticipatory noun phrases.

3   LINC stands for *Language in the National Curriculum*. It was a project funded by the Department of Education and Science under an ESG (Education Support Grant). The main aim of the project is to produce materials for teachers and to conduct activities to support implementation of English in the National Curriculum in England and Wales. Copies of the training materials are published in a printed desk-top version and are available from LINC project, Department of English Studies, University of Nottingham, Nottingham NG7 2RD, UK. For further exploration of LINC related issues of language and literacy see Carter (1996, 1997: Chapter 3). Richmond (1992) explores the political and ideological history of the LINC project, focusing in particular on different evaluations of the role of standard English in the training materials – an issue which contributed to an effective ban by the Conservative government of the time on formal publication of the training materials.

4   While not an issue focused on in this chapter, it should be recognised that the equation between standard English and written sources has historical roots in the development of the printing process in London in the fifteenth century and that the growth and development of standard English should not be seen in isolation from a material base in social, cultural, technological and political power.

Part III

PERSPECTIVES FROM OUTSIDE THE UK

INTRODUCTION TO PART III

Part III of this volume contains three chapters all of which present alternative approaches to the debate on 'Standard English'. It is perhaps not entirely by chance that they are written from a totally or partially non-British point of view, even though Lesley Milroy, despite her present position as full professor at the University of Michigan, stems from the British tradition in socio-linguistics. The aspects of the debate so far have all been focused on the question of 'Standard English' seen from a British perspective. But the protagonists of both sides are locked in an argument from which there is no escape. It is because of the urgent need to find an escape from this impasse that we offer three chapters containing salutary perspectives from outside Britain.

In Chapter 8, Lesley Milroy offers a comparison and contrast between the ways in which 'Standard English' is understood in non-linguistic circles in Great Britain and the United States. It is certainly not new to look at the processes of standardisation from an ideological point of view, but the term 'ideology' has been studiously and consistently avoided by lay commentators, sometimes even by linguists supporting such notions as 'correct' 'Standard English', 'educated' speakers of 'Standard English', 'good' English and 'bad' English. Honey (1997), for example, devotes a whole chapter (Chapter 6) to the demolition of the Milroys' notion of 'authority in language' without even mentioning the term 'ideology' once. Lesley Milroy, however, is quite open about what her aims are in this chapter, viz. to uncover and discuss 'the rather different ideologies which result in subtly but noticeably different language attitudes in Britain and the United States and can be related to contrasting national histories and social structures'. It is, indeed, this approach which we would like to see applied with more honesty and openness in the debate.

The second refreshing aspect of Milroy's approach is to insist on thorough sociohistorical research. She starts off by suggesting that the very notion of 'Standard English' in Britain is different from the equivalent notion in the United States. She also restricts her discussion to the 'spoken language', by which she means accent, i.e. the phonological codification of the standard which Trudgill maintains has not taken place. At this point we have to be careful, however, since Milroy is talking about an ideology, a set of beliefs about language shared by a community, and not about real attempts at codification and stabilisation. Any change in language is not held to be 'a neutral fact of social life', as sociolinguists would argue, but rather to lead to 'bad' or 'inadequate' language, allowing people who use these forms to be classified as morally or intellectually insufficient.

The main body of her chapter demonstrates how the language attitudes deriving from the British conceptualisation of standard spoken English are manifested in rather different ways in public life from language attitudes deriving from the American conceptualisation. In the USA the standard ideology reveals itself in attitudes that can be described as overtly racist or ethnically discriminatory. In Britain, on the other hand, the standard ideology is revealed in social-class prejudice. The language varieties most clearly marked for class are identified as those being the lowest in terms of public esteem. She illustrates these attitudes by discussing a number of real-life examples.

Milroy then sets out to ground these negative language attitudes deriving from the standard ideology in the very different sets of sociohistorical facts pertaining to language, social class, race and ethnicity that can be seen as contributing towards the historical development of British and American society.

In Chapter 9, Laura C. Hartley and Dennis R. Preston neatly corroborate Milroy's analysis by looking at folk evaluations of US English, through the analysis of which they are indeed able to locate the old Civil War boundary separating the South from other parts of the country. Hartley and Preston begin by making it clear to the reader that in the US it is not linguists who define language standards. The fresh approach that they bring to the study of the standard language is to make it crystal clear that, if we want to come closer to understanding the 'other' side of the divide in the debate, we had better begin to take the opinions of non-linguists seriously.

Hartley and Preston also make explicit what Milroy implies in Chapter 8 with respect to the USA, namely that every region in the country considers itself the 'locus of the standard' and that this is a result of the historical fact that no single centre of culture, economy and government has dominated others over long periods of time. In an attempt to display the truth of their adage that US linguists are unable to pin down the question of which regional variety can be considered Standard American English (SAE), they describe the fascinating but enormously complicated business of eliciting the lay opinions of non-linguists in four areas of the US; these are southeastern Michigan (MI), southern Indiana (IN), the South (S), and Oregon (OR). We will not go into detail here concerning Hartley and Preston's methodology or the parameters on which informants were asked to rate regional varieties of English in the US, except to say that the other side of the Civil War divide, the Northeast (or Yankee territory), appears to come off almost as badly in assessments as the South.

The research findings offered here show that the kinds of folk evaluations that were expressed mirror findings from other folk-linguistic research carried out elsewhere (cf. the research carried out in Wales by Williams et al. 1996).

There are two sorts of positive evaluation: the 'standard, prescribed, educated variety' and the 'often proscribed but cosy home style of one's own area'. The lesson to be learned is that we ignore these tendencies at our peril. If the 'standard, prescribed, educated variety' in Britain is indeed Received Pronunciation and, in terms cf the written language, the variety of 'Standard English' prescribed by the National Curriculum for England and Wales, those engaging in the debate on the linguistic side of the fence in Britain would do well to take this research seriously and to formulate a totally new set of pertinent questions.

In Chapter 10, Bent Preisler shows us that any assessment of the significance and the functions of 'Standard English' cannot be fully made unless one also takes the non-native English-speaking world into account. The new approach that he offers is to examine what role English plays in a rather typical EFL (English as a Foreign Language) situation and then to suggest what form of English might most profitably serve the present learners and potential learners of the language. The fact that the English language is vastly more significant in those countries in which it is taught as a foreign language than is generally appreciated in either Britain or the USA can be confirmed by one of the editors (Richard J. Watts) from his experiences in Switzerland. All of those functions of English that Preisler mentions with respect to Denmark are equally significant for Switzerland, if not more so, as it is an officially multilingual country with a supposed need for a lingua franca other than one of the official languages.

Preisler aims in Chapter 10 to examine the extent to which the debate about 'Standard English' is relevant in the Danish (and by extension the Swiss) context. He even goes so far as to suggest that it may not even be justified, thereby implying that most of the issues debated may simply confuse those responsible for setting up and running English teaching programmes. The problem with this argument is that it tends to overlook the simple fact that the debate in Britain is one about the teaching of English as a mother tongue to those who already speak a standard or a non-standard variety of the language. In addition, the language attitudes derived from the standard ideology in Britain concern matters of class consciousness and social-class discrimination whereas those in the USA focus on racial and ethnic discrimination. Hartley and Preston argue that it is not possible to define what SAE is in any case, and several of the other chapters in this volume put forward a similar set of arguments for the British form of 'Standard English'. Preisler, however, makes the valid point that the issues for a learner in the EFL situation are not about 'good' or 'bad' English, but, at least in the educational framework, about 'correct' or 'incorrect' English. In order for judgements such as these to be made, some standard is necessary.

What native speakers may not realise about the use of English in EFL countries is that, as Preisler quite correctly points out, although English in formal situations may be *spoken* in only very few situations, 'the domains in which English is *read* or *heard* are numerous and not necessarily special-ized'. His arguments are based on a very extensive survey carried out by the University of Roskilde on the use of English at all levels of the population in Denmark. The survey reveals that about 40 per cent of Danish adults are conscious that they encounter English at least once a day in Danish advert-ising, a figure which rises to 70 per cent of all informants who are aware of English in advertising several times a week.

In addition to the normal courses in English offered through the school system, there are more and more people, particularly young people, who 'learn' their English through Anglo-American oriented youth subculture in which the behavioural patterns of young people throughout the EFL world are being increasingly influenced. This can be confirmed through observation of what we might call 'snowboard subculture' in Switzerland. The major problem that a situation such as this poses is whether or not a form of 'Standard English' should be imposed as a grid to allow such learners 'from below' to find their feet on the English learning ladder.

Two things may be challenged in Preisler's argument. First, we challenge his claim that 'various scholars have recently been trying to persuade us that Standard English does not exist, and that, even if it did, it would not be a suitable or feasible model for EFL'. We respect his perception that this is so and understand the questions that he asks as a corollary of this assumption, viz. 'What kind of English have we been teaching our learners all these years?', 'What has made us think of it as a "standard"?' and 'Is a different kind of EFL called for, in view of how English is used around the world today?' The very fact that the questions are being asked indicates a high level of doubt and insecurity in the EFL world for which the continuing 'Standard English' debate is largely responsible. Second, if so much learning from below is going on, and we do not doubt for one moment that it is, we fail to see how those learners cannot benefit from a flexible approach towards the stand-ard which allows, at least within the medium of the spoken language, a wide range of styles corresponding to the various functions to which the standard will be put.

8

STANDARD ENGLISH AND LANGUAGE IDEOLOGY IN BRITAIN AND THE UNITED STATES

Lesley Milroy

1 Some beliefs about standard English

The term 'standard language ideology' as described by Milroy and Milroy (1998) and Lippi-Green (1994) characterises a particular set of beliefs about language. Such beliefs are typically held by populations of economically developed nation states where processes of standardisation have operated over a considerable time to produce an abstract set of norms – lexical, grammatical and (in spoken language) phonological – popularly described as constituting a standard language. The same beliefs also emerge, somewhat transformed by local histories and conditions, in these states' colonies and ex-colonies. For example, in all the countries discussed by contributors to Cheshire (1991) where English has been imported (I confine my comments in this chapter to English-speaking hegemonies), beliefs about language similar to those discussed below can be found. These are reported in a sizeable literature; for example Platt and Weber (1980) and Gupta (1994) both describe the operation of a British-style standard language ideology in Singapore. Although debates about standard English are a staple of the British press (in the United States the most contentious ideological debates are usually slightly differently oriented, as we shall see), experts and laypersons alike have just about as much success in locating a specific agreed spoken standard variety in either Britain or the United States as have generations of children in locating the pot of gold at the end of the rainbow.

I have suggested elsewhere that standardisation is best treated as a process, since attempts to locate a specific standard (product) are doomed to failure, given that all languages (except dead languages) vary and are in a constant state of change, phonology being particularly resistant to standardisation (Milroy and Milroy 1998: 22). In Britain and in former British colonies the

173

prestige accent Received Pronunciation (RP) is often treated not only by the general public, but also by some professional linguists, as a reference accent and described as 'standard English' (J. Smith 1996: 65). In the United States, so-called 'network American',[1] is often identified as standard English, although RP and network American are horses of a very different colour. Network American is a mainstream accent associated with the levelled dialects of the Northern Midwest, where salient locally marked features have been eradicated, so that they are commonly perceived as 'colourless' or 'characterless' (Wolfram 1991: 210). Speakers of such dialects commonly describe themselves and are described by others as having 'no accent' (Preston 1996). In Britain, it seems to be RP speakers who are typically described in this way, although unlike network American, RP is saliently marked for class and in no sense is nor ever has been a mainstream accent. Thus, with respect to spoken language, the term 'standard' means something quite different in Britain and America.

Preston's recent work on laypeople's evaluations of dialects (1996) shows clearly that there is little agreement on the geographical location of the best-spoken American English. People find it easier to specify what is *not* standard than what is; in a sense, the standard of popular perception is what is left behind when all the non-standard varieties spoken by disparaged persons such as Valley Girls, Hillbillies, Southerners, New Yorkers, African Americans, Asians, Mexican Americans, Cubans and Puerto Ricans are set aside. In Britain, where consciousness of the special status of RP as a class accent is acute, spoken standard English might similarly be described as what is left after we remove from the linguistic bran-tub Estuary English, Brummie, Cockney, Geordie, Scouse, various quaint rural dialects, London Jamaican, transatlantic slang and perhaps even conservative RP as spoken by older members of the upper classes. What remains is sometimes described as English spoken with 'no accent'. An important difference between Britain and the United States is the complication and confusion introduced by the special status of RP, an elite accent used by three per cent of the population. Yet it is often described as 'standard', particularly in teaching materials for learners of English as a second language.

The chief characteristic of a standard ideology is the belief that there is one and only one correct spoken form of the language, modelled on a single correct written form. Milroy and Milroy (1998) note that some linguistic channels and levels may be more successfully standardised than others, such that written language is more easily standardised than spoken, and morphological and syntactic systems more easily than phonological ones. Frequently, however, no clear distinction is made in discussions about standard English between spoken and written language. Smith points out that with reference to the written channel, the term standard language generally refers to 'the fixity of spelling, lexicon and grammar which derives from the work of the prescriptivist writers of the eighteenth century. To use standard English

is to signal competence in a set of well-established rules endorsed by a normative education system.' With respect to the spoken channel the situation is
much less clear. Drawing a useful distinction between 'focused' and 'fixed'
types of standard norm, J. Smith (1996) notes that scholars frequently discuss
language standards and language standardisation in a muddled and unsys-
tematic fashion. Referring to the spoken channel, he notes, 'standard language
is an extremely complex and notoriously loaded term' (ibid.: 65).

In Britain, many scholars view the spoken standard as a 'prestigious system
of grammar and lexis' which can, but need not be realised with a class specific
RP accent, but can be spoken with 'a Scottish, Welsh, American, Australian or Yorkshire accent'. However, to confuse the issue yet further, others
refer to standard English spoken with an RP accent as the standard language
(ibid: 65), thus treating RP as a reference accent, in response to its status as
a class accent. Yet there is no doubt that laypeople operate with a concept
of a correct or standard accent, as many of the ideology-driven comments
discussed in this chapter show.

Typically the standard-language ideology regards optional variation in either
channel as an undesirable deviation from a uniquely correct form. Such a
belief is widely and tenaciously held by people of all ages, intellectual levels,
political persuasions and social statuses in the face of ample evidence that
variation in patterns of language use is socially functional in a number of
ways. Furthermore, insofar as it is implicated in language contact ('foreign
accents') and processes of linguistic evolution (as are many stigmatised, non-
standard variants at all linguistic levels), patterned variation is necessarily
found in all speech communities. Yet, the standard ideology holds that far
from being a morally neutral fact of social life, language change equates with
language decay, and variation with 'bad' or 'inadequate' language. Metonymic
shift (or perhaps guilt by association) provides the logical slippage for such
negative judgements to be expressed in terms of undesirable moral, intellectual or social attributes of groups of speakers. After all, it may be believed
that sloppy or lazy speech must be produced by sloppy or lazy speakers, dim-
witted speech of the kind characterised by glottal stops is inevitably produced
by dim-witted speakers, and the speech of the gutter is also the speech of
people who habitually live in the proximity of the gutter. Examples of these
value-laden and often intemperately articulated beliefs will be cited at various
points in this chapter. Resistant to change or rational reflection, they tend
to be presented by those who hold them (including the stigmatised speakers
themselves) as 'common sense'. This expression generally denotes an
unanalysed ideological belief system. Thus, when we hear proclamations
by Republican senators in the USA along the lines that it is common
sense that English should be the only language used in the official documents
of the US federal government, or by Cabinet ministers of the last British
Tory government that standards of English will improve since common
sense is back in fashion, we can be sure that they are being driven by an

unacknowledged ideology. Open debate is avoided by an implication that it is superfluous. Unanalysed ideologies which are also widely held are useful tools for attracting public support, chiefly because of their capacity to elicit strong gut reactions.

2 Language ideology

Such beliefs about language as those described above have been systematically related to large-scale social and political institutions. Noting that the focus on particular social or linguistic issues varies, Woolard and Schieffelin (1994) review relevant contributions from ethnography of speaking, social psychology, sociology of language, history of public discourse on language, and contemporary public attitudes to language. Much of this material is explicitly presented within the framework of ideological analysis with the aim of producing a clear account of the processes which allow, without public protest or debate, the language of the least politically and economically powerful social groups to be stigmatised as 'bad', 'incomprehensible', 'sloppy', and worse. Woolard and Schieffelin characterise these processes as 'symbolic revalorisation', whereby discrimination against particular social groups is implemented by assigning negative values to their language:

> Symbolic revalorization often makes discrimination on linguistic grounds publicly acceptable, whereas corresponding ethnic or racial discrimination is not. However, simply asserting that struggles about language are really about racism does not constitute analysis. Such a tearing aside of the curtain of mystification in a 'Wizard of Oz theory of ideology' ... begs the question of how and why language comes to stand for social groups in a manner which is both comprehensible and acceptable.
>
> (Woolard and Shieffelin 1994: 62)

It is evident from newspaper reports and television programmes, from courtrooms and classrooms, that such symbolic revalorisation of language provides a useful resource for gatekeepers who wish to restrict access to goods and influence, thus affecting people's lives in many domains, both informal and institutional. For example, an article in the British magazine *Bella* entitled 'Can your accent blight your life?' describes the experiences of Helen, a Manchester woman who moved to London in search of employment: ' ... "in the arts where no-one has a regional accent ... my CV was good enough to get me interviews, but ... as soon as they heard me speak ... I wasn't taken seriously" ... and when Helen finally landed a job with a community theatre project in Islington, North London, she was told she'd only been selected because the area would benefit from a common touch'. Helen encounters similar reactions in casual interpersonal encounters: '"People can't see further than my voice and assume I'm aggressive and common. They think I should own pigeons and have an outside toilet.'" (*Bella*, 24 January 1996).

On the other side of the Atlantic we can cite the example of a 1987 screening of the Oprah Winfrey Show,[2] in which both studio audience and telephone callers contributed on the topic of African-American Vernacular English. Here are two extracts from the transcript of the show:

(1) *Second caller:*   Hi, Oprah?

    Winfrey: Yes

    Second caller: I guess what I'd like to say is that what makes me feel that blacks tend to be ignorant is that they fail to see that the word is spelled A-S-K, not A-X. And when they say aksed, it gives the sentence an entirely different meaning. And this is what I feel holds' blacks back.

    Winfrey: Why does it give it a different meaning if you know that's what they're saying?

    Second caller: But you don't always know that's what they are saying.

(2) *Ninth audience member:*   The problem seems to be that everybody tries to push something down your throat by arrogance. That's not the way to get something done. You could speak your own language, you could have your own way, but don't force someone else to have to suffer and listen to it.

    Winfrey: You say what?

    Tenth audience member: Well I'm an accountant and –

    Winfrey: Well, wait, wait, let me get back to you. What is causing you to suffer?

    Ninth audience member: Well I think there is a certain way of speaking that has been considered the acceptable way of speaking. And because of that this is the type of language you speak when you're out in the world. If you want to speak Spanish at home that's fine. If you want to speak black with your friends that's fine. But don't insult someone else's ears by making them listen to it.

The comments reported in the *Bella* magazine covertly articulate class prejudice, as is clear from the expressions 'common touch', 'aggressive and common' and the reference to pigeons and outside toilets which stereotypically characterise northern English working-class lifestyles. Some of the comments phoned in to Oprah Winfrey are presented as tolerant of an 'appropriate' variability, such as the ninth audience member's second contribution (but see Fairclough 1992 on the ideological nature of 'appropriateness'). For the most part, however, it is clear that the contributions in (1) and (2) covertly articulate racial prejudice. Lippi-Green (1994) has demonstrated that such covert discrimination is sanctioned even by the legal system; while employers are no longer able to implement overt racial discrimination in hiring and firing, demonstrably implausible linguistic claims that particular ethnic minority speakers are unintelligible – much as in (1) above – continue (as, mutatis mutandis, in Britain) to provide a publicly legitimised route to discrimination against disfavoured social groups.

3 Race, class and language ideologies

The research reviewed by Woolard and Schieffelin (1994) focuses overwhelmingly not on differences, but on commonalities underlying language ideologies in Britain, France, Canada, the United States and elsewhere, thus allowing different practices in speech communities of various types to be interpreted within a more general theoretical framework. Against this backdrop, my purpose here is to explore differences in the way language ideologies manifest themselves in public life and in the beliefs of individuals about language in two English-speaking countries: Britain and the United States. While we need to acknowledge similarities – in people's belief in the standard language ideology or in the passion with which issues of correctness are debated – it is also clear that there are differences, as exemplified above. Indeed, it is hard to imagine a long-running moral panic in the United States with all the ingredients of the great grammar debate discussed by Cameron (1995). Equally, it is hard to imagine the British press focusing over many years on an English Only movement or reacting quite as savagely as their American counterparts to the idea that Black English should have a role in the classroom, as in the Ebonics affair. Later in this chapter I consider the sociohistorical underpinning of current language ideologies in each nation.

Woolard (1989: 89) has commented on the strong and 'visceral' nature of language attitudes. In Britain the strongest gut reactions emerge in response to social class or class-related stereotypes, while in the United States they emerge in response to race and ethnicity, as illustrated above. In making this distinction, however, we need to acknowledge that the focus on race and ethnicity in the United States is mediated by class; African-American Vernacular English (AAVE) is essentially a working-class black variety. 'Foreign accents' also seem to be more subject to negative evaluation than in Britain, unless associated with prestigious groups – generally north

Europeans, as pointed out by Lippi-Green (1994) among others. For example, to the bemusement of many non-Americans in the University community, the 'unintelligibility' of overseas Graduate Student Instructors is a regular source of undergraduate grievance. In 1996 objections were vociferous enough to impel a senior administrator of the University of Michigan to react in a fashion which bears the hallmark of an ideologically driven response. Specifically, British GSIs were not thought to be in need of special assessment and remedial instruction, while monolingual English-speaking Irish students were. A major instantiation of American language ideology thus presents itself overwhelmingly as a negative and sometimes demonstrably irrational attitude to languages other than English, and by association to English spoken with a 'foreign' accent. Spanish and Spanish-accented English are viewed with particular disfavour; see (2) above. Such hostile public discourse both underpins and is supported by a fierce and longstanding political conflict, most clearly visible in the so-called 'English Only' movement.

The lobbying effort known as 'US English' emerged in the early 1980s and is currently (in 1997) particularly active, although its precise objectives are not clear. Broadly speaking, it opposes the use at all official levels of languages other than English. Although it originated as and remains essentially an anti-Hispanic, anti-immigrant coalition (Castro 1992: 182), it is hostile also to official educational provision for the needs of AAVE-speaking children, as shown by its interventions in the Ebonics debate which became particularly acrimonious in January 1997 (see further Rickford 1997; Pullum 1997; Baugh 1998). Associated with right-wing political groups, US English has an extremely high public profile, characteristically eliciting and expressing intemperately strong, irrational and polarised reactions. For example, Cardenas (1992) presents a moderate and carefully argued case for initial instruction in Spanish for Texas children who are monolingual when they start school. Citing a somewhat geographically and historically challenged but supposedly religious objection – 'If English was good enough for Jesus Christ it ought to be good enough for the children of Texas' – he continues:

> The emotional responses to bilingual education sometimes get so intense that they defy all reason. On two occasions I have read articles in which the writers object to the use of the phrase 'English as a second language.' The argument presented in both cases was that English is the greatest language on earth and therefore second to none. How does one argue with such an individual that the word 'second' refers to chronological order?
>
> (Cardenas 1992: 349–50)

Fishman (1992) notes the prominence of language policy as an internal issue for the first time in American history in the years following the emergence of US English. Commenting on the 3:1 majority in favour of the English Language Amendment passed in California's state legislature, in November 1986, he identifies the English Only movement as uniquely and characteristically American:

> No similar legislative effort to redress the internal insults to English, real or imaginary, have surfaced in any other core countries of English, such as England, Australia or New Zealand, all of which have substantial non-English-mother-tongue populations of their own. The general view toward non-English languages in governmental use in these countries is quite benevolent and even supportive in ways undreamt of here.
>
> (Fishman 1992: 166)

While Fishman's comments give a somewhat misleading impression of government benevolence towards linguistic minorities in these countries, it is certainly true, in Britain at least, that language rights of ethnic minorities seldom emerge as a major public issue. However, the legitimacy and acceptability of indigenous British non-standard dialects elicits irrationality and intensity comparable to discourse on AAVE and Spanish in the United States, and (as exemplified in Section 1 above) such discourse generally alludes directly or indirectly to social class or social mobility. Linguistic prejudice thus surfaces with quite characteristically different ambiences in the two nations. An example of a particularly British reaction was evident following the British linguist Jean Aitchison's presentation of The 1996 Reith Lectures on BBC Radio (Aitchison 1997). Entitled 'The language web', the series discussed a wide range of language issues, including acquisition, bilingualism, language minorities, historical change, language mixing and language attitudes. Public responses were focused not on bilingualism and language minorities (as one might predict they would be in the United States), but on issues of correctness and on Aitchison's argument that forms associated with low-status British speakers were historically valid, structured, potential harbingers of long-term language change and embodiments of a variability present in all natural languages. A year after the event, the Guardian newspaper's summary of this wide range of topics and of responses to them highlights the characteristically British language ideology: 'Trying to dispel fears about the corruption of English by emphasising its evolution, she evinced much restating of these fears' (*Guardian*, 23 January 1997, G2, p. 5).

A concern with class and mobility much more directly underpins public reactions to so-called 'Estuary English', a variety which is currently spreading both socially and geographically as a reflex of Britain's changing mobility patterns and class structure (see Dorling 1995, particularly Chapter 6). For example, the following newspaper headlines are drawn from a wide selection of comparable comments on a topic which received particularly extensive media exposure between 1994 and 1996, following reports of research on dialect levelling in the town of Milton Keynes, South Eastern England, by Paul Kerswill and Ann Williams of the University of Reading. It is noticeable that they usually focus on phonological details, sometimes treating RP explicitly as a reference accent:

(3) Between Cockney and the Queen: 'Estuary English' describes
    the speech of a growing number of Britons. Poised between
    RP and Bow Bells it minds its 'p's and 'q's but drops its 't's.
        (*Sunday Times*, 28 March 1993, Wordpower Supplement)

(4) Britain's crumbling ruling class is losing the accent of
    authority . . . the upper-class young already talk Estuary
    English, the cockneyfied accent of the South-east.
        (Neal Ascherson, *Independent on Sunday*, 7 August 1994)

(5) Pity the young who converse only in Oik.
        (Peter Tory, *International Express*, 7 August 1994)

Offering intemperately phrased and implausible objections similar to those expressed in the US English Only debate, Tory continues:

According to Reading University, this repellent sub-world speech is originating in Milton Keynes . . .

All sorts gather there from every corner of the land, most of them making a career out of soldering on microchips and have produced, from dozens of once respectable dialects, a hellish, slowspreading universal yob-tongue.

Is this fair on Milton Keynes? Perhaps not. There could be another answer, which may not seem obvious to many.

We should find out, through sociological research, why it is that today's oik-speaking young insist on wearing their baseball caps back to front.

The two problems, in my view, could be profoundly connected.
        (Peter Tory, *International Express*, 7 August 1994)

It is not only American culture (assuming that is the inference intended) which is blamed for the emergence of a new levelled dialect in South Eastern England. Other commentators, notably John Osborne (*The Mail on Sunday*, 7 August 1994) and Keith Waterhouse (*Daily Mail*, 4 August 1994) have proposed school teachers, Australian television soap operas and presenters of children's television programmes as agents of drastic linguistic decay. Like Tory, Waterhouse makes a distinction between the urban dialect of Milton Keynes ('slack-mouthed patois') and a genuine rural dialect:

Most regional accents – Northern, Scottish, Welsh, West Country, East Anglian – are attractive enough (although I'm afraid I can see no case for Brummagem [the urban dialect of Birmingham]). They have evolved from local conditions and local history – the Yorkshire truncated t' for *the*, for example, comes out of the mills where you had to speak loudly and succinctly to be heard above the clatter of the looms.

(Keith Waterhouse, *Daily Mail*, 4 August 1994)

I'll comment later on this genuine dialect/degenerate speech distinction, which emerges regularly in British ideologically motivated comment. Interestingly, however, it has not been reported in major accounts such as those of Lippi-Green (1997) or Preston (1996) of standard-language ideologies in America.

The underlying British concern with class emerges particularly clearly in Bradbury's (1994) description of Estuary English as 'the classless argot'. In response to his own question 'Is there today a standard English?' he offers an answer:

Estuary English, sometimes called Milton Keynes English, seems to be bidding for the position. It seems to have been learnt in the back of London taxis, or from alternative comedians. It's southern, urban, glottal, easygoing, offhand, vernacular. It's apparently classless, or at any rate a language for talking easily across classes. The Princess of Wales is supposed to speak it: graduates cultivate it, presumably to improve their 'street-credibility'.

Interestingly, Bradbury goes on to suggest that the 'classless argot' may be comparable to the English used by American fiction writers: 'Contemporary American fiction . . . is often admired for its vernacular tone and the easy flow of its speech, which is said to compare well with the "literary" language in which the British write many of their novels.' Although Bradbury's discussion slides between speech and writing, he seems here to be sensitive to the emergence of a relatively socially unmarked levelled variety in Britain, similar to the mainstream American variety which is often described in the US as the standard language (cf. Section 1 above).

So far I have tried to give some idea of the somewhat differently flavoured language ideologies in Britain and the United States. As we might expect, these national discourses are associated also with different public attitudes to class and race in the two countries, and Bradbury's comparison in his final paragraph is suggestive of these broader ideological differences. These are neatly summarised by Karpf (1997), quoting American lawyer and the 1997 BBC Reith Lecturer Patricia Williams: 'The United States deems itself classless with almost the same degree of self-congratulation that Britain prides itself as being free of racial animus.' While, in fact, race and class are demonstrably both socially divisive, and moreover are generally interacting social categories, race appears to be particularly divisive in the United States. This is suggested by a comparison of black/white interracial marriage rates which are higher in Britain than in the US: in Britain 30 per cent of all British-born men of Caribbean origin and 50 per cent of such women have white partners (Policy Studies Institute 1997). In her interview with Karpf, Williams cites a parallel US figure of 2 per cent.

To draw this comparison is not to deny that in the US there are asymmetries of power and status which are usually described as class differences. The point is that such asymmetries are strongly associated with racial and ethnic divisions. Nor on the other hand is the intention to deny the existence of racism in Britain, or the bitter conflict between black Britons and (particularly) the British police. Vicious racially motivated attacks take place regularly, a recent example being the Stephen Lawrence affair which received much media attention at the time (February 1997) and subsequently.[3] Nevertheless, class remains much more saliently divisive than race in Britain, and class distinctions operate more independently of race than in the US. A conservative, scandal-ridden but still intact monarchy and aristocracy continues to provide a powerful and visible focal point for the country's traditional class hierarchy.

The contrast between the British and American situations can be illustrated by an adaptation of Haugen's image of the sociolinguistic hierarchy as a layer cake. Haugen's original layer cake represents the respective positions of Finns, Lapps (Sami), Swedish dialect speakers and standard Swedish speakers in the Swedish province of Norrbotten (Haugen 1992: 407). An elaborate, colourful and rather heavy topping on a British layer cake is made up of the monarchy and aristocracy. This is the part of the cake which is most visually striking. This British-baked cake is also rather taller and less broad-based than the American one, narrowing sharply in the layers close to the topping. In both countries, the upper layers are formed by relatively standardised speakers, with successive layers below of rejected and disparaged social groups. As the knife reaches the lower layers, another difference becomes apparent: in Britain, speakers of stigmatised urban dialects constitute the lowest layer of all, while in the United States that position is occupied by AAVE speakers, and perhaps also some Spanish speakers. It is these differences in the way the respective national cakes are assembled, particularly at the top and the bottom, which give rise to the stereotypical perception that America is classless and Britain free of racial animus.

In the following sections, historical, social and political factors underlying these rather different national sociolinguistic structures and different language ideologies will be reviewed. We shall start with contrasting social and political histories of Britain and the United States, moving on to contrasting linguistic histories and linguistic historiographies.

4 An historical perspective

4.1 Britain and Ireland

In general, different sociolinguistic consequences are likely to spring from the contrasting histories of New World immigrant countries and European countries (as briefly discussed by Chambers 1995: 58, and Baugh 1997: 711). Most obviously, since Britain, like other European nation states, has supported an ancient monarchy and aristocracy, the variety spoken at the royal court was recommended as early as the sixteenth century as the 'best' English. Wakelin (1972a: 27) notes a number of clear references which begin to appear only in the sixteenth century to educated, upper-class London and southern speech as a social model[4] (J. Smith 1996: 92). The best known example is taken from *The Arte of English Poesie* (1589; attributed to George Puttenham), where the aspiring poet is recommended to 'take the vsuall speach of the Court, and the shires lying around London within lx miles'. In the seventeenth century similar statements single out the speech of London or that of the universities of Oxford and Cambridge as the best. Conversely, regional dialects receive adverse comment and are regularly used to characterise naive or rustic speakers. Thus, when Edgar in King Lear takes on the guise of a 'base peasant' he switches to Kentish dialect. These evaluations characterise an early stage in the long process of the standardisation of English (see further Milroy and Milroy 1998: 29–36). But in interpreting such data from the early modern period, we need to remember that until the emergence of RP and the British public schools in the 1870s and the subsequent development of an 'accent bar' (Abercrombie 1965), many powerful Englishmen spoke with regional accents (see further below).

The sixteenth-century identification of the best English with the English of the social and geographical territory around London and the ancient Universities and the concomitant stigmatisation of regional dialects continue to this day, as evidenced by the terms 'The Queen's English' and 'Oxford English'. However, massive social and economic changes since the Industrial Revolution (in England conventionally dated 1760–1851; see Corfield 1991: 2) had the effect of revalorising regional dialects as class dialects, as the population shifted from the countryside to the cities.

In Ireland the massive depletion of the rural population by emigration and death in the famine years (1845–49) created a significantly different situation. Furthermore, the only area of large-scale industrialisation in Ireland was Belfast and surrounding areas of Eastern Ulster. Migration from rural areas to Belfast reached its peak rather later than rural–urban migration in England, the city growing from a population of 75,000 in 1841 to 387,000 in 1911 (Foster 1988: 342). The western urban sector was the slowest to expand and, as reported by L. Milroy (1987a), some older working-class inhabitants of West Belfast who were interviewed in 1975 described either their own or their parents' memories of migration. Many maintained ties with rural kin, and consciousness of these rural links is much greater than in English cities where we find a larger and longer established urban proletariat. Commenting on the project of researching Belfast's urban dialect in 1975, a West Belfast priest urged me to remember that 'no matter what kind of airs they try to put on, no one in Ireland is more than a kick in the pants away from the countryside'. This chronology, in conjunction with a detailed account of the dialects of Belfast and its rural hinterland (see further J. Milroy 1992; L. Milroy 1987b), grants insight into the development of a language ideology coloured by the rural–urban migration which accompanies industrialisation. We shall look shortly at the details of the Irish situation, but first let us consider the bigger picture.

Roughly speaking, in nineteenth-century Britain the focus of the standard-language ideology shifted very clearly to spoken English and to class dialects. Crossick (1988) discusses the language of social description which emerged in nineteenth-century England along with the social changes contingent on the Industrial Revolution. Mugglestone (1995) and Bailey (1997) discuss the nineteenth-century preoccupation with linguistic correctness and socially acceptable speech. Writing in 1873, Oliphant uses the discourse of class rather than region or rusticity to criticise [h]-dropping:

> Those whom we call 'self-made men' are much given to this hideous barbarism ... Few things will the English youth find in after-life more profitable than the right use of the aforesaid letter.
> (cited by Milroy and Milroy 1998: 2)

J. Milroy (1983) describes the sociolinguistic history of /h/, the zero variant of which seems to be an ancient marker of nearly all regional dialects of English except the most northerly (currently the isogloss dividing variably from categorically [h]-pronouncing areas seems to be located at Sunderland, Wearside). To this day, [h]-dropping is a particularly salient class marker in British cities; we have suggested elsewhere that it shares with the glottal stop the status of the most stigmatised British urban variant (Milroy et al. 1994).

4.1.1 The history of Received Pronunciation

Honey (1989: 12–37) documents the process by which the elite class accent known as RP developed in Britain in the nineteenth century. He points out that no standard accent was detectable among those who had received a privileged education before 1870; for example the Prime Minister Gladstone, who was a pupil at Eton in the 1820s, retained his Liverpool accent throughout his life.[5] However, from 1870 onwards the English public school system (i.e. a network of high prestige private schools) expanded greatly to provide a boarding-school education which supplied valuable social credentials. Such an education (apparently regardless of intellectual attainment) opened for pupils the doors to those ancient guardians of the standard language, the Universities of Oxford and Cambridge, and to careers such as the Anglican clergy, an Army commission, colonial administration, and teaching. Not only was the accent explicitly taught, but boys entering a school such as Eton or Harrow with regional accents were shamed into conformity. By the end of the nineteenth century, according to Honey, an RP accent proclaimed either that its user was a public school man, or that he had gone to some trouble to acquire an accent which signalled his adherence to the values of the elite for whom it constituted important social capital.

Accent was the most important requirement for an Army officer in the First World War until mass slaughter in the trenches forced the Army to promote men with regional accents. These were the 'temporary gentlemen' referred to by the novelist Pat Barker's public-school educated officer Charles Manning as he listened to a young officer from Salford, near Manchester: 'noting Prior's flattened vowels . . . the amazing thing was how persistent one's awareness of the class distinction was . . . the mind seemed capable of making these minute social assessments in almost any circumstances' (Barker 1993: 240–1). In the Second World War, also, the accent requirement for Army officers was thought still to hold, although much less rigidly than before. For example, the public-school educated actor Dirk Bogarde has claimed that he was promoted from the ranks solely because of his accent.

The acquisition of a highly focused RP accent was clearly a matter of some social and economic importance well into the twentieth century. Certainly its function is not paralleled by any single class specific accent of English in the United States, and at this point RP might, in Smith's terms, be described as a fixed standard rather than a standardised centripetal norm towards which speakers tended. By this he means that RP was effectively a 'fixed collection of prescribed rules, from which any deviation at all is forbidden' (J. Smith 1996: 66). Confident control of RP was an advantage (and often a necessity) in a wide range of professions, indexing not only class but a sound educational background. The accent requirement diffused downwards in employment domains with a 'linguistic market' orientation such as teaching and secretarial work. Famously, Wyld, the Merton Professor of English at Oxford, linked Received Pronunciation (his term was RS for Received Standard) with class and argued for its intrinsic aesthetic advantages:

If it were possible to compare systematically every vowel sound in RS with the corresponding sound in a number of provincial and other dialects, assuming that the comparison could be made, as is only fair, between speakers who possessed equal qualities of voice and the knowledge how to use it, I believe no unbiased listener would hesitate in preferring RS as the most pleasing and sonorous form, and the best suited to the medium of poetry and oratory.

(Wyld 1934: 605)

Wyld defines the social domain of RS extremely narrowly as follows:

If I were asked among what class the 'best' English is most consistently heard at its best, I think, on the whole, I should say among officers of the British Regular Army. The utterance of these men is at once clear-cut and precise, yet free from affectation; at once downright and manly, yet in the highest degree refined and urbane.

(ibid.: 614)

Conversely, Wyld's scathing comments on the levelled accents of English cities ('Modified Standards') highlight the distinction drawn in Section 1 between a levelled variety and an institutionalised class accent defined by a set of prescriptive norms:

It is urged, however, that to introduce provincial sounds into what is intended to be Standard English, addressed to educated people, is distressing and distracting. For the various forms of Modified Standard of towns which reflect class influence, and are of the nature of plain vulgarisms, there is little to be said except in dispraise.

(ibid.: 613–14)

In a paper written in 1951 and published in 1965, Abercrombie writes critically of the class ideology still underlying RP:

It is not easy to put into words how this accent-bar works. Your social life or your career or both may be affected by whether you possess it [RP] or do not ... I believe it is not putting it too strongly to say that in all occupations for which an educated person is required, it is an advantage to speak RP, and it may be a disadvantage not to speak it.

(Abercrombie 1965: 13)

Still later, Edwards (1993: 217) draws attention to a letter written in 1974 to John Stevens, the son of a London docker and a highly competent student teacher. The letter explicitly rejected him as a suitable candidate as a lecturer in a teachers' training college purely because of his spoken language.

Clearly then, there was a considerable incentive for speakers to modify local accents, and in the twentieth century the BBC provided a model for those who wished to do so. Only in the 1960s was the policy of insisting on RP speakers on radio and television abandoned, and at about the same time the requirement of a prescribed and relatively homogeneous accent became relaxed also in the public schools and the Church of England. According to Honey, it was only in 1959 that the first Anglican suffragen bishop with a clearly non-standard accent was appointed. The situation was similar in the Roman Catholic hierarchy, with the difference that traces of educated Scottish or Irish accents were not thought to compromise the speaker's educational status. Foreign accents also were acceptable, certainly in the Roman Catholic hierarchy (as they were in the Universities of Oxford and Cambridge) where English regional accents were not (see also Abercrombie 1965: 14). Given the stringency with which the accent-bar operated against the interests of native speakers of Anglo-English dialects like John Stevens, this detail constitutes a very significant contrast with American attitudes, which stigmatise foreign accents particularly heavily, more so apparently than regional or class accents of American English.

4.1.2 Language ideology and class conflict

So much for the role of RP in the continuing evolution of a class-based language ideology. However, to understand why linguistic discrimination deals particularly severely with the dialects of major industrial cities such as Manchester and Birmingham, even (as is clear from Wyld's comments) the levelled varieties spoken by educated people, we need to consider class relations in Britain, particularly in England. At the beginning of the twentieth century class conflict became much more overtly bitter than before, to the extent that industrial relations were in effect a running class war (Crowley 1989: 209–15). It is truly difficult to exaggerate the bitterness of British class conflict then and subsequently. The English urban proletariat was viewed as a threat to social order and was described in such intemperate and fearful terms as 'Barbarians at our gates', 'a menace to the future', 'emerging like rats from a drain', 'a weird and uncanny people'. Class conflict became institutionalised as the Trade Union movement gathered strength in the early twentieth century. This conflict was particularly evident quite recently during Margaret Thatcher's premiership. One of Thatcher's avowed aims was to destroy the Trade Unions, and at the time of the 1984 miners' strike, she employed quite traditional rhetoric in her reference to trade-unionised British miners as 'the enemy within'.

As language became closely linked with class following the evolution of the RP accent requirement, an intense awareness of class-based linguistic differences thus developed, fed by hostile class relations. In 1924 the author John Galsworthy asserted that 'there is perhaps no greater divide in society than the differences in viva-voce expression' (quoted by Crowley 1989). C. H. Rolph (b. 1901) rose from modest employment as a clerk in a clothing firm to become a London police inspector and writer for the high quality left-wing journal the *New Statesman*. He describes in his memoirs his reaction at the age of seventeen to hearing the voice a young woman whom he had for some time admired from afar:

> ... the period voice of the East End Cockney, ugly and abrasive. Having heard her speak, and registered to my secret rage that she should have been saddled for life with this ugliest of all versions of my native tongue, I immediately lost interest in her as a girl, and now recall her merely as a method of producing unpleasant noises.
>
> (cited by Honey 1989: 35)

Such evidence suggests that in Britain, in the nineteenth century and well into the twentieth century, the kind of visceral reactions described by Woolard are indeed reserved for language varieties which symbolise feared and stigmatised social classes. Modern social-psychological research shows that the ideological discourse developed in the nineteenth century determines to this day the prestige ranking assigned to British accents (Giles and Powesland 1975; Giles and Coupland 1991; Honey 1989: 51–78). Many separate investigations have confirmed that the most stigmatised varieties of English are those of Glasgow, Birmingham, Liverpool (Scouse) and London (Cockney); indeed, we have already encountered disparaging remarks about both Birmingham English and Cockney. Most studies, including one carried out in Ireland (Milroy and McClenaghan 1977), show that RP is ranked highest, followed by the relatively standardised varieties used by educated Scottish, Welsh and Irish speakers; Scottish doctors of medicine appear to be evaluated particularly positively. The rural dialects of Northumberland, Cornwall, Devon or Wiltshire, however impoverished these areas may be, are generally thought to be attractive. Both urban and rural Yorkshire accents are usually positively rated, and viewed as 'trustworthy'.

No comparable split in evaluative reactions to urban and rural dialects is reported in the US (Preston 1996), but such a split can be associated with the apparently characteristically British tendency noted earlier to distinguish between 'genuine' dialects and 'sloppy' or 'degraded' speech. This distinction is drawn not only by laypeople but also by British dialectologists and probably springs from the variously motivated interests of nineteenth-century scholars in legitimising dialects. Rural dialects were often presented as 'pure' or 'genuine' and, insofar as they were unaffected by prescriptive phenomena such as elocution and spelling pronunciation, were thought to offer a clearer view of universal laws of language.[6] Lower in the hierarchy, the ranking of urban accents other than the most stigmatised set varies a little in different parts of the country. However, while such ethnically marked varieties as London Jamaican and Indian-accented English are rated fairly low, they do not occupy the most disparaged position. The following comment of a British child of Caribbean origin, writing in 1981, suggests such a perception of parity between London Jamaican and Cockney, itself an historically disparaged dialect:

> I feel that there is nothing wrong in speaking Creole as there is nothing wrong in speaking Cockney, but I feel that when you go for an interview or you are speaking to someone important you should try to speak as close as possible to Standard English.
>
> (Sebba 1993: 14)

Some of these details of the British linguistic market are reflected in the comments of Stephanie Callister, a Sky News reader:

> Most people find accents acceptable nowadays. I was BBC trained in Belfast for 7 years – they knocked off the rough edges off [sic] my accent. I've never been advised to speak RP ... I think a Celtic accent is far more acceptable than a dodgy London one.
>
> (*Independent on Sunday*, 24 November 1996, p. 7)

Interestingly, the British preference for rural dialects does not hold in Ireland, where the linguistic stock market appears to reflect not only demographic and economic structural differences and a later experience of urbanisation, but responses to the disastrous consequences during and after the Famine years to nineteenth-century rural poverty (see Section 4.1 above). Bilingualism in rural Ireland may also be a factor, as a rural speaker born in the West of Ireland in the first half of this century is likely to be bilingual (see ÓRiágan 1997). Informal evidence such as letters to local newspapers and metapragmatic comments of speakers gathered during fieldwork (Milroy 1987a) suggest that in Ireland rural accents are particularly heavily stigmatised. In Belfast, palatalised variants of /k/ and dental variants of /t/ attracted particularly scathing comments. While these variants are characteristic of Hiberno-English (as opposed to Ulster Scots) rural speech, by 1975 they had all but disappeared from the levelled urban dialect of Belfast.

So far I have attempted to assemble the sociohistorical scaffolding which underpins the specifics of contemporary British standard-language ideology. The elaborate class distinctions of Britain are rather different from those in the industrial north of the United States, with which they might reasonably be compared. According to Rogers and Wilenz, terminology such as 'labor', 'capital', 'working class', 'middle class' became used less and less as Southern black migration to Northern cities began, and successive waves of immigrants formed a new hierarchy, each new wave occupying the lowest position in the layer cake. Evaluatively loaded names for racial categories proliferated: 'slav, teuton, paddy, dago, hunkie, polack' and so forth, and a taxonomy of race developed parallel to the British taxonomy of class. In other words, race rather than class was consolidated as the chief social divisor as America developed into an industrial nation. Nothing shows more clearly the contrast between America and Britain at this crucial period than the manner in which the American analogue to Booth's (1892) classic work on class in London was carried out. Booth surveyed working-class London using a set of simple class taxonomies, half above and half below the poverty line. In 1907 the Russell Sage Foundation carried out a survey of Pittsburgh modelled on Booth, but gave up any attempt to impose his categories, settling instead for a number of 'racial studies'. Only in the 1920s with free immigration at an end were attempts made by the Census Bureau, following the English model, to express inequality in terms of a careful gradation of classes (Rogers and Wilenz 1991: 249; Marwick 1980). In Britain, on the other hand, the widespread race consciousness and conflict which clearly exists seems to be a relatively recent feature of British life, erupting from a relatively latent state only in the years following extensive immigration from former colonies after the Second World War. At this point, many immigrants constituted a new, lower social class (Giddens 1990).

4.1.3 Regional indicators and class markers

Let us conclude this discussion of the sociohistorical underpinnings of Britain's characteristically class-oriented language ideology with a comment on work outside the language ideology tradition which gives some idea of how regional dialect markers became revalorised (in Woolard and Schieffelin's terms) as class markers in the developing industrial cities of the British Isles. The fact that Belfast's period of major expansion was later than that of comparable cities in Great Britain allows us to investigate the linguistic trajectory of the revalorisation process a little more directly than is possible in English cities such as London, Liverpool or Manchester. Drawing on historical, dialecto-logical and contemporary linguistic evidence, Milroy and Milroy (1985) describe the conversion of two rural Ulster Scots regional variants of /a/ and /e/ into sociolinguistic markers of class and other social categories in Belfast. Similarly, L. Milroy (1982) attempts a more general reconstruction of the development of socially structured heterogeneity in the working-class dialect of Belfast. The emergence of structured heterogeneity is one aspect of the ongoing process of dialect levelling; such levelling takes place as new dialects emerge in the wake of contact between incoming migrants from many (some-times dramatically different) dialect areas.

With respect to the contemporary sociolinguistic situation in Britain, the new, levelled variety popularly known as 'Estuary English' has apparently extended both geographically, to oust locally marked varieties in a very large area of South Eastern England, and socially, in that – as pointed out by Neil Ascherson; see (4) above – it is now used by upper-class speakers. This change in British sociolinguistic structure apparently reflects current patterns of mobility following deindustrialisation and the end of the ninety-year monopolisation of the linguistic market by RP. The emergence of an urban dialect in the new town of Milton Keynes is currently being studied in detail by Kerswill and Williams (Kerswill 1996). Negative reactions to Estuary English of the kind documented earlier in this chapter have appeared alongside (and sometimes become conflated with) equally negative reactions more specifically to the dialect of Milton Keynes. Thus, despite the demise of the RP accent requirement, the standard-language ideology in Britain seems still to be focused primarily on class.

4.2 America

4.2.1 Multilingualism and language ideology

American social and linguistic history and linguistic historiography presents even to the casual reader a very different picture from the dominant one in Britain. In the early twentieth century we find both a parallel and a contrast to the British situation. The parallel lies in the widespread but intemperately expressed fear of engulfment. However, the groups which are seen to threaten the social fabric are not an urban proletariat speaking varieties of English rooted in historically established dialects, but immigrants who are speakers of languages other than English. Here is Theodore Roosevelt's frequently cited comment:

> We have room but for one language here and that is the English language, for we intend to see that the crucible turns our people out as Americans, of American nationality, and not as dwellers in a polyglot boarding house.
>
> (quoted by Crawford 1992: 100)

Leibowicz (1985) notes that bilingualism becomes an important issue in the United States at times of particularly heavy immigration. Thus, at the turn of the century and currently, the pendulum has swung away from a movement to cultural pluralism towards Anglo conformity. Commenting on the English Language Amendment (ELA), a measure designed to protect English in the United States, Leibowicz sees the English Only movement as parallel to the early-twentieth-century Americanisation Campaign:

> Most proponents of the ELA embrace an astonishingly pure form of Anglo-conformity. Sadly, it appears that in doing so some supporters also have an affinity for using language issues as a weapon against those who are already the objects of cultural or racial prejudice. Where the Americanizers were afraid of Slavic or Mediterranean hordes, supporters of ELA are afraid of Spanish and the people who

speak it. It is almost as if we had traveled back in time seventy-five years; once again the United States is facing unprecedented numbers of non-English speakers, seemingly unassimilable, and possibly hostile to American ideals and institutions. In ominous echoes of the Americanizers, the supporters of the ELA not only insist that the problem posed by Spanish speakers is unique; they also view this new situation exactly as their predecessors viewed the new immigrants at the turn of the century – as a threat, not as an opportunity or a challenge.

(Leibowicz 1985: 109–10)

While the United States is inherently a multicultural and multilingual nation, the historical roots of an ideological focus on monolingualism and assimilation run as deep as the corresponding British focus on class and rank. In this section I will attempt to pull together several different strands of relevant sociohistorical information, referring freely to Crawford's (1992) comprehensive collection of readings on the official English controversy. I shall consider later the issue of African-American Vernacular English (AAVE), which seems to be underpinned by a rather different but sometimes interacting set of sociohistorical developments.

Before the nineteenth century, national multilingualism and personal bilingualism were generally accepted in the United States as a fact of life, for several compelling reasons. First, there are two colonial languages other than English in the United States: Spanish has been spoken in the South West and Florida for more than 400 years, and antedates English speaking settlements in these areas; French was spoken in the eastern areas formerly held and populated by the French and is still spoken in parts of the North East (particularly Maine) and the South. Second, a large number of indigenous American languages were spoken. Finally the large German population of the United States has a particularly long history of effective mother-tongue maintenance. Consider the remarks of Benjamin Rush, one of the signatories of the Declaration of Independence:

What Pennsylvanian of British or Irish extraction would not prefer German [German speakers] as fellow citizens learned in the arts and sciences than in a state of ignorance of them all? A man who is learned in the dialect of a Mohawk Indian is more fit for a legislator than a man who is ignorant even in the language of the early Greeks. The German language has existed for fifty years in Pennsylvania. It never can be lost while German churches and schools exist in it. A German college will serve to preserve it, but it will preserve it, not in its present state, but in its original force and purity.

(quoted by Heath 1992[1976]: 23)

Evidence abounds of such ready acceptance of multilingualism by members of the Continental Congress, and of the enlightened eighteenth-century priorities expressed by Rush to spread learning regardless of the learner's native tongue. Several different discourses can be distinguished, all of which promoted English as a national language, although it was apparently not yet seen (as it was later by Theodore Roosevelt) as an ideological instrument associated with national loyalty and American values. Benjamin Franklin (1992[1753]) provides an early example of the defensive, fearful and intolerant rhetoric characteristic of the late twentieth-century English Only movement. Complaining about the Pennsylvanian Germans' large numbers ('they come in droves . . . '), their success in maintaining their mother tongue ('few of their children learn English') and their general uncouthness ('those who come hither are generally the most ignorant and stupid Sort of their own nation'), he fears that these apparently unassimilable speakers will create cultural and political anarchy: 'They will soon so outnumber us, that all the advantages we have will not, in My Opinion, be able to preserve our language, and even our government will become precarious' (Franklin 1992[1753]: 19).

Not all advocates of the English language shared Franklin's intolerance of multilingualism in the new nation, some simply wishing to codify an American language as a means of promoting American achievements. John Adams proposed a language academy to promote the English language, to which he declared his allegiance, aware that the British had failed to do so: 'An Academy instituted by the authority of Congress, for correcting, improving, and fixing the English language would strike all the World with Admiration and Great Britain with Envy' (quoted by Heath 1992[1976]: 27). However tempting it might have seemed to compete successfully with Britain in this symbolic way, the idea of a national language academy did not appeal to men who wanted to create a state free of the elitism associated with European monarchies and aristocracies. Hence, a rather different kind of thinking promoted the ideal of a classless form of the English language, known as 'Federal English'. In 1789 Noah Webster argued that it was in the nation's interest to foster the continued divergence of American and British English, and to this end he compiled not only his famous dictionary with its new spelling system, but numerous elementary grammar textbooks.

It seems then that, although English was always the language of government, the original Continental Congress deliberately chose for very good reasons not to adopt an English Only stance. But equally, since multilingualism has always been seen by some as problematic, an English Only movement has been around in various guises since the beginning of the United States:

> While English-only rhetoric is often cloaked in the rationality of language unification, it has frequently been associated either with crackpot linguistic schemes or xenophobia or sometimes both. For many proponents its real purpose has been to oppose the

naturalization of non-English speakers, whether French, Spanish, German, Scandinavian, Central European, African or Asian.

(Barron 1992: 30)

We have already noted that a massive increase in immigration from Europe peaked at the turn of the century, and it is not difficult to see why this and earlier key developments in the US in the nineteenth century cumulatively gave rise to a political climate where multilingualism became viewed less tolerantly and an English Only philosophy was able to surface. The Gold Rush attracted a wave of Chinese immigrants to the west who inspired violent xenophobia. In 1848 the Mexican territories of the South West were annexed. Thus, 75,000 Spanish-speaking people who had been established in the region since the mid-sixteenth century were forced under American rule. The Treaty of Hidalgo was intended to protect their political, civil and religious rights, as well as their culture and language, but a massive increase in the English-speaking population created a Spanish-speaking minority and transformed the Mexican-Spanish-Indian lifestyle of the region. The resultant cultural conflict produced a series of laws which discriminated against Mexican-American language and culture and affects Mexican-Americans to this day. Notably, in 1878 California became the first English Only state; official proceedings were restricted to English and guarantees for Spanish-language publications agreed at the Treaty of Hidalgo were eliminated.

Nor did the Native American population fare any better in the climate of fear, intolerance and repression accompanying the conquest of the West, which turned Native Americans into linguistic minorities subject to severe discrimination. The following is an extract from the 1887 annual report of the commissioner for Indian affairs, J. D. C. Atkins:

Schools should be established which children should be required to attend; their barbarous dialects should be blotted out and the English language substituted . . . the object of greatest solicitude should be to break down the prejudices of tribe among the Indians; to blot out the boundary lines which divide them into distinct nations, and fuse them into one homogeneous mass. Uniformity of language will do this. Nothing else will. . . . It is also believed that teaching an Indian youth in his own barbarous dialect is a positive detriment to him. The first step to be taken towards civilisation, towards teaching the Indians the mischief and folly of continuing in their barbarous practices is to teach them the English language.

(Atkins 1887, cited by Crawford 1992: 48/51)

The cruel policy recommended here was energetically pursued, with the disastrous effect that, after years at school, children could neither find employment and assimilate to the white mainstream nor find a place in their home communities. Thus, in the late nineteenth century not only the Spanish-speaking population of the South West but also the indigenous population of a previously multilingual United States became victims of a severe and subtle form of discrimination which set them up not only for an invidious sense of inferiority about their own language and culture, but for educational failure and disadvantage in the employment market (Crawford 1992: 23).

Atkins' disparagement of Native American languages contrasts sharply with Rush's confident assertion a century earlier that 'a man who is learned in the dialect of a Mohawk Indian is more fit for a legislator than a man who is ignorant even in the language of the early Greeks'. Furthermore, for Rush language was a pragmatic instrument, a means of spreading learning and democratic principles, while by Atkins' time the English language had become an ideological instrument such that American egalitarian, democratic ideals and generally proper and civilised behaviour were seen as related to English monolingualism. Such a change in thinking represented by the Rush/Atkins contrast is current to this day, and it is evident from many of the nineteenth- and twentieth-century readings in Crawford (1992) that Anglo-conformists of all kinds claim this relationship as an ideological cornerstone. Such thinking is also evident in the discourse of present-day English Only activists, who see bilingualism both as a social and personal stigma and as a threat to the cohesion of the state. For example, without attention to the historical, political and demographic differences between Canada and the United States, bilingualism is often cited as the cause rather than the effect of that country's ethnic conflicts and political schisms (Crawford 1992: 3).

4.2.2 Race and language ideology

African-American Vernacular English (AAVE) is probably the most stigma-tised linguistic code of all in the United States. Both negative attitudes to the language – see again (1) above – and the continuing and amply docu-mented discrimination experienced by African Americans, whether or not they are vernacular AAVE speakers, appear to spring from the bitter economic, political and social cleavages created by slavery and subsequently by the Civil War. In her capacity as a jurisprudence scholar, Williams (1991, 1995) provides detailed evidence of quite profound levels of discrimination both from her personal experience and from statistical evidence in domains such as law, education and employment. In America, as in Britain, developments in the nineteenth and early twentieth centuries provide a particularly illuminating perspective on current language ideology.

Rogers and Wilenz (1991) stress the interaction in the American English vocabulary of social description between racial categories and class or rank categories. Delegates to the first Continental Congress followed the British practice of labelling social categories as 'sorts': 'the better sort' (i.e. the rich), 'the middling sort' and 'the lower sort' (i.e. the poor). The fourth category, often obscured as an embarrassment to those creating a model democratic state, was 'Negro slaves', and Jefferson was not unusual in considering Africans to have inferior intellects (King et al. 1997: xx). The Southern slaveholding elite in the pre-Civil War period operated also with a four-tier social system: gentlemen, common planters, white servants and ' "negroes" so rarely free that the slave relation was on most occasions subsumed in the language of race'. Even after emancipation, this pattern did not change, although for a short period into the 1870s African Americans had the vote and elected national representatives. The slaves for their part 'fostered a broad sense of themselves as a people and an exploited class' (Rogers and Wilenz 1991: 242–8). This social structure, driven by an economy founded on slavery, differed substantially from the system which developed in the northern cities in the late nineteenth century following the emergence of market capitalism and the formation of an industrial workforce.

Heavy immigration to northern cities between 1880 and 1920 gave rise to conflicts for dominance between immigrant groups and older elites. Labour conflicts and America's emergence as a capitalist economy par excellence with the associated money-making ethos had the effect of crowding out demo-cratic ideals of equal rights in both north and south. Consequently, the situation for African Americans deteriorated, and in the south the anti-demo-cratic backlash resulted in such statutory procedures as literacy tests. Poll taxes[7] were set in place between 1890 and 1902 to disenfranchise black Southerners (and also very poor whites) and the situation hardly improved until the civil rights movement of the 1960s: 'Abandoned by the North, Southern blacks were powerless after 1877 to halt the tide of reaction which would leave them trapped in chronic poverty, segregation and disenfran-chisement' (Rogers and Wilenz 1991: 257).

4.3 The Afro-British intellectual tradition[8]

Africans in Britain have traditionally occupied a very different position in the social hierarchy, and I shall briefly compare their position in the eight-eenth and nineteenth centuries with that of their American counterparts as outlined above. The most important point of contrast is that, although most of the 15,000–20,000 Africans who lived in Britain at the end of the eight-eenth century worked as either slaves or servants in British households, they did not constitute a separate underclass as in America. For example, Samuel Johnson left his entire estate to his African manservant Francis Barber, to whom he was greatly attached and whom he educated at his own expense at Bishop Stortford school. In fact, Johnson's anti-American sentiments around the time of Independence were expressed as disgust at the hypocrisy of American democratic ideals of which leading exponents were slave-owners: 'How is it that we hear the loudest yelps for liberty among drivers of Negroes?' (quoted by Hibbert 1990: 117).

Some Africans like Barber were educated by their employers, sometimes in elite establishments; Julius Soubise, a well-known dandy and man about town, was sent to Eton by the Duchess of Queensberry. Others, like the political writer Olaudah Equiano (1745–97), received their education aboard the large warships. Certainly by the end of the eighteenth century a sizeable body of Afro-British writing had been produced by a literate and articulate body of men who used their position to campaign against slavery and whose work was used to good effect by abolitionists such as the Irishman Thomas Digges (Edwards and Dabydeen 1991: xi). Equiano's polemic autobiography, surely the foundation slave narrative text, was a bestseller, published in eight English editions and one American edition in his lifetime, and translated into Dutch, German and Russian (ibid.: 54). Africans knew that their English language abilities were crucial in securing and maintaining freedom. The maxim that 'the power of white over black was the power of the English language' (ibid.: xi) is illustrated by two passages from Equiano's autobiography. At these points in the narrative, Equiano had purchased his own freedom and could not legally be reenslaved:

> 'Then,' said he, 'you are now my slave.' I told him my master could not sell me . . . 'and by the law of the land no man has the right to sell me.' And I added, that I had heard a lawyer and others at different times tell my master so. . . . Upon this Captain Doran said I talked too much English.
>
> (Edwards 1989: 58–9)

> On this they made up to me, and were about to handle me; but I told them to be still and keep off; for I had seen those kind of tricks played upon other free blacks and they must not think to serve me so. At this they paused a little, and the one said to the other – it will not do; and the other answered that I talked too good English.
>
> (ibid.: 117)

The existence of a free black, and sometimes literate, population in Britain, the heart of an Empire which itself was the heart of the slave trade, seems to be a consequence less of British altruism than of the inability of the authorities to control and enslave those Africans who found their way to Britain (King et al. 1997). At a time of conflict and inequality in Britain when Scottish Highland clans were being forced from the land to emigration, Lowland Scots dissenters exiled to Barbados as indentured labourers, and a constant threat to civil order was presented by a poverty-stricken rural population, one might surmise that Africans were perceived as a less urgent threat than these other more troublesome disaffected groups. African servants often appear in the paintings of William Hogarth, which chronicle contemporary life, and portraits of Africans by the society portrait painter Thomas Gainsborough hang in London's National Portrait Gallery. The existence of this small but well-connected cultural elite in literary London points up the British/American contrast in the eighteenth century particularly clearly. One prominent member of this elite was George Bridgewater, child prodigy, virtuoso violinist and friend of Beethoven (Beethoven originally dedicated the Kreutzer Sonata to Bridgewater, but after a quarrel changed the dedication; King et al. 1997). The career of the eminent writer Ignatius Sancho (1729–80) is described in detail by King.

Sancho was a substantial literary figure known chiefly for his letters, particularly those addressed to the novelist Laurence Sterne, whose style he imitated. When Sancho's collected letters were published two years after his death in 1780 they created a literary sensation; the prime minister, Lord North, subscribed to the edition, showing clearly the level of Sancho's assimilation to mainstream British culture. In discussions with Thomas Jefferson, English radicals were accustomed to cite Sancho as evidence that Africans were intellectually equal to Europeans. Further evidence of his high standing is his portrait by Thomas Gainsborough.

Sancho first made his reputation under the patronage of the Duke of Montagu, later using the allowance granted to him by the Montagu family to set up a grocer's shop in London. He was happily married for many years to Anne Osborne, a Jamaican woman with whom he had six children. His letters record that he voted in the 1780 parliamentary election for the English radical Charles Fox, having acquired the right to vote as a property owner and shopkeeper in Westminster fifty-two years before the Great Reform Act which provided for universal male suffrage in Britain. When we compare his position with that of Africans in America shortly after the Declaration of Independence, the most significant point perhaps is that he was able to vote at all. Unless we assume the essential irrelevance of race to English domestic politics, it seems odd that at the height of the British slave trade an African was able to cast a vote in a British election.

King's account of Sancho and others in his circle (King et al. 1997) gives some idea of how the social categories of race and rank interacted in eighteenth-century Britain, and of the contrast with American social structure. Although at that time the plight of the British poor was grim, it was by no means the inevitable fate of an African to join them. While many African servants were poor, they certainly did not constitute a distinct, racially defined underclass, as in America. Phillips (1997) notes the existence in Britain (but not in America) of an identifiable black middle class, some members of which became absorbed into fashionable society. Thus, taking into account the condition of the poor in eighteenth-century Britain, we can conclude that the Africans were not institutionally categorised in that country as a subordinate social group.

The American group which most closely parallels this black intellectual elite is probably the trio constituted by Frederick Douglass, Booker T. Washington and W. E. B. Dubois (Meier 1970).[9] Crucially, however, these writers emerged after emancipation only in the late nineteenth century, a full hundred years after Sancho and his contemporaries in Britain. Nor does their work seem to have been accepted into the contemporary American cultural mainstream, as that of Sancho certainly was.

The Afro-British intellectual tradition persisted into the nineteenth century, and I shall comment very briefly on issues relevant to this chapter which emerge from their writings (see further Edwards and Dabydeen 1991). Harriet Jacobs (1815–80, a.k.a Linda Brent) provides very useful testimony, as she experienced conditions in both America as a slave, and in Britain where she was employed as a governess. She is one of several Black American visitors to Britain around the mid-nineteenth century who, despite their experience of both overt and covert racism, found it a haven of security in comparison with America. The distinctions she draws between the two countries supports the general argument that, on the whole, black persons in Britain were not treated as a distinctive underclass but incorporated into an existing rank system:

> The supper [at London's Adelaide Hotel] seemed to me less luxurious than those I had seen in American hotels; but my situation was indescribably more pleasant. For the first time in my life I was in a place where I was treated according to my deportment, without reference to my complexion. ... Ensconced in a pleasant room ... I laid my head on my pillow, for the first time, with the delightful consciousness of pure, unadulterated freedom.
>
> (quoted in Edwards and Dabydeen 1991: 182)

Later in her narrative, Harriet Jacobs comments revealingly on the position of agricultural labourers in Steventon, Berkshire, a small and very poor town:

> I had heard much about the oppression of the poor in Europe. The people I saw around me were, many of them, among the poorest poor. But when I visited them in their little thatched cottages, I felt that the condition of even the meanest and most ignorant among them was vastly superior to the condition of the most favoured slaves in America. They laboured hard; but they were not ordered out to toil when the stars were in the sky, and driven and slashed by an overseer, through heat and cold, till the stars shone out again. Their homes were very humble; but they were protected by law. No insolent patrols could come at the dead of night and flog them at their pleasure. ... There was no law forbidding them to read and write; and if they helped each other in spelling out the Bible they were in no danger of thirty-nine lashes. ... I repeat that the most

ignorant and most destitute of these peasants was a thousand fold
better off than the most pampered American slave.
(quoted in Edwards and Dabydeen 1991: 183)

William Davidson (1786–1820) and Robert Wedderburn (1761–1835) were
both mulatto sons of wealthy Scots in Jamaica – Davidson's father was
Governor of Jamaica, and Wedderburn's was a doctor of medicine who turned
to the more lucrative profession of slave-owning, thus earning his son's
undying contempt. They are of interest here because of their status as mainstream members of the British Radical movement of the late eighteenth and
early nineteenth century and are described as such by McCalman (1989)
without particular reference to their race (see also Edwards and Dabydeen
1991). Indeed, black Londoners had been involved in earlier acts of civil
disorder such as the storming of Newgate jail in 1770 and the Gordon Riots
of 1780. However, these protestors and their supporters, who were chiefly
working-class British radicals, were certainly not defined by race; the poet
William Blake was a member of the mob which stormed Newgate, while on
the other hand Ignatius Sancho wrote a conservative and anti-radical letter
in sanctimonious disapproval of the Gordon Riots. It thus seems fair to suggest
that Afro-British protestors took their place alongside others in the mainstream of the British Radical movement, which eventually succeeded in 1832
in ridding the country of a vicious and reactionary Tory government. Slavery
was abolished in 1833 by the new Whig government as one of a number of
far-reaching electoral and social reforms. As radicals engaged in the struggle
to achieve these reforms, Davidson and his co-conspirators were executed for
their roles as leaders of the 1820 Cato Street Conspiracy (a plot to blow up
the Tory Cabinet during a dinner time meeting at Grosvenor Square).
Wedderburn, a notoriously outspoken radical and colourful polemicist, eventually stood trial for blasphemy.

No account of eminent Afro-British writers could neglect to mention the
intriguing J. J. Thomas (1840–89), an accomplished linguist, and Trinidad's
best known nineteenth-century intellectual. In 1869 he published *Theory and
Practice of Creole Grammar* (reprinted as Thomas 1989) and in 1888 visited
the British Museum in London to research for an enlarged second edition.
Instead, however, he published a different book, *Froudacity* (Thomas 1889),
in response to J. A. Froude's *The English in the West Indies*. Froude held the
powerful position of Regius Professor of Modern History at the University of
Oxford, and his book was marred by British chauvinism, by ignorance of the
people he described and by some unpleasant examples of Victorian racism.
Froudacity was proclaimed as an historically sound, polished and elegant piece
of work which succeeded moreover in discrediting Froude's scholarship (see
further Edwards and Dabydeen 1991: 224–35).

The different social histories of African communities in Britain and America partly explains why the extremely low status of AAVE is not paralleled

in British Black English; recall that while Jamaican creole is stigmatised it is not one of the most consistently disparaged varieties. Distasteful public disparagement of AAVE on the other hand is common, and is often openly racist; for example, an article has appeared in a scholarly journal entitled 'The shuffling speech of slavery Black English' (Morse 1973). Consider also the following comment on AAVE by the journalist John Simon:

> As for 'I be', 'you be', 'he be', etc. which should give us all the heebie-jeebies, these may indeed be comprehensible, but they go against all accepted classical and modern grammars and are the product not of a language with roots in history but of ignorance of how language works.
>
> (quoted by Pinker 1994: 385)

The closest British parallel to such unpleasant rhetoric is to be found not with respect to British Black English but in comments by columnists such as Peter Tory (see p. 181 above) on working-class or Milton Keynes English.

5 Standard English and the dialects in America

Recall that standard languages in colonial settings are something very different from standard languages in Europe, where aristocratic models and deeply entrenched social-class differences favour the development of institutionally prescribed standards and the emergence of class rather than ethnicity as the chief basis of social and political cleavage. How then does this affect the relation between language and class and class-oriented discrimination in the United States? Labov's description of New York City (and by association its accent) as 'a sink of negative prestige' (Labov 1966) suggests that we need to address this question.

Preston (1996) makes some relevant comments on the popular belief in a neutral variety of spoken American English which can be identified as 'the best English'. Demonstrating the lack of agreement amongst professional linguists on the locus of such a variety, he notes that even influential text-book writers do little more than present their personal beliefs (which are not shared even by all linguists) as linguistic fact. Certainly there does not exist in America a focused and identifiable class accent corresponding to Received Pronunciation in Britain, although some might argue that network American and the famous Brahmin accent of Boston are candidate varieties (Wolfram 1991). As noted earlier, network American differs from RP in a number of respects, chiefly in being an unmarked, mainstream accent, from which localised features have been eradicated, and (despite its name) in its lack of institutional support. Boston's Brahmin accent on the other hand has a sharp class distribution, but has never had the institutional support accorded to RP, or its nationwide geographical distribution. Nor has it been associated with the operation of a nationwide 'accent-bar' (see further below).

Preston (1996) tackles the question of where the best English is spoken by examining Americans' perceptions of distinctive speech areas in the US and of the 'pleasantness' and 'correctness' of the varieties thus identified. An important and very general perception of all Preston's informants is the unique status of the American South as a distinct linguistic and cultural area. Revealingly, one Carolina informant represented linguistic divisions in terms of the Civil War: south of a diagonal line running across the United States from North East to South West 'southerners' are to be found; elsewhere reside 'damn yankees'. A Michigan informant identified much the same area, but labelled it as 'Southern' with the pejorative description 'hill-billy' in parentheses. The Great Lakes area was marked off with the legend 'midwestern English', described parenthetically as 'normal'.

While judgements such as this provide evidence of widely held perceptions of a neutral, levelled variety in the Northern Midwest, there was little agreement on a single locus of the most correct variety. For example, Southerners identified the Boston area of New England (presumably they had in mind the Brahmin accent) while Michigan speakers identified their own variety as the most correct. However, agreement on the *least correct* variety was much more striking; judges from the South, Michigan and Indiana all agreed that this might be found in an area of the South (the extent of which varied somewhat between judges) and New York City. We have seen that the sociohistorical scaffolding which supports such beliefs is extremely culture specific and that British and American beliefs about language are consequently very different. It seems reasonable to suggest that the beliefs reported to Preston derive from the major historical divisions outlined in Section 4.2, notably the Civil War conflict between (what is perceived to be) an urban, progressive north and a rural, conservative, slave-owning south. The status of New York City as the first destination of the poorest immigrants may well be the source of its negative image.

The judgements of Preston's informants reveal beliefs quite different from those current in Britain. In America the urban dialects of industrial cities generally do not seem to be as stigmatised as the speech of the South, which is associated not only with an historic and divisive conflict but with rural poverty. As we have seen, British attitudes to urban industrial accents are particularly negative and are rooted in class consciousness.

6 Conclusion

I have attempted in this chapter to suggest that the term 'standard English' means something quite different in Britain and the United States, and to contrast national-language ideologies as instantiated in language policies and language discrimination against particular social groups. The sociohistorical scaffolding of these contrasting ideologies has been examined, along with British and American linguistic historiographies.

While the language-standardisation process in Britain is historically associated with the existence of a monarchy which has provided a focal point for a strong class system, early American English developed in a more egalitarian context. Thus, a candidate spoken American standard such as network American is a levelled *Gemeinsprache*, a focused mainstream dialect lacking institutional support, while in Britain Received Pronunciation is quite differently embedded in social structure. Specifically, the norms of RP have been quite explicitly prescribed, the accent is historically associated with upperclass and upper-middle-class speakers and has enjoyed (in the past at least) strong institutional support.

In the United States, on the other hand, rather distinctive language ideologies took shape under the pressure of quite different social and historical developments. The bitter divisions created by slavery and the Civil War shaped a language ideology focused on racial discrimination rather than on the class warfare which erupted particularly fiercely in Britain in the early years of the twentieth century and remained evident during the tenure of successive Conservative governments between 1979 and 1997. In the United States, the need to accommodate large numbers of non-English speakers, from both long-established communities (such as Spanish speakers in the South West) and from successive waves of immigrants gave rise early in the history of the nation to policies and attitudes which discriminated against these speakers. These policies and attitudes are to this day embodied in a version of the standard-language ideology which is negatively disposed to speakers of languages other than English – again an ideology quite different from that characteristic of Britain.

Scholarly approaches to language discrimination – as opposed to political ideologies and laypeople's attitudes – emerge also as quite different in Britain and the United States. Furthermore, the work of historians of language is quite different in the two countries, a striking point being the evident class consciousness and elitism of British scholars. A clear example is Henry Cecil Wyld (1920, 1934), writing at the height of RP's hegemony. Wyld's views on the intrinsic functional and aesthetic superiority of RP and his taxonomy of various kinds of regional and modified standard in Britain revealed the class ideologies underlying his scholarly work particularly clearly. Abercrombie's sensitivity to the parallels between class discrimination, race discrimination and linguistic ideology provide us with a particularly relevant concluding comment:

> In England standard English speakers are divided by an 'accent-bar', on one side of which is RP, and on the other side all the other accents. And very often the first judgment amade on a stranger's speech is the answer to the question: which side of the accent-bar

is he? . . . The accent-bar is like the colour bar – to many people on the right side of the bar it appears eminently reasonable.

(1965: 13–14)

We can only add that what is reasonable and common-sensical for one community constitutes baffling and far from common-sense behaviour for another. It is as difficult for scholars as for laypeople to identify the numerous effects of historically well-established language ideologies upon their thinking.

Acknowledgements

Thanks to Rosina Lippi-Green for useful discussion of many of the issues raised here and to Jim Milroy, John Rickford, Theresa Satterfield and Kathryn Woolard for comments on an earlier draft.

Notes

1   In reality many high profile American broadcasters speak with regional accents. For example, Walter Kronkite's successor as CBS newsreader is the audibly Texan accented Dan Rather.
2   I am indebted to Keith Walters for his discussion of these extracts (Walters 1996).
3   Stephen Lawrence, a middle-class black teenager, was murdered by racist white youths. The police were alleged to have been slow in investigating the murder and, for lack of evidence, no one was convicted although the identity of the killers was widely known (or at least strongly suspected). In February 1997 there was a strong judicial, public and media reaction in support of the Lawrence family. At the time of writing (1997) Stephen's family continue to pursue his alleged murderers through the courts.
4   The association between the aristocracy and the emergent spoken prestige form documented by Puttenham and others needs to be interpreted with care. From the time of the emergence of the so-called Chancery Standard in the 15th century – effectively a levelled variety used by medieval lawyers – upper-class forms have been replaced by middle-class innovations as spoken and written Standard English has evolved.
5   At that time in Liverpool a Lancashire dialect was spoken, antedating mass Irish migration to Liverpool and subsequent emergence of the modern Anglo-Irish contact dialect known as 'Scouse'.
This is what Ellis has to say:

> By 'natural' as distinguished from 'educated' English pronunciation is meant a pronunciation which has been handed down historically, or has changed organically, without the interference of orthoepists, classical theorists, literary fancies, fashionable heresies and so forth, in short untamed English everywhere, from the lowest vulgarity . . . to the mere provinciality.
>
> (Ellis 1869–89, Part IV, pp.1243–4)

This view is quite parallel to Labov's insistence a hundred years later that the vernacular is the most reliable source of information on language structure, free from the effects of hypercorrection. See also Crowley (1989: 141) for a discussion of nineteenth-century and early-twentieth-century discourses on dialects.

7   Again we find a telling parallel with the way poll taxes were used in Britain. In 1988 Margaret Thatcher attempted to set in place a poll-tax system which had the effect of disenfranchising the urban poor of both migrant and indigenous origin.

8   I am indebted to Richard Milroy for assistance in locating material used to research this section.

9   I am indebted to Theresa Satterfield for providing me with this reference.

THE NAMES OF US ENGLISH: VALLEY GIRL, COWBOY, YANKEE, NORMAL, NASAL AND IGNORANT

Laura C. Hartley and Dennis R. Preston

1 Standard US English

A commonplace in United States (hereafter US) linguistics is that every region supports its own standard; none is the locus (or source) of *the* standard. Historically that is a fair assessment, for no long-term centre of culture, economy and government has dominated in the US. Falk puts it this way:

> In the United States there is no one regional dialect that serves as the model. What is considered standard English in New York City would not be considered standard in Forth Worth, Texas. Each region of the country has its own standard.
>
> (Falk 1978: 289)

It is doubtful, however, that non-linguists in the US believe that there is no region which is more (or less) standard than others. Falk's position is a confusion of a sophisticated linguistic relativism, deriving from well-intentioned attempts to debunk notions of so-called primitive and deficient linguistic systems, with what she believes to be popular perception. The latter, of course, is the point which deserves investigation, for, at least in the US, it is not linguists who define language standards.

Other introductory texts propose a mysterious, nonexistent variety:

> SAE [Standard American English] is an idealization. Nobody speaks this dialect; and if somebody did, we wouldn't know it because SAE is not defined precisely. Several years ago there actually was an entire conference devoted to one subject: a precise definition of SAE. This convocation of scholars did not succeed in satisfying everyone as to what SAE should be. The best hint we can give you is to listen

to national broadcasters (though nowadays some of these people may speak a regional dialect).

(Fromkin and Rodman 1983: 251)

From this it is clear that Fromkin and Rodman contrast the standard with regional varieties, and they earlier show that they find some regional varieties distinctly non-standard:

> It is true that many words which are monosyllabic in Standard American are disyllabic in the Southern dialect: the word *right*, pronounced as [rayt] in the Midwest, New England, and the Middle Atlantic states and in British English, is pronounced [rayt] in many parts of the South. [N.B.: This pronunciation is, in fact, not disyllabic. Why a centering glide, not there in most varieties of Southern speech anyway, produces two syllables and a rising one does not is a mystery to us.]
>
> (ibid.: 249)

Fromkin and Rodman here come much closer to a popular description of a standard as their own prejudices peek through. SAE exists in the Midwest, New England and the Middle Atlantic states (and even British English is sanctioned), but the South does something else – by implication, not standard. Falk would correctly accuse Fromkin and Rodman of linguistic prejudice, but a legitimate search for the source and locus of SAE will have to consider just such prejudices. What non-linguists believe constitutes precisely that cognitive reality which needs to be described – one which takes speech community attitudes and perceptions into account.

Fromkin and Rodman err by stating personal folk beliefs cloaked in the mantle of linguistic expertise. If they want to report what attitudes people hold about varieties, they should make it clear either that they have that information from research or that they cite it as their own belief (or what they suspect about others' beliefs). To do otherwise confuses scientific reporting with linguistic prejudices. At least Langacker appears to be citing what he believes many people may believe (albeit without documentation) when he observes the following:

> British English enjoys special favor in the eyes of many Americans. Boston English is considered by many people to be more prestigious than Southern speech or Brooklynese.
>
> (Langacker 1973: 55)

This must be true for Fromkin and Rodman, for they believe that some Southern vowels, despite their use by educated and uneducated speakers alike, are not standard.

208

More recent introductions to general linguistics do not contain such glaring errors as those cited from Fromkin and Rodman, but, like Falk, they continue to exhibit the linguist's laudable but unfortunately minority relativistic attitude towards the question of standardness and geographical variety. In O'Grady et al. (1993), for example, one is told the following:

> While sociolects are defined by linguistic differences associated with definable social groups in a single geographical area, regional dialects are associated with the linguistic traits shared by social groups in a single geographical area.
>
> (O'Grady et al.: 426)

We might ignore the linguistic inaccuracy here, for, as Trudgill (1995: 29) points out, the general rule of regional distribution is that the lower the social status, the greater the regional difference, but it is difficult to excuse the continuing linguistic ignoring of the fact that social ('standard', 'correctness') issues of language for non-linguists have clear geographical correlates. Again, linguists are simply not making clear the distinction between their professional attitude and the prevailing popular one. Although one might not criticise geologists, chemists or astronomers, for example, for failing to make folk beliefs about their areas of study explicit, perhaps even in introductory texts, in a 'human science' like linguistics, it seems far less reasonable to exclude a careful explication of the tension between the scientific and folk views.

Language attitude studies have explored affective dimensions of diversity, beginning by sampling attitudes towards different languages (Lambert et al. 1960) and moving on to different varieties of the same language (see, for example, Tucker and Lambert 1969). Giles and associates (summarised in Ryan and Giles 1982) have investigated a large number of reactions (to taped voices) and have suggested a general pattern: speakers of regional varieties (where that implies non-standardness) find speakers of their own varieties warm, friendly, honest, sympathetic and trustworthy, but often slow, unintelligent and plodding; they regard speakers of the standard as cold, dishonest and unsympathetic, but quick, intelligent and ambitious. To the extent that listeners find their own varieties less prestigious, they suffer from what Labov (1966) called 'linguistic insecurity'. Some of this insecurity doubtless has its source in speakers' awareness of the fact that the local variety will not serve extra-regionally. That is, it will not convince outside listeners that the intelligence, education and authority of the speaker or writer are high, and it will not, therefore, inspire confidence in the content of some messages. There are exceptions: information of the sort most likely to be delivered in a local or non-standard variety (street-wise facts, farming information, sports calls and expressions, hunting and fishing facts) might, indeed, be seen as more trustworthy if delivered in a non-standard variety, but the evaluation of other ('intellectual') characteristics of the speaker would continue to be low.

Language-attitude studies confirm, then, that regional varieties are not all equal, even when only phonological features are contrasted (that is, when lexicon and grammar are not variables). Such findings help establish the basis for another perspective on varieties, an essential one for languages with no clear-cut standard model – an account of what speakers of various regions (and classes and sexes and ethnic groups and ages and so on) believe about linguistic variety. Language-attitude surveys hope to avoid the observer's paradox (Labov 1972), which here includes the effect awareness has on respondents' reactions to, as well as on their performances of, language. The general approach taken here – generally 'folk linguistics', more specifically 'perceptual dialectology' – seeks to discover, on the other hand, the overt categories and definitions speakers have of such linguistic matters.[1]

2 The perception of regional variety

Folk dialectology first intrigued Europeans, who sought the degree of differ-ence which respondents felt existed between their home areas and nearby ones (see, for example, Rensink 1955). That work has had a continuing influ-ence in Europe (see, for example, Daan and Blok 1970; Kremer 1984) and in Japan (see, for example, Grootaers 1959).

Preston began looking at such data from a purely dialectological point of view (see, for example, Preston 1982) by asking respondents to draw and label US speech areas on a relatively blank map. He soon found, however, inspired partly by the labels which are the focus of this paper, that there was more pre-scription than description in such folk accounts and began seeking data other than respondent beliefs about where different varieties exist. Several of these approaches and findings are summarised here.

If, for example, speakers are presented with the task of identifying the areas of the US where the most 'correct' English is spoken, how will they respond? If they are all relativists like Falk, they will simply indicate that the task cannot be done, claiming that each area supports a standard. If, however, as Fromkin and Rodman show and Langacker claims, they have regional linguistic prejudices, they will readily rank areas of the country for language correctness. If Langacker is right, there should also emerge some preference for 'British' speech (however that may be represented) and a preference for Boston over Brooklyn and the South; if Fromkin and Rodman's prejudices are widely represented, a preference for Eastern and Midwestern speech over Southern should also emerge.

Additionally, if the studies by Giles and associates apply to US varieties, one might also find that speakers who consider their accents to be 'non-standard' (i.e. who suffer from linguistic insecurity) will rank their home areas lower for correctness. On the other hand, since Giles and his associates found that there was a decided preference for the local area along affective dimen-sions, one should find such a preference for the local area in a ranking task

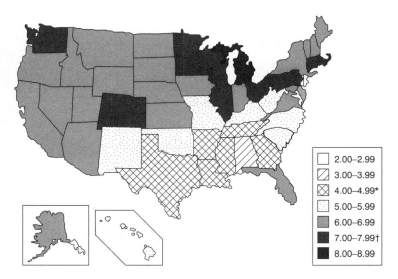

Figure 9.1 Mean scores for language 'correctness' by MI respondents for US English (on a scale of 1 to 10: 1 = least correct and 10 = most correct)

Note: * New York City
      † Washington, DC

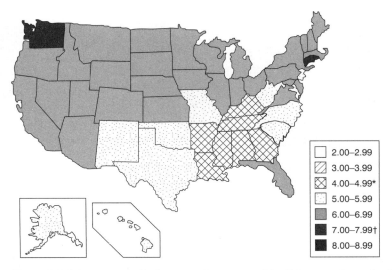

Figure 9.2 Mean scores for language 'correctness' by IN respondents for US English (scale as in Figure 9.1)

Note: * New York City
      † Washington, DC

211

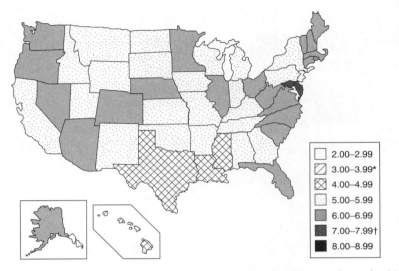

Figure 9.3 Mean scores for language 'correctness' by S respondents for US English (scale as in Figure 9.1)

Note: * New York City
     † Washington, DC

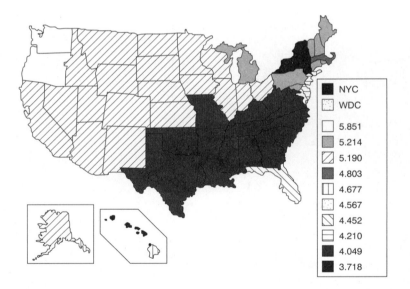

Figure 9.4 Regions ranked for language 'correctness' by OR respondents (based on a scale of 1 to 7; 1 = least correct and 7 = most correct)

Note: * New York City
     † Washington, DC

which asks where the most 'pleasant' variety is spoken. Figures 9.1 to 9.8 summarise findings from 'correct' and 'pleasant' ratings of US speech areas by respondents from the four areas which will be the focus of this chapter. The following abbreviations are used: MI for southeastern Michigan, IN for southern Indiana, S for the South, and OR for Oregon.[2]

These folk evaluations of US English mirror the finding from many language attitude studies that there are two sorts of admired language. The first is the standard, prescribed, educated variety; the second, the often proscribed but cosy home style of one's own area (see, for example, Ryan et al. 1982: 8). A linguistically secure region like MI assigns evaluations as shown in Figure 9.1. For MI residents, the best English is spoken in the Great Lakes area, most specifically in MI itself; the worst in the South – the farther south and the more central, the worse.

Figure 9.2 shows correct ratings from IN, an area of considerably less linguistic security, due, no doubt, to its proximity to the prejudiced-against US South. Local speech is not bad, but it is not so uniquely correct as the linguistically secure MI raters believe theirs is. IN speakers see themselves as part of a huge, apparently undifferentiated, more-or-less correct northern and western area of the entire country. Doubtless southern IN speakers are eager to cut themselves off from the nearby stigmatised South, showing that the traditional dividing line of the Ohio River is still powerful for the folk, in spite of the minor role it plays in traditional dialect studies.

The Southern map of correctness (Figure 9.3), however, does not reveal an unequivocal pattern of linguistic insecurity. Some Southerners do not find themselves any less well-spoken than the southern IN respondents did, giving SC, NC, VA and WV ratings (see Appendix for full forms of abbreviated state names) in the 6.00–6.99 range and, even though 'homeland' parts of the South are rated low (5.00–5.99), these ratings are assigned to many 'non-southern' parts of the country. New York City (NYC) and NJ are the only big Northern losers, but such ratings are ubiquitous. The interesting 4.00–4.99 incorrectness zone seen here is the 'western' South – MS, LA and TX. In summary, although their linguistic insecurity is supported by the low home-area scores, Southerners 'deflect' some of this 'correctness insecurity' by assigning similar low scores to a large area (including areas outside the South) and by finding an even 'worse' South (the western areas).

Finally, as Figure 9.4[4] shows, OR is only very slightly different from MI, allowing only neighbouring WA to bask in the relatively unique glory of its 'correctness'.

'Pleasantness' ratings often reverse these patterns. Figure 9.6 shows that the linguistically insecure IN respondents rate their own territory as uniquely pleasant, just as the MI raters did theirs for correctness. They do not, however, rate southern states any lower for pleasantness than they do northern states, a hint that, in their heart of hearts, they know that there is southernness on their tongues. In contrast, Figure 9.5 shows that the linguistically secure MI

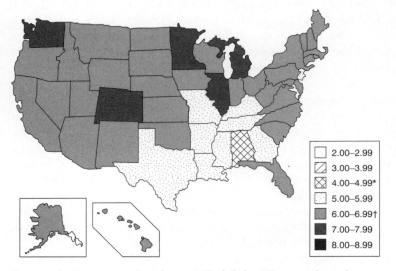

Figure 9.5 Mean scores for 'pleasant' English by MI respondents (ratings as in Figure 9.1)

Note: * New York City
      † Washington, DC

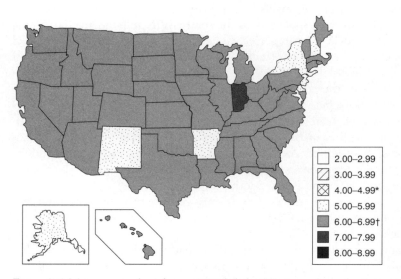

Figure 9.6 Mean scores for 'pleasant' English by IN respondents (ratings as in Figure 9.1)

Note: * New York City
      † Washington, DC

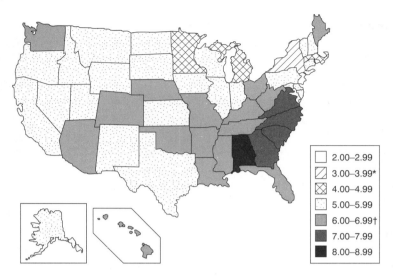

Figure 9.7 Mean scores for 'pleasant' English by S respondents (ratings as in Figure 9.1)

Note: * New York City
    † Washington, DC

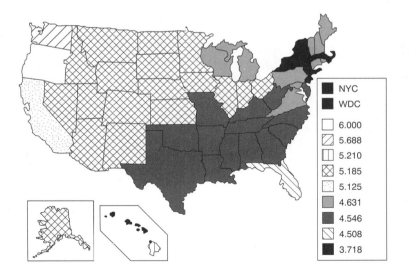

Figure 9.8 Ratings for 'pleasant' English by OR respondents (ratings as in Figure 9.4)

Note: * New York City
    † Washington, DC

raters give nearby IL and MN (and distant CO and WA) as high scores for pleasantness as they give the local area, but the South remains bad – AL downright awful. Southern raters (Figure 9.7) rate the entire Southeast very high, but, like the IN raters, elevate AL (the site where the ratings were done) to 8.00–8.99, a level paralleled only by MI's evaluation of its own correctness. Southern 'unpleasantness' ratings are harsh. The only 2.00–2.99 rating in any of these studies shows up for NJ; NYC and even NY are given a 3.00–3.99; MA, MI and MN are assigned 4.00–4.99, a rating reserved by MI raters for only the 'worst' Southern state (AL) and IN raters for only NYC in the same task. OR, nearly uniquely correct, is in fact uniquely pleasant (Figure 9.8), although WA is seen to be nearly as pleasant. This pattern is somewhat different from that of other linguistically secure areas (e.g. MI).

These ratings provide confirmation of the general patterns of linguistic security and insecurity outlined above. Areas with greater insecurity focus on regional solidarity (as expressed in 'pleasantness') to express local identity. Areas with considerable security do not use local speech to express such identity, for their 'uniqueness' is already taken up in the expression of status rather than solidarity matters. Only the OR ratings (where nearly unique local high assessments for both 'correctness' and 'pleasantness' emerge) break this pattern somewhat, suggesting, perhaps, that these categories are less salient in western areas of the US (Hartley 1996).

The evaluative influences which seem to guide these tasks are further confirmed when a rather different approach to folk perception is used. These same respondents were asked to characterise the degree of difference (e.g. Grootaers 1959) or similarity (e.g. Rensink 1955) between home and nearby areas, and no voice stimuli were provided. Each rated the fifty states – and New York City (NYC) and Washington, DC (WDC) – for their degree of difference from the home site on the following scale: 1 = same, 2 = a little different, 3 = different, 4 = unintelligibly different.

Figures 9.9 to 9.12 show that most raters seem to be operating in general on their perceptions of pleasantness (Figures 9.5 to 9.8) rather than on those of correctness (Figures 9.1 to 9.4) in the assignment of '1' – 'the same'. Although IN respondents rate IL and OH 'the same', theirs is still an extremely local area. MI raters, on the other hand, see exact similarity between themselves and a relatively large upper midwestern or 'Great Lakes' area.

IN raters treat the South, however, from a correctness rather than pleasantness perspective. Figure 9.6 shows that they do not distinguish between it and much of the West and Midwest for 'pleasantness', while Figure 9.2 shows that the South is distinct for its incorrectness and is two degrees different in the task shown in Figure 9.10. Since MI raters find the South distinct on both pleasant and correct dimensions, it is not possible to tell which caricature is at work in Figure 9.9, for they still find it distinct. Additionally, they locate their only '4' ratings ('unintelligibly different') in the core South,

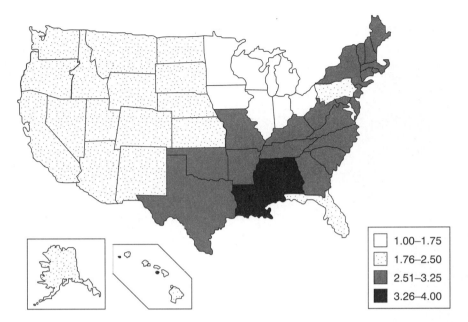

Figure 9.9 Degree of difference between MI (the home area) and the fifty states, NYC and WDC (scores converted to means ranges)

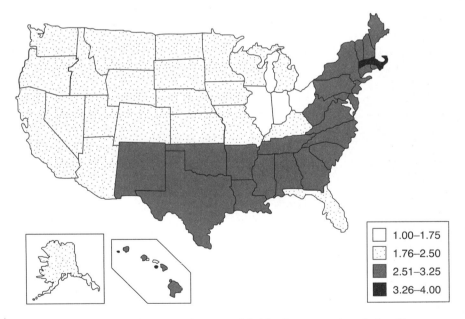

Figure 9.10 Degree of difference between IN (the home area) and the fifty states, NYC and WDC (scores converted to means ranges)

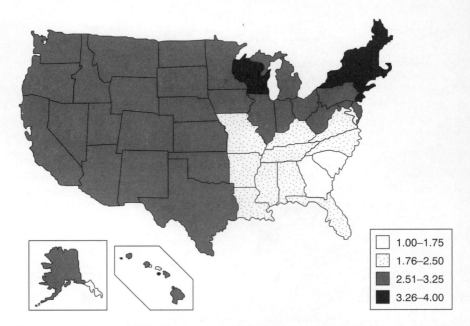

Figure 9.11 Degree of difference between S (the home area) and the fifty states, NYC and WDC (scores converted to means ranges)

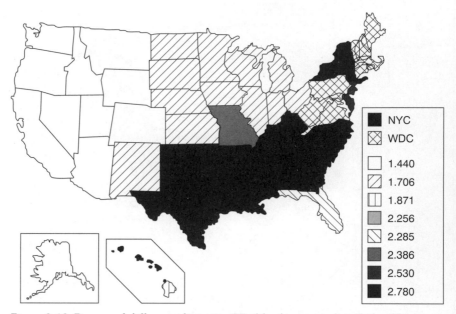

Figure 9.12 Degree of difference between OR (the home area) and the fifty states, NYC and WDC (scale as in Figures 9.9 to 9.11; ratings as in Figure 9.4)

but, since AL was singled out for special treatment on both the correct and pleasant tasks by MI raters, it is not possible to tell which protocol is at work here either.

Perhaps most interesting is the fact that IN raters, who found MA no different from IN in correctness (Figure 9.2) and only one step down in pleasantness (Figure 9.6), find only it unintelligibly different. The cluster of poorly rated Northeastern states on the pleasantness dimension, however, is the clue for this IN response. There is perhaps further dislike (a sort of *covert prestige*) on the part of the linguistically insecure against those varieties which may be felt to be 'excessively' correct, and that is a frequent caricature of New England speech. Since it is safe to assume that southern IN linguistic insecurity has its source in its association with the South, it is perhaps enough for those respondents to indicate that the South is simply 'different'.

For southern IN, the more linguistically insecure area, both extreme degree of difference categories are reflections of pleasantness judgements. For the more linguistically secure respondents from MI, the pleasantness dimension is most important for exact similarity, but pleasantness and correctness converge in the characterisation of unintelligible difference.

Figure 9.11, the Southern raters' map of degree of difference, although more like the IN map in one important way, is different from the two earlier difference maps in a number of ways. Like IN raters, Southerners find the heart of major difference in the Northeast, but they expand the zone of unintelligibility to include the entire area, and they expand it all the way west to WI (although MI just misses being included). Like MI raters, therefore, their zone of unintelligibility is larger, suggesting that the 'Midland' position of IN is less likely to produce such radical evaluations.

Again like IN raters, the Southerners have their own core zone of similarity (GA and SC, oddly since many are from AL), but, unlike IN or MI raters, they expand it to a secondary 'local' zone. Like many of the maps from every region and for every task, it excludes LA and TX; however, unlike nearly all the generalisations about the South shown so far, it includes FL, MO and AR. For these Southern raters, the large Western zone of states is all lumped together, but it is a '3', not a '2' as it was in the IN and MI surveys. The two-level differentiation within the South seems to have promoted more distinctive ratings of all non-southern areas – the West, North and Northeast.

The OR raters (Figure 9.12) are the odd ones out in this survey so far. Although they exhibit relatively 'exclusivist' characterisations of their own 'correctness' and 'pleasantness', they seem to be able to operate on a more 'objective' level when asked to rate 'degree of difference'. As Figure 9.12 shows, they rate themselves together with a large western group of states. Hartley (1996) suggests that the historical knowledge of the various immigrant streams to the West helps explain this apparently contradictory rating.

The last task in this review of perceptual findings from four areas suggests that conclusive research on attitudes towards varieties cannot be done without knowledge of what regions exist for the respondents. If we play a sample of a South Midland voice for respondents who judge it to be thus, and so on any variety of attitudinal measures, we are not completely justified in saying that those attitudinal responses are the respondents' attitudes towards a South Midland voice. Why not?

First, unless we ask (and surprisingly few studies of language attitude have), we do not know where the respondents believe the voice is from. A report might accurately state that respondents had certain attitudes towards a South Midland voice sample, but the respondents might have gone home believing that they had heard an Inland Northern one.

Second, we do not really know where our respondents believe voices *can* be from, for we do not know their taxonomies of regional speech areas, in which such professionally determined areas as Inland Northern, South Midland and the like may not exist. That would be a trivial objection if folk taxonomies of speech regions simply had different names from those assigned by professional dialectologists.

Figures 9.13 to 9.16 show the results of research which addresses this problem of taxonomy. Respondents from the areas discussed here outlined and labelled speech regions of the United States. Computer-assisted digitisation of the hand-drawn maps allowed a quantitative generalisation of where the respondents felt significant differences exist (Preston and Howe 1987) in Figures 9.13 and 9.14. A hand-count assessment of areas included in the drawings (introduced in Preston 1982 and refined in Hartley 1996) was used to produce Figures 9.15 and 9.16.

It should come as no surprise that the South is the most salient area for all groups of raters (i.e. the area outlined most frequently). On the other hand, the unique correctness self-assessment by MI raters, the unique pleasantness self-assessment by IN speakers and the nearly unique assessment on both measures by OR raters did not cause any of these states to be singled out as a separate dialect area (as, for example, Texas clearly is). On the other hand, Southerners' distinctions within the South, seen in all the above tasks, are also evident here.

These hand-drawn map data show that the study of attitudes to regional speech requires knowledge not only of evaluative caricatures of dialects but also of what possible areas for classification lie behind such caricatures (a suggestion repeatedly urged on the field; see, for example, Preston 1989: 3). Basing research on scholarly intuitions about folk categories or on the results of scientific dialectology alone may result in serious misinterpretations.

These several approaches show that affective dimensions, at least in US English, are notions which, for non-linguists, have geographical significance. Though it is not easy to arrive at the folk perception of such concepts, it is important to seek it out, since it represents a set of beliefs both strongly held and highly influential in the linguistic life of speech communities. As with other folk linguistic matters, such a multidimensional approach to what are

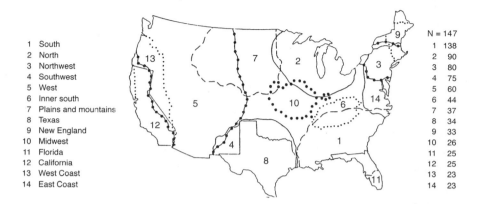

		N = 147
1	South	1 138
2	North	2 90
3	Northwest	3 80
4	Southwest	4 75
5	West	5 60
6	Inner south	6 44
7	Plains and mountains	7 37
8	Texas	8 34
9	New England	9 33
10	Midwest	10 26
11	Florida	11 25
12	California	12 25
13	West Coast	13 23
14	East Coast	14 23

Figure 9.13 Computer-assisted generalisations of hand-drawn maps showing where MI respondents believe speech regions to exist in the US

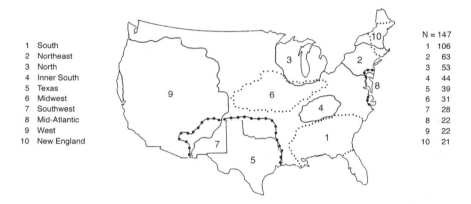

		N = 147
1	South	1 106
2	Northeast	2 63
3	North	3 53
4	Inner South	4 44
5	Texas	5 39
6	Midwest	6 31
7	Southwest	7 28
8	Mid-Atlantic	8 22
9	West	9 22
10	New England	10 21

Figure 9.14 Computer-assisted generalisations of hand-drawn maps showing where IN respondents believe speech regions to exist in the US

ultimately folk questions provides a surer consideration of the limited data gathered in language-attitude surveys and from anecdotal and participant observer information. It serves, moreover, to help build a more complete and accurate picture of the regard for language use and variety within a speech community, providing questions about such issues as language standards with answers from the communities themselves.

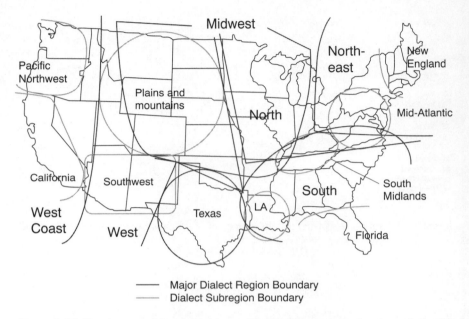

— Major Dialect Region Boundary
— Dialect Subregion Boundary

Figure 9.15 Hand-counted generalisations of hand-drawn maps showing where SC respondents believe speech regions to exist in the US

The names of US speech regions

As noted, a feature of this research which suggested, in the earliest map-drawing studies (Preston 1982), that prescription was perhaps the greatest force behind folk notions was the presence of labels assigned areas (and their speakers). We turn our attention to a study of such labels for the four groups whose general perceptions are outlined above. In every case except for the southern data, the respondents' labels reported on are from a random subset of fifty individual hand-drawn maps drawn by the same respondents as those who provided the degree of difference, pleasantness and correctness assessments given above (see Notes 2 and 4).

Three previous studies focus on labels: Coupland et al. (1995), Hartley (1996) and Preston (1982), and in any such study, there are two principal classificatory problems: the labels and the regions. Before we describe how we have dealt with both, we present, in Figures 9.17 to 9.20, four hand-drawn maps, one from each of the regions focused on here, to illustrate the source (and 'spirit') of our data.

We freely confess that these four maps were not randomly chosen (although the subsets of fifty from each area were so selected); some of these are particularly rich in the labels we intend to investigate here. Many we looked at were not, but a very large number contained just the sorts of geographic and

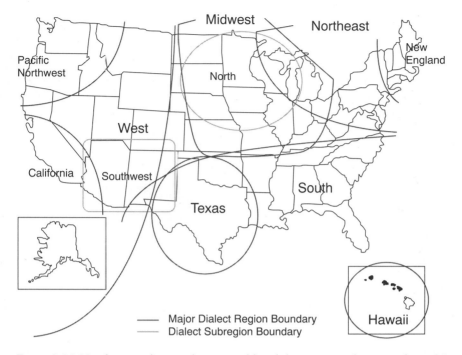

Figure 9.16 Hand-counted generalisations of hand-drawn maps showing where OR respondents believe speech regions to exist in the US (Hartley 1996: 78)

linguistic labels so evident in these, and we turn now to the problems of their classification and their placement in geographic space; the latter first.

A sense of the problem emerges immediately from an investigation of Figures 9.17 and 9.19. For the Michigander, the 'Boring Midwest' is MI, WI, OH, IN, IL, most of MO, the eastern one-third of KS and IA. For the South Carolinian, the area labelled 'Midwest bland' is ND, SD, NE, the southwestern half of MN, most of IA, the northeastern half of MO, most of KS, CO, most of NM, the northeastern one-quarter of AZ, the eastern half of UT, WY and the southeastern one-third of MT. In short, very little overlap. It is clear, therefore, that there must be some 'unifying' classification of areas, one which allows us to say where areas were drawn and what labels were assigned to them. As the above illustration shows, that unifying classification cannot come from the labels assigned to the areas by the respondents themselves.

Cultural geographers know that the question of 'regions' is a complex one of mental maps (see, for example, Gould and White 1974) and a host of other cultural, political, topographic and other factors. Preston (1986) resolves this difficulty in part by relying on Zelinsky (1980), an ingenious compilation

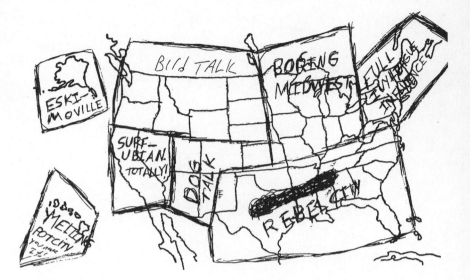

Figure 9.17 Hand-drawn map by an MI respondent

Figure 9.18 Hand-drawn map by an IN respondent

Figure 9.19 Hand-drawn map by an SC respondent

of US areas based on self-naming of regions in the 'yellow pages' of business and professional listings in telephone directories. We have been guided in part by such cultural, physical and political labels, but we have modified our need for regions by the areas our respondents have drawn. For example, Zelinsky does not report any internal divisions of the South, but the maps we have worked with indicate a need for a 'South Midland' or 'Outer South' (as dialectologists would have it) or an 'Appalachia' or 'Upland South', as most topographical and/or cultural geographers would likely designate it.

In fact, Figures 9.13 to 9.16 also reflect a similar resolution of this problem, for the generalised areas represented there are determined from the outlines that the respondents drew, not from the labels they assigned. In this presentation, the main difference is that we have not based the regions on data from any one of the four areas but on data from all four. If we had chosen regions based only on the need indicated by, for example, OR data, we would have needed no 'West Coast' or 'Mid-Atlantic' areas. Figure 9.21 displays the regions which we eventually decided on as the basis for this study. Although the areas are complex (especially the overlaps among 'Plains and Mountains', 'Midwest' and 'North'), they capture not only the diversity of regional outlines from these studies but also the generalisations reached by such cultural geographers as Zelinsky (1980).

When we say, therefore, that the label 'Hillbilly' applies to the area 'South Midland', we refer to the area designated by that latter term in Figure 9.21.

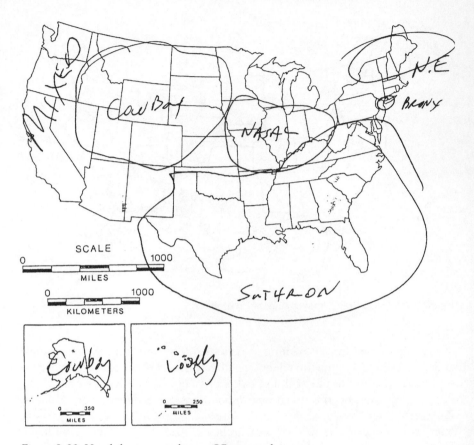

Figure 9.20 Hand-drawn map by an OR respondent

The complete list of regions from that figure includes the following: AK, CL, FL, HI, Mid-Atlantic, Midwest, New England, North, Northeast, Pacific Northwest, Plains and Mountains, South, South Midland, Southwest, TX, West, and West Coast. The regions 'East Coast' and 'Great Lakes' were used only in the preparation of generalisations from the hand-drawn maps and not in the following analysis of labels.

The classification of the labels is more straightforward, following a 'topical' analysis introduced in Preston (1982). The system used here differs only a little, reflecting the classification of all labels into an evaluative ('neutral', 'negative', 'positive') set, regardless of their topical classification, as suggested in Coupland et al. (1995). The entire set is as follows:

1 *Area*: references to geographical and topographical as well as political or popular divisions (e.g. 'west', 'New York City', 'plains') (It is important

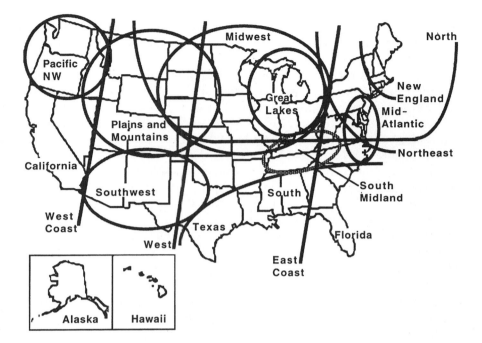

Figure 9.21 Regions of the US used in this study

to remember that this 'area' label may be misleading; the respondent may have encircled an area whose name in Figure 9.21 is quite different from the label he or she gave it.)

2   *Sound*: references to the acoustic/auditory features of language, including 'respellings', such as 'twang', 'nose-talking', 'harsh', 'Suthron' (i.e. 'Southern')

3   *Identity*: references to the inhabitants of a region in terms of a stereo- typical profession (e.g. 'cowboys') or some other characteristic (e.g. 'ignorants')

4   *Ethnicity*: references to ethnic identity (e.g. 'Cubans', 'Asians', 'White Trash')

5   *Media*: references to popular culture figures or events (e.g. 'Beverly Hillbillies', 'Beach Boys')

6   *Attributes*: caricatures of activity, practices, personality and the like (e.g. 'slow', 'rude')

7   *Standardness*: direct references to language variety status (e.g. 'bad English', 'proper English')

8   *Distribution*: indications that the label refers to a situation in which either more than one variety exists in the area labelled (e.g. 'mixture') or that the area supports one variety exclusively (e.g. 'just Southern')

9   *Intelligibility*: references to understanding ('hard to understand')
10 *Variety*: specific references to linguistic variety (e.g. 'Creole', 'dialect')
11 *Comments*: extended comments on the variety, region or 'typical' speakers

In the following pages, we provide a quantitative treatment of the labels based on the above classification system and on groupings into the evaluative categories 'neutral', 'negative' and 'positive'. These labels and ratings are related to areas as given in Figure 9.21. In each case, the labels extracted are from a random selection of fifty hand-drawn maps.

An examination of Table 9.1 shows clearly that the most salient category for regional identification is geographical, since respondents in each region incorporated references to area in 58–77 per cent of the labels. This result is unsurprising, but is clearly not very helpful for uncovering evaluative folk perceptions, since these terms are largely neutral in their connotations. An examination of the other categories, though much less frequent in usage, is thus more insightful in terms of understanding the ways in which varieties of US speech are popularly viewed.

For both MI and OR respondents, the second most used category for language identification was that of *variety*. Interestingly, while these variety references appear in 54 MI labels and 59 OR labels, they are used only 3 and 5 times respectively to refer to the respondents' home areas. In the case of MI, 2 of these home references were to 'English' and only 1 identified the local area as having a 'North Accent'. For the OR respondents, 4 of the 5 variety references are to 'English', and the remaining label characterises the West Coast as having a 'Normal Accent'. In describing the varieties of speech in other regions of the US, both MI and OR respondents most frequently use the terms 'accent' and 'dialect', which suggests that for these areas of high linguistic security, the local area is seen as being the place where 'correct' or 'standard' English is spoken, while 'accents' and

Table 9.1 Frequency of *label* category by area of respondent (number; percentage in brackets)

Category	MI (n = 344)	IN (n = 225)	SC (n = 348)	OR (n = 319)
Area	265 (77.0)	146 (64.9)	205 (58.9)	207 (64.9)
Sound	43 (12.5)	37 (16.4)	48 (13.8)	50 (15.7)
Identity	37 (10.8)	37 (16.4)	108 (31.0)	29 (9.1)
Ethnicity	30 (8.7)	32 (10.1)	28 (8.0)	31 (9.7)
Media	0 (0.0)	1 (0.4)	6 (1.7)	1 (0.3)
Attributes	14 (4.1)	18 (8.0)	35 (10.1)	11 (3.4)
Standardness	9 (2.6)	9 (4.0)	8 (2.3)	19 (6.0)
Distribution	15 (4.4)	14 (6.2)	15 (4.3)	10 (3.1)
Intelligibility	4 (1.2)	2 (0.8)	1 (0.3)	2 (0.6)
Variety	54 (15.7)	20 (8.9)	91 (26.1)	59 (18.5)
Comments	10 (2.9)	14 (6.2)	25 (7.2)	11 (3.4)

'dialects' (which, for non-linguists, always implies 'non-standard') are found elsewhere. This idea is further supported by examining the labels which fall into the *standardness* category, which appears to be used by MI and OR respondents, primarily for the purpose of identifying their local areas as the places where 'Normal', 'Standard' or 'General' English is spoken, as well as where there is 'No Accent'.

For residents of SC, the category of Variety is used more frequently than it is by residents of the other areas (although it occurs less than *identity* labels for SC respondents) and is used at a higher rate to refer to the South, the local area (12 of 91 labels). Four of these labels identify the South as having an 'accent' or a 'dialect'. More importantly, the labels which refer to varieties in other areas of the US overwhelmingly use the neutral term 'talk', rather than a more evaluative term such as 'dialect'.

The IN respondents rely on the category of variety much less than respondents from other areas. Only 1 of the 20 variety labels used by this group refers to the home area, and this label admits the fact that southern Indianans have 'a slight southern accent'. Where variety labels are used by IN residents, they generally identify highly caricatured accents such as 'Brooklyn', 'Boston' and 'mountain dialect' (in reference to South Midland). It thus seems that the IN respondents are more hesitant to make reference to others' accents, for fear that attention might be drawn to their own, another indication of their linguistic insecurity.

The category which is more important than variety for both IN and SC respondents is that of *identity*. In fact, this appears to be an important category for identifying non-locals for these two groups, at least as important as variety was for MI and OR. In the case of the SC respondents, only 13 of the 108 labels in this category were used to refer to themselves, and these 13 were almost all 'Southerners', 'Us' or 'Home Folks'. In describing the identities of other regions, however, the South Carolinians were quite colourful, e.g. 'Crazies' (CA), 'Baker Talk' (Midwest), 'Cheese Talk' (WI), 'Potato Heads' (ID), 'L. L. Bean Talk' (ME) and 'Them – the bad guys' (Northeast), used in contrast with 'Us – the good guys'. By far the identity label most frequently employed by the SC respondents was 'Yankee', used to refer to New England, Northeast, North and sometimes even West and Midwest. For the IN respondents, a slight amount of insecurity again rears its head in the one time that the category of identity is used to describe the local area, i.e. 'Country people'. Like the South Carolinians, these respondents use this category almost exclusively to refer to other areas.

The category of identity, though not as frequent in the MI and OR data, is nonetheless still used as a way of identifying other regions. Like the SC respondents, MI and OR residents often draw on cultural icons or occupational caricatures to describe areas. Examples from the MI data include 'Islander' (HI), 'Okey' [sic] (Midwest) and 'Yuppy' (Northeast), while

'Cowboy' (Plains and Mountains), 'Rebel slang' (South) and 'Central Farmers' (Midwest) show up in the OR data. Interestingly, this category is never used by the OR respondents to refer to themselves, not even in neutral ways such as 'Westerners'.

For all four sets of respondents, the identity category was used almost exclusively to characterise the speech of the South Midlands (when it was identified as a separate speech area), usually as 'Hillbillies' or 'Hicks'. Only the MI respondents (and a minority at that) seem willing to identify this region in more neutral terms, such as 'Appalachian'. This is perhaps due to the significant historical immigration of people from this region into southeastern MI. The only other regions to receive a large number of identity labels across the board are 'Texans' and to a lesser extent 'New Yorkers'.

Ethnicity is another category which appears to be used primarily to refer to specific states. It shows up most frequently in all respondent sets in reference to 'Cajuns' in LA, 'Cubans' in FL, 'Eskimos' in AK, 'Dutch' in PA and 'Mexicans' or 'Spanish' in the Southwest and TX. In addition, SC respondents include a number of references to 'Geechees', a term which refers to (historically) Gullah creole-speaking African-Americans along the South Carolina Coast.

The other category which is used relatively frequently by all four respondent groups is that of *sound*. Some stereotypes again emerge from all four respondent sets: Southerners and Texans have a 'drawl' (often spelled as 'draw' on the maps and clearly pronounced that way in interviews by numerous respondents) and talk 'slow' while Northeasterners talk 'fast', sound 'nasal' and have a 'brogue'. As with variety, MI and OR respondents rarely refer to sound qualities of their own speech; just one OR respondent referred to it as 'Soft – TV like', while many South Carolinians and one honest Indianan recognize the 'drawl' in their own speech.

In terms of the remaining categories, *attributes* are most important to SC respondents, again as a way of setting up an 'Us' vs. 'Them' dichotomy. Midwesterners are 'bland', Northeasterners are 'Mean' and 'Rude', Texans are 'big' and 'bad', and people on the West Coast are 'only interested in fun'. In contrast, Southerners are 'down home folks' and 'good'. The category of *distribution* is most frequently employed by the IN respondents, an indication of their greater sensitivity to dialect variation within a given area, no doubt a result of its position as a transition zone between traditionally northern and southern areas. One respondent even points out that in IN you find '150 miles big diff'. MI residents are more concerned with *intelligibility*, depicting people from AK and NY as 'hard to understand', while Westerners and Midwesterners are 'easy to understand'.

One final point perhaps worth noting in this discussion of category distributions, is the fact that SC respondents not only used the most labels (348) but also employed longer labels (including those catalogued as *comments*) than any other regional group. Since these respondents were exclusively

Table 9.2 Frequencies of labels used for hand-drawn maps for respondents from the four areas studied (number; percentage in brackets)

	Labels (n = 50)			
	South	Northeast	South	Northeast
MI (n = 147)	138 (94)	80 (54)	63 (17)	45 (13)
IN (n = 123)	106 (86)	63 (51)	58 (25)	39 (17)
OR (n = 65)	60 (92)	49 (75)	58 (18)	42 (13)
SC (n = 50)	47 (94)	23 (46)	85 (24)	48 (14)

college students, however, it may not be correct to attribute that tendency to their regional background.

Even in this characterisation of the distribution of categories, it is obvious that evaluative comments play an important role, and we turn now to a direct investigation of that fact. Tables 9.3 to 9.6 show the areal and evaluative distribution of labels for the four respondent groups.

Not surprisingly, for all four regional groups, the most frequent labels are assigned to the South and the Northeast (see Tables 9.3 to 9.6), the areas most frequently drawn (see Figures 9.13 to 9.16). Those frequencies are summarised in Table 9.2.

Table 9.3 MI results for labelling of other US accents (n = 50; 344 labels, referring to 361 areas; 'West' and 'Midwest' overlap most frequently; number; percentage in brackets)

Area	Labels	Positive	Negative	Neutral
Alaska	12 (3.3)	0 (0.0)	1 (8.3)	11 (91.7)
California	16 (4.4)	1 (6.2)	2 (12.5)	13 (81.2)
Florida	13 (3.6)	1 (7.7)	2 (15.4)	10 (76.9)
Hawaii	12 (3.3)	1 (8.3)	0 (0.0)	11 (91.7)
Mid-Atlantic	23 (6.4)	0 (0.0)	1 (4.3)	22 (95.7)
Midwest	24 (6.6)	1 (4.2)	3 (12.5)	20 (83.3)
North	25 (6.9)	7 (28.0)	3 (12.0)	15 (60.0)
Northeast	45 (12.5)	1 (2.2)	7 (15.6)	37 (82.2)
New England	20 (5.5)	1 (5.0)	0 (0.0)	19 (95.0)
Northwest	7 (1.9)	1 (14.3)	0 (0.0)	6 (85.7)
Plains and Mountains	9 (2.5)	0 (0.0)	2 (22.2)	7 (77.8)
South	63 (17.4)	4 (6.3)	10 (15.9)	49 (77.8)
South Midland	19 (5.3)	2 (10.5)	8 (42.1)	9 (47.4)
Southwest	18 (5.0)	0 (0.0)	5 (27.8)	13 (72.2)
Texas	27 (7.5)	1 (3.7)	6 (22.2)	20 (74.1)
West	22 (6.1)	2 (9.1)	2 (9.1)	18 (81.8)
West Coast	6 (1.7)	1 (16.7)	2 (33.3)	3 (50.0)
Totals	361	22 (6.1)	46 (12.7)	293 (81.2)

Table 9.4 IN results for labelling of other US accents (n = 50; 225 labels, referring to 232 areas; 'South' and 'South Midland' overlap most frequently; number; percentage in brackets)

Area	Labels	Positive	Negative	Neutral
Alaska	1 (0.4)	0 (0.0)	0 (0.0)	1 (100.0)
California	9 (3.9)	3 (33.3)	1 (11.1)	5 (55.6)
Florida	6 (2.6)	0 (0.0)	0 (0.0)	6 (100.0)
Hawaii	3 (1.3)	0 (0.0)	0 (0.0)	3 (100.0)
Mid-Atlantic	5 (2.1)	0 (0.0)	1 (20.0)	4 (80.0)
Midwest	20 (8.6)	3 (15.0)	2 (10.0)	15 (75.0)
North	22 (9.5)	2 (9.1)	5 (22.7)	15 (68.2)
Northeast	39 (16.8)	4 (10.2)	7 (17.9)	28 (71.8)
New England	8 (3.4)	1 (12.5)	1 (12.5)	6 (75.0)
Northwest	1 (0.4)	1 (100.0)	0 (0.0)	0 (0.0)
Plains and Mountains	2 (0.8)	0 (0.0)	0 (0.0)	2 (100.0)
South	58 (25.0)	2 (3.4)	14 (24.1)	42 (72.4)
South Midland	23 (9.9)	0 (0.0)	15 (65.2)	8 (34.8)
Southwest	11 (4.7)	0 (0.0)	2 (18.2)	9 (81.8)
Texas	13 (5.6)	1 (7.7)	4 (30.8)	8 (61.5)
West	8 (3.4)	0 (0.0)	0 (0.0)	8 (100.0)
West Coast	3 (1.3)	0 (0.0)	0 (0.0)	3 (100.0)
Totals	232	17 (7.3)	52 (22.4)	163 (70.2)

In the hand-drawn map task, no one of the four regional groups singled out an area more frequently than it did the South, and only the MI respondents singled out an area more frequently than the Northeast for second position (the 'North', their home area). In the labels count, no group assigned labels to any area more frequently than to the South, and the Northeast was in second position for all four groups as well. In fact, for all four regional groups, the third most frequently labelled area never reached even double-digit percentages (of all labels assigned).

Why all this attention to the South and the Northeast? The answer is easily found, we believe, in a closer look at Figures 9.1 to 9.4 (and, to a lesser extent, Figures 9.5 to 9.8). In every case in the 'correctness' rankings, the South and NYC (usually accompanied by NJ) are the lowest-ranked areas. This is even true of southern ratings of the South (Figure 9.3), and the only exception to this general rule when applied to 'pleasantness' occurs in IN and S ratings of the South.

In short, what is 'incorrect' (and to a lesser extent, less 'pleasant') in US English is most salient. This appears to be true of respondents from all over the country, and the areas prejudiced against are the same – the South and the Northeast (generally restricted to NYC and NJ, occasionally NY).

If this first attempt at an assessment of the qualitative assignment of labels is true, there should be confirmation of it in the characterisation of labels as

Table 9.5 SC results for labelling of other US accents (*n* = 50; 348 labels, referring to 348 areas; number; percentage in brackets)

Area	Labels	Positive	Negative	Neutral
Alaska	2 (0.6)	0 (0.0)	0 (0.0)	2 (100.0)
California	18 (5.2)	1 (5.6)	6 (33.3)	11 (61.1)
Florida	15 (4.3)	0 (0.0)	3 (20.0)	12 (80.0)
Hawaii	5 (1.4)	0 (0.0)	0 (0.0)	5 (100.0)
Mid-Atlantic	13 (3.7)	1 (7.7)	5 (38.5)	7 (53.8)
Midwest	33 (9.5)	0 (0.0)	10 (30.3)	23 (69.7)
North	11 (3.2)	0 (0.0)	6 (54.5)	5 (45.4)
Northeast	48 (13.8)	0 (0.0)	31 (64.6)	17 (35.4)
New England	15 (4.3)	0 (0.0)	2 (13.3)	13 (86.7)
Northwest	9 (2.6)	1 (11.1)	4 (44.4)	4 (44.4)
Plains and Mountains	10 (2.9)	0 (0.0)	5 (50.0)	5 (50.0)
South	85 (24.4)	6 (7.0)	13 (15.3)	66 (77.6)
South Midland	9 (2.6)	0 (0.0)	6 (66.7)	3 (33.3)
Southwest	11 (3.2)	0 (0.0)	3 (27.3)	8 (72.7)
Texas	32 (9.2)	0 (0.0)	10 (31.2)	22 (68.8)
West	19 (5.4)	0 (0.0)	3 (15.8)	16 (84.2)
West Coast	13 (3.7)	0 (0.0)	3 (23.1)	10 (76.9)
Totals	348	9 (2.6)	110 (31.6)	229 (65.8)

'positive', 'negative' and 'neutral'. This is clearly true for MI respondents (Table 9.3). The South, South Midland and TX show a combined score of 24 negative labels and the Northeast 7. IN respondents (Table 9.4) assign 33 negative labels to the South Midland, South and TX and 7 to the Northeast. Even the SC respondents (Table 9.5) continue this derogation, assigning 29 negative labels to the South Midland, South and TX. Their greater dislike for the Northeast, however, is revealed in their assigning fully 33 negative labels to it alone, the highest number of evaluative labels (positive or negative) assigned any one region by any group in these studies. Even the generally well-liked Midwest was assigned 10 negative labels by the SC raters, but much of that area was often indiscriminately called 'Yankee' by these southern respondents. Finally, OR respondents agree with these general trends. They assign 28 negative labels to the South Midland, South and TX and 10 to the Northeast.

The qualitative labels support, then, our claim that incorrectness and salience go hand in hand in the perception of US English varieties and that the South and the Northeast (as represented by NYC, NY and NJ) are the leading recipients of these classifications. Those familiar with the gross caricatures of US regions will not need to be told of the popular culture support for these views. Although 'everyone knows better', the following (at least) are common. Gangsters and crooks, immigrants (who speak poor

Table 9.6 OR results for labelling of other US accents (*n* = 50; 319 labels, referring to 319 areas; number; percentage in brackets)

Area	Labels	Positive	Negative	Neutral
Alaska	17 (5.3)	2 (11.8)	0 (0.0)	15 (88.2)
California	14 (4.4)	2 (14.3)	1 (7.1)	11 (78.6)
Florida	9 (2.8)	1 (11.1)	2 (22.2)	6 (66.7)
Hawaii	16 (5.0)	3 (18.8)	1 (6.2)	12 (75.0)
Mid-Atlantic	11 (3.4)	0 (0.0)	1 (9.1)	10 (90.9)
Midwest	33 (10.3)	0 (0.0)	6 (18.2)	27 (81.8)
North	11 (3.4)	1 (9.1)	1 (9.1)	9 (81.8)
Northeast	42 (13.2)	0 (0.0)	10 (23.8)	32 (76.2)
New England	17 (5.3)	0 (0.0)	1 (5.9)	16 (94.1)
Northwest	11 (3.4)	4 (36.4)	1 (9.1)	6 (54.5)
Plains and Mountains	7 (2.2)	0 (0.0)	2 (28.6)	5 (71.4)
South	58 (18.2)	0 (0.0)	17 (29.3)	41 (70.7)
South Midland	3 (0.9)	0 (0.0)	2 (66.7)	1 (33.3)
Southwest	10 (3.1)	0 (0.0)	1 (10.0)	9 (90.0)
Texas	22 (6.9)	0 (0.0)	9 (40.9)	13 (59.1)
West	30 (9.4)	9 (30.0)	2 (6.7)	19 (63.3)
West Coast	8 (2.5)	2 (25.0)	1 (12.5)	5 (62.5)
Totals	319	24 (7.5)	58 (18.2)	237 (74.3)

English) and other ethnic minorities, hoodlums and street people live in NYC (and, by association, in NY and NJ). A disproportionately large African-American population along with redneck, barefoot, poorly educated, intermarried, moonshiner KKK members reside in the South. Popular culture abounds with the continuing employment of these caricatures, although we believe they are deeply embedded in folk 'wisdom' outside their popular culture use. (Note in Table 9.1 that *media* labels were assigned only 8 times in the 1,236 total labels.)

The salience of the incorrect (or the human preference to play on weaknesses) is further revealed in the catalogue of 'positive' labels. The MI respondents (Table 9.3) like the North (where they live), but they assign it only 7 positive labels. The IN respondents (Table 9.4) give no area even as many as 5 positive labels. The SC respondents (Table 9.5), who ought to be gung-ho southern promoters, give the South only 6 approving designations, and the OR raters, like those in MI, find only the general home area (West) worth praise (9 times). The overall assignment of evaluative labels shows that the preference for negative labels is ubiquitous. MI respondents gave 46 (0.127) negative and 22 (0.061) positive labels; IN respondents gave 52 (0.224) negatives and only 17 (0.073) positives. SC raters (the harshest, stemming from their dislike for the Northeast) gave 110 negative labels (0.316) and only 9 (0.026) approving ones. OR raters gave 58 (0.182) negative labels and 24 (0.075) positive ones.

Finally, these labelling performances can be surveyed by sampling some of the specific negative and positive labels assigned stereotypical areas by all four regional groups.

MI respondents gave the South, South Midlands and Texas various negative labels, but those with the word 'drawl' were most common for the South and Texas (most often simply 'Southern Drawl' although many were elaborated with such extensions as 'southern drawl slower-speaking').[5] In contrast, labels with the word 'hillbilly' or 'hick' predominated for the South Midland, an interesting division between a straightforward linguistic caricature on the one hand and an identity or stereotypical person label on the other (e.g. 'Tennessee Kentucky Southern Ohio "Hicks" Hillbillies'). The Northeast was assigned such negative labels as 'East New York nasal accents' and 'Eastern twang broad a's', both playing on phonological caricatures. Additionally, however, restricted negative labels in the Northeast included such items as 'Buffalo sometimes hard to understand' and 'Pennsylvania Dutch slang', showing that not all negative labels for the Northeast have their source in the unfavourable view of NYC and NJ varieties.

On the positive side, MI raters labelled their home area (North) 'Midwest – standard English', 'no accent', or simply 'normal', and nearby areas (e.g. WI) were called 'easy to understand'. Most positive characterisations were straightforwardly linguistic, although one respondent labelled much of the North 'central midwest my comfort zone'.

IN respondents agree with the MI assessment that South and TX speakers are users of a 'drawl'. One respondent, however, provides this very detailed label: 'Alabama "Twang" and accents are placed on different syllables from ours. Also runs sounds together.' They also call South Midland speakers 'hillbillies' (although they do not use the label 'hick'). From a 'production dialectology' point of view, by the way, these IN respondents are speakers of South Midland dialect themselves. Their 'distancing' their KY and other near-south neighbours (by calling them 'hillbillies') is, no doubt, a part of their own linguistic insecurity. Finally, IN respondents identified the Northeast with such labels as 'sissy talking' (a common southern and African-American male caricature of Northern US male speech) or 'North East fast talking'. One respondent identified all New Yorkers as speakers of 'slang'. Although not given to much praise, one IN respondent found that in CA there were 'natives with good diction', and another found the Midwest 'like england [sic] more proper less slang'.

As noted above the SC respondents were extremely harsh on the Northeast. Most common was the identity label of Northerners as 'Yankees' (e.g. 'the north "Yankees"' and 'North Northern Yankees'). In some cases this dichotomy was expressed without the term – 'Them – the bad guys' or simply 'Them'. Linguistic caricatures were present however, most playing on the southern caricature of northern speech as 'nasal' – 'nose plugs', 'NJ accents twist words in mouth nasal sounding', and the interestingly spelled 'North nasal pärk', with the umlaut perhaps indicating nasalisation. In a few cases the identity and linguistic caricature occurred together: 'Yankees talk through nose'. 'Drawl' is also very common in SC references to southern speech ('Southern Drawl Y'all'), and one SC respondent believes that SC in particular is 'lost in language and time'. Other negative comments, however, often refer to pretentious rather than 'incorrect' use, particularly with reference to Charleston, SC: 'Weird Charlston drawl that is supposed to be an indication of blue bloods' and 'Aristocratic pretentious white trash'. We believe these evaluations supplement the self-praising 'good-ole-boy' evaluations of southern speech which figure in some of the positive comments. As previously mentioned, SC respondents refer disapprovingly to a coastal SC variety (Gullah) and its speakers as 'Geechee', and one uses the only overtly racist label, 'spic talk', to refer to the language of the Southwest. Like the MI respondents, SC labellers refer to South Midland speakers as both 'hillbilly' and 'hick', but they do not refer to TX speech so frequently with the word 'drawl' as the other respondents did. They as frequently play on the TX caricature of 'big': 'Texas Talk & Tall Tales Biggest Best of Everything.'

On the positive side (only 9 total), the SC raters give 6 to themselves. They are the opposite of 'Yankees' and 'Them'; they are 'Us – the good people' and 'The South "God's People" '. As suggested just above, they are the opposite of fancy or aristocratic types: they call themselves 'Deep South Home Folks Good Ole' Boys' and 'Down Home Folks'.

OR respondents agree that the South has a 'drawl', and several remark on the rate ('slow'). One plays on the North–South dichotomy (like many SC raters) by labelling the entire area 'Rebel slang'. Of the nine negative labels of TX speech, eight use 'drawl'; the last uses 'Heavy Texas twang'. There are only two OR identifications of the South Midland, and both use the term 'hillbilly'. OR labels of the Northeast are even harsher (although not as numerous as those of the South). Speakers there have a 'thick brogue', and a common ethnic stereotype is played on in the label 'harsh, talk fast sound Jewish'. The linguistic caricature used by the SC respondents is repeated in the label 'nasal sound', but a more negative evaluative comment appears in 'meaningless mumble'. Also like the SC respondents, the populist distaste for aristocratic speech surfaces, here in reference to the entire Northeast: 'Eastern upturned nose British immigrant wannabees in love with the Queen Mum'. On the positive side, the OR respondents like the West and call it in 5 of the 9 positive labels 'normal'. The even more local Northwest is also 'normal' or has 'no accent'.

In general, our survey of labels supports other findings from perceptual dialectology in the US. The South and the Northeast, particularly NYC and NJ, are not, as linguists would have it, just other regions with their own local standards. Even to locals in the South, that region and the largest metropolitan area of the East Coast are the home bases of 'incorrect' US English. Although the vast majority of respondents simply label dialect regions with regional names, the survey of affective dimensions in labels reveals the continuing regional prejudices in US English and minor, but intriguing, populist and historical trends.[6] These labels are significantly different both in their evaluative dimensions and in the classificatory types from those uncovered in Wales in Coupland et al. (1995), and we hope that further research in other areas which we know to be underway (for example, France, Germany, Turkey and Japan) will reveal further patterns of the popular use of labels in perceptual dialectology tasks. For this volume, we hope this paper adds popular and folk detail to the discussion of language standards. Without it, the enterprise is purely academic, a damning popular label if there ever was one.

Notes

1   'Folk linguistics' here refers to beliefs held about language by non-linguists. The value and scope of such work is briefly outlined in Hoenigswald (1966); a more thorough review is provided in Niedzielski and Preston (in progress).

2   The work reported on here for MI and IN was supported by a grant from the National Science Foundation to Dennis R. Preston. The respondents were subdivided into relatively well-balanced subgroups based on age, status and gender but, in the findings reported here, these groups are combined and only data for European-American respondents are considered. There are two groups of S respondents. First, we are indebted to Michael Montgomery for the southern maps; they are from respondents from South Carolina and also represent both sexes, a considerable variety of social status and age groups, and only European-Americans. For the quantitative southern data ('degree of difference' and 'pleasant' and 'correct' studies) we are grateful to Ann Pitts who provided these data from European-American Auburn University students. The areal and age and status ranges of this group, therefore, are not comparable to the others (although a number of studies, such as Preston [1988], have shown that such factors are not particularly powerful). The Oregon data, again from both genders and a variety of age and status groups but uniformly European-American, are taken from Hartley (1996).

3   The ratings scores for OR 'correctness', 'pleasantness' and 'degree of difference' were calculated with a non-parametric technique (multidimensional scaling). These maps, therefore, represent the clusters discovered by that technique (and further isolated by a 'K-means' procedure). To make these maps comparable to the others, however, we have calculated the means scores for each cluster and arranged them in an ascending order on the maps, although these scores were not used in the statistical determination of the areal groupings.

4   Since the hand-drawn maps are all from South Carolina residents, we shall refer to these data in what follows as 'SC' rather than 'S'.

5   One might argue that the designation 'drawl' is neutral, but our experience with folk users of the term makes us believe it most often suggests negative evaluation.

6   With the study of these labels, we hope to have shown that the findings from other modes of perceptual dialectology are further attested. As in those studies, and in those by other researchers, the dominating folk linguistic idea for US respondents is rather obviously one of 'correctness'. It should be clear to readers of this volume that when we call 'correctness' a 'dominating folk linguistic idea', we mean to refer to what others in this volume call a 'language ideology'.

Appendix

The United States state abbreviations (and ones for New York City and Washington, DC) used throughout this paper are as follows:

AL	Alabama	AK	Alaska	AZ	Arizona
AR	Arkansas	CA	California	CO	Colorado
CT	Connecticut	DE	Delaware	FL	Florida
GA	Georgia	HI	Hawaii	ID	Idaho
IL	Illinois	IN	Indiana	IA	Iowa
KS	Kansas	KY	Kentucky	LA	Louisiana
ME	Maine	MD	Maryland	MA	Massachusetts
MI	Michigan	MN	Minnesota	MS	Mississippi
MO	Missouri	MT	Montana	NE	Nebraska
NV	Nevada	NH	New Hampshire	NJ	New Jersey
NM	New Mexico	NYC	New York City	NY	New York
NC	North Carolina	ND	North Dakota	OH	Ohio
OK	Oklahoma	OR	Oregon	PA	Pennsylvania
RI	Rhode Island	SC	South Carolina	SD	South Dakota
TN	Tennessee	TX	Texas	UT	Utah
VT	Vermont	VA	Virginia	WDC	Washington DC
WA	Washington	WI	Wisconsin	WV	West Virginia
WY	Wyoming				

10

FUNCTIONS AND FORMS OF ENGLISH IN A EUROPEAN EFL COUNTRY

Bent Preisler

Traditionally, the concept of Standard English, or rather Standard British English, has been essential in the teaching of English as a Foreign Language (EFL) in Europe. Until 1945 Standard British English was practically the only EFL norm at most European universities and, although American English and, to a lesser extent, other varieties have been making inroads since then, the European tradition in the teaching of English is still largely based on Standard British English and Received Pronunciation. However, in recent years the concept of Standard English has, for a number of reasons, come under attack. This chapter examines to what extent the problematisation of Standard English is relevant and justified in the context of EFL, in view of the actual functions of English in an EFL country, pointing out in the process some important functions and related EFL problems which seem so far to have been overlooked.

The main arguments against the usefulness of Standard English as a concept, whether or not they are relevant to the EFL context, can be broadly summarised as follows:

1   In countries where English is a native language, Standard English is often synonymous with the arbitrary norms of purists wishing to assert their own social and intellectual superiority as 'guardians' of the language (compare, for example, Milroy and Milroy 1998; Leith 1997).
2   Standard English is not even a linguistic reality. 'Standard' presupposes invariability, but Standard English is anything but invariable. At best the term should be reserved for a functionally reduced or simplified variety (see Bex 1993).
3   In an international context, Standard English is associated, in particular, with the standards of Britain and North America. Thus, by implication, it challenges the autonomy of all the other Englishes in the world

(compare, for example, Verma 1982; Kachru 1992b: 53; Singh et al. 1995).

4   By the same token, as an instrument of cross-cultural communication Standard English is too culture specific. A functionally reduced model is preferable (compare, for example, L. Smith 1983a; Johnson 1990) – or even diversity, in the hope that cross-cultural 'empathy' (compare Hübler 1985) can make up for any problems of communication among local and non-native-speaker varieties – perhaps aided by a survival kit of pragmatic 'dos and donts' (compare, for example, L. Smith 1983b).

As far as EFL is concerned, at least one of these arguments, viz. (1), appears to be irrelevant in the assessment of the usefulness of Standard English as a teaching model, or would have to be restated in terms of its possible implications for learners of English in EFL countries. The learners' interlanguage is typically penalised with reference to 'correct' vs. 'incorrect' English, not 'good' vs. 'bad' English, nor is Standard English usually an issue affecting the learner's social or individual identity. As for the remaining arguments, their relevance to the particular EFL situation seems to vary according to the level of proficiency. In a class of adults learning English from scratch, questions of variability in the model, and associated values, would appear to be less important than imparting the basics of a model. In fact, the entire issue of Standard English – though relying on assumptions related to the general debate, about formal properties, social functions (in mother-tongue and second-language countries) and appropriateness for cross-cultural communication – has to be viewed in a special perspective when the context is EFL. This chapter will provide such a perspective, being based on a detailed analysis of the status and functions of English in one particular EFL country, Denmark.

I have organised my discussion into 6 sections: (1) The official status of English in Denmark; (2) Use of EFL; (3) Acquisition of EFL; (4) Attitudes towards English; (5) Danish–English bilingualism?; (6) Forms of EFL.[1] My data, unless otherwise indicated, derive from a large-scale investigation into the use of English in everyday life in Denmark, and on attitudes and problems related to this, which was recently carried out at the University of Roskilde. The project consists of two complementary investigations: (1) a quantitative analysis of responses to a questionnaire given to a random sample of the Danish adult population, and (2) a discourse analysis of ethnographic interviews with representatives of some of the youth subcultures assumed to be spearheading the use of English in Denmark.[2]

1 The official status of English in Denmark

Denmark is an EFL country – as opposed to countries where English is a second language (ESL) – to the extent that English does not have official status in government and administration generally. However, English (like other foreign languages, particularly German and French) is promoted by the educational system (EFL is an obligatory subject from the 4th grade), as well as – directly or indirectly – by particular official and semi-official agencies involved in international communication (e.g. foreign trade and tourism). According to a ministerial notice from 1976, the official aim of the teaching of English in Danish schools is to make the Danish population bilingual, with English as the second language, and although this statement has disappeared in more recent notices, the same idea is still very much alive among politicians concerned with education.[3] Yet it has never been justified in functional terms, beyond the general notion of the need to know English for purposes of 'international communication', nor have its implications been analysed in terms of language policy or, indeed, feasibility. So far educational policies have resulted in roughly 80 per cent of the adult population having had some English in Primary School, the figure being almost 100 per cent for those under 40 years of age. In Primary School, they have been taught English for an average of almost 5 years. And more than half of the adult population have had English in their post-Primary-School education.

2 Use of EFL

Apart from linguistic minorities, Danes as a rule use Danish across the whole range of formal and informal domains in which English is used in countries where English is the first language. However, in determining the extent to which English is used in Denmark, as increasingly in the EFL world generally, it is extremely important to distinguish between active and passive uses. While it is still true, as far as formal uses are concerned, that English is *spoken* only in a limited number of specialised domains involving international communication – e.g. within higher education, foreign affairs, tourism, big business – the domains in which English is *read* and *heard* are numerous and not necessarily specialised. Specialised domains in which English is spoken (or written) are characterised by specialised registers geared for specialised receivers. Domains in which English listening and reading skills are required, on the other hand, often represent activities common to the whole or large parts of the population, such as listening to popular music, watching films and using computers in the home. Even if some of them have special registers (e.g. computers and advertising), these are still meant to appeal to a general public, not (or, in the case of computers, not only) specialists. The influence of English is obviously a function of rapidly growing internationalisation, but it is important to realise that, to the extent that many of these domains represent popular activities – and indeed depend on popular demand for their existence – participation in the process of internationalisation is no longer the privilege of an educational elite. In fact, the promotion of English by the hegemonic culture for purposes of 'international communication' ('English from above') now has its popular counterpart ('English from below'),

241

often representing the use of English by Danes to communicate with other Danes. In the following I will discuss some important manifestations of 'English from below.'

2.1 Formal domains of 'English from below'

As far as popular music is concerned, a substantial proportion of popular lyrics heard on Danish radio and TV are in English. More than 70 per cent of the adult population listen to English lyrics at least once a day. Furthermore, many Danish bands, representing genres such as 'rock'n'roll', 'death-metal' and 'hip-hop' music, compose and sing their lyrics exclusively in English, and are expected to by their Danish audiences. These genres would therefore seem to constitute formal subdomains of language use in which the use of English has become conventionalised and is in fact obligatory, in a form of intra-Danish (mass) communication.

As in the other Scandinavian countries, foreign films shown in the cinema or on TV, as well as other foreign TV programmes, are shown in the original language – with Danish subtitles – the only exception to this rule being cartoons and other programmes for small children. Whatever the motives behind this policy – and whatever problems of comprehensibility it may present that cause most other EFL societies (compare Moag 1982: 25) to dub in their indigenous language – it has the firm support of close to 90 per cent of the Danish population, according to the survey. The vast majority of imported films and TV programmes are in the English language, making this another domain where regular exposure to spoken English is unavoidable for the majority of the population. It also means that proficiency in English is an advantage with a view to full semantic and pragmatic understanding of the dialogue, and a necessity in case of poor reading skills. About 45 per cent of the population watch English-language films or TV programmes with subtitles every day, an additional 30 per cent doing it several times a week. And then, of course, we have not taken into account the fact that English-language programmes are also accessible, in the original language and *without* subtitles, on satellite and cable TV, and that more than a third of the adult population (besides an unknown proportion of children and adolescents, compare below) watch these at least once a week.

In other domains where the general public is constantly exposed to the English language, code-switching within texts is more common than complete (multi-sentence) texts in English. Code-switching is the rule rather than the exception, and words and messages in English abound everywhere, most conspicuously on shop signs, posters, menus, etc. Advertisements especially are often partially or completely in English, and these appear in super-markets, on the sides of buses, in newspapers and magazines, etc. The same is true of commercials on Danish radio and TV. According to a recent student project (Frederiksen et al. 1995), 45 per cent of all commercials on Danish

TV2 involve code-switching to English, and 6 per cent are wholly in English. Some of these ads and commercials are international ones which have not been translated. Others are Danish ones produced for Danes, having been rendered into English to give them an international flavour. According to the present survey, about 40 per cent of Danish adults are aware of encountering the English language at least once a day in advertising aimed at the Danish public, the figure rising to nearly 70 per cent if the frequency is several times a week.

Manufacturers are required, through EU regulations, to provide instruction manuals in Danish for machines involving a safety risk,[4] but no similar obligation is enforced for the benefit of consumers having to assemble and operate other goods resulting from the manufacturing process. Many foreign products are accompanied by an instruction manual in several languages, including at least one Scandinavian language,[5] but often the instruction is in English only. Respondents corresponding to 23 per cent of the population estimate that they come across instructional texts in English at least once a week, and as many as 52 per cent of employees say they encounter texts in English at their place of work, including instruction manuals, at least once a week – 32 per cent saying daily!

In the news media, code-switching to English is extremely common, partly because the translation of foreign news tends to become sloppy under time pressure, partly because many topics are inspired by Anglo-American cultural trends, and partly because bilingual journalists often seem not to be aware that they are code-switching. One newsreader, for example, explained in Danish that many V.I.P.s (pronounced in English) had arrived for an international conference in Copenhagen. She went on to explain, conscientiously, that 'V.I.P. betyder [means] *very important person*' – but omitted to translate *very important person* into Danish.

Another area is Personal Computers, which are extremely popular in Denmark. Most software originates in the United States, and users without any knowledge of English have a serious handicap. Some major international products are available in a Danish version, but the Danish version is often more expensive than the English version, and often the translation is only partial. My *Word* programme, which is the translated version, contains English words such as *Word, office, zoom* and *support*; my Trio DataFax Program, also the Danish version, has a function called *edit log*, which has not been translated, and a click-on option called 'information' opens a file with information in straight English. Games for children and adolescents are usually in the original, English-language version, and English is encountered in computer programmes by about 45 per cent of adult Danes at least once a week, and by 25 per cent every day.

These examples of the use of English in the media and other formal domains that are part of everyday life in Denmark are by no means exhaustive (see, for example, Risager 1993). Table 10.1 gives approximate figures summarising

Table 10.1 Extent to which English is experienced by adult Danes

Experience	Frequency (%)	
	At least once a day	At least once a week
Active experience		
Speak English	9	27
Write in English	4	12
Passive experience		
Hear/listen to English	80	93
See/read English	50	88

the extent to which English is experienced across domains, actively as well as passively, by adult Danes.

2.2 Informal domains of 'English from below'

According to Moag, English is excluded from informal domains in EFL societies:

> Occasional individuals might use a bit of English with family members at home now and then, but this would be conditioned by personal whim, not by sociolinguistic factors.
>
> (Moag 1982: 28)

Although this may still have been an adequate description in 1982, it does not fit the situation in the late 1990s. As I will show, informal use of English – especially in the form of code-switching – has become an inherent, indeed a defining, aspect of the many Anglo-American-oriented youth subcultures which directly or indirectly influence the language and other behavioural patterns of young people generally, in Denmark as well as in other EFL countries. It is impossible to explain the status of English in, and impact on, Danish society (as this is reflected, for example, in advertising and other areas of the Danish media) without understanding the informal function of the English language, and indeed its sociolinguistic significance, in the Anglo-American-oriented youth subculture. The following account is based on ethnographic interviews which I carried out with central representatives of subcultural groups relying heavily on the use of English, who refer to their subcultural form of expression as (1) rock'n'roll, (2) death-metal music, (3) hip-hop dancing and graffiti, and (4) computers. The transcripts were subjected to discourse analysis within a framework of subcultural theory formulated by the Danish cultural sociologist Kjeld Høgsbro (Høgsbro 1995; see also Corbin and Strauss 1990). The main aspects of the theory are:

1   A subculture is a practice: it does not have members, only performers. According to Høgsbro, a subculture is defined, across time and place, in terms of performers' shared paradigms of meaning. It is a variant of a source culture, or combines elements of meaning from different source cultures. Elements of meaning differentiating one subculture from another are marked by symbols. The pattern of symbols constitutes the style of the subculture, through which it appears as a separate social organisation. In my investigation, the subcultures are all variants of a source culture which is international, rooted primarily in the USA. The symbols of meaning whereby the subculture acquires its identity are therefore first of all linguistic ones, the use of code-switching to English in the subcultural discourse. Written texts, such as pamphlets, are often completely in (colloquial) English. English, furthermore, is a necessary medium of communication with groups belonging to the same subculture in other countries. Høgsbro points out that the national groups would barely survive by themselves. They exist only by virtue of belonging to a subculture which is international. My investigation shows that core performers spend a lot of time and money on direct communication with, and visits to, groups in other countries.

2   Performers' status in the subculture, according to Høgsbro, is not dependent on their qualities as individuals, but only on the degree to which they have been able to internalise the subcultural paradigms of meaning, as these are symbolised in style of living, patterns of social behaviour, style of language, body language and dress. My own data confirm that, in English-language-oriented subcultures, the ability to use and understand English is indeed an important status symbol.

3   The core of the subculture consists of those who have internalised the subcultural paradigms of meaning. Around this core there is a zone of performers who master these paradigms to a varying degree, and whose less perfect mastery may to some extent be compensated for by a show of style. As this show of style determines a performer's position in the hierarchy, it leads to the development of a 'public' vs. 'private' self, as well as anxiety-and-bluff mechanisms to avoid revelation of the private self because it constitutes a potential threat to one's status. This description, by Høgsbro, is confirmed for the subcultures investigated in so far as core performers are either fluent in English, or at least seem to have the whole range of relevant and distinctive English terminology at their fingertips. More marginal performers, in this case people who by their own admission are less consistent and/or skilful performers, appear to be less inclined to codeswitch.

4   Høgsbro finally points out that, as a further consequence of (2), the mythology of the subculture is not about the lives of individuals, but about a chain of collective conquests vis-à-vis a hegemonic culture or other subcultures. And, indeed, performers of the English-language-oriented

youth cultures seem used to having to justify their subcultural activities to outsiders, which they do with indirect reference to the 'collective conquests' of the subculture. The death-metal singer, conscious of the violence and aggressiveness of his music, talks with pride about the radio programme in which his death-metal singing technique, called 'growling', received remarks of approval by an established opera singer. A group of hip-hop street dancers performed on television, and one performer, who is also a graffiti artist, has had a picture exhibited at a recognised art exhibition. A computer-culture informant admits that his subculture depends on the illegal copying of software, but his knowledge of computers has nevertheless landed him a job at a school, installing computers, i.e. his subculture still provides access to increased status in the hegemonic culture. Stories such as these also seem to illustrate, at the micro-level, how, as a form of social organisation the subculture has come to pervade most social strata and social movements and is now, according to Høgsbro, perhaps the most important contributor to the processes through which popular cultural demands lead to the gradual revision of social institutions.

3 Acquisition of EFL

It is commonly believed (and was the case probably up until the early 1980s) that in EFL countries English is learned almost exclusively through formal instruction (see, for example, Moag 1982: 34). However, as a corollary of the developments in everyday functions of English as described in Section 2, this is no longer the case, at least not in Denmark. Few children arrive for their first English lesson in the 4th grade without already knowing some English. Of the types of English text discussed in Section 2, many have subtypes that are targeted for, or particularly popular with, children and adolescents, who use and develop skills in English in peer-group contexts. Examples of such contexts are watching English-language cartoons on the satellite TV stations, then perhaps progressing to 'splatter movies' (graphically violent or gory movies) or martial-arts videos without Danish subtitles, listening to rap lyrics, and code-switching in discussions of the latest in English-language rock'n'roll or computer games acquired on the Internet. These are a few of the many English-language-oriented activities that occupy young people today, and that are linked (directly or indirectly) to youth subcultures such as those described in Section 2.

This development has important implications in terms of motivation. Distinguishing – with Lambert and Tucker (1972: 347ff) and others – between types of motivation, Moag characterises the purpose of learning English in an EFL country as predominantly instrumental: people learn English because it is a necessary tool in their work (Moag 1982: 32), and not primarily because they have a desire to identify with the cultures whose language they are learning (the integrative type of motivation). However, while this is still the case as far as 'English from above' is concerned, the motivating force behind the learning of 'English from below' is basically integrative, being the desire to symbolise subcultural identity or affiliation, and peer group solidarity. Thus, in Denmark and probably other EFL countries, code-switching to English is an inherent aspect of adolescent speech, and +/– code-switching has some of the characteristics of a sociolinguistic variable. The hierarchical organisation of the English-language-oriented subcultural group described above is essentially that of the adolescent boys' group (see Maltz and Borker 1982), and group leaders – whose speech style of frequent code-switching marks their superior status within the group – are usually boys.

4 Attitudes towards English

The public speech norm (as opposed to particular written registers) does not endorse code-switching to English, and even people who codeswitch habitually will say or imply, when asked, that it is 'wrong' to use English where Danish would do as well. However, as a foreign language, English is highly prestigious in Denmark, as is a degree of Danish–English bilingualism in the individual. Thus, nearly two thirds of respondents in the quantitative investigation agreed that all Danish adults ought to be able to speak, and understand, spoken English without any problems (agreement about the importance of reading and writing skills being considerably less). The predominantly positive attitude towards the presence of English in Danish society is reflected in the gradient from the same investigation that is shown in Table 10.2.[6]

Knowing the particular benefits that the use of English is associated with can tell us something about the functions that a model for EFL is expected to fulfil. The figures below suggest instrumental functions, first of all as a key to participation in the internationalisation process. However, more than

Table 10.2 Views on the presence of the English language in Danish society

'The presence of the English language in Danish society is . . .	Agree (%)
(a) . . . a practical consequence of increased internationalisation.'	92
(b) . . . useful because it helps improve people's English.'	89
(c) . . . useful because it broadens people's cultural horizon.'	69
(d) . . . a threat to the Danish language.'	26
(e) . . . a threat to Danish culture.'	19
(f) . . . a craze not to be taken seriously.'	16

two-thirds of respondents expect the presence of the English language in Danish society to 'broaden their cultural horizon'. Another set of results – though indicating that the majority of the population do not primarily see the use of English as a culturally specific influence – shows that more than one-third regard it as representing the cultural influence of the USA, an additional 5 per cent attributing it to British influence. Danes, furthermore, want their children's command of English to extend to formal educational domains, as indicated by the (perhaps astonishing) fact that as many as 37 per cent were willing to go along with a suggestion that English replace Danish as the language of instruction in school subjects such as geography.

A series of questions were devoted to finding out to what extent there is an awareness of different regional Englishes – in particular the distinction between the two major varieties, American and British English – and (if this is so) to what extent they are associated with particular cultural activities and positive or negative values. Initially, to get an indication of any differential attitudes towards American and British culture, respondents were asked whether they liked Americans or Britons better, and whether they would prefer to live in Great Britain or the USA. The answers show a slightly stronger orientation towards Britons: 27 per cent 'like' Britons better, as opposed to 20 per cent in favour of Americans, and 52 per cent would prefer to live in Great Britain, as opposed to 43 per cent favouring the USA.[7]

As regards the English language, people were asked whether they consider themselves capable of distinguishing between American and British English, and they were given examples of popular TV series in which the characters speak one or the other of the two varieties. As many as 81 per cent answered in the affirmative, whereas 19 per cent said they were not capable of distinguishing between American and British English (there were no scores in 'don't know').

Table 10.3 Reasons for preference of either American or British English

'I prefer . . .	British English . . .	American English . . .
(a) . . . because this variety is more cultivated.'	66%	3%
(b) . . . because this variety is more natural.'	30%	65%
(c) . . . because this variety represents progress and individualism.'	1%	7%
(d) . . . because this variety represents tradition and spiritual values.'	36%	3%
(e) . . . because the other variety is ugly.'	17%	4%
(f) . . . because the other variety is stiff and formal.'	2%	52%
(g) . . . for other reasons.'	10%	10%

Given the British tradition in the teaching of English in European schools, it is hardly surprising that Danes find it somewhat more difficult to 'like' the American variety of English than Americans and American society (compare Flaitz 1993: 187). Still, as many as 33 per cent of those capable of distinguishing between American and British English prefer American English, against 50 per cent in favour of British English; 17 per cent are undecided.

Throughout these results there was a tendency for younger respondents to be more American-oriented than older respondents, and for respondents who had left school early (before the 10th grade) to be more American-oriented than respondents with the Danish equivalent of a High School degree or General Certificate of Education.

To further explore attitudes to American and British English in the Danish population, those preferring either one or the other of the two varieties were asked to explain their preference by selecting reasons from a list of stereotypical value judgements often associated with either American or British English. More than one preference could be given. The results are shown in Table 10.3.

Of those who prefer British English, a vast majority (66 per cent) appear to do so because they regard this variety as more 'cultivated' than American English; other, less frequently chosen, reasons for preferring British English include the notion that British English represents 'tradition and spiritual values' (36 per cent), and the opinion that American English is 'ugly' (17 per cent). Most of those who prefer American English do because they regard this variety as more 'natural' (65 per cent), and because they think British English is 'stiff and formal' (52 per cent).

It was thought likely that attitudes towards British and American English would to some extent depend on notions of the relative suitability of each variety for particular cultural contexts. Thus the informants were given the opportunity to select the variety of their choice for each of the contexts shown in Table 10.4, or to indicate that either variety would do.

Table 10.4 Survey on the relative perceived suitability of American or British English in various contexts

		American English	British English	Either
(a)	The teaching of English in Danish schools	15%	68%	17%
(b)	Films and TV series with action	45%	18%	37%
(c)	Comedies (films and TV series)	21%	42%	37%
(d)	Documentaries (films and TV series)	15%	45%	40%
(e)	Films and TV series about love and romance	27%	27%	45%
(f)	Song lyrics (pop music, rock'n'roll)	22%	22%	56%
(g)	Advertising, commercials	22%	20%	58%

Table 10.5 Survey on the relative perceived suitability of American or British English by those who like American English better than British English

		American English	British English	Either
(a)	The teaching of English in Danish schools	38%	39%	23%
(b)	Films and TV series with action	72%	2%	26%
(c)	Comedies (films and TV series)	45%	24%	31%
(d)	Documentaries (films and TV series)	37%	22%	41%
(e)	Films and TV series about love and romance	57%	5%	38%
(f)	Song lyrics (pop music, rock'n'roll)	42%	10%	48%
(g)	Advertising, commercials	45%	5%	50%

These results show, to begin with, that it is possible to order contexts according to how important the distinction between American and British English appears to be for context: only 17 per cent of respondents think either variety will do in (a) the teaching of English, whereas, at the other extreme, 58 per cent think it does not matter whether American or British English is used in (g) advertising and commercials. These summary results also show that British English is the preferred variety for (a) the teaching of English, (c) comedies and (d) documentaries, whereas American English is preferred for (b) action films.

However, the summary results conceal the fact that the individual's choice of variety for almost every context is determined by his or her *general* orientation. Those who 'like American English better than British English' prefer American English for every single context and to roughly the same extent as those 'liking' British English prefer British English for the same context. A significant exception is (a) the teaching of English in Danish schools. Those with no *general* preference tend to side with British English when it comes to choosing a variety for the particular context. Compare Table 10.4 with the results for those who 'like American English better than British English' given in Table 10.5.

It is a measure of the influence of tradition that even those who 'like American English better than British English', and who choose American English over British English for every other context, are divided equally between the two varieties in their choice of a variety for (a) the educational context.[8] By comparison, the only context for which those who 'like British English better than American English' choose American English as frequently as British English is that of (b) action films.

One conceivable source of influence with regard to who develops a 'liking' for American English as opposed to British English is the variety and attitude of one's English teacher. Respondents were asked if they had ever had an English teacher who did not accept the use of American words or American pronunciation, and whether they had ever had an English teacher who spoke American English. However, correlation of the teacher variable with attitudes to American and British English did not explain the 33 per cent preference for American English among those able to make the distinction. Another possible explanation might have been travel activities – Danes paying extended visits to the US on business, as exchange students, au pairs, etc. – but the survey shows that the relevant travel activities only involve about 3 per cent of the population.

On the other hand, a series of questions constituted a survey of cultural leisure-time interests, some of which (but not all) are influenced by American or British culture and language, and which might conceivably correlate with language attitude as style markers of either subculture or class. For example:

Do you listen to, or play: *Do you play:* *Do you:*
Rock'n'roll   Computer games   Ride horseback . . .
Jazz   Golf . . .
Classical music
Rap / hip-hop music
Country music
Danish pop music . . .

The options, for each activity, are (1) 'not at all', (2) 'a little', (3) 'quite a bit', (4) 'a lot'. As it turns out, people's preference for American vs. British English correlates significantly with such leisure-time interests. Thus a preference for American English correlates positively with an interest in rock'n'roll, hip-hop music, country music, Danish pop music and computer games, and negatively with classical music, golf and horseback-riding.[9] Compare the results for country and classical music which are given in Figures 10.1[10] and 10.2,[11] respectively.

Results such as these seem to provide evidence that the major varieties of English have symbolic value in the Danish population as markers of class-related or subcultural style, and – as in a previous investigation, concerning the English language in France (Flaitz 1993) – evidence *against* the view that international English has become 'a medium pure and simple rather than . . . either a symbol or a message' (Fishman 1982: 24).

5 Danish–English bilingualism?

In discussing the extent to which English is used in Denmark, as increasingly in the EFL world generally, I emphasised the distinction between active and passive uses of language, and the fact that a majority of the Danish population seem able at least to read and understand spoken English well enough to cope with code-switching and texts in English encountered many times

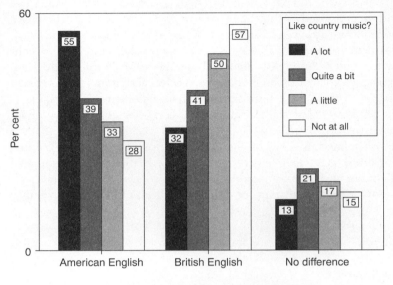

Figure 10.1 Correlation between preference for American or British English and interest in country music

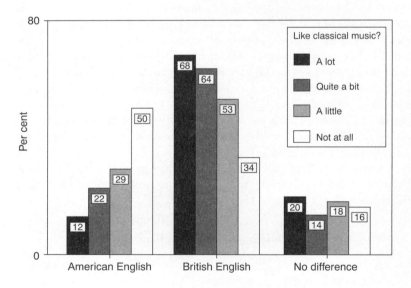

Figure 10.2 Correlation between preference for American or British English and interest in classical music

each day. In fact, an index averaging respondents' own ratings of their ability to use English in particular situations shows that about 60 per cent of the adult population regard themselves as very or reasonably proficient in English. For those who have had English in school beyond the 9th grade, the figure is 85 per cent.

I have presented evidence, furthermore, that attitudes towards the use of English in Danish society are generally positive, partly because it reflects the instrumental functions of English as an international lingua franca, and partly on account of cultural values associated with the English language. A vast majority of Danes regard themselves as capable of distinguishing between American and British English, and these main varieties of English have even become symbolic of different cultural values in the Danish population.

Still, in spite of the aspirations of Danish politicians towards 'bilingualism' in the population as such, at least 20 per cent of the population have little or no knowledge of English (or, for that matter, any other foreign language; compare Bacher et al. 1992). What is worse, there seems to be little awareness of this, in the population or in government, or of the problems faced by that large minority of Danes who are experiencing a new kind of functional illiteracy by not having access to texts that are being used and understood as a matter of course by the rest of the population by virtue of their knowledge of English. However, any discussion of the forms and functions of English in a European EFL country will have to consider the social characteristics, language attitudes and EFL needs of those whom the development towards varying degrees of bilingualism has left behind.

The 20 per cent of the population who have little or No Knowledge of English (NKE from here on) include especially the older generations (aged 45 and above), who went to school at a time when English did not play the role in society or school that it does today. The figure of 20 per cent is probably a conservative estimate (compare Bacher et al. 1992: 107), as the NKE category has been defined here in fairly exclusive terms: respondents were asked to assess their own command of English in terms of seven different skills/contexts:

Ability to . . .
1   . . . understand English song lyrics listened to on the radio
2   . . . understand English films without Danish subtitles
3   . . . read and understand a short instruction in English
4   . . . read a book in English
5   . . . write a letter in English
6   . . . explain in English how to get to the nearest bus stop
7   . . . discuss opinions in English

Only those who thought they had 'little' or 'no' ability in every single context were included in the NKE category.[12]

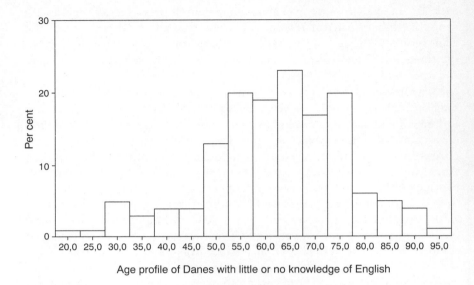

Age profile of Danes with little or no knowledge of English

Figure 10.3 Histogram displaying an NKE age profile of Danes

Figure 10.3 shows the NKE age profile with the age of 62–63 as mean and median. There are few young members – the younger people are, the more likely they are to know English. On the other side of age 62–63, the drop is proportional to the decrease in the representation of these groups in the population.

The ratio of men to women in the NKE group is not significantly different from 1:1. None of the respondents went to school beyond the 10th grade; almost 75 per cent left school after the 7th grade, and close to 60 per cent did not do any kind of vocational training after leaving school. Today, in accordance with the high age profile, 60 per cent are retired, while 33 per cent are active on the job market, undergoing education or doing military service; the remaining 7 per cent are not currently in employment outside the home.

The following, more detailed description of the NKE section's situation (as experienced by themselves) is to be regarded as diagnostic, indicating the size of the NKE problem in terms of how it affects people's lives, and some of the obstacles – not least attitudinal ones – which a specially designed, adult EFL course or programme would have to overcome to reach this group. Behind this description lies the assumption that it is the duty of a democratic society to ensure that everybody is taught enough English, in the relevant forms, to be able to cope with the linguistic manifestations of internationalisation in the media and elsewhere in their daily lives.

Initially, it is important to obtain an indication of the frequency with which NKE people think they encounter the English language.[13] Fifty per cent of them say by way of an overall estimate that they *hear* the

English language at least once a day, another 26 per cent saying once a week. When asked how often they *see* the English language in writing, the overall estimate is down to 12 per cent ('at least once a day') and 20 per cent ('at least once a week'), but separate frequencies for specific contexts show that the true figures are much higher. It seems that NKE people's *awareness* of the extent to which they are exposed to English is low until they are confronted with examples of relevant contexts, i.e. it seems that they have learned to ignore, to some extent, messages that they don't understand.

Those who, according to their own awareness, are the least exposed to English are the elderly (aged 70 and above), and/or those qualified only for unskilled work. Gender, too, may be important, to the extent that women seem to encounter English less frequently than men.

Respondents were asked to select two reasons why anyone would want to learn English. There were five options, the first two representing an instrumental, the next two an integrative attitude to language learning. Table 10.6 shows the relative frequency with which each reason was selected by NKE respondents. The most conspicuous figure here is the 50 per cent for whom learning English would be a *practical* measure. The other instrumental reason, increased job opportunities, is regarded as far less important.[14] The implication seems to be that not knowing English is a practical problem influencing people's everyday lives. Note that the integrative reason, being able to meet people from other countries, counts for as much as 26 per cent.

NKE people's *reaction* when they find themselves addressed in a language they don't understand depends on how often it happens, as shown in Table 10.7.[15] Those who think they hear spoken English *less* frequently than once a week tend to say either that they don't care (54 per cent) or that it makes them wish they knew (more) English (37 per cent). However, only 36 per cent of those who think they hear spoken English *at least* once a week say they don't care, and 21 per cent say it makes them angry that they are excluded from communication in this way. This suggests that, as the use of English in Danish society increases, NKE persons will experience this as a growing personal problem.

These findings make it all the more surprising that many NKE persons deny that they *need* to know (more) English, though again there is variation accord-

Table 10.6 Reasons for learning English

'Knowing English . . .	
(a) . . . is practical.'	50%
(b) . . . increases job opportunities.'	14%
(c) . . . makes one more respected.'	5%
(d) . . . enables one to meet people from other countries.'	26%
(e) (. . . is good for other reasons.)	5%

Table 10.7 Reaction to being addressed in a language one does not understand

	Those who hear English	
	. . . at least once a week	. . . less than once a week
(a) 'I don't care.'	36%	54%
(b) 'It makes me angry.'	21%	3%
(c) 'It makes me wish I knew (more) English.'	34%	37%
(d) (Other reactions)	10%	6%

ing to how frequently they think they encounter English, as shown in Table 10.8.[16] Both groups say they need to know English to some extent (23–25 per cent), but only those who encounter English frequently have a sizeable score in 'very much' (25 per cent). Conversely, as many as 71 per cent of those who hear spoken English *less* frequently than once a week say they *don't* need to know (more) English. It is particularly surprising that as many as 50 per cent of the group who encounter English frequently say they *don't* need to know (more) English. Despite the emotional responses, e.g. anger, of this group (see above) at being addressed in a language they do not understand, many of them are still not ready to draw a conclusion which, by implication, might seem to commit them to a course of action (i.e. learning English).

It is commonplace in language-attitude studies that it is necessary to distinguish conceptually between attitudes towards bilingualism and attitudes towards the specific languages involved. In other words, we need to ask whether we are really measuring the attitudes of monolinguals[17] trying to cope in a society presupposing a degree of bilingualism in the individual, or whether their attitudes towards bilingualism are actually manifestations of, for example, protectiveness towards Danish language and culture, and (by the same token) a fear of the influence of Anglo-American language and culture. The summary for the NKE section in Table 10.9 – reflecting their relative agreement with the same statements as those applied to the whole population, above – is in fact very similar to the pattern for the whole population. In other words, NKE people do not differ significantly from the rest of the population in this

Table 10.8 Extent to which respondents feel they need to know English

	Those who hear English	
	. . . at least once a week	. . . less than once a week
'I need to know (more) English . . .		
(a) . . . very much.'	25%	6%
(b) . . . to some extent.'	25%	23%
(c) . . . not at all.'	50%	71%

Table 10.9 Views on the presence of the English language in Danish society

'The presence of the English language in Danish society is . . .	Agree	
	Responses (%)	Respondents (%)
(a) . . . a practical consequence of increased internationalisation.'	28	89
(b) . . . useful because it helps improve people's English.'	27	86
(c) . . . useful because it broadens people's cultural horizon.'	20	64
(d) . . . a threat to the Danish language.'	12	38
(e) . . . a threat to Danish culture.'	7	23
(f) . . . a craze not to be taken seriously.'	7	21

respect, showing a predominantly positive attitude to the general presence of the English language in Danish society. The right-hand column, showing the percentage of respondents expressing relative agreement, indicates high scores in the instrumental categories (a) and (b), and to a lesser extent in the integrative one, (c). Scores in the negative categories (d–f) are, however, not quite negligible, in particular the indication in (d) that 38 per cent of NKE respondents think the English language is a threat to the Danish language.

Finally, to measure how serious NKE Danes really are in wishing to broaden their cultural horizon, respondents were confronted with the suggestion that foreign TV programmes – rather than being shown, as they are now, with the original sound track, but with Danish subtitles – should be shown with the Danish language dubbed in. Results are shown in Table 10.10.[18] As the large majority of foreign programmes on Danish TV are of Anglo-American origin, this seems to suggest that the negative attitudes towards English expressed in some of the previous questions do not primarily reflect concern about Danish language and culture. Rather, negative attitudes towards English in the NKE section of the population appear to reflect the individual's sense of personal communication problems.

The purpose of this description of the section of the Danish population who have little or no knowledge of English has been to point out some contrasts, and also some similarities, between this minority and the majority

Table 10.10 Views on subtitling or dubbing of foreign TV programmes

'Foreign TV programmes should be shown with the Danish language dubbed in.'	
(a) 'I agree very much.'	18%
(b) 'I agree with some reservations.'	15%
(c) 'I disagree to some extent.'	11%
(d) 'I strongly disagree.'	56%

who have learned English at least so well as to be able to cope with the uses of English in Danish society. These contrasts and similarities are the conditions that would have to be considered in a discussion of what kinds of EFL programme, and forms of English, would be needed in providing everyone in Denmark with the necessary minimum of proficiency in English. With regard to similarities, we have noted that English is generally considered prestigious in the Danish population, and that it is not to any great extent regarded as a threat to Danish language or culture. On the contrary, several of the results point to English being regarded as a source of cultural enrichment. This means that basic motivation for learning English is not a problem. However, in the case of NKE people – while they are clearly affected, in practical as well as psychological terms, by their inability to understand English – basic motivation for learning English may be overruled by other factors, as implied by some of the findings. Thus NKE people have a high age profile – and competing priorities to go with it – and are likely to lack faith in their ability to start learning a foreign language relatively late in life. Their brief school careers in the past, furthermore, suggest a negative attitude towards intellectual pursuits as such. These factors point to a need for adult EFL campaigns to be designed especially to reach the NKE section of the population, including the older generations.[19] Any qualified discussion of the forms and functions of English to be taught in an EFL country such as Denmark would have to consider this important problem. Furthermore, it is not a problem that will disappear as the current younger generation becomes older (the older generations were, admittedly, not taught English in school to the same extent as children are nowadays). Thousands of potential members of the NKE section are added each time a new generation leaves school (see Bacher et al. 1992). These are people who leave school early because they are tired of it and do not do well at school subjects. Many immigrant children come from cultural enclaves where Anglo-American influences are effectively kept out, so that by the time they start school they – unlike Danish children – have had little or no contact with the English language, and some of them may never manage to catch up with the average Danish child in terms of proficiency in English.[20] People with negative school experiences will often try to avoid or ignore, in later life, situations reminding them of this 'failure'. Under such circumstances, what little English they may have learned in school will eventually disappear: attrition of English skills has been shown to begin after a few years as far as women are concerned, whereas men tend to experience it especially as they approach middle age (Lieberson, cited in Moag 1982: 39).

6 Forms of EFL

According to Moag (1982: 13), variation within English in an EFL country can be characterised as minimal or slight, as opposed to interlanguage features, which are maximal or extensive. In this final section of the chapter I will examine – under the headings of (1) Variation within EFL, and (2) Models of EFL – to what extent this description is still adequate, in light of the preceding analysis of Denmark as an EFL country. I will draw some conclusions with regard to the functions of Standard English as a model for EFL and as an international lingua franca.

6.1 *Variation within EFL*

In the discussion on the uses of English we had to distinguish between 'English from above' and 'English from below', the former constituting the promotion of English by the hegemonic culture for purposes of 'international communication' (primarily through formal education), the latter representing the informal – active or passive – use of English as an expression of subcultural identity and style. In view of such radically different functions, it is hardly surprising to find that the question of variation within English even in an EFL country is now much more complex than suggested by Moag's early 1980s characterisation of such variation as 'slight'.

The degree of variation within 'English from above' is carefully differentiated to suit the assumed communicative or educational needs of a particular target group, considering their age level, level of proficiency and possible specialised interests. This is done through syllabus designing, which, on the part of the school teacher – and to a limited extent the children themselves – involves the particular selection of texts that they will be exposed to, and will use as input for learning. Though these texts may, right from the start, represent some functional and regional variation (e.g. rhymes as well as prose, British as well as American English), variation will hardly be extensive until the advanced levels. Variation in 'English from above' seems to have the following characteristics:

1   It depends on the level of proficiency.
2   It is a function of the *teaching materials*, and of the students' ability to recognise and understand different types of text, involving only to a very limited degree the students' ability to vary their own spoken or written English according to functional criteria.
3   Whatever the range of variation taught, it is reproduced in the passive repertoire of the individual learner, so that – to the extent that requirements were everywhere the same for comparable levels of proficiency – we would expect all learners of a particular level to be passively proficient within more or less the same range of variation.
4   Variation within English means variation within Standard English – texts in, or modelled on, native non-standards are hardly ever used, though they may occur in projects defined by the students themselves, as a manifestation of 'English from below'.

With regard to variation within 'English from below', we still have to distinguish between active and passive uses of English, but there is a considerable degree of functional variation in both types, and it follows a different pattern:

1 While obviously presupposing a minimum of 'general' competence in English, the degree of functional variation – primarily in the area of lexis – that the individual is expected to handle is not directly related to his or her general proficiency. Not only is there no limit to the kind of text in English that can occur in advertising and other areas of public discourse, and which the 'average' reader or listener is expected to understand – functional variation in the individual's active English vocabulary is an essential feature of the discourse of English-language-oriented subcultures, regardless of the degree of grammatical and phonological competence.

2 The social forces of the subcultural environment are thus, generally speaking, more successful than the classroom at ensuring the learning of active functional variation in English. All that most English teachers can hope for is that students acquire a distinction between informal and (generally) formal style. Within the peer group of the English-language-oriented subculture, on the other hand – while this particular distinction is of no importance – the status of the individual depends on the extent to which his (or less usually, her) English repertoire reflects the complete range of different domains and activities in the subculture.

3 Still, functional variation in the active use of 'English from below' is confined within the domains of one subculture, in the speech and writing of the subcultural core figure or 'expert'. Functional variation across subcultures takes place at the 'societal' level, but the repertoires of readers/listeners vary systematically according to social and cultural affiliations. Functional variation across subcultures is never part of the individual's active competence.

4 Finally, variation within 'English from below' occasionally involves texts – and so requires passive skills – in non-standard English, e.g. African-American vernacular. However, non-standard grammar and vocabulary are not as typical of 'English from below' as one might think: even in the particular domains concerned, most variation involves other parameters such as register, jargon, slang and taboo. This is true also of the active use of English by Danish speakers, whose interlanguage in grammatical terms may have features in common with, but is rarely modelled on, native non-standards (*it don't matter*, etc.).

The Danish hip-hop group 'Out of Control' is a paradigmatic example of an English-from-below source and was interviewed for part of the research reported in this chapter. 'Out of Control' is a group of street dancers (their own term) from Copenhagen, but some of them are into other branches of hip-hop culture as well. They have danced in the streets of many cities in Europe, and a wide network of hip-hop friends and contacts in Europe and the US enables them to keep up with the latest developments in their form of underground art. They, in turn, are considered among the 'avant-garde' of hip-hop dancing in Denmark – they are consulted by more commercialised dancing schools featuring hip-hop, and they are very proud of having been on Danish television several times. They spoke straight English during the first interview, because some of their hip-hop friends from Germany were present, whereas the second interview was in Danish with constant code-switching to English. Their vocabulary represents at least four distinct registers, corresponding to as many basic hip-hop domains, and two levels of formality (compare 1–3 with 4 below):

1. Techniques and styles in break-dancing, e.g. *boogie, electric boogie, wind-mills, back spin, head spin, turtle, foot work, shop, crock, poppin', bobbin', back slide, moon walk, pop, freezer, cracking, float, waves, isolation, back spreads, ground moves, hydraulics, call-forty-five, King Tuts, the Window, boo-ballooing, lock, locking, points, rolls, skeets, bus stop, showdance, running man, swipes,* etc.

2. Techniques and styles in Rap and DJ, e.g. *ragamuffin, scratch, scratcher, mixer, cut-backs, cross-fader, break, break-beat, toast,* etc.

3. Techniques and styles in graffiti, e.g. *tag, tagging, bomb, bombing, jams, cipher, burn-off, wild-style, semi-wild-style, straight-letters, 3D-letters, white-lines, piece, throw-up, whole-cars, windows, window-down-whole-car,* etc.

4. Hip-hop mythology: street life in New York City, e.g. *battle* (noun 'compe-tition between gangs', or verb), *biting* ('plagiarism'), *biter, wanna-be, dope, pusher, graffiti-trip, fuck* ('not care about'), *hang-out, low-life, riot, stick-up kid,* etc.

To sum up, although variation within EFL is indeed slight in terms of the active proficiency skills transmitted through 'English from above', there is considerable variation in the passive repertoire acquired. Learners' passive repertoires are further developed and specialised as a result of informal contact with manifestations of 'English from below.' Depending on the degree of iden-tification with a particular subculture associated with the English language, furthermore, EFL users may even develop an active command of a range of variational parameters reflecting the different domains and activities of the subculture. On the other hand, while such EFL users may have frequent contact with other speakers of non-native English (i.e. English characterised by transfer from the speaker's mother tongue), their exposure to native non-standard varieties of English is often more limited.

6.2 Models of EFL

It used to be a commonplace that the formal teaching of active skills in a foreign language begins with the selection of that particular regional and/or social variety of the language which is to provide the learners' linguistic model. Whereas any selection of vocabulary through a particular syllabus will represent only a small part of the entire lexical repertoire of the variety chosen, the phonological and grammatical systems selected will soon be generally reflected every time a learner speaks in the foreign language. Progress in lexical proficiency is related to quantity – perfecting grammar and pronunciation is a qualitative process. The development of passive skills is less dependent on the exclusive use of one linguistic and cultural model, allowing – particularly at the advanced levels – the occasional use of texts representing different regional, social and even historical varieties.

The teaching of English as a foreign language, in Denmark and elsewhere, has rested on the assumption that, as far as learners' active grammar and vocabulary are concerned, it is based on one model variety, Standard English. The fact that various scholars have recently tried to persuade us that Standard English does not exist and that, even if it did, it would not be a suitable or feasible model for EFL, presents some interesting theoretical problems: What kind of English have we been teaching our learners all these years? What has made us think of it as a 'standard'? Is a different kind of EFL called for, in view of how English is used around the world today?

For some scholars the problem with Standard English is its variability. Its various manifestations are too different (e.g. personal letters vs. legal documents) to make up a 'standard', and so Standard English must be a myth (Bex 1993: 260). However, functional variation is not antithetical to the concept of 'standard' in linguistics; in fact the standard has been *defined* in terms of its functional 'elaboration' (Haugen 1966), through which it has become uniquely capable of serving the complete range of important social functions such as government, administration, the courts, the church, commerce, education, etc. Whereas the question of standard vs. non-standard concerns especially the sentence-grammatical levels of description, functional or genre differences involve mainly discourse-grammatical and lexical features. Even poetry, unless marked by regional and/or non-prestigious forms, can be regarded as a functional variety of Standard English in spite of various linguistic idiosyncrasies ('poetic license'), to the extent that such idiosyncrasies are conscious deviations from the standard, and so depend on the existence of a standard for their artistic effect. In classical sociolinguistics, the standard–non-standard contrast is bound up with the concept of linguistic prestige. Standard English is the overtly prestigious variety that speakers of non-standard English will accommodate to according to the formality of the situation, because features of relative prestige are within speakers' conscious awareness as such (compare Labov's 'sociolinguistic markers', e.g. Labov 1970;

see also Stalker 1986). The 'dialect' of a particular urban speech community can be described in terms of its 'Inherent Variability' (see Trudgill 1974a); recently a theoretical framework has been suggested within which Standard English might itself be described in terms of its Inherent Variability (Preisler 1995). As functional variability, therefore, is not a valid criterion for denying the existence of Standard English, neither can functional variability in the linguistic model used for EFL be a relevant criterion in denying its status as Standard English.

Irrelevant too – in an EFL context – is the argument that a concept of Standard English associated, in particular, with the standards of Britain and North America challenges the autonomy of the other Englishes of the world. Such political correctness fails to distinguish between the functions of autonomous, national varieties of English, and the functions of an international variety. The form of English taught in an EFL country should be determined only by the degree in which it will enable non-native speakers to cope with the linguistic aspects of internationalisation as it affects their own lives.

In the preceding, I have in fact presented a fairly detailed picture of how English is used in Denmark, and hence, of the various ways in which the English language affects the lives of different sections of the Danish population. It should, therefore, be possible to draw some conclusions with regard to the forms of English that need to be taught.

We have seen that internationalisation and the language of internationalisation (English) affect the whole population, not just an educational elite. We have also seen that there are huge differences in the *way* the use of English affects people, depending on their demographic and cultural (or subcultural) background. To some people English becomes an aspect of their professional or subcultural identity. The majority with at least a limited ability to read English, and understand spoken English, usually have no problems with the growing presence of English in public communication. However, about one fifth of the population are unable to read or understand English. These are people who leave school early, often because school has been a negative experience; most of them are middle-aged or older, and inclined to think that learning English – or trying to brush up what little English they may once have had – is simply not an option. Finding some way of reaching these people before that stage is reached, and motivating them to acquire and keep up sufficient passive skills in English to cope with everyday messages and texts – perhaps enabling them, for example, to use the Internet as a matter of course – is a major challenge for educators.

A democratic language policy affecting education would try to bridge the gap between the haves and the have-nots in terms of English, by providing EFL teaching experienced as relevant and attractive by groups of different backgrounds, not only children and adolescents but also adults. The aim of bilingualism should be variably defined in order to accommodate people of different abilities and perceived communicative needs. Variability in these terms refers primarily to domain/register and level of linguistic/pragmatic proficiency. It does not imply the teaching of a wide range of English regional and social varieties, which would be both unrealistic and irrelevant.

'English from above' should be seen as having three main functions:

1   constituting a formal element of education by way of preparing people for the international aspects of their professional lives
2   providing a foundation for the individual's informal acquisition of 'English from below' in any of its particular manifestations, including the ability to participate in activities representing subcultural interests and self-expression
3   ensuring that nobody leaves school without a minimum of reading and listening skills in English and a realisation of the importance of maintaining such skills.

Because of its variability in functional terms, as pointed out above, the variety of English best suited for all of these functions is undoubtedly Standard English in its two major regional forms, not least because only Standard English has a thoroughly codified written version. Outside the classroom, too, by far the most frequent native forms of English that Danes come into contact with are functional varieties of Standard American English or Standard British English, including (as I have argued) most of the varieties of 'English from below'. Channels of international communication such as the Internet, to which everybody will in the future have direct and unlimited access, are dominated by texts in Standard American or British English. Standard English is already the model used all over the world for EFL purposes, but usually it is taught in either one or the other of its two main forms – British English and American English – depending on the society and its historical or geographical relationship with either Britain or the USA. However, in the age of the Internet and e-mail, physical distances and linguistic spheres of interest are becoming less relevant, and so, from an instrumental point of view alone, passive skills in English (listening and reading) should be taught on the basis of *both* British and American English.

Furthermore, the preceding analysis of integrative attitudes towards the two varieties in Denmark showed that they are differentially associated with more general cultural and subcultural values in the Danish population. From a motivational point of view, then, this confirms that not only should EFL courses or programmes employ American English as well as British English teaching materials, but that the development of passive skills should routinely involve comparison between American and British English as distinct varieties, with particular emphasis on cultural characteristics as they are represented in lexis. Active skills (speaking and writing) naturally tend to reflect the British English model taught in school – even in subcultures rooted in the USA, as far as grammar and pronunciation are concerned. Ideally, however, learners should be able to choose either variety as a model for the formal development of their active proficiency, which is entirely possible. Even if teachers speak only one variety they may be able to offer some guidance based on theoretical knowledge, relevant teaching materials and audio-visual facilities.

A crucial question regarding the function of Standard English as an international lingua franca is the role of pragmatics in EFL, and the problem of how a culturally specific language can function as a lingua franca in cross-cultural contexts. Some scholars have suggested that EFL should be taught in a culturally 'neutral' variety, at least in terms of native-speaker culture. However, pragmatic transfer from, or adaptation to, the learner's mother tongue would be an acceptable way of safeguarding the learner's own socio-cultural identity (Hübler 1985: 192) or of making the foreign language 'real' in the context of the learner's own world (Widdowson 1994: 386). Others have given a highly restricted definition of 'English as an international language', according to which EFL should be taught within narrow functional domains such as 'business culture', 'computer culture', 'tourist culture', etc. (L. Smith 1983a; R. Johnson 1990).[21]

However, if EFL is based on models such as these, English as a lingua franca may become even more pidginised than it already is as a result of its use at many levels of society, i.e. it might evolve into a number of different, linguistically and functionally simplified, varieties. If English is learned simply as a lingua franca – i.e. if the teaching of EFL is not firmly rooted in the cultural context of native speakers – there is a danger that it will become unidiomatic, and that EFL speakers may wrongly come to regard unidiomatic echoes of their own mother tongue as the 'natural' (and therefore universally understood) mode of expression in English. The grammatical corollary of this is the tendency for native-English grammatical rules to be ignored if they are not within learners' conscious awareness as factors affecting comprehensibility. Accent, too, is likely to be left undeveloped because, beyond the basics, it is the least important level in communication, as a result of which EFL users may become deaf even to marked phonemic deviations from native phonological models, and learners may even be warned against improving their accent because this might lead to misunderstandings when culturally naive foreigners are mistaken for native speakers. The pidginised Englishes of, for example, Danes, Germans and Italians are systematically different due to interference from the respective native languages. This is also a measure of the extent to which their cultural specificity, rather than relating to Anglo-American culture, relates to cultures where English is spoken only as a foreign language.

With the evolution of a multiplicity of culturally autonomous Englishes, Standard English maintained as an instrument of cross-cultural communication will only be effective at the level of communicative competence to the extent that it is based on shared cultural assumptions. English has evolved as the result of a historical process, and the history of the language is an inescapable factor influencing its use even as a lingua franca. For this reason it seems inevitable that those shared cultural assumptions, to be reflected in the teaching of pragmatics in EFL, should derive from the cultural contexts of Standard English in its two most influential varieties. Taking a long-term perspective – as the global information society imposes its own supranational norms and values on the language of wider communication – this worldwide lingua franca (as distinct from the regional Englishes) is quite likely to undergo spontaneous and continuous standardisation in the direction of one model.

In the meantime, internationalisation in Europe has reached a point where young learners can expect to become fluent in English. This level of proficiency is often not attained until the post-school years, in environments and situations where English is used as a lingua franca, and only in a minority of cases in communication with native speakers of English. A recent study has indicated that the extent of transfer from the mother tongue is likely to be inversely proportional to (1) the amount of formal instruction which the lingua-franca user received in school, and (2) the extent to which this instruction was based on the standard variety of the foreign language (Rasmussen 1993: 18). It therefore seems essential that the foreign-language classroom experienced by learners during their school years should concentrate specifically on Standard English in its central cultural contexts, and on comparison with corresponding contexts in the learners' own culture.[22]

Acknowledgements

I am indebted to Karen Risager and Hartmut Haberland for valuable comments and suggestions. These colleagues are not, of course, responsible for any errors that remain.

Notes

1 Compare Moag's taxonomy of English-using societies (Moag 1982), whose categories are defined in terms of eight composite, distinctive features. For a discussion of this and other models, see Leitner (1992).
2 The data were collected in 1995 and 1996, in cooperation with the Institute of Social Development and the Danish National Institute of Social Research. The sample for the quantitative investigation consisted of 856 adult Danes. The project was made possible by a grant from the Danish Research Council for the Humanities.
3 Compare Undervisningsvejledning for folkeskolen 2, Fremmedsprog, Undervisningsministeriet, 1976, p. 9. The same idea was recently reiterated almost verbatim by the chair of the Education Committee of the Danish Parliament, Ms Hanne Severinsen, in an interview on the role of English in Denmark in one of the daily papers (Kristeligt Dagblad, 15 November 1996).
4 Bekendtgørelse om indretning af tekniske hjælpemidler. Arbejdstilsynets bekendtgørelse nr. 561 af 24. juni 1994.

5 Written Danish, Norwegian and Swedish are so similar that texts of this kind in any one of the three languages can be understood in the whole of Scandinavia.

6 For each statement the options were (1) 'I agree very much', (2) 'I agree with some reservations', (3) 'I disagree to some extent', (4) 'I strongly disagree', (5) 'I don't know'. The summary is a count of (1) and (2) lumped together.

7 These percentage differences are statistically significant: $p < 0.05$. Flaitz, too – with regard to France (Flaitz 1993: 187) – found a generally positive attitude towards English language and culture, though the American variety was preferred as far as culture was concerned.

8 The difference between 38 per cent and 39 per cent is not statistically significant.

9 Compare the stereotype of British English being the more 'cultivated' variety: Table 10.3.

10 Chi^2: $p = 0.007$.

11 Chi^2: $p = 0.000$.

12 The NKE category is in fact slightly under-represented in the data compared with its size in the population. The figures of this presentation are based on unweighted data.

13 In accordance with the phenomenological nature of this investigation, the question is how often people *think* they encounter the English language. It would be difficult to determine the truth about this or whether NKE people are always able to *identify* the language correctly.

14 The less importance of 'increased job opportunities', in comparison with both the 'practical' and the integrative ('meeting people') reason, is statistically significant ($p < 0.01$ and $p < 0.05$, respectively).

15 Chi^2: $p < 0.05$.

16 Chi^2: $p < 0.05$.

17 The majority of Danes who do not know English do not know any other foreign language, either. There are, of course, exceptions, just as we are ignoring immigrants who do not know English but who are not monolinguals.

18 The 'don't know' category was negligible and has been treated here as 'missing cases'.

19 With regard to a similar situation, e.g. in Germany and Sweden, see Findahl (1989: 140f.).

20 I owe this observation to Karen Risager.

21 For a critique of these models see Preisler (1995).

22 Compare Rasmussen (1993: 18–19); Firth (1990).

EPILOGUE

11

CURIOUSER AND CURIOUSER: FALLING STANDARDS IN THE STANDARD ENGLISH DEBATE

Tony Crowley

And so the standard English debate rumbles on. What seems to me to be the contribution made by this collection of essays is that it highlights two enduring features of the arguments around the term and concept. First, the confusions around the term itself, difficulties which have dogged it since its first recorded use. Second, the fact that this is not simply a linguistic debate, but one which is immersed in, and has had significant impact upon, larger social and political questions. In order to set out my own views I will consider a work which I consider to be confused, confusing and pernicious: John Honey's *Language is Power* (1997). I have chosen Honey's work on the grounds that it is a good example of a particular approach to the Standard English question, and that Honey is a frequent contributor to the debates around it.[1]

There are two significant confusions around the phrase 'Standard English': that around 'standard' and that relating to 'English'. With regard to 'standard', it is still evidently a word which shifts in its meaning between 'uniformity' and 'level of excellence'. I will return to this elision and its political implications later. In respect of 'English' in the phrase, its ambiguity lies in the failure to distinguish between speech and writing. I will show the problems caused by these confusions by looking at Honey's text.

On page 1 of *Language is Power* Honey defines the problematic term: 'By standard English I mean the language in which this book is written, which is evidently the same form of English used in books and newspapers all over the world.' This is clear: standard English is the medium of writing in the English language, grammatically stable and codified. And in fact this is the definition of the term used by its first recorded (1858) coiners, the lexicographers of the *New/Oxford English Dictionary*. On page 3 of *Language is Power*, however, we are informed that 'standard English can be spoken in any accent of English, though in practice it is seldom (indeed perhaps never) spoken in the broadest forms of regional accent'. This is a quite different use of the phrase in that it refers to speech rather than writing. The thinking behind this elision is presumably as follows: just as standard English, in the sense of writing, can be transcribed in *any* handwriting and remain stable, identifiable and codifiable, likewise standard English, in the sense of speech, can be spoken in *any* accent and remain similarly able to be identified and codified on the basis of its stability.

Honey's use of 'standard English' to refer to both writing and speech, without clarification, is a common error. Its danger lies in the presupposition that there is in some sense standard (written) English and standard (spoken) English and that they share a common structure. It is as though standard English were an ideal form of the language which is realised in practice by 'the best' users of English in the forms of standard written and spoken English. Honey's position on this point seems clear in his comments on the historical development of standard English. For example:

> The study of school text books for spelling, reading, writing, and speaking make it abundantly clear that between the sixteenth and the beginning of the nineteenth centuries there was an ever more widely held notion of a standard form of English, all the elements of which were realistically accessible through book-learning.
>
> (Honey 1997: 81)

It is also clear in his later assertion that in order to acquire standard English a child needs 'constant exposure to written forms, to educated speech, and to explicit teaching' (ibid.: 53); presumably the aim of the explicit teaching being to give the child the common structure which underpins standard spoken and written English.

There are in fact a number of difficulties with Honey's definitions of both standard English writing and speech even in his explicit formulations. Thus the standard written language is said to have 'its own structures, vocabulary, styles, qualities, and functions' (ibid.: 49). What, we might ask, might a standard written vocabulary be? In a definition which reveals the usual lack of precision the answer appears to be simple: 'the word-stock of any normal English dictionary, shorn of all words marked as dialect words' (ibid.: 191); what does 'normal' mean? What of the qualities of standard written English? Are these intrinsic to the language? Like the amorous nature of Italian, the philosophical rigour of German, the lilt of Irish? Or are these judgements made of the language which are then transferred to it? In turn, standard spoken English is said to have its own 'grammar, vocabulary and idiom'. How do we know what is to be excluded from the standard vocabulary of spoken English? And how are its idioms to be decided upon?[2]

Difficulties of definition apart, however, let us stay with Honey's general point about Standard English: that it has two forms, written and spoken, and that they share a common, ideal structure. This, along with the conviction that both forms must be taught to children and encouraged socially, is Honey's underlying proposition. Yet this is such an important theoretical point that even Honey wavers in his conviction. Samuel Johnson held that the best speech reflects writing; Honey, despite his apparently supreme confidence, is not quite so sure. In answer to the Milroys' assertion of the incorrectness of the assumption that 'the model of spoken language lies in the written channel' and their proposition that 'the structure and function of written language is *altogether different* from that of spoken language' (ibid.: 122), Honey's response is peculiar in the extreme. 'This is not the place to debate in fine detail,' he writes, 'that latter proposition.' An argument in 'fine detail' in a book of some three hundred pages is clearly an unreasonable expectation; an argument in some detail, however, might have been useful. For this is the claim which underpins a great deal of the confusing use of the term 'standard English.' How are we to resolve the difficult questions associated with it if not by the sort of finely detailed research carried out by, for example, Jenny Cheshire (see Chapter 6 of this volume), research which leads her to assert that the dominance of the model of formal written English constitutes in itself 'an important reason for our ignorance about the structure and syntax of spoken English'. Honey's answer is simply to duck such complicated research and to resort, in a common tactic in these debates – frequently used by conservative politicians for example – to received social attitudes and beliefs (one might say prejudices):

> It is important, though, to emphasise here that many educated people, including some respectable linguists, and also huge numbers of ordinary and not particularly educated people, act as though they believed that those forms of spoken English which are the most acceptable for a number of functions, especially functions associated with formality, are the forms which most closely reflect written forms.
>
> (ibid.: 122–3)

Later Honey appears to accept that the Milroys are right to 'point out several differences between spoken and written English' (ibid.: 131) and adds that 'the application of the rules of written language to spoken language is especially inappropriate when those differing rules of English are not codified and made available to teachers and students' (ibid.: 148). Yet in a neat twist of rhetoric he restates the problem thus:

> What they [the Milroys] fail to address is the problem of how linguists or educationalists can persuade the great British public to abandon their longstanding and deeply held respect for the widely available forms of a highly standardised written English, and to treat the

spontaneous and context-dependent forms of a much less standardised and codified spoken English with the same deference they give
to forms enshrined in centuries of admired literature.

(ibid.: 132)

There are a number of tricks here. The first is to claim that linguists and
educationalists would ask for an abandonment of respect for standard written
English. The second is to slip in an admission that the spoken language is
in fact not merely less codified but less standardised than the written language.
The third is to imply that the standard written language is valued and autho-
rised by 'the great British public' because it is enshrined in 'centuries of
admired literature', another favourite commonplace among conservative
contributors to the debate. Its incoherence can be indicated by some simple
questions: Which authors are to guide us in syntax? Milton, Sterne and
Edgeworth? In punctuation? Swift and Henry James? In vocabulary? Nashe,
Shakespeare, Joyce?

The most important point raised in the quotation above is Honey's conces-
sion that speech and writing are distinct, a difference asserted again when he
admits that '[t]he Milroys are completely right to argue for schools (and examination boards) to offer clearer guidance on where the norms of spoken and
written English may differ' (ibid.: 133). This is somewhat odd given his earlier
declaration of the importance of the belief of 'many educated people, including some respectable linguists, and also huge numbers of ordinary and not particularly educated people' that standard English speech forms 'most closely
reflect written forms' (ibid.: 122–3). How is the circle to be closed? How can
the question of the factual difference between writing and speech in English
be ducked simply on the grounds that 'people' act as though they don't believe
there to be such a difference, only to reappear later as a necessary part of the
school curriculum and examining process? The answer is provided by means
of a formulation which acts to restore the lost unity between standard English
writing and speech. After conceding the point that education should offer
instruction 'on where the norms of spoken and written English may differ',
Honey continues: 'but it must be emphasised that in both cases the norms that
students will expect to be taught will be the realistic norms of educated speakers of standard English' (ibid.: 133). Leaving aside the silly imprecision of the
term 'realistic' and the clumsiness of 'speakers' for users, the basis for reunit-
ing standard English speech and writing is clear. It is not a common structure,
nor apparently does it include common intrinsic features at all. The unifying
principle is to be the fact of social use by a particular group.

This brings me to a point raised earlier in this chapter, the familiar and
long-lasting confusion between 'uniformity' and 'excellence' and the whole
question of value and authority which lies at the core of the standard English
debate. As I indicated above, I do not think that this aspect of the debate
is much concerned with the standard written language. Though if there are

educationalists or linguists who argue against literacy in standard written English, I would be interested in opposing them; I consider that to be a straw target set up by thinkers and ideologues of the right. The question of the standard spoken language, however, is quite different and again it is instructive to follow Honey's argument in so far as it replays so many of the mistakes and muddled arguments of the past.

What is standard spoken English and where is it to be found? A key to these questions is provided by Honey's identification of

> the general point from which it seems impossible to escape, that there is a long-standing and now overwhelming association, right across British society, between the use of the grammar, vocabulary, and idiom of standard English, and the concept of 'educatedness'.
>
> (ibid.: 39)[3]

The answer to the problem of identifying standard spoken English clearly does not have to involve research into forms of language since there is a handy short-cut by way of popular perceptions: standard spoken English is quite simply the form of the spoken language used by the 'educated'. 'Ordinary people' and 'very ordinary people' (key players in the argument, though none are quoted) along with John Honey, are very clear on this point: 'the most acceptable uses' are 'those which find most favour among educated people' (ibid.: 164).[4]

Honey's exemplification of this point is made towards the end of the book:

> [E]ducatedness ... in this book has been identified as a defining quality of those forms of spoken and written English which are regarded as standard, and ... is the touchstone of prescription.
>
> (ibid.: 235)

There is of course an evident problem with this way of pinpointing the standard spoken language: what constitutes 'educatedness'? Honey is sensitive to this problem which he addresses thus: 'educatedness is a *changing* concept which must be recognised as reflecting the way the most educated members of society actually speak and write English in the present day' (ibid.: 236). It is certainly possible to agree that 'educatedness' is a changing concept, but surely it refers to what counts as 'being educated' means at a particular point in a particular society. To say that 'educatedness' must simply reflect what 'the most educated' (note the slippage) members of society do is either tautological or tendentious. It also avoids the central questions: what counts as being 'educated', or, more pressingly, who are we to recognise as 'the educated'?

Again Honey is aware of the difficulty of his position and he refines it. Referring to 'the most educated members of society' he declares that 'those members [are] to be identified by objective criteria'. What are they? The answer is given when alluding to 'people who satisfy every normal criterion of "educatedness"'. That is:

> graduation from (often famous) universities, or literary reputation, or the ability in all other respects to use the language in highly acceptable ways – or [people] who are in some way other high-status figures (like royalty).
>
> (ibid.: 161–2)[5]

Specifically the people he has in mind are 'university professors (including well-known professors of English, distinguished Oxbridge theologians) . . . politicians (including several party leaders and three education ministers)' (ibid.: 161). Somewhat amusingly, however, these criteria for educatedness and this list of figures is derived from a survey of the 'incorrect use' of 'I–me', 'we–us' by the educated. This of course leads to the question: when is an 'incorrect use' a 'change' in the language. The answer appears to be, when it is used by the 'educated'.

Or not quite. For although Honey cedes authority in language to the 'educated', he notes that this means that in practice this may cause confusion with such items as pronoun alteration. How then are value, excellence and authority to be guaranteed? How are both standard spoken and standard written English to be protected and disseminated? These are questions which lie behind a great deal of the argumentation in the standard English debates and they are related directly to the social and political issues which I mentioned at the beginning of this chapter. They lie close to the core of one form of conservative thought on language, whether that be eighteenth-century high toryism or the crudities of the new right in the 1980s and 1990s.

John Honey resents the use of the phrase 'new right' in relation to his thought on the grounds that he judges it to be 'far too extreme to be applicable to me' (ibid.: 219); he cites the use of the phrase in America to refer to political forces financed by Christian fundamentalism, in Britain with regard to 'hard-line groups who tried to influence Margaret Thatcher' (ibid.: 219), and in Germany in relation to neo-Nazi groupings. Let us accommodate Honey's rejection of these uses of the phrase 'new right' and accept instead the formulation to which he is happy to adhere:

> (a) freedom from unnecessary state influence in the lives of ordinary citizens; (b) freedom of expression in speech, in broadcasting, in the arts, and in publications; and (c) freedom to organise social movements, and to dissent openly from government.
>
> (ibid.: 218)

In accordance with this definition, Honey is happy to align himself with the new right. How then does his model for authority in language use fit the definition? Is Honey a new-right thinker even given his own stipulation of the meaning of the phrase?

Linguistic authority for Honey, as noted above, lies with a specific group:

> As soon as a language is taught, you must have standards, regularities, and you must involve pedants, whose reference point will always be those who are widely perceived as the 'best users'.
>
> (ibid.: 105)

'Pedants' and the 'best users' then are to guarantee 'standards' (note the vagueness of the terminology) and all changes, 'usually brought about by less educated people, must pass through the filter of approval by educated people generally' (ibid.: 147). He continues:

> That filter, and that criterion – acceptability to the educated – constitute for English the mechanism of authority, and embody the notion of prescription which is then codified by dictionary-makers and grammarians.
>
> (ibid.: 147)

The task of prescription, we are informed, is simply 'to represent the real consensus of educated usage in the present day' (ibid.: 148).

There is, unfortunately, a problem with the model. Honey has already noted the difficulty with pronouns evident among the educated (even the 'most educated' apparently). He goes on to cite further examples where 'educated usage' is not only unreliable but involves damage to the language. One case is the use of the word 'decimate':

> From its Latin root involving 'ten' (compare *decimal*), it was used for many centuries to indicate the taking of one in ten. ... With the decline in a widespread knowledge of Latin among the educated of the late twentieth century, the one-in-ten meaning of decimate was lost, and people who heard the word judged from its context simply that something drastic had happened.
>
> (ibid.: 154)

Further 'examples of words which are undergoing a similar change in the way they are used even by apparently educated people' (ibid.: 155) are 'reticent' and 'cohort'. With regard to 'reticent', Honey asserts that it is being 'confused' with 'reluctant' and asks the question:

Does this confusion matter? It does, because it makes it more difficult to use *reticent* in its original and more specific sense, and this
involves a loss to the language. In this case it is an avoidable and
unnecessary loss, the result of ignorance and careless use.

(ibid.: 156)

Honey would appear to be on dangerous ground here since the damage he
alleges is being caused by BBC broadcasters, a Black American Civil Rights
Activist, the biographer of Sylvia Townsend Warner, the novelist Tom Clancy,
an Oxford Professor of Politics, and Linguistics Professor John Joseph (among
others). Most of these people would, presumably, fall under the category of
'the educated', thereby seemingly undermining Honey's contention that it is
'the educated' who preserve standards. How then is Honey to avoid the charge
that he has become the self-appointed guardian of the standards of spoken
and written English?

The answer to the accusation lies in his stipulation of the concentration
of linguistic authority in a central body which exists at a level beyond any
one individual such as Honey, but not apparently at the level of all the
educated. At first sight the resolution of problems around 'correctness'
suggested by Honey seems to be potentially democratic. In relation to
number concord, for example, we are informed that in cases of dispute 'there
would be an advantage in some public discussion of which form to prefer'
(ibid.: 151). 'Some public discussion', however, is unhelpfully vague and the
mechanism needs to be made explicit:

> This is why I have come to the conclusion that the time has arrived
> to agitate for the creation of an authoritative body to issue advice
> on the 'correct' use of English – i.e. the most acceptable usages, those
> which find most favour among educated people.
>
> (ibid.: 164)

How is this to be done?

> [B]y creating an *official* Academy on the French model, or by encoura-
> ging the formation of an unofficial group of respected users of the
> language who will offer guidance on a whole range of specific points,
> updating their judgements at regular intervals – but always bearing in
> mind that their codified 'rules' of usage will only have as much credi-
> bility as the wider community of the educated is prepared to give them.
>
> (ibid.: 164)

Once the judgements have been made, they must be 'codified as "rules" of guidance' and be given to everybody: 'taught to children in schools and made accessible through reference books available in public libraries' (ibid.: 164).

This is a curious model of linguistic authority, but not, as Honey notes, a new one; indeed its formulation could have been taken from any one of hundreds of eighteenth-century texts.[6] Is this model, to return to a question raised earlier, one which if adopted would ensure Honey his place among the new right? The answer to this must be no, if we accept Honey's definition of the aims of the new right. For two important bases of that definition were freedom from unnecessary state interference in the lives of ordinary citizens and freedom of expression in speech. Honey's call for an 'authoritative body' infringes both tenets of the alleged manifesto of the new right. An 'official Academy' would constitute unnecessary state interference in the lives of 'ordinary' citizens. And both the *official* Academy' and the 'unofficial group' would have precisely as part of their remit the aim of limiting freedom of expression by the issuing of 'guidance' and 'rules' about 'correctness' in speech and writing. Neither, of course, would be democratically elected. Perhaps, however, I am serving an injustice upon John Honey; it may be that he is a member of the new right after all. But that can only be the case, given his attitudes to the language which his works embody, if we are to accept another definition of the new right based on the practical experience of the 1980s and 1990s. My definition of the new-right policy would be that it sought ever-increasingly centralised forms of power, that it reduced choice by removing local forms of democracy and replaced them instead by unelected bodies appointed by those in power, and that it sought to banish dissent and control freedom of expression by the promotion of narrow codes of 'correctness'.[7] By that definition of what the new right stands for, Honey's attachment to it is correct. Though not of the 'punctuation means punctuality' and 'grammar means grammar schools' brigade, Honey belongs in the new right.

It is in fact a great pity that the standard English debate is marred by the sort of conceptual confusions and political posturings (no matter how poorly expressed) which I have outlined by looking at one contribution to the debate. For in fact I think there are genuine questions to be asked about what we might mean by 'standards' in relation to speech and writing. There is a great deal to be done in this respect, and proper arguments to be made, but one thing is clear for sure. The answer does not lie in some simple-headed recourse to the practice of 'the best authors' or the 'admired literature' of the past, valuable though that writing is. Nor does the answer reside in 'rules' for speech laid down by either the 'educated' or any official or unofficial body held to be able to guarantee spoken 'correctness'. The answers to the real questions will be found to be much more complex, difficult and challenging than those currently on offer. For those reasons they might be more successful.

Notes

1 It would be easy simply to ridicule Honey's work since it is marred by errors and lapses of all sorts. It starts, for example, with the abandonment of a fundamental

principle of scholarship: 'I have not always followed the conventions of indicating when emphasis is the author's or was added by me' (Honey 1997: x). Apart from prompting concern about Honey's understanding of the nature of conventions (presumably important in engaging in the question of standards) this does rather lay the author open to the charge of tampering with the evidence. Things get worse. In relation to the question of evidence, though Honey's criticism of Labov is based on the claim that Labov presents 'no evidence' as to whether his interviews and interviewees are representative, 'evidence' presented by Honey to support his own case is often suspect. It includes his use of a Bantu language as an example on the basis of what 'one [unattested] linguist colleague tells me' (ibid.: 17); reference to an (unidentified) conference in the USA at which 'two white American professors, in a knee-jerk reaction' protested 'against the use of the word "deficit" in this or any linguistic context' (ibid.: 26); the citation of a 'survey of standards of English among undergraduate students at a sample of Britain's "traditional" universities' (ibid.: 178). Honey's reference to this survey is particularly instructive. He establishes its credentials: 'as a guide to the reliability of its scientific method, it should be noted that Dr. Lamb [the researcher] is a Reader in Genetics – a discipline rooted in statistics – at Imperial College in the University of London' (ibid.: 178). He continues by denying the reader access to the statistical facts, glossing them instead with the usual imprecision: 'the response was very satisfactory', 'a small proportion of respondents . . . showed themselves unsympathetic to the body conducting the survey', and 'almost all respondents admitted a serious problem' (ibid.: 178). One further example may serve to illustrate Honey's idea of convincing evidence. In a point about the social consequences of 'speaking a non-standard dialect rather than standard English' (ibid.: 41) he cites 'a relative of my wife's [sic]' who 'speaks the rich [presumably one of its 'qualities'] dialect of an old-established British mining community':

> In any encounter with officialdom when he travels around the world, he compensates for the limitations of his native dialect by the use of two strategies: he shouts, and if that fails, he swears.
>
> (ibid.: 42)

We might note here the author's grasp of the significance of objective, attested observations and compare it favourably with Labov's evident and shoddy disregard for scientificity.

The problems are more than methodological, however, and range to intellectual curiosities which are worthy of note if not comment. There appears to be, in Honey's view, the possibility of a 'preliterate tribal language' in which the vocabulary consists of 'a few thousand words, most of which carry only one meaning' (ibid.: 13). No such language is specified, of course, though linguists might be interested in the notion of finding words in any language which have one meaning. Other oddities arise from Honey's use of the language, which is peculiar given his clear confidence in his status as an 'educated' writer and speaker. Examples include reference to 'standard English (of the kind that we write)' (ibid.: 52), which seems to imply that there are other kinds of standard English, an illogical assertion given his definition of 'standard'. Later he asserts that 'the standard accent was non-local except insofar as it represented a South of England provenance' (ibid.: 97). This rather does raise the question of what the word 'local' means to Honey.

Other lapses are more sinister and difficult to accept. Bakhtin is described as a 'Soviet linguist', presumably in order to smear his work by associating it with the Soviet Union, which is not particularly fair given that Bakhtin was extremely harshly treated by the Soviet state and displayed considerable courage in continuing his research in conditions of suffering and exile. Foucault is inaccurately described as a Marxist theorist; it is in reference to Foucault, too, that Honey's work slips well below the standards required of academic debate. Foucault's writing is described with reference to the 'fact' that he was 'tortured by his homosexual nature' (ibid.: 109). And the impetus behind his research is attributed thus: 'Partly perhaps because his own sexuality involved bizarre forms of sado-masochism, he was intensely interested in the ideas of discipline and punishment, domination, subjection and subjugation, power and oppression . . . ' (ibid.: 109). This type of crudity is repeated later in discussing the politics of the work of Raymond Williams:

> Critics [none specified] have pointed out that from his emotionally frigid home background (he came from a poor family, and won his way to grammar school and Cambridge) Williams learned to love 'the People' rather than actual people.
>
> (ibid.: 115)

Honey is too skilled a rhetorician not to know what he is doing with such words, though whether he understands academic standards is again called into doubt. In case he does not know, it should be made clear that such attacks on (dead and thus not able to be libelled) fellow members of the profession, on the basis of sexual or domestic life, have no place in academic debate. This is not a question of falling standards but of shamefully fallen standards of decency and professionalism.

2 An amusing idiomatic problem is raised in a quote on the back cover of *Language is Power* used to recommend Honey's earlier text *Does Accent Matter?* (1989). The *Mail on Sunday* reviewer is quoted as declaring that 'You can't pull the wool over Professor Honey's *ears*' (emphasis added). Given that the more frequent idiom mentions eyes rather than ears it would be interesting to know if the author would classify this as (1) a mistake, (2) non-standard, (3) idiomatic or (4) a change in the language.

3 Note that there is no distinction here between standard English speech and writing.

4 'Standard English' was defined in the 1933 *OED* Supplement (Murray et al. 1933) as follows:

> Applied to a variety of the speech of a country which, by reason of its cultural status and currency, is held to represent the best form of that speech. *Standard English*: that form of the English language which is spoken (with modifications, individual or local) by the generality of the cultured people in Great Britain.

In Henry Wyld's *Elementary Lessons in English Grammar* (1909) it was defined thus:

> Our business is only with one main form of English, that form that is generally called 'Educated English', that is a sort of general average English which has a wide circulation among educated people, and is what is generally referred to by the rather vague name 'correct English', or better, *Standard English*.

5   It is reassuring to know that there are some regal continuities in these debates. When George Sampson defined standard English speech in *English for the English* in 1925, he commented:

> There is no need to define standard English speech. We know what it is, and there's an end on't. We know standard English when we hear it just as we know a dog when we see it, without the aid of definition. Or, to put it another way, we know what is *not* standard English, and that is a sufficiently practical guide. If anyone wants a definite example of standard English we can tell him that it is the kind of English spoken by a simple unaffected young Englishman like the Prince of Wales.

6   Its structure, an unelected body which decides on 'rules' and which judges on disputes, also resembles an even older institution: the relationship between the Law Lords and the House of Commons.

7   New-right policies in the 1980s and 1990s saw increasing centralisation of state power (the capping of the powers of local authorities, the imposition of a national curriculum in England and Wales); reduction of local choice (the abolition of health boards, the proliferation of quangos); unnecessary interference in the lives of citizens (Clause 28, the return to 'Victorian values' such as street-begging); attacks upon freedom of expression (the Broadcasting Ban), the freedom to organise (the banning of Trade Unions at GCHQ) and the freedom to dissent (the Criminal Justice Act).

BIBLIOGRAPHY

Aarsleff, H. (1983) *The Study of Language in England, 1780–1860*, new edition, Minneapolis, MN: University of Minnesota Press.

Abercrombie, D. (1965) 'RP and local accent', in D. Abercrombie (ed.) *Studies in Phonetics and Linguistics*, Oxford: Oxford University Press, 10–15. Originally printed in 1951.

Aitchison, J. (1997) *The Language Web: 1996 BBC Reith Lectures*, Cambridge: Cambridge University Press.

Alford, H. (1889) *The Queen's English*, 8th edn, London: George Bell. First edn 1864.

Atkins, J. D. C. (1992[1887]) 'Barbarous dialects should be blotted out', in Crawford (1992), 47–50.

Bacher, P., Clemmensen, N., Jacobsen, K. and Wandall, J. (1992) *Danskerne og fremmedsprog*, Copenhagen: Udviklingscenteret for Folkeoplysning og Voksenundervisning.

Bailey, N. (1721) *Universal Etymological Dictionary*, London.

Bailey, R. (1997) *Nineteenth Century English*, Ann Arbor, MI: University of Michigan Press.

Bailey, R. and Görlach, M. (eds) (1982) *English as a World Language*, Cambridge: Cambridge University Press.

Bain, R., Fitzgerald, B. and Taylor, M. (1992) *Looking into Language*, Sevenoaks: Hodder and Stoughton.

Bakhtin, M. (1981) 'Discourse in the novel', in *The Dialogic Imagination*, Austin, TX: University of Austin Press.

Barker, Pat (1993) *The Eye in the Door*, printed as Book 1 of *The Regeneration Trilogy*, London: Allen Lane.

Barron, D. (1992) 'Federal English', in Crawford (1992), 36–9.

Baugh, A. C. and Cable, Thomas (1978) *A History of the English Language*, 3rd edn, London: Routledge.

Baugh, J. (1996) 'Linguistic discrimination', in Goebl, Hans, Nelde, Peter H., Stary, Zdenek and Woelck,Wolfgang (eds) *Contact Linguistics: A Handbook of Contemporary Research*, Berlin: Mouton de Gruyter, 709–14.

—— (1998) 'Linguistics, education and the law: Educational reform for African-American minority students', in Mufwene, S. et al. (1998), 282–301.

Beal, J. (1993) 'The grammar of Tyneside and Northumbrian English', in Milroy and Milroy (1993), 187–213.

Bennett, J. A. W. and Smithers, G. (1966) *Early Middle English Verse and Prose*, Oxford: Oxford University Press.

Berg, D. L. (1993) *A Guide to the Oxford English Dictionary*, Oxford: Oxford University Press.

Berger, P. and Luckmann, T. (1991) *The Social Construction of Reality: A Treatise in the Sociology of Knowledge*, 6th edn, Harmondsworth: Penguin.

Berrendonner, A. and Reichler-Béguelin, M.-J. (1989) Décalages: les niveaux de l'analyse linguistique, *Langue française* 81, Février.

—— (1997) 'Left dislocation in French: Varieties, norms and usage', in J. Cheshire and D. Stein (eds) *Taming the Vernacular: Fom Dialect to Written Standard Language*. London: Longman, 200–17.

Bex, Tony (1993) 'Standards of English in Europe', *Multilingua* 12, 3: 249–64.

—— (1996) *Variety in Written English*, London: Routledge.

Blommaert, Jan (in press) *Language Ideological Debates*, Berlin: Mouton de Gruyter.

Bloomfield, L. (1935) *Language*, London: George Allen & Unwin.

Blount, T. (1656) *Glossographia; or a Dictionary Interpreting all such Hard Words*, London.

Bolinger, D. (1981) *Language; the Loaded Weapon*, London: Longman.

Bolinger, D. and Sears, D. A. (1981) *Aspects of Language*, New York: Harcourt Brace Jovanovich.

Booth, Charles (1892) *Life and Labour of the People in London*, Vol. 1, London: Williams and Norgate.

Borroff, M. (1985) 'Fowler and the rest', *Yale Review* 74, 3: 353–67.

Bourdieu, Pierre (1982) *Ce que parler veut dire: L'économie des échanges linguistiques*, Paris: Fayard.

—— (1991) *Language and Symbolic Power*, ed. J. B. Thompson, trans. G. Raymond and M. Adamson, Cambridge: Polity Press.

Bourdieu, Pierre and Passeron, Jean-Claude (1994) 'Introduction: Language and relationship to language in the teaching situation', in Bourdieu et al. (1994), 1–34.

Bourdieu, Pierre, Passeron, Jean-Claude and de Saint Martin, Monique (1994) *Academic Discourse: Linguistic Misunderstanding and Professional Power*, with contributions by Christian Baudelot and Guy Vincent, trans. Richard Teese from *Rapport Pédagogique et Communication*, Paris: École Pratique des Hautes Études, 1965.

Bradbury, M. (1994) 'Eschew the Estuary', *London Times*, 1 September.

Brown, G. and Yule, G. (1983) *Discourse Analysis*, Cambridge: Cambridge University Press.

Bullokar, W. [1586] *Pamphlet for Grammar*, ed. and introduction J.Turner, 1980, Leeds: School of English, University of Leeds.

Burton-Roberts, N. (1986) *Analysing Sentences*, London: Longman.

Butterfield, H. (1931) *The Whig Interpretation of History*, London: Bell and Sons.

Byatt, A. S. (1997) *Babel Tower*, London: Vintage.

Cameron, D. (1990) 'Demythologizing sociolinguistics: Why language does not reflect society', in Joseph, John E. and Taylor, Talbot J. (eds) *Ideologies of Language*, London: Routledge, 79–93.

—— (1995) *Verbal Hygiene*, London: Routledge.

Cameron, D., McAlinden, F. and O'Leary, K. (1988) 'Lakoff in context: The social and linguistic functions of tag questions', in J. Coates and D. Cameron (eds) *Women in their Speech Communities*, London: Longman, 74–93.

Cardenas, Jose A. (1992) 'An educator's rationale for native language instruction', in Crawford (1992), 342–51.

Carew, Richard (1586) 'The excellency of the English tongue', in Camden, William (1870) *Remains Concerning Britain*, London: John Russel Smith, 42–51.

Carter, R. (1995) *Keywords in Language and Literacy*, London: Routledge.

—— (1996) 'Politics and knowledge about language', in R. Hasan and G. Williams (eds) *Literacy in Society*, London: Longman, 1–28.

—— (1997) *Investigating English Discourse: Language, Literacy and Literature*, London: Routledge.

Carter, R. and McCarthy, M. (1995) 'Grammar and the spoken language', *Applied Linguistics* 16: 141–58.

—— (1997) *Exploring Spoken English*, Cambridge: Cambridge University Press.

Castro, Max (1992) 'On the curious question of language in Miami', in Crawford (1992), 178–85.

Cawdrey, R. (1604) *Table Alphabeticall*, London: Edward Weaver.

Chafe, W. (1994) *Discourse, Consciousness and Time: The Flow and Displacement of Conscious Experience in the Speaking and Writing*, Chicago, IL and London: University of Chicago Press.

Chambers, J. K. (1995) *Sociolinguistic Theory*, Oxford: Blackwell.

Chambers, J. K. and Trudgill, P. (1997) *Dialectology*, 2nd edn, London: Cambridge University Press.

Channell, J. (1994) *Vague Language*, Oxford: Oxford University Press.

Cheshire, J. (1982) *Variation in an English Dialect*, London: Cambridge University Press.

—— (1987) 'Syntactic variation, the linguistic variable and sociolinguistic theory', *Linguistics* 25: 257–82.

—— (1991) *English around the World: Sociolinguistic Perspectives*, Cambridge: Cambridge University Press.

—— (1996) 'That jacksprat: An interactional perspective on English *that*', *Journal of Pragmatics* 25: 369–93.

—— (1997) 'Involvement in "standard" and "nonstandard" English', in J. Cheshire and D. Stein (eds) *Taming the Vernacular: From Dialect to Written Standard Language*, London: Longman, 68–82.

Cheshire, J. and Milroy, J. (1993) 'Syntactic variation in non-standard dialects: Background issues', in J. Milroy and L. Milroy (eds) *Real English: The Grammar of English Dialects in the British Isles*, London: Longman, 3–33.

Cheshire, J. and Ouhalla, J. (1997) 'Grammatical constraints on variation', paper presented to the First Workshop on Linguistic Variation, University of Reading, Reading, March 1997.

Cheshire, J. and Stein, D. (1997) 'The syntax of spoken language', in J. Cheshire and D. Stein (eds) *Taming the Vernacular: From Dialect to Written Standard Language*, London: Longman, 1–12.

Chomsky, N. (1965) *Aspects of the Theory of Syntax*, Cambridge, MA: MIT Press.

—— (1995) *The Minimalist Program*, Cambridge, MA: MIT Press.

Chomsky, N. and Halle, M. (1968) *The Sound Pattern of English*, New York: Harper Row.

Clark, C. (1992) 'The myth of the Anglo-Norman scribe', in M. Rissanen, O. Ohalainen, T. Nevalainen and I. Taavitsainen (eds) *History of Englishes*, Berlin: Mouton de Gruyter, 117–29.

Clyne, Michael (ed.) (1992) *Pluricentric Languages*, Berlin: Mouton de Gruyter.

Coates, J. (1987) 'Epistemic modality and spoken discourse', *Transactions of the Philological Society*, 110–31.

—— (1997) 'One-at-a-time: The organization of men's talk', in S. Johnson and U. Meinhof (eds) *Language and Masculinity*, Oxford: Blackwell, 107–29.

Cohen, M. (1977) *Sensible Words: Linguistic Practice in England 1640–1785*, Baltimore, MD: Johns Hopkins University Press.

Coles, E. (1676) *An English Dictionary*, London: Samuel Crouch.

Corfield, P. J. (1991) *Language, History and Class*, Oxford: Blackwell.

Corley, Mary-Ann (ed.) (1991) *Program and Provider Perspectives on Developing Indicators of Program Quality for Adult Education Programs*, Washington DC: Pelavin Associates.

Cornish, F. (1988) 'Predicate anaphors as "discourse operators"', *Journal of Semantics*, 233–64.

Coupland, N., Williams, A. and Garrett, P. (1995) '"Welshness" and "Englishness" as attitudinal dimensions of English language varieties in Wales', paper presented to the ICOLC, Valencia, Spain, and submitted for publication in the proceedings, to be published by Benjamins Amsterdam.

Cox, B. (1991) *Cox on Cox: An English Curriculum for the 1990s*, London: Hodder and Stoughton.

Crawford, J. (ed.) (1992) *Language Loyalties: A Sourcebook on the Official English Controversy*, Chicago, IL: University of Chicago Press.

Creider, C. (1986) 'Constituent-gap dependencies in Norwegian: An acceptability study', in D. Sankoff (ed.) *Diversity and Diachrony*, Amsterdam: John Benjamin, 415–24.

Crossick, G. (1991) 'From gentlemen to the residuum: Languages of social description in Victorian Britain', in Corfield (1991), 150–78.

Crowley, T. (1987) 'Description or prescription? An analysis of the term "Standard English" in the work of two twentieth-century linguists', *Language and Communication* 7: 199–220.

—— (1989) *The Politics of Discourse: The Standard Language Question and British Cultural Debates*, London: Macmillan. Published in the USA as *Standard English and the Politics of Language*, Urbana and Chicago IL: University of Illinois Press.

—— (1991) *Proper English? Readings in Language, History and Cultural Identity*, London: Routledge.

—— (1996) *Language in History: Theories and Texts*, London: Routledge.

—— (1997) 'Uniform, excellent, common: reflections on standards in language', *Language Sciences* 19, 1: 15–21.

Crystal, D. (1980) 'Neglected grammatical factors in conversational English', in S. Greenbaum, G. Leech and J. Svartvik (eds) *Studies in English Linguistics*, London: Longman, 153–66.

—— (1984) *Who Cares About English Usage*, Harmondsworth: Penguin.

Daan, J. and Blok, D. P. (1970) 'Von randstad tot landrand', Bijdragen en Mededelingen der Dialecten Commissie van de Koninklijke Nederlandse Akademie van Wetenschappen te Amsterdam, 37, Amsterdam: N. V. Noord.

Davis, H. G. (1994) 'The interdependence of lexicography and linguistic theory', *Journal of Literary Semantics: An International Review* 23, 2: 189–99.

De Maria, R. Jr. and Kitzinger, R. (1989) 'Introduction' to transformations of the word', *Language and Communication* 9: 83–102.

Dear, I. C. B. (compiler) (1986) *Oxford English*, Oxford: Oxford University Press.

DfE/WO Department for Education/the Welsh Office (1995) *English in the National Curriculum*, London: HMSO.

Dictionnaire de la langue française (1694) Académie Française.

Dobson, E. J. (1968) *English Pronunciation 1500–1700*, 2 vols, Oxford: Clarendon Press.

Dorling, D. (1995) *A New Social Atlas of Britain*, New York: Wiley.

Downes, W. (1984) *Language and Society*, London: Fontana.

Duncan, Daniel (1731) *A New English Grammar*, London: Prevost.

Duncan, S. (1972) 'Some signals and rules for taking speaking turns in conversations', *Journal of Personality and Social Psychology* 23: 283–92.

Edwards, J. (1979) *Language and Disadvantage*, London: Arnold.

Edwards, J. and Middleton, D. (1986) 'Joint remembering: Constructing an account of shared experience through conversational discourse', *Discourse Processes* 9: 423–59.

Edwards, P. (ed.) (1989) *The Life of Olaudah Equiano*, London: Longman.

Edwards, P. and Dabydeen, D. (eds) (1991) *Black Writers in Britain 1760–1890*, Edinburgh: Edinburgh University Press.

Edwards, V. (1993) 'The grammar of Southern British English', in Milroy and Milroy (1993), 214–38.

Ehlich, K. (1982) 'Anaphora and deixis: Same, similar or different?', in R. J. Jarvella and W. Klein (eds) *Speech, Place and Action: Studies in Deixis and Related Topics*, Chichester and New York: Wiley.

Eisenstein, E. L. (1980) *The Printing Press as an Agent of Change: Communications and Cultural Transformations in Early Modern Europe*, Cambridge: Cambridge University Press.

Eisikovits, E. (1991) 'Variation in subject-verb agreement in Inner Sydney English', in J. Cheshire (ed.) *English around the World: Sociolinguistic Perspectives*, Cambridge: Cambridge University Press, 235–55.

Ellis, Alexander (1869–89) *On early English Pronunciation with especial Reference to Shakespeare and Chaucer. Containing an Investigation of the Correspondence of Writing with Speech in England from the Anglo-Saxon Period to the Present Day. Preceded by a Systematic Notation of all Spoken Sounds by Means of the Ordinary Printing Types*, 5 parts, London: Transactions of the Philological Society.

Enright, D. J. (1997) 'Review of The New Fowler's Modern English Usage', *Times Literary Supplement*, 4897: 6.

Fairclough, N. (1992a) 'The appropriacy of "appropriateness"', in Fairclough, (1992), 33–56.

—— (ed.) (1992b) *Critical Language Awareness*, London: Longman.

Falk, Julia (1978) *Linguistics and Language: A Survey of Basic Concepts and Implications*, 2nd edn, New York: Wiley.

Findahl, Olle (1989) 'Language in the age of satellite television', *European Journal of Communication* 4: 133–59.

Finnegan, R. (1989) 'Communication and technology', *Language and Communication*, 9, 2/3: 107–27.

Firth, Allan (1990) '"Lingua franca" negotiations: towards an interactional approach', *World Englishes* 9, 3: 269–80.

Fishman, Joshua A. (1982) 'The sociology of English as an additional language', in Kachru, Braj B. (ed.) *The Other Tongue: English Across Cultures*, Urbana, IL: University of Illinois Press, 15–22.

—— (1988) 'The displaced anxiety of Anglo Americans', in Crawford (ed.), 165–70.

—— (1992) 'Sociology of English as an additional language', in Kachru (1992a), 19–26.

Flaitz, Jeffra (1993) 'French attitudes toward the ideology of English as an international language', *World Englishes* 12: 179–91.

Foster, R. F. (1988) *Modern Ireland 1600–1972*, London: Allen Lane.

Fowler, H. W. (1926) *Modern English Usage*, Oxford: Clarendon Press.

—— (1965) *Fowler's Modern English Usage*, revised edn by Sir Ernest Gowers, Oxford: Clarendon Press.

—— (1996) *The New Fowler's Modern English Usage*, revised edn by R. Burchfield, Oxford: Oxford University Press.

Fowler, H. W. and Fowler, F. G. (1931) *The King's English*, 3rd edn, Oxford: Clarendon Press.

Franklin, Benjamin (1992 [1753]) 'The German language in Pennsylvania', in Crawford (1992), 18–19.

Frederiksen, M. K., Knudsen, N., Michaelsen, S., Ringgaard, C., Saxild, K. (1995) 'Er dansk lost', unpublished project report, International Cultural Studies, University of Roskilde.

287

Fromkin, V. and Rodman, R. (1983) *An Introduction to Language*, 3rd edn, New York: Holt, Rinehart & Winston. 5th edn, (1993).

Garfinkel, H. (1967) *Studies in Ethnomethodology*, Englewood Cliffs, NJ: Prentice Hall.

Gelyukens, R. (1992) *From Discourse Process to Grammatical Construction: On Left-dislocation in English*, Amsterdam: John Benjamin.

Giddens, A. (1990) *Sociology*, London: Polity.

Giles, H. (1973) 'Accent mobility: A model and some data', *Anthropological Linguistics* 15: 87–105.

—— (1987) 'Our reactions to accent', in B. M. Mayor and A. K. Pugh (eds) *Language, Communication and Education*, London: Croom Helm, 64–72.

Giles, H. and Coupland, N. (1991) *Language: Contexts and Consequences*, Buckingham: Open University Press.

Giles, H., Coupland, J. and Coupland, N. (eds) (1991) *Contexts of Accommodation: Developments in Applied Sociolinguistics*, Cambridge: Cambridge University Press.

Giles, H. and Powesland, P. F. (1975) *Speech Style and Social Evaluation*, New York and London: Academic Press.

Görlach, M. and Schröder, K. (1985) '"Good usage" in an EFL context', in S. Greenbaum (ed.) *The English Language Today*, Oxford: Pergamon Press.

Gould, P. and White, R. (1974) *Mental Maps*, Harmondsworth: Penguin.

Gowers, E. (1954) *The Complete Plain Words*, London: HMSO.

—— (1957) *H. W. Fowler: The Man and His Teaching*, London: The English Association.

—— (1973) *The Complete Plain Words*, 2nd edn revised by Sir Bruce Fraser, London: HMSO.

—— (1986) *The Complete Plain Words*, 3rd edn revised by S. Greenbaum and J. Whitcut, London: HMSO.

Grace, G. (1991) 'How do languages change? More on "aberrant" languages', paper presented at the Sixth International Conference on Austronesian Linguistics, Honolulu, HI.

Graddol, D., Leith, D. and Swann, J. (eds) (1996) *English: History, Diversity and Change*, London: Routledge.

Greenbaum, S. (ed.) (1985) *The English Language Today*, Oxford: Pergamon Press.

—— (1986) 'English and a grammarian's responsibility: The present and the future', *World Englishes* 5: 189–95.

—— (1996) *The Oxford English Grammar*, Oxford: Oxford University Press.

Greenbaum, S. and Whitcut, J. (1988) *Longman Guide to English Usage*, London: Longman.

Greenwood, James (1711) *An Essay towards a Practical English Grammar*, London.

Grootaers, Willem A. (1959) 'Origin and nature of the subjective boundaries of dialects', *Orbis* 8: 355–84.

Gupta, A. (1994) *The Step-Tongue: Children's English in Singapore*, Philadelphia, PA: Multilingual Matters.

Halford, B. (1990) 'The complexity of oral syntax', in B. Halford and H. Pilch (eds) *Syntax gesprochener Sprachen*, Tübingen: Gunter Narr, 33–43.

Hall, R. A. (1950) *Leave Your Language Alone!*, Ithaca, NY: Cornell University Press.

Halliday, M. A. K. (1989) *Spoken and Written Language*, Oxford: Oxford University Press.

—— (1994) *An Introduction to Functional Grammar*, 2nd edn, London: Edward Arnold.

Harris, J. (1993) 'The grammar of Irish English', in Milroy and Milroy (1993), 139–86.

Harris, R. (1980) *The Language Makers*, London: Duckworth.

—— (1986) *The Origin of Writing*, London: Duckworth.

—— (1987) *The Language Machine*, London: Duckworth.

—— (1988) 'Murray, Moore and the myth', in R. Harris (ed.) *Linguistic Thought in England 1914–1945*, London: Duckworth, 1–26.

—— (1989) 'How does writing restructure thought?', *Language and Communication* 9: 99–106.

—— (1996) *Signs, Language and Communication*, London and New York: Routledge.

Hartley, Laura (1996) 'Oregonian perceptions of American regional speech', unpublished MA thesis, East Lansing, MI: Department of Linguistics and Languages, Michigan State University.

Haugen, E. (1966) 'Dialect, language, nation', in J. B. Pride and J. Holmes (eds) (1972) *Sociolinguistics: Selected Readings*, Harmondsworth: Penguin, 97–111.

—— (1992 [1972])) 'The curse of Babel', in Crawford (ed.) 399–409.

Havelock, E. A. (1976) *Origins of Western Literacy*, Ontario: Ontario Institute for Studies in Education, Monograph Series 14.

—— (1982) *The Literate Revolution in Greece*, Princeton, NJ: Princeton University Press.

Heath, S. B. (1976) 'Why no official tongue?', in Crawford (1992), 220–30.

Heller, Monica (1995) *Crosswords: Language, Education and Ethnicity in French Ontario*, Berlin: Mouton de Gruyter.

Heryanto, A. (1990) 'The making of language: Developmentalism in Indonesia', *Prism* 50: 40–53.

Hewson, T. H. (1955) *The Command of English: A Certificate Course for Practical People*, London: John Murray.

Hibbert, C. (1990) *Redcoats and Rebels: The War for America, 1770–1781*, London: Grafton Books.

Higginson, E. (1864) *An English Grammar Specifically Intended for Classical Schools and Private Students*, London.

Hobsbawm, E. J. (1990) *Nations and Nationalism since 1780: Programme, Myth, Reality*, Cambridge: Cambridge University Press.

Hoenigswald, Henry (1966) 'A proposal for the study of folk-linguistics', in W. Bright (ed.) *Sociolinguistics*, The Hague: Mouton, 16–26.

Høgsbro, Kjeld (1995) 'Arbejdspapir vedrørende de metodiske forudsætninger for analysen af subkulturers brug af talemåder og begreber fra det engelske sprog', unpublished working paper, Copenhagen: Institute of Social Development.

Holmes, J. (1986) 'Functions of *you know* in women's and men's speech', *Language in Society* 15: 1–22.

—— (1989) '*Sort of* in New Zealand women's and men's speech', *Studia Linguistica* 42: 85–121.

Honey, J. (1983) *The Language Trap: Race, Class and the 'Standard English' Issue in British Schools*, Kenton, Middlesex: National Council for Educational Standards.

—— (1989) *Does Accent Matter?*, London: Faber.

—— (1997) *Language is Power: The Story of Standard English and its Enemies*, London: Faber.

Hübler, Axel (1985) *Einander verstehen: Englisch im Kontext internationaler Kommunikation*, Tübingen: Narr.

Huddleston, Richard (1984) *Introduction to the Grammar of English*, Cambridge: Cambridge University Press.

Huddleston, W. (1987) 'The misdirected policy of bilingualism', in Crawford (1992), 114–17.

Hudson, R. and Holmes, J. (1995) 'Children's use of spoken Standard English', a report prepared for the School Curriculum and Assessment Authority, London: SCAA.

Hughes, G. A. and Trudgill, P. (1979) *English Accents and Dialects*, London: Arnold.

Johnson, R. K. (1990) 'International English: Towards an acceptable, teachable target variety', *World Englishes* 9, 3: 301–15.

Johnson, Samuel (1747) *The Plan of an English Dictionary: Addressed to the Right Honourable Philip Dormer Stanhope, Earl of Chesterfield*, London: J. & P. Knapton.

—— (1755) *A Dictionary of the English Language. To which are prefixed, a history of the language, and an English grammar*, 2 vols, London.

—— (1816) *The Works of Samuel Johnson: A New Edition in Twelve Volumes*, London: Nichols and Son.

Jones, D. (1917) *English Pronouncing Dictionary Containing 58,000 Words in International Phonetic Transcription*, 11th Everyman's edn 1957, London: Dent.

Jones, Hugh (1724) *An Accidence to the English Tongue*, London.

Joseph, J. E. (1987) *Eloquence and Power: The Rise of Language Standards and Standard Languages*, London: Frances Pinter.

Kachru, B. B. (1985) 'Standards, codification and sociolinguistic realism: The English language in the outer circle', in R. Quirk and H. G. Widdowson (eds) *English in the World: Teaching and Learning the Language and Literatures*, Cambridge: Cambridge University Press, 11–30.

—— (1986) *The Alchemy of English: The Spread, Functions and Models of Non-native Englishes*, Oxford: Pergamon.

—— (ed.) (1992a) *The Other Tongue*, 2nd edn, Urbana, IL: University of Illinois Press.

—— (1992b) 'Models for non-native Englishes', in Kachru (1992a), 48–74.

Karpf, Anne (1997) 'Fighting talk', *Guardian*, G2, 23 January, 4–5.

Kerswill, P. (1996) 'Children, adolescents and language change', *Language Variation and Change* 8: 177–202.

King, R., Sandhu, Sukhdev, Walvin, James and Girdham, Jane (1997) *Ignatius Sancho: African Man of Letters*, London: National Portrait Gallery.

Kingman, J. (1988) *Report of the Committee of Enquiry into the Teaching of the English Language*, London: HMSO.

Klein, L. (1994) '"Politeness" as linguistic ideology in late seventeenth- and early eighteenth-century England', in D. Stein and I. Tieken-Boon van Ostade (eds) *Towards a Standard English 1600–1800*. Berlin: de Gruyter, 31–50.

Kloss, H. (1967) 'Abstand languages and Ausbau languages', *Anthropological Linguistics* 9: 29–41.

Kremer, Ludger (1984) 'Die Niederländisch-Deutsch Staatsgrenze als subjective Dialektgrenze', in *Grenzen en grensproblemen, een bundel studies nitgegeren door het Nedersaksich Instituut van der R. U. Gronigen ter gelegenheid van zijn 30-jarig bestaan*, Nedersaksiche Studies 7, zugleich: *Driemaandelijkse Bladen* 36, 76–83.

Labov, W. (1966) *The Social Stratification of English in New York City*, Washington DC: Center for Applied Linguistics.

—— (1970) 'The study of language in its social context', in Giglioli (ed.) (1972) *Language and Social Context*, Harmondsworth: Penguin, 283–307.

—— (1972) *Sociolinguistic Patterns*, Philadelphia, PA: University of Pennsylvania Press.

—— (1994) *Principles of Linguistic Change: Internal Factors*, Oxford: Blackwell.

Lakoff, R. (1974) 'Remarks on *this* and *that*', Proceedings of the Tenth Regional Meeting of the Chicago Linguistics Society, 321–44.

—— (1977) 'You say what you are: Acceptability and gender-related speech', in S. Greenbaum (ed.) *Acceptability in Language*, The Hague: Mouton, 73–86.

Lambert, W. E. (1960) 'Evaluational reactions to spoken languages', *Journal of Abnormal and Social Psychology* 50: 197–200.

Lambert, W. E. and Tucker, G. R. (1972) 'A social psychology of bilingualism', in J. B. Pride and J. Holmes (eds) *Sociolinguistics*, Harmondsworth: Penguin, 336–49.

Lambert, W. E. et al. (1960) 'Evaluational reactions to spoken language', *Journal of Abnormal Social Psychology* 60: 44–51.

Langacker, Robert W. (1973) *Language and its Structure: Some Fundamental Linguistic Concepts*, 2nd edn, New York: Harcourt Brace Jovanovich.

Lass, R. (1987) *The Shape of English: Structure and History*, London: Dent.

—— (1996) 'Language universals and evolutionary bottlenecks: A methodological trial balloon', in Robin Sackmann (ed.) *Papers in Honor of Hans-Heinrich Lieb*, Amsterdam: Benjamins, 191–200.

—— (1997) *Historical Linguistics and Language Change*, Cambridge: Cambridge University Press.

Lawton, D. L. (1982) 'English in the Caribbean', in R. W. Bailey and M. Görlach (eds) *English as a World Language*, Cambridge: Cambridge University Press, 251–80.

Le Page, R. and Tabouret-Keller, A. (1985) *Acts of Identity*, London: Cambridge University Press.

Lehmann, W. P. (1962) *Historical Linguistics*, New York: Holt, Rinehart and Winston.

Leibowicz, J. (1992 [1985]) 'Official English: another Americanisation campaign?', in Crawford (1992), 101–11.

Leith, D. (1980) *Social History of English*, London: Routledge.

—— (1996) 'The origins of English', in Graddol et al. (1996), 95–132.

—— (1997) *A Social History of English*, 2nd edn, London: Routledge.

Leith, R. and Graddol, D. (1996) 'Modernity and English as a national language', in Graddol et al. (1996), 136–66.

Leitner, Gerhard (1992) 'English as a pluricentric language', in M. Clyne (ed.) *Pluricentric Languages*, Berlin: Mouton de Gruyter, 179–237.

Lippi-Green, R. (1994) 'Accent, standard and language ideology, and discriminatory pretext in court', *Language in Society* 23: 163–98.

—— (1997) *English with an Accent*, London: Routledge.

Locke, J. (1690) *An Essay Concerning Human Understanding*, ed. P. H. Nidditch, Oxford: Clarendon Press [1975].

Lowth, Robert (1762) *A Short Introduction to English Grammar*, London.

Lyons, J. (1968) *Introduction to Theoretical Linguistics*, Cambridge: Cambridge University Press.

—— (1972) 'Human Language', in R. A. Hinde (ed.) *Non-Verbal Communication*, Cambridge: Cambridge University Press, 49–85.

—— (1977) *Semantics*, Cambridge: Cambridge University Press.

Macaulay, R. (1973) 'Double standards', *American Anthropologist* 75: 1324–37.

Maltz, Daniel and Borker, Ruth (1982) 'A cultural approach to male–female miscommunication', in J. J. Gumperz (ed.) *Language and Social Identity*, Cambridge: Cambridge University Press, 196–216.

Marsh, G. P. (1865) *Lectures on the English Language*, London: John Murray.

Marwick, A. (1980) *Class: Image and Reality in Britain, France and the USA since 1930*, Oxford: Oxford University Press.

—— (1982) *British Society Since 1945*, Harmondsworth: Penguin.

McArthur, T. (1986) *Worlds of Reference: Lexicography, Learning and Language from the Clay Tablet to the Computer*, Cambridge: Cambridge University Press.

McCabe, C. (1990) 'Language, literature and identity: Reflections on the Cox report', *Critical Quarterly* 32, 4: 11.

McCalman, Iain (1989) *Radical Underworld, Prophets, Revolutionaries and Pornographers in London, 1795–1840*, Cambridge: Cambridge University Press.

McCarthy, M. (1998) *Spoken Language and Applied Linguistics*, Cambridge: Cambridge University Press.

McCarthy, M. and Carter, R. (1994) *Language as Discourse: Perspectives for Language Teaching*, London: Longman.

291

Meechan, M. and Foley, M. (1994) 'On resolving disagreement: Linguistic theory and variation – *there's bridges*', *Language Variation and Change* 6: 63–85.

Meier, A. (1970) *Negro Thought in America 1880–1915: Racial Ideologies in the Age of Booker T. Washington*, Ann Arbor, MI: University of Michigan Press.

Miège, Guy (1688) *The English Grammar*, London.

Milroy, J. (1977) *The Language of Gerard Manley Hopkins*, London: Deutsch.

—— (1981) *Regional Accents of English: Belfast*, Belfast: Blackstaff.

—— (1983) 'On the sociolinguistic history of /h/-dropping in English', in M. Davenport, E. Hansen and H.-F. Nielsen (eds) *Current Topics in English Historical Linguistics*, Odense: Odense University Press, 37–53.

—— (1991) 'Social network and prestige arguments in sociolinguistics', in K. Bolton and H. Kwok (eds) *Sociolinguistics Today: International Perspectives*, London: Routledge, 146–62.

—— (1992) *Linguistic Variation and Change*, Oxford: Blackwell.

——(1995) 'Foreword', in Rona K. Kingmore and Michael Montgomery (eds) *Ulster Scots Speech*, Tuscaloosa, AL: University of Alabama Press.

—— (1996) 'Linguistic ideology and the Anglo-Saxon lineage of English', in J. Klemola, M. Kyto and M. Rissanen (eds) *Speech Past and Present: Studies in English Dialectology in Memory of Ossi Ihalainen*, Frankfurt: Peter Lang, 169–86.

Milroy, J. and Milroy, L. (1985) 'Linguistic change, social network and speaker innovation', *Journal of Linguistics* 21,2: 339–84.

—— (eds) (1993) *Real English: The Grammar of English Dialects in the British Isles*, London: Longman.

—— (1998) *Authority in Language: Investigating Language Prescription and Standardisation*, 3rd edn, London: Routledge. 1st edn 1985, 2nd edn 1991.

Milroy, J., Milroy, L., Hartley, S. and Walshaw, D. (1994) 'Glottal stops and Tyneside glottalization: Competing patterns of variation and change in British English', *Language Variation and Change* 6,3: 327–57.

Milroy, L. (1982) 'Social network and linguistic focussing', in S. Romaine (ed.) *Sociolinguistic Variation in Speech Communities*, London: Arnold, 141–52.

—— (1987a) *Language and Social Networks*, 2nd edn, Oxford: Blackwell.

——(1987b) *Observing and Analysing Natural Language: A Critical Account of Sociolinguistic Method*, Oxford: Blackwell.

Milroy, L. and McClenaghan, P. (1977) 'Stereotyped reactions to four educated accents in Ulster', *Belfast Working Papers in Language and Linguistics* 2, Paper No. 4.

Moag, Rodney (1982) 'English as a foreign, second, native, and basal language: A new taxonomy of English-using societies', in Pride (1982), 11–50.

Monboddo, Lord (Burnett, James) (1774–1792) *On the Origin and Progress of Language*, 6 vols, London.

Montgomery, M. (1989) 'Choosing between *that* and *it*', in R. W. Fasold and D. Schiffrin (eds) *Language Change and Variation*, Amsterdam: Benjamin, 241–54.

Morse, J. Mitchell (1973) 'The shuffling speech of slavery Black English', *College English* 34: 834–43.

Mufwene, Salikoko S., Rickford, John R., Bailey, Guy and Baugh, John (1998) *African-American English: Structure, History and Use*, London: Routledge.

Mugglestone, L. (1995) *'Talking Proper': The Rise of Accent as a Social Symbol*, Oxford: Clarendon Press.

Mühlhäusler, P. (1996) *Linguistic Ecology: Language Change and Linguistic Imperialism in the Pacific Region*, London: Routledge.

Murray, James A. H. (1884) 'General Explanations', *OED*, Vol. 1.

—— (1900) *The Evolution of English Lexicography: The Romanes Lecture*, Oxford: Clarendon Press.

Murray, James A. H., Bradley, Henry and Craigie, W. A. (eds) (1993) *The Oxford English Dictionary: Being a corrected reissue with an introduction, supplement and bibliography of A New English Dictionary on Historical Principles*, Oxford: Clarendon.

Murray, K. M. E. (1978) *Caught in the Web of Words: James A. H. Murray and the Oxford English Dictionary*, Newhaven, CT: Yale University Press.

Niedzielski, N. and Preston, D. R. (in progress) *Folk Linguistics*, Oxford: Oxford University Press (under review).

O'Grady, W., Dobrovolsky M. and Aronoff, M. (1993) *Contemporary Linguistics: An Introduction*, 2nd edn, New York: St Martin's Press.

ÓRiágan, P. (1997) *Language Maintenance and Language Shift as Strategies of Social Reproduction*, Oxford: Oxford University Press.

Ochs, E. (1979) 'Planned and unplanned discourse', in T. Givón (ed.) *Syntax and semantics 12: Discourse and Syntax*, New York: Academic Press, 51–80.

Ochs, E., Schegloff, E. and Thompson, S. A. (eds) (1996) *Interaction and Grammar*, London: Cambridge University Press.

Oliphant, T. K. (1873) *Sources of Standard English*, London: Macmillan.

Oprah Winfrey Show (1987) *Standard and Black English*, 19 November, WLS-TV, Chicago, IL. Transcript No. W309, New York: Journal Graphics Inc.

Oxford English Dictionary (1933), ed. J. A. H. Murray, Oxford: Clarendon Press. 2nd edn 1989.

Partridge, E. H. (1947) *Usage and Abusage: A Guide to Good English*, London: Hamish Hamilton.

Pawley, A. and Syder, F. H. (1983) 'Natural selection in syntax: Notes on adaptive variation and change in vernacular and literary grammar', *Journal of Pragmatics* 7: 551–79.

Perera, K. (1990) 'Grammatical differentiation between speech and writing', in R. Carter (ed.) *Knowledge about Language and the Curriculum*, Sevenoaks: Hodder and Stoughton: 216–33.

—— (1993) 'Standard English in attainment target 1: Speaking and listening', *Language Matters*, Centre for Language in Primary Education, 3: 10.

—— (1994) 'Standard English: The debate', in S. Brindley (ed.) *Teaching English*, London: Routledge, 79–88.

Phillips, Caryl (1997) 'Foreword,' in King et al.

Phillips, E. (1658) *A New World of English Words; or, a General Dictionary, Containing the Interpretation of Words Derived from Other Languges, Terms that Relate to the Arts and Sciences*, London.

Philological Society (1859) *Proposal for the Publication of a New English Dictionary by the Philological Society*, London: Trubner.

Pinker, S. (1994) *The Language Instinct*, Harmondsworth: Penguin.

Platt, J. and Weber, H. (1980) *English in Singapore and Malaysia: Status, Features, Functions*, Oxford: Oxford University Press.

Platt, J., Weber, H. and Ho, M. L. (1984) *The New Englishes*, London: Routledge Kegan Paul.

Policy Studies Institute (1997) *Ethnic Minorities in Britain*, London: PSI.

Porter, Roy (1982) *English Society in the Eighteenth Century*, Harmondsworth: Penguin.

Preisler, Bent (1995) 'Standard English in the world', *Multilingua* 14, 4: 341–62.

Preston, D. R. (1982) 'Perceptual dialectology: Mental maps of United States dialects from a Hawaiian perspective', *Working Papers in Linguistics, University of Hawaii* 14, 5–49. Summarised in H. Warkentyne (ed.) 1981, Methods/Méthodes IV, papers from the Fourth International Conference on Methods in Dialectology, Victoria, BC: University of Victoria, 192–8.

—— (1985) 'Southern Indiana perceptions of "correct" and "pleasant" English', in H. Warkentyne (ed.) Methods/Méthodes V, papers from the Fifth International Conference on Methods in Dialectology, Victoria, BC: University of Victoria, 387–411.

—— (1986) 'Five visions of America', *Language in Society* 15,2: 221–40.

—— (1989) *Perceptual Dialectology*, Dordrecht: Foris.

—— (1996) 'Where the worst English is spoken', in Schneider, Edgar W. (ed.) *Focus on the USA*, Amsterdam, Benjamin, 297–361.

Preston, D. R. and Howe, G. M. (1987) 'Computerized generalizations of mental dialect maps', in Denning et al. (eds), *Variation in Language: NWAV–XV at Stanford*, Stanford, CA: Department of Linguistics, Stanford University, 361–78.

Pride, John B. (ed.) (1982) *New Englishes*, Rowley, MA: Newbury House.

Protherough, R. and Atkinson, J. (1994) 'Shaping the image of an English teacher', in S. Brindley (ed.) *Teaching English*, London: Routledge, 5–15.

Pullum, Geoffrey K. (1997) 'Language that dare not speak its name', *Nature* 386, 27 March, 321–2.

Puttenham, G. (1589) *The Arte of English Poesie*, London.

Quirk, R. (1957) 'Relative clauses in educated spoken English', *English Studies* 38: 97–109.

—— (1985) 'The English language in a global context', in R. Quirk and H. G. Widdowson (eds) *English in the World: Teaching and Learning the Language and Literatures*, Cambridge: Cambridge University Press, 1–6.

Quirk, R., Greenbaum, S., Leech, G. and Svartvik, J. (1972) *A Grammar of Contemporary English*, London: Longman.

—— (1985a) *A Contemporary Grammar of the English Language*, London: Longman.

—— (1985b) *The Comprehensive Grammar of the English Language*, London: Longman.

Radford, A. (1981) *Transformational Syntax*, Cambridge: Cambridge University Press.

Rasmussen, Gitte (1993) 'Lingua Franca: en forskningsberetning', *Merino* 15 (Center for Erhvervssproglige Studier, Odense University): 1–26.

Rensink, W. G. (1955) 'Dialectindeling naar opgaven van medewerkers', *Mededelingen der centrale commissie voor onderzoek van het nederlandse volkseigen* 7: 20–3.

Richardson, C. (1815) *Illustrations of English Philology*, London: Gale and Fenner.

—— (1836) *A New Dictionary of the English Language*, London: Pickering.

Richmond, J. (1992) 'Unstable materials', *The English Magazine* 26: 13–18.

Rickford, J. (1997) 'Commentary: Suite for Ebony and Phonics', *Discover*, Dec 1997: 82–7.

Ricks, C. (1980) 'Prefatory note', in Leonard Michaels and Christopher Ricks, *The State of the Language*, Berkeley, CA: University of California Press, xi–xii.

Risager, Karen (1993) 'Buy some petit souvenir aus Dänemark: Viden og bevidsthed om sprogmødet', in K. Risager, A. Holmen, A. Trosborg (eds) *Sproglig mangfoldighed: om sproglig viden og bevidsthed*, University of Roskilde: Publication of Association Danoise de Linguistique Appliquée 30–42.

Rogers, Daniel T. and Wilenz, Sean (1991) 'Languages of power in the United States', in Corfield (1991), 240–63.

Romaine, S. and Lange, D. (1991) 'The use of *like* as a marker of reported speech and thought: A case of grammaticalization in progress', *American Speech* 66, 3: 227–79.

Ross, A. S. C. (1954) 'Linguistic class-indicators in present-day English', *Neuphilologische Mitteilungen* 55.

Ryan, E. B. and Giles, H. (1982) *Attitudes towards Language Variation*, London: Arnold.

Ryan, E. B., Giles, H. and Sebastian, R. J. (1982) 'An integrative perspective for the study of attitudes towards language variation', in E. B. Ryan and H. Giles (eds) *Attitudes towards Language Variation*, London: Arnold, 12–19.

Sampson, George (1925) *English for the English*, Cambridge: Cambridge University Press.

Saussure, F. de (1922) *Cours de linguistique générale*, trans. Roy Harris, London: Duckworth, 1983.

Saxon, Samuel (1737) *The English Scholar's Assistant*, London.

Schegloff, E. (1979) 'The relevance of repair to syntax for conversation', in T. Givón, (ed.) *Discourse and Syntax*, New York: Academic Press, 261–86.

Schiffrin, D. (1987) *Discourse Markers*, Cambridge: Cambridge University Press.

—— (1994) *Approaches to Discourse*, Oxford: Blackwell.

Schutz, A. (1962) *Collected Papers*, vol. 1, ed. by M. Natanson, The Hague: Nijhoff.

Sebba, M. (1993) *London Jamaican*, London: Longman.

Seppänen, Aimo (1997) 'The genitives of the relative pronouns in present-day English', in Cheshire and Stein (eds), 152–69.

Sheridan, Thomas (1762) *A Course of Lectures on Elocution: Together with Two Dissertations on Language; and some Tracts relative to those Subjects*, London.

Sigley, R. (1997) 'The influence of formality and informality on relative pronoun choice in New Zealand English', *English Language and Linguistics* 1: 207–32.

Simon, J. (1980) 'The corruption of English,' in L. Michaels and C. Ricks (eds) *The State of the Language*, Berkeley: University of California Press.

Singh, Rajendra, D'souza, J., Mohanan, K. P. and Prabhu, N. S. (1995) 'On "new/non-native" Englishes: A quartet', *Journal of Pragmatics* 24: 283–94.

Skeat, W. W. and Sisam, K. (1915) *The Lay of Havelok the Dane*, Oxford: Clarendon Press.

Smith, J. (1996) *An Historical Study of English: Function, Form and Change*, London: Routledge.

Smith, L. (ed.) (1983a) *Readings in English as an International Language*, Oxford: Pergamon.

—— (1983b) 'English as an international language: No room for linguistic chauvinism', in L. Smith (1983a), 7–11.

Smith, O. (1984) *The Politics of Language 1791–1819*, Oxford: Clarendon Press.

Sperber, D. and Wilson, D. (1986) *Relevance Theory*, Oxford: Blackwell.

Stalker, J. C. (1986) 'A reconsideration of the definition of standard English', in G. Nickel and J. C. Stalker (eds) *Problems of Standardization and Linguistic Variation in Present-Day English*, Heidelberg: Julius Groos, 50–8.

Stein, D. (1994) 'Sorting out the variants: Standardization and social factors in the English language 1600–1800', in D. Stein and I. Tieken-Boon van Ostade (eds) *Towards a Standard English 1600–1800*, Berlin: de Gruyter, 1–18.

—— (1997) 'Syntax and varieties', in J. Cheshire and D. Stein (eds) *Taming the Vernacular: From Dialect to Written Standard Language*, London: Longman, 35–50.

Stein, G. and Quirk, R. (1995) 'Standard English', *The European English Messenger* 4,2: 62–3.

Strang, B. M. H. (1970) *History of English*, London: Methuen.

Strauss, Anselm and Corbin, Juliet (1990) *Basics of Qualitative Research*, Newbury Park, CA: Sage.

Stubbs, M. (1983) *Discourse Analysis: The Sociolinguistic Analysis of Natural Language*, Oxford: Blackwell.

—— (1986) *Educational Linguistics*, Oxford: Blackwell.

—— (1993) 'Educational language planning in England and Wales: Multicultural rhetoric and assimilationist assumptions', in J. Maybin (ed.) *Language and Literacy in Social Practice*, Clevedon: Multilingual Matters, 193–214.

Sturtevant, E. M. (1917) *Linguistic Change*, Chicago, IL: University of Chicago Press.

Sundby, B., Bjørge, A. K. and Haugland, K. E. (1991) *Dictionary of English Normative Grammar 1700–1800*, Amsterdam: Benjamin.

295

Sutcliffe, P. (1978) *The Oxford University Press: An Informal History*, Oxford: Clarendon Press.

Sweet, H. (1964) *The Practical Study of Languages*, Oxford: Oxford University Press.

—— (1971) *The Indispensable Foundation*, ed. Eugenie Henderson, Oxford: Oxford University Press.

Swift, Jonathan (1712) *A Proposal for Correcting, Improving and Ascertaining the English Tongue*, London: Benjamin Tooke.

Tagliamonte, S. (1997) 'Grammaticalization in apparent time: Tracing the pathways of *gonna* in the city of York', paper presented at NWAVE 24, Quebec City.

—— (in press) '*Was/were* variation across the generations: View from the city of York', *Language Variation and Change*.

Taylor, Talbot and Joseph, John E. (eds) (1990) *Ideologies of Language*, London: Routledge.

Thomas, J. J. (1889) *Froudacity: West India Tales by J. A. Froude*, London: Fisher Unwin.

—— (1989) *The Theory and Practice of Creole Grammar*, London: Beacon Books. Reprint of book first published in 1869.

Thompson, S. and Mulac, A. (1991) 'The discourse conditions for the use of the complementizer *that* in conversational English', *Journal of Pragmatics* 15: 237–51.

Tooke, J. H. (1786) *The Diversions of Purley*, London: J. Johnson.

Toon, T. E. (1982) 'Variation in contemporary American English', in R. W. Bailey and M. Görlach (eds) *English as a World Language*, Cambridge: Cambridge University Press, 210–50.

Tottie, G. (1991) *Negation in English Speech and Writing: A Study in Variation*, London: Academic.

Trench, R. C. (1851) *On the Study of Words*, London: Kegan Paul, Trubner.

—— (1857) *On Some Deficiencies in Our English Dictionaries, Being the Substance of Two Papers Read before the Philological Society*, London: Parker.

Trudgill, Peter (1974a) *The Social Differentiation of English in Norwich*, Cambridge: Cambridge University Press.

—— (1974b) *Sociolinguistics*, Harmondsworth: Penguin.

—— (1975) *Accent Dialect and the School*, London: Edward Arnold.

—— (1984) 'Standard English in England', in P. Trudgill (ed.) *Language in the British Isles*, Cambridge: Cambridge University Press, 32–44.

—— (1992) *Introducing Language and Society*, London: Penguin.

—— (1995) *Sociolinguistics: An Introduction to Language and Society*, Harmondsworth: Penguin.

Trudgill, P. and Cheshire, J. (1989) 'Dialect and education in the United Kingdom', in J. Cheshire, V. Edwards, H. Münstermann and B. Weltens (eds) *Dialect and Education: Some European Perspectives*, Clevedon: Multilingual Matters, 94–109.

Trudgill, P. and Hannah, J. (1985) *International English*, revised edn, London: Edward Arnold.

Tucker, G. R. and Lambert, W. E. (1969) 'White and Negro listeners' reaction to various American English dialects', *Social Forces* 47: 463–8.

Verma, S. K. (1982) 'Swadeshi English: Form and function', in Pride (1982), 174–87.

Wakelin, M. (1972a) *English Dialects: An Introduction*, London: Athlone Press.

—— (1972b) *Patterns in the Folk Speech of the British Isles*, London: Athlone Press.

Wallis, John (1653) *Grammatica Linguæ Anglicanæ*, London.

Walters, K. (1996) 'Contesting representations of African American language', Proceedings of SALSA III, Austin, TX: University of Texas Press, 137–51.

Watts, Richard J. (1990) 'The role of early grammar writers in creating a linguistic tradition', in Riccarda Liver, Iwar Werlen and Peter Wunderli (eds) *Sprachtheorie und Theorie der Sprachwissenschaft*, Tübingen: Gunter Narr, 299–315.

296

—— (1996) 'Justifying grammars: A socio-pragmatic foray into the discourse community of early English grammarians', in Andreas H. Jucker (ed.) *Historical Pragmatics*, Amsterdam: Benjamin, 145–85.

—— (in press) 'Mythical strands in the ideology of prescriptivism', in Laura Wright (ed.) *The History of Standard English*, London: Cambridge University Press.

Weiner, E. S. C. (1990) 'The Federation of English', in C. Ricks and L. Michaels (eds) *The State of the Language*, London: Faber, 492–502.

Weinreich, Uriel, Labov, William and Herzog, Marvin (1968) 'Empirical foundations for a theory of language change', in W. Lehmann and Y. Malkiel (eds) *Directions for Historical Linguistics*, Austin, TX: University of Texas Press, 97–195.

Wells, J. C. (1982) *Accents of English: An Introduction*, Cambridge: Cambridge University Press.

Whitney, W. D. (1897) *The Life and Growth of Language*, New York: Appleton.

Widdowson, H. G. (1993) 'Proper words in proper places', *ELTJ* 47, 4: 317–29.

—— (1994) 'The ownership of English', *TESOL Quarterly* 28, 2: 377–89.

Wilkinson, G. (1995) *Introducing Standard English*, Harmondsworth: Penguin.

Williams, Angie, Garrett, Peter and Coupland, Nikolas (1996) 'Perceptual dialectology, folklinguistics and regional stereotypes: Teachers' perception of variation in Welsh English', *Multilingua* 15, 2: 171–99.

Williams, P. (1991) *The Alchemy of Race and Rights*, Cambridge, MA: Harvard University Press.

—— (1995) *The Rooster's Egg: On the Persistence of Prejudice*, Cambridge, MA: Cambridge University Press.

Wolfram, W. (1991) *Dialects and American English*, Washington DC: Center for Applied Linguistics.

Woods, E. (1995) *Introducing Grammar*, Harmondsworth: Penguin.

Woolard, Kathryn A. (1989) *Double Talk*, Stanford, CA: Stanford University Press.

Woolard, Kathryn A. and Schieffelin, Bambi (1994) 'Language ideology', *Annual Review of Anthropology* 23: 55–82.

Wright, Laura (ed.) (in progress) *The History of Standard English*, Cambridge: Cambridge University Press.

Wyld, H. C. (1920) *A Short History of Modern Colloquial English*, London: Fisher Unwin.

—— (1927) *A Short History of English*, London: J. Murray.

—— (1934) 'The best English: A claim for the superiority of Received Standard English', *Proceedings of the Society for Pure English* 4, Tract 39, 603–21.

Zelinsky, Wilbur (1980) 'North America's vernacular regions', *Annals of the Association of American Geographers* 70, 1: 1–16.

INDEX

NOTE: Page numbers followed by *fig* indicate information is to be found only in a figure; page numbers followed by *tab* indicate information is to be found only in a table. Although the orthography can vary, the term Standard English has initial capital letters throughout the index.

Aarsleff, H. 76
AAVE *see* African-American Vernacular English
Abercrombie, D. 19, 184, 187, 188, 204
Abstand principle 3
Académie Française: as authority model 69, 278; dictionary project 79
accent: 'accent bar' 184, 187, 188, 204; and British Army 186, 187; in broadcasting 190, 205n1, 208; and discrimination 19, 176–8, 184; 'drawl' 235, 237n5; in education 162; foreign 178–9, 188; historical perspective 184, 185–6; nasal 235–6; and prestige 175, 189; public school accent 184; in Received Standard English 105; rural 190; and social class 118; and spoken Standard English 163; and Standard English 70, 113, 114, 118–19, 169, 271; Standard English is not 123; stigmatised 184, 188, 189, 190, 213, 216; and universities 184, 186, 188; urban 185, 190, 203; US folk evaluation of 174, 202–3, 207–38; variation in 162; *see also* Belfast accent; Birmingham accent; Brahmin accent; Cockney accent; dialect; Indian-accented English; Jamaican accent; 'network American';

pronunciation; Scouse; Ulster Scots accent; Yorkshire accent
'acceptability' of language 25
Adamic theory of language 77, 79, 84
Adams, John 194
advertising 4; in Denmark 172, 241, 242–3, 250; 'Shamed By Your Mistakes' advert 106
African-American Vernacular English (AAVE) 177, 178, 179, 183, 193, 196, 201–2; in EFL context 260; *see also* Black English
African-Americans: historical perspective 196–7; intellectual tradition 200; 'Negro slaves' 197
Afro-British intellectual tradition 197–202
agreement *see* concord
Aitchison, Jean 180
Alford, H. 29
alphabetical order 74–5, 78, 83
America *see* United States
American English 3; Danish perceptions of 248–51, 252*fig*, 253, 264; folk evaluations of 170–1, 174, 202–3, 207–38; *see also* Standard American English
American languages, indigenous 193, 195–6
American South *see* South, American
American Standard English *see* Standard American English
Americanisation Campaign 192–3
Amory, Leo 96
Anglo-conformity 192–3, 196
Anglo-Norman scribes 34–5
Anglo-Saxon language 28–9, 99
Appalachian English 5

aristocracy and best English 184, 204, 205n4
Arte of English Poesie (treatise) 184
Ascherson, Neil 181, 191
Atkins, J.D.C. 195, 196
Atkinson, J. 92
attributes and US regional speech areas 227, 228tab, 230
Ausbau languages 3, 118
Australian English 3, 124
authority in language: Honey on 169, 274–9; language pronouncements 21–4, 87n3; National Language Authority proposal 69, 278–9; and standard ideology 26; US academy for 194; on usage 89–108; *see also* codification of language; prescriptivism
authors: errors committed by 94, 98; as models for language 44, 59, 60, 91, 182, 274

Bacher, P. 253, 258
Bailey, N.: *Universal Etymological Dictionary* 79–80
Bailey, R. 5, 185
Bakhtin, M. 162, 280–1n1
Barber, Francis 197
Barker, Pat 186
Barron, D. 194–5
Baugh, A.C. 184
Baugh, J. 179
BBC: meaning confused by 277–8; as model of spoken Standard English 187–8; Reith Lectures 180, 183
Beal, J. 133
Beethoven, Ludwig van 199
Belfast, Northern Ireland: accent 184–5, 190, 191
Bella (magazine) 176–8
Bennett, J.A.W. 35
Berg, D.L. 86
Berger, P. 14, 41, 66
Berrendonner, A. 134–5, 141
Bex, Tony 9, 14–15, 239, 262
Bible: as model of language 87n4
bilingualism: Danish–English 241, 247, 251, 253–8, 263–4; in Ireland 190; in US 192, 196
Birmingham accent 182, 189
Black English 178, 201–2; *see also* African-American Vernacular English
Blake, William 201

Blommaert, Jan 2
Bloomfield, L. 73
Blount, T. 78
Bogarde, Dirk 186
Bolinger, D. 20, 73
Booth, Charles 191
Borker, Ruth 247
Borroff, M. 94
Boston English 208; Brahmin accent 202–3
Bourdieu, Pierre 14, 15, 41–2, 63, 106, 107
Bradbury, Ray 182–3
Bradley, Henry 100
Brahmin accent, Boston 202–3
Bridgewater, George 199
Brightland, John 49
Britain: Black English in 201–2; historical perspective 184–92; language discrimination in 19; language ideology in 173–206
British Broadcasting Corporation *see* BBC
British English 3; Danish perceptions of 248–51, 252fig, 253, 264; US view of 208, 210
British Standard English *see* Standard English
broadcasting: BBC English 187–8; confusion of meanings 277–8; in Denmark 242, 243, 246, 250, 257; 'network American' accent 174, 202, 204, 208; *Oprah Winfrey Show* 177–8; regional accents in 190, 205n1, 208
Brown, G. 130
Bullokar, W. 101
Burchfield, Robert 93, 100–1
Butterfield, H. 7
Byatt, A.S. 108n2

California: English Language Amendment 180; as English Only state 195
Callister, Stephanie 190
Cambridge University: and accent 184, 186, 188
Camden, William 61
Cameron, D. 20, 22, 90–1, 134, 163, 164, 178
Canadian English 3, 135, 136
CANCODE corpus and research project 115–16, 149–52, 154–8, 159–60, 165–6n1

canonical forms of language 16–17
capital: cultural 15, 42, 63; material
  41–2, 63; symbolic 14, 15, 41, 42, 51,
  63, 107, 108
Cardenas, Jose A. 179
Carew, Richard 61, 67–8
caricatures, linguistic 233–4, 235–6
Carter, Ronald 2; corpora 115–16,
  130–1, 142, 165–6n1; ellipsis 155,
  156; heads and tails 151, 152;
  meaning of standard 71; teaching of
  Standard English 116, 158, 160
Castro, Max 179
Cawdrey, R.: Table Alphabeticall 75, 76,
  77
Census Bureau (US): taxonomies of class
  191
Chafe, W. 137
Chambers, J.K. 36, 118, 184
Chancery Standard English 205n4
change see linguistic change
Channell, J. 161
Cheshire, Jenny 2, 6, 118, 173;
  existential there 135; non-standard
  varieties of English 131–2; Reading
  English 138–9; -s suffix 139;
  standardisation 133; syntax 114–15,
  130, 273; that 134, 135, 144
child language, degenerate input to 34
Chomsky, Noam 22, 25, 34, 72, 136, 141
Church of England: and accent 186, 188
Churchill, Winston 93
civil servants 108n7; handbooks of usage
  for 101–2
class see social class
class markers 191–2
classical music in Denmark 251, 252fig
classics: classical education 51, 64, 65–6,
  99, 101, 102, 106–7, 108n7; Standard
  English as classical language 64–5; see
  also Greek, classical; Latin
clause components 156
Clyne, Michael 4
Coates, J. 146
Cobbett, William 102
Cockney accent/dialect 31, 67, 189, 190
code-switching in Denmark 242–3, 244,
  246, 247, 251, 261
codification of language 13, 114, 115,
  130; dictionaries 117, 277; grammars
  117, 130; of written form of Standard
  English 158, 278

Coles, E. 77, 83
Colet, John 66
colonial languages 193
colonialism: and Standard English 9, 63
commercials see advertising
comparative linguistics 28
'complaint tradition' 13, 20, 90, 108n8
computers: and English usage in
  Denmark 241, 243, 244, 246, 251
concord 135–9, 157, 161
Conservative government (Major,
  1990-7) 175, 204
Conservative government (Thatcher,
  1979–90) 1, 166n3, 188, 204, 205–6n7
context dependent features 133–4
Conversational Analysis 27
conversational speech 23–4, 32, 33;
  grammar of 149–59; heads and tails
  151–2, 154
Corfield, P. J. 184
Cornish, F. 144
corpora of transcribed speech 133, 142,
  145; CANCODE corpus and research
  project 115–16, 149–52, 154–8,
  159–60, 165–6n1; Reading English
  corpus 138–9; use in grammars 130–1,
  166n2
correctness: authority for 278, 279; and
  discrimination 13; as ideology of
  language 237n6; notions of 7, 13, 18,
  19–20, 21; text normalisation 34–5;
  US ratings of 210–13, 219, 232,
  237n6; see also prescriptivism
corruption of language 30–1
country music in Denmark 251, 252fig
Coupland, N. 189, 222, 226, 237
Cox, B. 1, 91
Crawford, J. 193, 196
Creider, C. 25
Creole 190, 201, 202
Crossick, G. 185
Crowley, Tony 9, 15, 28, 85, 106; dialect
  205n5; meanings of standard 71, 90;
  and RP 114; on Wyld 31
Crystal, David 107
cultural capital 15, 42, 63

Dabydeen, D. 198, 200–1
Daily Mail 181
Davidson, William 201
Davis, Hayley 6, 14, 71, 78, 83
De Maria, R. Jr 76

Dear, I.C.B. 108–9n9
death metal music subculture, Denmark 242, 244, 246
definition of words 79–85
degenerate input to child language 34
degree of difference ratings (US) 216–19
Denmark: Danes with no knowledge of English 253–8, 263, 267n12; 13; 17; Danish–English bilingualism 241, 247, 251, 253–8, 263–4; functions of English in 171–2, 239–67; Standard English in 262–6; subculture groups in 242, 244–6, 247, 260–1
Department for Education and Employment (DfEE) 91; see also National Curriculum for English in England and Wales
descriptivism 6–7, 8–9; descriptive linguistics 13, 28–34, 107–8, 131, 145–6; in folk linguistics 210
determination of language 114, 117
DfEE see Department for Education and Employment
dialect: as degenerate form 29–30; dialect switching 121, 122–3; Estuary English 180–2, 191–2, 202; formal use of 121, 122–3; and grammar 161; heads and tails in 154; historical perspective 67–8, 184–5; in histories of language 31, 205n5; Honey on 280n1; inherent variability of 263; levelling of 180–2, 191; non-standard lexis of 127; regional markers 191–2; revalorisation of 184, 191; rural 29, 182, 189, 190; social dialects 123–4; and spoken Standard English 164; Standard English as 123–5; US folk evaluation of 170–1, 174, 202–3, 207–38; see also accent; Cockney dialect/accent
dialectology 17–18, 108; perceptual 207–38
dictionaries 94, 108n5; alphabetical order in 74–5, 78, 83; codification by 117, 277; development of 76–87; etymological 79–80, 82, 83; pronouncing 85, 147; Victorian 29; see also lexicography; Oxford English Dictionary (OED)
Dictionnaire de la langue française (Académie Française) 79
Digges, Thomas 198

discourse communities 14, 15; defined 43; grammar writers as 40–68; see also speech communities
discrimination: social 13, 19, 176–8; see also linguistic discrimination
distribution and US regional speech areas 227, 228tab, 230
Dobson, E.J. 31
Dorling, D. 180
double negatives 156–7
Douglass, Frederick 200
Downes, W. 146
Dryden, John 98
Dubois, W.E.B. 200
Duncan, Daniel: A New English Grammar 43, 44, 51, 60, 65; addressees 57–8, 64; on parts of speech 49; references to Latin 52, 53
Duncan, S. 144

Ebonics debate (US) 1, 178, 179
educatedness: and speech 30, 139–41, 149–59; and Standard English 5, 8, 14, 15, 30, 118, 130, 275–6, 277–8
education: classical 51, 64, 65–6, 99, 101, 102, 106–7, 108n7; curriculum debate 7, 8, 22, 40–1, 89–92, 274; Denmark, English-language teaching in 240–1, 246, 250–1, 259, 262–6; grammars aimed at 44–5, 61; native American languages obliterated 195–6; prescriptivism in 8, 14, 21, 275; registers taught in 121–2; and social construction 40–1, 42, 62–8; Standard English teaching 5, 21, 66, 113, 116, 118, 158–61, 163–5, 272–3, 274; teaching of English, historical perspective 91–3; university teaching of English 108; US English movement 179; see also educatedness; English as a foreign language (EFL); English as a second language (ESL); National Curriculum for English in England and Wales; public school system
Edward VII, King of the United Kingdom 38
Edwards, J. 142
Edwards, P. 198, 200–1
Edwards, V. 19, 187
EFL see English as a foreign language
Ehlich, K. 144
Eisenstein, E.L. 76

Eisikovits, E. 135
ellipsis in speech 154–5, 156, 161, 166n2
Ellis, Alexander 205n5
English: canonical form 17; historical perspective 23–39, 184–202; for international communication 4, 241–2, 259, 264; as lingua franca 171, 253; national varieties of 5; non-standard varieties 30; pronunciation of 31; teaching of 91–3, 274; university teaching of 108; varieties of 118; *see also* African-American Vernacular English; American English; Anglo-Saxon language; Appalachian English; Australian English; Black English; British English; Canadian English; English as a foreign language; English as a second language; Estuary English; Jamaican English; Middle English; non-standard English; Queen's English; Reading English; Standard English
English as a foreign language (EFL) 5, 6; concept of Standard English in 239–40; forms of English in Denmark 239–67; forms of 171–2, 258–66; motivation for learning 246–7, 255–8; RP in 33; Standard American English in 239, 264; Standard English in 118, 127, 239–40
'English from above' learning in Denmark 241, 247, 259, 261, 264
'English from below' learning in Denmark 241, 242–6, 247, 259, 260–1, 264
English Language Amendment (ELA)(US) 180, 192
English Only movement (US) 178, 179–80, 192–3, 194–5, 196
English as a second language (ESL) 3, 5; in Denmark 172, 241; RP in 174; in US English debate 179
Enright, D.J. 93
Equiano, Olaudah 198
ESL *see* English as a second language
Estuary English 180–2, 191–2, 202
ethnic minorities: language rights 179–80; *see also* race
ethnicity and US regional speech areas 227, 228*tab*, 230
etymological dictionaries 79–80, 82, 83
evolutionary linguistics 84
existential *there* 135–8, 139, 157, 161

Fairclough, N. 178
Falk, Julia 207, 208, 209, 210
'Federal English' 194
feminine endings 96–7
fiction *see* authors
field 42
fillers 133
films in Denmark 241, 242, 246, 250
Finnegan, R. 74
Fishman, Joshua A. 179–80, 251
fixed-code theory 72, 73
Flaitz, Jeffra 249, 251, 267n7
Foley, M. 131, 135–6, 137, 138
folk linguistics 9, 90; Danish evaluations of use of English 239–67; folk evaluations of US dialects 170–1, 174, 202–3, 207–38
foreign accents 178–9, 188
foreign words 80
formality: of Danish English speakers 261; dialect use 121, 122–3; in speech 146–7; and Standard English 119–21, 128, 262
Foster, R.F. 185
Foucault, Michel: Honey on 281n1
Fowler, F.G. 93, 99
Fowler, H.W. 91, 101, 103, 104, 105, 106, 107, 108; *The King's English* 93, 99–100; background 93–4; *Dictionary of Modern English Usage* (MEU) 93, 94–9, 100
Fox, Charles 199
Franklin, Benjamin 194
Fraser, Sir Bruce 103, 108n7
Frederiksen, M.K. 242–3
French: English damaged by 29; oral syntax 141; standard 69–70; as US colonial language 193
Fromkin, V. 70, 207–8, 209, 210
Froude, J.A. 201
fused constructions 139–40
fused participles 99, 103–4

Gainsborough, Thomas 199
Galsworthy, John 188
Garfinkel, H. 130
Gelyukens, R. 152
generative tradition in linguistics 114, 116, 131, 132, 138, 145
genre-specific constructions 142–5
German 52, 193–4
Germany: 'new right' in 276
Gibbon, Edward 98

Giddens, A. 191
Gildon, Charles 49
Giles, H. 98, 119, 189, 209, 210, 213
Gimson, A.C. 33
Gladstone, William Ewart 185–6
glottal stop 38, 162, 185
Görlach, M. 5
Government and Binding Theory 136, 137
Gowers, Ernest 91, 106, 107, 108; background 100–1; *Complete Plain Words* (CPW) 100–3, 108n7&8; on Fowler 95, 101; on idiom 104, 105; revises Fowler 93, 96, 97
Grace, G. 17, 34
Graddol, D. 147
Graduate Student Instructors (US): intelligibility of 179
graffiti subculture, Denmark 244, 246
grammar: codification of 13; eighteenth-century grammarians 13–14, 40–68, 132; formality in 120; Gowers on 102; Partridge on 104; of spoken forms of Standard English 129–48, 149–66; and Standard English 124–6; and standard ideology 25–6; teaching of 92–3, 108
grammars 94, 108n5, 147; addressees 55–62, 64; based on written language 27, 152–3; codification of language 117, 130; corpora data used for 130–1, 166n2; descriptive 131; for education 44–5, 61; eighteenth-century grammar writers 13–14, 40–68, 132; Latin used as model for 44, 46, 47, 50–4, 61, 64–5; prescriptive 125, 131, 277; *see also* handbooks of English
Greece, classical 74
Greek, classical 14, 52, 53, 62, 64
Greenbaum, Sidney 5, 107, 108n7, 109n11, 166n2
Greenwood, James: *An Essay toward a Practical English Grammar* 43, 44, 50, 51, 61–2, 64–5; on grammar 46–7, 48; on parts of speech 47, 49; references to Latin 52, 53–4
Guardian, the 180
Gupta, A. 173

h-dropping 35, 185
habitus 42, 64
Halford, B. 140
Hall, Robert A. 19–20, 21

Halle, M. 25
Halliday, M.A.K. 156
handbooks of English 7, 14–15, 29, 89–109; *see also* grammars
Hannah, J. 5
Harris, Frank 38
Harris, J. 133
Harris, R. 73, 74, 75, 107, 109n10, 133
Hartley, Laura C. 9, 170, 216, 219, 220, 222, 237n2
Haugen, E. 183, 262
Havelock, E.A. 74
Havelock (Middle English romance) 35
head structures 151–2, 154, 166n2
Heller, Monica 2
Heryanto, A. 34
Herzog, Marvin 17, 36
heterogeneity 36–7, 191
Hewson, T.H. 92
Higginson, E. 87n4
hip hop music subculture, Denmark 242, 244, 246, 251, 260–1
Hobsbawm, E.J. 40, 63
Hoenigswald, Henry 237n1
Hogarth, William 199
Høgsbro, Kjeld 244–6
Holmes, J. 121, 163
Honey, John: *Language is Power* 1, 9, 16; and accent 70, 188, 189, 280n1; authority concept 169, 276–9; debated 271–82; on dialect 280n1; history of Standard English 71; linguists as enemy 2, 21, 22, 24, 26, 91; National Language Authority proposal 69, 87n3, 278–9; and 'new right' 276–7, 279; on RP 185–6; scholarship of 279–81n1; Standard English defined 6, 70, 271–2, 280n1; Standard English and educatedness 15, 275–6, 277–8
Honey, John: *Does Accent Matter?* 281n2
Hopkins, Gerard Manley 31
Howe, G.M. 220
Hübler, Axel 265
Hudson, R. 121, 163

idealisation: Standard American English as 207–8; Standard English as 32–3, 70, 272–3; standard languages as 18, 26, 27
identity and language: national 3, 28, 96, 162–3; subcultural 247, 259, 261, 263; and (US) regional speech areas 227, 228tab, 229–30

ideology of language: and authority 26; correctness as 237n6; immigration and 192–6, 204, 219; language attitudes 169–70, 171, 173–206; in linguistics 24–39; and prestige 37–9; of Standard English 1–2, 13–15, 45, 169–70; of standard languages 18, 20, 22, 23, 28–34, 35, 173–206
idiom 104–5, 272
immigration and language ideology 192–6, 204, 219; see also migration
Independent: grammar correspondence 90
Independent on Sunday 181
Indian-accented English 189
Indiana, southern: group composition 237n2; language ratings 17C, 203, 211fig, 213, 214fig, 216, 217fig, 219, 220, 232; speech area maps 221fig, 224fig, 228tab, 229, 230, 231, 233, 234, 235
industrial relations and social class 188
Industrial Revolution 184–5
infrequent constructions 139–42
inherent variability of dialect 263
'institutionalization' theory 41
instruction manuals in Denmark 243
intelligibility 4, 71–2; of Graduate Student Instructors in US 179; US speech area ratings 216–19, 228, 230
international communication: English used for 4, 241–2, 259, 264
International Express 181
Internet use of English 264
interracial marriage rates 183
intuitions of linguists 25, 131–2, 132, 133, 135, 138
Ireland 184–5, 190, 191

Jacobs, Harriet 200–1
Jamaican English 5, 189–90; see also Creole
Jefferson, Thomas 197, 199
Jespersen, Otto 95, 98, 103–4
Johnson, R. 265
Johnson, Samuel 24, 28, 87, 197, 273; A Dictionary of the English Language 80–3
Jones, Daniel 33, 85
Jones, Hugh: An Accidence to the English Tongue 43, 44, 65; addressees 58–9, 64; on grammar 47–8; on parts of speech 48, 49; references to Latin 50–1

Joseph, John E. 2, 3, 4, 108, 134, 278
journalists see media; newspapers

Kachru, B.B. 3–5, 10n2
Karpf, Anne 183
'Kenyon–Knott grammar' 25
Kerswill, Paul 181, 192
King, R. 198, 199
Kingman, J.: report 6, 89–90, 91, 92
Kitzinger, R. 76
Klein, L. 147

labelling of speech areas (US) 210, 220–37; positive and negative 232–7
Labov, William 8, 210; Honey on 280n1; linguistic insecurity 209; prestige 37, 38, 202; sociolinguistic markers 262; structured heterogeneity 17, 36; style 119, 120; vernacular 205n5
Lakoff, R. 131, 134
Lambert, W.E. 209, 246
Langacker, Robert W. 208, 210
Lange, D. 134
language attitudes 209–10, 213; in Denmark 247–51, 256–7, 258; and ideologies 169–70, 171, 173–206; see also folk linguistics; public opinion
language guardians 20, 21, 22, 239; Honey as 278
Language in the National Curriculum (LINC) project 157–8, 159–60, 166n3
language pronouncements 21–4
Lass, R. 30
Latin 14, 62, 64, 76–7, 101, 104; Fowler and 95, 98–9; Honey on 277; as model for English grammars 44, 46, 47, 50–5, 61, 64–5
Lawrence, Stephen 183, 205n3
Lawton, D.L. 5
lay opinion see folk linguistics; public opinion
lay tradition in linguistics 114, 115
layer cake hierarchy 183
Le Page, R. 117
left dislocation 134–5, 137, 139, 142, 152
legitimacy of language 28, 30–1
'legitimate language' 42–3, 46; models of 44, 59, 60, 87n3; and 'public' education 51, 62–5, 66
Lehmann, W.P. 31
Leibowicz, J. 192–3
leisure activities in Denmark 251

Leith, D. 31
Leith, R. 147
lexicography: and Standard English 14, 69–88; standards of 76–87; *see also* dictionaries
lexis: lexical choice 119–20; lexical items 122; of non-standard English 127; and Standard English 119–21, 121–3, 127; *see also* register; vocabulary; words
Lily, William 66
Limburg, Netherlands: use of dialect 121
LINC project 157–8, 159–60, 166n3
lingua franca: English as 171, 253, 259, 265–6
linguistic caricatures 233–4, 235–6
linguistic change: from above 38; from below 38; not corruption 30, 31; and prestige 37; and public opinion 175, 180; and standardisation 27–8, 35, 39, 126–7
linguistic discrimination 173–206; and race 170, 171, 177, 178–80, 183, 190–1, 195–6, 202, 204; and social class 13, 19, 170, 171, 174–5, 176–8, 180–3; *see also* linguistic prejudices
linguistic habitus 42, 64
linguistic insecurity 209, 210, 213, 216, 219, 229
linguistic prejudices 208, 210; *see also* linguistic discrimination
linguistics: attacks on 2, 21, 22, 24–39, 91; comparative 28; descriptive 13, 28–34, 107–8, 131, 145–6, 210; evolutionary 84; generative tradition 114, 116, 131, 132, 138, 145; intuitions of linguists 25, 131–2, 132, 133, 135, 138; prescriptive 107, 108; and standardisation 13, 16–39, 19, 130–1; structural 18, 28, 36–7, 39; three traditions 114–15; *see also* folk linguistics; sociolinguistics
Lippi-Green, R. 19, 173, 178–9, 182
literacy 76, 152; of Danes with no knowledge of English 253–8, 263; oracy 153; and Standard English 130
Literary Standard English 105
Liverpool: Scouse 189, 205n5
Locke, John 78–9, 81
London Jamaican accent 189–90
London–Lund corpus 133
Lowth, Robert: *A Short Introduction to English Grammar* 44, 59–60, 65, 87n4;

addressees 59, 64; on grammar 49–50; on parts of speech 50; references to Latin 51–2
Luckmann, T. 14, 41, 66
Luxembourg: formal use of dialect 121
Lyons, John 72, 73, 75, 131

Macaulay, R. 146
McCabe, C. 149, 165
McCalman, Iain 201
McCarthy, M. 142, 155, 156, 160, 165–6n1; heads and tails 151, 152
McClenaghan, P. 189
Mail on Sunday 181, 281n2
Maltz, Daniel 247
maps of US speech areas 210, 220–37
marriage: interracial 183
Marsh, G.P. 30, 31
Marwick, A. 103, 107, 191
material capital 41–2, 63
Mead, Richard 61
media: 'complaint tradition' in 90; and Estuary English 180–2; literacy debate 157; notions of correctness 22; *Sun* uses Standard English 124; symbolic revalorization of language 176–8; Victorian fear of newspaper jargon 31; view of linguists and educators 1, 2; view on speech 151; *see also* broadcasting; newspapers; public opinion
Meechan, M. 131, 135–6, 137, 138
Meier, A. 200
Michigan, southeastern: group composition 237n2; language ratings 170, 203, 211*fig*, 213, 214*fig*, 216, 217*fig*, 219, 220; speech area maps 221*fig*, 224*fig*, 228–30, 231, 232, 233, 234, 235
Middle English: standardisation of 34–5
Middleton, D. 142
Miège, Guy: *The English Grammar* 44, 61
migration: and language change 184–5; *see also* immigration and language ideology
Milroy, James 28, 113–14; accent 191; 'complaint tradition' 20; dialect 185; Honey on 273, 274; linguistic change 39; phonology 173; standard language ideology 13, 18, 34, 130, 146, 173, 174, 184; syntax 130
Milroy, Lesley 9, 113–14; accent 189, 190, 191; 'complaint tradition' 20;

dialect 185; Honey on 273, 274; ideology of Standard English 169–70; phonology 173; standard language ideology 18, 34, 67, 130, 146, 173, 174, 184

Milton Keynes: Estuary English 180–2, 191–2, 202

Mitford, Nancy 107

Moag, Rodney 242, 244, 246, 258–9, 266n1

Modified Standard English 32, 105, 187

Monboddo, James Burnett, Lord 87n4

Montagu, Duke of 199

Montgomery, Michael 139, 142, 237n2

morality: in language pronouncements 21, 22; of languages 16–17

Morse, J. Mitchell 202

motivation for EFL learning 246–7, 255–8

Mugglestone, L. 31, 114, 185

Mühlhaüsler, P. 34, 36

Mulac, A. 133

multilingualism 171, 192–6; see also bilingualism

Murray, James A.H. 84–5, 86, 88n5, 107

Murray, K. 84

music in Denmark 251, 252fig; popular 241, 242, 244, 246, 250, 251, 260–1

National Curriculum for English in England and Wales: on American and Australian English 124; curriculum debate 1, 7, 8, 22, 40–1, 89–92, 274; 'important real-world implications' 115, 132; Language in the National Curriculum (LINC) project 157–8, 159–60, 166n3; and spoken forms of Standard English 114, 115, 116, 129, 147, 153–4, 165, 171; variations ignored 162; vocabulary 113, 122, 127

national identity and language 3, 28, 96, 162–3

National Language Authority proposal 69, 278–9

Native American languages 193, 195–6

'network American' accent 174, 202, 204, 208

'new right' 276–7, 279, 282n7

New York City: accent 202, 203; and Standard American English 203

Newbolt report 91–2, 93

newspapers: on Estuary English 180–2; as models of legitimate language 44, 59; on Standard English 173; use of Standard English 124

Niedzielski, N. 237n1

Nietzsche, Friedrich Wilhelm 108n2

non-native speakers see English as a foreign language

non-standard English: lexis of 127; and linguistic change 126–7; negative view of 163; and style 120–1; varieties of 30, 31, 131–2

norms of language 25–6, 27, 34–5, 274

North, Frederick, 8th Lord North 199

Norway: formal use of dialect 121

Nottingham, University of see CANCODE research project

Ochs, E. 146

OED see Oxford English Dictionary

O'Grady, W. 209

Oliphant, T.K. 29, 31, 185

Onions, Charles Talbut 103–4

Oprah Winfrey Show 177–8

oracy 153

'oral syntax' 139–41

Oregon: group composition 237n2; language ratings 170, 212fig, 213, 215fig, 216, 218fig, 219, 220, 237n3; speech area maps 223fig, 225, 226fig, 228–9, 230, 231, 233, 234, 236

ÓRiágan, P. 190

orthography 9, 27, 34–5, 74, 75, 79, 98

Osborne, Anne 199

Osborne, John 181–2

Ouhalla, Jamal 139, 141

Out of Control (Danish hip hop group) 260–1

overseas learners see English as a foreign language

Oxford English 108–9n9

Oxford English 184

Oxford English Dictionary (OED) 14, 71–2, 76, 77, 82, 89; Fowler uses phonetic system from 97; historical approach 81, 86; proposal for 83–4; scope of 88n5; Standard English defined in 271, 281n4

Oxford University: and accent 184, 186, 188

Pacific languages 34

Partridge, Eric H. 91, 93, 107; on Standard English 105–6; Usage and Abusage 103–6

parts of speech 47, 48–9, 50, 54–5
Passeron, Jean-Claude 42, 106
Pawley, A. 137
Pearsall Smith, Logan 104–5
perceptual dialectology 207–38
Perera, K. 108n1, 151, 158, 164
permissiveness and language 20
Peterborough Chronicle (Middle English manuscript) 35
Phillips, Caryl 199
Phillips, E.: *A New World of English Words* 78
Philological Society 83–4
philology 28; comparative 84
phonetics 33, 97, 114
phonology 114, 120, 169, 173; *see also* sound; speech
Pinker, S. 20, 202
Pitts, Ann 237n2
Pittsburgh, US: survey 191
Platt, J. 5, 173
pleasantness: US ratings of 213–16, 219, 232
plural forms 157
poets: as models of language 44, 59, 60
poll taxes (UK) 205–6n7
popular music: in Denmark 241, 242, 246, 250, 251
popular press *see* media; newspapers
Port Royal Grammarians 78
Porter, Roy 68n1
Powesland, P.F. 189
Preisler, Bent 4, 171–2
prejudices *see* linguistic prejudice
prescriptivism 6–7, 8, 9; and authority and morality 22–4; conversational speech condemned by 23–4; in dictionaries 79, 277; in education 8, 14, 21, 275; in English teaching 92; in folk linguistics 210; of grammarians 13–14, 40–68, 125, 131, 277; and handbooks of English 14–15; and notions of correctness 18, 19–20; pronouncements 29; Victorian 73
prestige: and accent 175, 189; of English in Denmark 247; and Standard English 7, 8, 31–2, 113, 114, 124, 262; and standard ideology 37–9; *see also* discrimination; educatedness; social class; stigma
Preston, Dennis R. 182, 189; folk evaluations 9, 170, 174, 237n1; US speech areas 202, 203, 210, 220, 222, 223, 226

printing process: and development of Standard English 166n4; and standardisation of language 74, 76
pronunciation: dictionaries of 85, 147; Fowler on 97–8; historical description of 31; omitted from first *OED* 84; and spelling 98; and Standard English 31–2, 113, 118–19; *see also* accent; received pronunciation
Protherough, R. 92
'public' education 68n1; grammars aimed at 44–5, 50; and legitimate language 62–7; and social construction 40–1, 42, 62
public opinion: awareness of standard language 18; and Estuary English 180–2; and linguistic change 175, 180; notions of correctness 13, 19, 20, 22; on spoken standards 175; on Standard English 89, 90–1, 173; 'symbolic revalorization' 176–8; view of linguists and educators 20; *see also* folk linguistics; 'language guardians'; media
public school system 106–7; public school accent 184; Public School English 105; and RP 186
Pullum, Geoffrey K. 179
punctuation: change in 27
Puttenham, George 184, 205n4

Queen's English 29, 184
Queensberry, Duchess of 198
Quirk, Randolph 10n1, 33, 132; definitions of Standard English 130; existential *there* 136; use of corpora data 115, 130, 131, 166n2; on variety of standards 2–3, 6, 124

race: and linguistic discrimination (US) 170, 171, 177, 178–80, 183, 190–1, 195–6, 202, 204; Stephen Lawrence case (UK) 183, 205n3; taxonomies of (US) 190–1; Victorian racism 201; *see also* African-American Vernacular English; African-Americans; Afro-British intellectual tradition; ethnic minorities; ethnicity
Radford, A. 25
Radical movement, Britain 201
Rather, Dan 205n1
Reading English corpus 138–9, 142
Reading University: Estuary English research 181

received pronunciation (RP): historical perspective 31–3, 184, 185–8, 204; and idea of Standard English 85; and language discrimination 19; as prestige accent 114, 189; as standard of spoken English 118, 171, 173–4; and stigma 38; teaching of 66; US equivalent 202–3

Received Standard English 31–2, 32–3, 105, 186–7

reference works *see* dictionaries; grammars; handbooks of English

regional speech maps (US) 210, 220–37

register 121–3; in English use in Denmark 241, 260, 261, 264; and Standard English 128

Reichler-Béguelin, M.-J. 134–5, 141

Reith Lectures 180, 183

Relevance Theory 141

revalorisation: of regional dialect 184, 191; symbolic 176–8

Richardson, Charles 82–3, 84

Richmond, J. 166n3

Rickford, J. 179

Ricks 86–7

right dislocation 152

rock'n'roll subculture, Denmark 242, 244, 251

Rodman, R. 70, 207–8, 209, 210

Rogers, Daniel T. 190, 191, 196, 197

Rolph, C.H. 188–9

Romaine, S. 134

Roman Catholic Church: accents in 188

Roosevelt, Theodore 192, 194

Roskilde, University of, Denmark 172, 240

Ross, A.S.C. 38

Royal Society of London for the Improvement of Natural Knowledge 77, 79

royalty and 'best' English 184, 204

RP *see* received pronunciation

Rush, Benjamin 193–4, 196

Russell Sage Foundation: Pittsburgh survey 191

Ryan, E.B. 209

-s suffix 138–9

Sampson, George 282n5

Sancho, Ignatius 199, 200, 201

Sapir, Edward 28

Saussure, Ferdinand de 14, 71, 73, 74, 75, 77, 87n2; Saussurean paradox 36; 'speech circuit' 72

Saxon, Samuel: *A Short Introduction to English Grammar* 43, 44, 51; addressees 55–7, 64; on parts of speech 48–9; references to Latin 52

Saxonisms 99; *see also* Anglo-Saxon language

Scandinavian written languages 267n5

Schegloff, E. 27

Schieffelin, Bambi 2, 176, 178, 191

Schiffrin, D. 137, 138, 142

Schröder, K. 5

Schutz, Alfred 72

science: language for 77–8, 78–9; registers for 121–3, 128

Scottish accent 189

Scouse accent/dialect 189, 205n5

Sears, D.A. 73

Seppänen A. 135

Shakespeare, William: *King Lear* 184

'Shamed By Your Mistakes in English?' (advertisement) 106

Sheridan, Thomas 67

Sigley, R. 132

Simon, John 20, 202

Singapore: standard language ideology in 173

singular forms 157

Sisam, K. 35

Skeat, W.W. 35

slavery 197, 198, 200–1

Smith, J. 174, 174–5, 184, 186

Smith, L. 265

Smith, Logan Pearsall 104–5

Smithers, G. 35

social background and language 130, 164

social behaviour: language as 14

social class 8–9; and accent 118; class markers 4, 191–2; in eighteenth century 199; Estuary English classless 180–2, 191–2; and industrial relations conflict 188; and linguistic discrimination 13, 19, 170, 171, 174–5, 176–8, 180–3; and prestige in language 37–9; revalorisation of regional dialects 184, 191; and spoken English 184–92; and spoken Standard English 147; taxonomies of 190–1; US taxonomy of 196–7; and varieties of English 8; *see also* working classes

social construction: and education 40–1, 42, 62–8; in Fowler 97; of Standard English 40–68; subcultures in Denmark 242, 244–6, 247, 260–1 social dialects 115; Standard English as 123–4

'social institution' theory 41, 62, 66

sociolinguistics 8–9; appropriacy 7; hierarchy of 183; notions of correctness 19; prestige explanations 37–9; sociolinguistic tradition 114, 115; Standard English as dialect 123–5; and standard ideology 36–7; standardised languages 117; and teaching of spoken Standard English 163

Soubise, Julius 198

sound in US regional speech areas 227, 228*tab*, 230, 235–6

South, American: accent stigmatised 213, 216; dialect of 170; group composition 237n2; language ratings 203, 212*fig*, 213, 215*fig*, 216, 218*fig*, 219, 220, 232; social system 197; South Carolina speech area maps 222*fig*, 225*fig*, 228*tab*, 229, 230–1, 233, 234, 235–6

Spanish: as colonial language in US 193; status in US 1, 179, 183, 192–3, 195, 204

speech *see* conversational speech; corpora of transcribed speech; oracy; oral syntax; speech areas; speech communities; spoken forms of language; spoken forms of Standard English; spoken forms of standard languages; vernaculars

speech areas (US), taxonomies of 210, 220–37

speech communities 36, 38, 39, 71–2; variation in 175, 178; *see also* discourse communities

speech fellowships 3

spellcheckers 3

spelling 9, 27, 34–5, 74, 75, 79, 98

Sperber, D. 141

spoken forms of language: relationship with written forms 73–5, 97–8, 115–16

spoken forms of Standard English 2, 6, 8, 70, 113–16; in Britain and US 173–4; classroom case study 159–61; corpora of 130–1; debate on 271–82; and definitions 271–2; and educatedness 69, 275; formality in 146–7; grammar of 149–66; historical perspective 184–92; Honey's view 271–5; and

language attitudes 169–70; and National Curriculum for English in England and Wales 114, 115, 116, 129, 147, 153–4, 165, 171; relationship to written forms 97–8, 130, 158–61, 271–5; RP as standard 171; in schools 163–5; and syntax 114–15, 129–48; *see also* pronunciation

spoken forms of standard languages 18, 22, 27, 174; conversational speech 23–4; variation in 36–7, 175

spoken Standard American English 174, 202–3

stabilisation of language 114, 117

Stalker, J.C. 263

standard: meanings of 90, 108n1, 271

Standard American English (SAE) 70, 124; in EFL teaching 239, 264; folk evaluations of 170, 174, 203, 207–38; as idealisation 207–8; linguistic change 126–7; location of 174, 207–38; problems of defining 171, 207–8

Standard English: access to 21; characterisation of 117–28; as classical language 64–5; debate on 13–14, 271–82; definitions of 6, 13, 15, 70–1, 89–90, 117, 130, 171, 271–2, 280n1, 281n4, 282n5; grammatical features 124–6; historical perspective 1, 7, 13–15, 69–88, 272; as idealisation 32–3, 70, 272–3; ideology of 1–2, 13–15, 45, 169–70; not an accent 118–19, 123; not a language 118; not a register 121–3; not a style 119–21; as official language 240–1; rigidity of 132; spelling of term 117, 123; varieties of 5, 6, 239–40, 259, 262–6; *see also* spoken forms of Standard English; written forms of Standard English

standard ideology 24–39

standard languages 16–39; histories of 28; as idealisations 18, 26, 27; ideology of 18, 20, 22, 23, 28–34, 35, 173–206; legitimacy of 28; and prestige 37–9; 'standard-language cultures' 18, 23, 26, 39; variation in 18, 162; written and spoken forms of 18, 22, 23–4, 27, 36–7, 174–5; *see also* Standard American English; Standard English; standardisation

standardisation 71, 117, 132–4, 173; characteristics of 26–8; historically of English 184; ideology of 18, 23; and linguistic change 27–8, 35, 39, 126–7; and linguistics 16–39; problems of 80; processes of 114; *see also* standard languages

Stein, D. 130, 133, 135, 139
Stein, G. 124
Sterne, Laurence 199
Stevens, John 187, 188
stigma 38–9; and accent 184, 188, 189, 190, 213, 216; and African-American Vernacular English (AAVE) 196; *see also* linguistic discrimination; prestige
Strang, B.M.H. 27
structural linguistics 18, 28, 36–7, 39
structural oppositions 134–5
Stubbs, M. 164
style 119–21, 146, and Standard English 128; *see also* formality
subculture groups in Denmark 4, 242, 244–6, 247, 259, 260–1
Sun: Standard English used by 124
Sunday Times 181
Sundby, B. 135
Sutcliffe, P. 93
Sweden: layer cake hierarchy 183
Sweet, Henry 29–30, 84
Swift, Jonathan 20, 79
switching: code-switching in Denmark 242–3, 244, 246, 247, 251, 261; dialect switching 121, 122–3
Switzerland: formal use of dialect 122–3; functions of English in 171, 172
Syder, F.H. 137
symbolic capital 14, 15, 41, 42, 51, 63, 107, 108
'symbolic revalorization' 176–8
synonyms 80–1
syntax: and authority 274; oral syntax 139–41; and spoken forms of Standard English 114–15, 129–48; *see also* grammar

Tabouret-Keller, A. 117
tag questions 134, 144
Tagliamonte, S. 134, 135, 136
tail structures 152, 154, 166n2
Taylor, Talbot 2
technical register 121–3, 128
television programmes: in English in Denmark 242, 243, 246, 250, 257

text normalisation 34–5
Thackeray, William Makepeace 94
that 134, 135, 139–40, 141–2, 144
Thatcher, Margaret 188, 205–6n7; and 'new right' 276; *see also* Conservative government
there, existential 135–8, 139, 157, 161
Thomas, J.J. 201
Thompson, S. 133
Times Educational Supplement 162
Tooke, J. Horne 82, 83
Toon, T.E. 5
Tory, Peter 181, 202
Tory government *see* Conservative government
Tottie, G. 133
Trade Union movement 188
Treaty of Hidalgo (US) 195
Trench, Richard Chenevix 83–4
Trudgill, Peter 2, 5, 6, 8, 37; on dialect 209, 263; and Standard English 70, 113, 114, 118, 130, 169; standardisation 117; style 119
Tucker, G.R. 209, 246

Ulster Scots accent 190, 191
United States: Civil War 170, 196, 203; Continental Congress 194, 196–7; correctness ratings 210–13, 219, 232, 237n6; degree of difference ratings 216–19; Ebonics debate in 1, 178, 179; English Only movement 178, 179–80, 192–3, 194–5, 196; folk evaluation of dialects 170–1, 174, 202–3, 207–38; foreign accents stigmatised 188; Graduate Student Instructors, intelligibility of 179; historical perspective 192–7; indigenous American languages 193, 195–6; language ideologies in 173–206; multilingualism of 192–6; 'new right' in 276; pleasantness ratings 213–16, 219, 232; Spanish language in 1, 179, 183, 192–3, 195, 204; speech research 116; Standard English concept in 169; taxonomies of speech areas 210, 220–37; xenophobia in 195; *see also* American English; Boston English; 'network American' accent; New York City; Standard American English
universities: and accent 184, 186, 188; English language teaching 108

urban accents 18<del>7, in</del> *[handwritten: Standard English]*
US English *see* American English;
  Standard American English
US English movement 179–80
usage handbooks *see* handbooks of
  English

'vague' language 161
variety and US regional speech areas
  228, 229
vernaculars 27, 205n5
vocabulary *see* lexis; words

Wakelin, M. 18, 184
Walker, William 49
Wallis, John: *Grammatica Linguæ
  Anglicanæ* 44, 46, 61–2, 65
Washington, Booker T. 200
Waterhouse, Keith 181–2
Watts, Richard J. 13, 55, 67, 171
Weber, H. 173
Webster, Noah 194
Wedderburn, Robert 201
Weiner, E.S.C. 86
Weinreich, Uriel 17, 36
Wells, J.C. 38
Welsh accent 189
Welsh Office 113; *see also* National
  Curriculum for English in England
  and Wales
wh-descriptive clause 142–5
wh-type clauses 155–6, 166n2
Whitcut, J. 108n7
Whitney, W.D. 31
Widdowson, H.G. 91, 265
Wilenz, Sean 190, 191, 196, 197
Williams, Angie 170
Williams, Ann 181, 192
Williams, Patricia 183, 196
Williams, Raymond 281n1

Winfrey, Oprah: TV show 177–8
Wolfram, W. 174, 202
women: Fowler on 100
Woolard, Kathryn A. 2, 176, 178, 189,
  191
word order in speech 155–6
word processors: spellcheckers 3
words: definitions of 79–85; lexical items
  122; meanings of 79–85, 277–8,
  280n1; *see also* dictionaries; lexis;
  orthography
working classes disadvantaged by
  linguists 21
Wright, Joseph 30
Wright, Laura 66
written forms of language: grammars
  based on 27, 152–3; linguists
  immersed in 130–1; relationship with
  spoken forms 73–5, 97–8, 115–16; as
  standard 152–3
written forms of Standard English 6, 8,
  70; definitions of 271–2; Honey's view
  on 271–5; relationship to spoken
  forms 97–8, 130, 158–61, 271–5
written forms of standard languages 27,
  174
Wyld, Henry Cecil 30, 31–3, 37, 39,
  105, 188; on RP 186–7, 204; Standard
  English definition 281n4

xenophobia in US 195

Yorkshire accent 182, 189
you know X construction 138, 139
youth cultures, Denmark 242, 244–6,
  247
Yule, G. 130

Zelinsky, Wilbur 223, 225